DIVERTING AUTHORITIES

Diverting Authorities

Experimental Glossing Practices in Manuscript and Print

JANE GRIFFITHS

OXFORD
UNIVERSITY PRESS

OXFORD
UNIVERSITY PRESS

Great Clarendon Street, Oxford, OX2 6DP,
United Kingdom

Oxford University Press is a department of the University of Oxford.
It furthers the University's objective of excellence in research, scholarship,
and education by publishing worldwide. Oxford is a registered trade mark of
Oxford University Press in the UK and in certain other countries

© Jane Griffiths 2014

The moral rights of the author have been asserted

First Edition published in 2014

Impression: 1

All rights reserved. No part of this publication may be reproduced, stored in
a retrieval system, or transmitted, in any form or by any means, without the
prior permission in writing of Oxford University Press, or as expressly permitted
by law, by licence or under terms agreed with the appropriate reprographics
rights organization. Enquiries concerning reproduction outside the scope of the
above should be sent to the Rights Department, Oxford University Press, at the
address above

You must not circulate this work in any other form
and you must impose this same condition on any acquirer

Published in the United States of America by Oxford University Press
198 Madison Avenue, New York, NY 10016, United States of America

British Library Cataloguing in Publication Data
Data available

Library of Congress Control Number: 2014942178

ISBN 978–0–19–965451–2

Printed and bound by
CPI Group (UK) Ltd, Croydon, CR0 4YY

Links to third party websites are provided by Oxford in good faith and
for information only. Oxford disclaims any responsibility for the materials
contained in any third party website referenced in this work.

*for my parents
and for Smokey,
who has slept on it all*

Acknowledgements

I have incurred many debts during the seven years of writing this book, in the course of which I experienced three changes of job and five house moves, not all of them voluntary. I should like to thank friends and former colleagues in the Department of English at Edinburgh, especially Randall Stevenson and Sarah Carpenter, for superlative kindness and rationality; those in the Department of English at Bristol, especially Pamela King, Elizabeth Archibald, and Jane Wright, for humour and support in interesting times. I should also, rather belatedly, like to thank Lucy Newlyn and Sharon Achinstein of St Edmund Hall, Oxford, for my first academic post and for their friendship; and, most emphatically, the Warden and Fellows of Wadham College and the English Faculty at Oxford, for providing a happy resolution to all those moves, and for making me so welcome.

I am extremely grateful to the staff of the many libraries I have visited, notably Cambridge University Library; the libraries of Trinity College and Magdalene College, Cambridge; Durham University Library; Edinburgh University Library; Glasgow University Library; Lambeth Palace Library; the library at the Herbert, Coventry; the libraries of All Souls College, Christ Church, and Magdalen College, Oxford; Columbia University Library; Princeton University Library; the Pierpont Morgan Library, New York; and the Rosenbach Foundation, Philadelphia. A special mention must go to the staff of the British Library, especially those in Manuscripts who have done so very much heavy lifting of Lydgate and Laurent de Premierfait on my behalf, and the staff of the Bodleian Library, without whom this book would certainly not exist; here, I should like particularly to thank the staff pent in durance vile in Special Collections, in hopes of their speedy release, and (in all seriousness) Vera Ryhajlo, whose astonishing depth of knowledge was invaluable, and who is so very much missed.

A shorter version of Chapter 3 was previously published in *English Manuscript Studies* (2009) as 'Exhortations to the Reader: The Glossing of Douglas's *Eneados* in Trinity College MS O.3.12', and part of Chapter 5 previously appeared in *Interfaces* (2006) as 'Voicing the Commonplace: Emblem, Interpretation, and Civil Society in William Bullein's *Dialogue against the Fever Pestilence*'. I should like to thank the editors of *Interfaces* for their permission to include that material here, and the University of Chicago Press for its enlightened policy of allowing authors to reprint articles previously published in their journals. I am also grateful to the organizers of the Scottish Editing Conference at De Montfort University (2008), the Material Cultures Conference at Edinburgh (2010), the History of the Book Conference at York (2011), and the Reading of Books and the Reading of Literature Conference at Columbia University (2012), as well as to the convenors of the University of Bristol Medieval Research Seminar and Department of English Research Seminar for the opportunity to present parts of my research, and to Jeanette Beer and Mary Wellesley for the opportunity to do so at Kalamazoo.

I should like to thank the Bodleian Library, the British Library, and the Master and Fellows of Trinity College, Cambridge, for permission to publish images from manuscripts and early printed texts in their ownership; Aditi Nafde and Stephen Partridge for their permission to quote from unpublished work; Jacqueline Baker at OUP for her encouragement; and the three anonymous readers of the manuscript for their perceptive and helpful comments. Among the less formal debts I have acquired, I am particularly grateful to A. S. G. Edwards and Julia Boffey for their encouragement and practical suggestions, and to Pamela King and Daniel Wakelin for reading parts of this book in draft. I should also like to thank my former PhD student at Bristol, Rachel Stenner, for stimulating discussion of all things paratextual. All errors and misconceptions in this book are, of course, my own.

Finally, in addition to those friends mentioned in the first paragraph, I should like to thank all those who have managed to keep their address books updated over the last few years, and in particular my parents, Mary and Derek Griffiths, Peter Scupham, and Margaret Steward for their constant support, Nicola Blackwell and Nick Tigg for their steadfast friendship, Joan Griffiths for her frequent hospitality and left-field questions, Lottie Hoare for reminding me that there are more things in heaven and earth than glosses, Sally Speirs for coffee, cat-tending, and theatre, Andrew Doney for tea and for keeping things on the road, Paul Vibert for spectacular improbability, and Smokey for supreme feline loyalty.

Contents

List of Illustrations	xi
Introduction	1
1. Material Processes: The Glossing of Lydgate's *Siege of Thebes* and *Fall of Princes*	19
2. Authors, Translators, and Commentators: Glossing Practices in Bodleian MS Fairfax 16	54
3. Exhortations to the Reader: The Double Glossing of Douglas' *Eneados*	81
4. Glossing the Spoken Word: Erasmus' *Moriae Encomium* and Chaloner's *Praise of Folie*	103
5. A Broil of Voices: The Printed Word in Baldwin's *Beware the Cat* and Bullein's *Dialogue against the Fever Pestilence*	123
6. 'Masking naked in a net': Author and Text in the Works of Gascoigne and Harington	149
7. 'Playing the Dolt in Print': The Extemporary Glossing of Nashe's *Pierce Penilesse his Supplication to the Devil*	175
Afterword	205
Bibliography	211
Index	235

List of Illustrations

1.1.	Bodleian MS Digby 230, f. 2	31
1.2.	MS Harley 2251, f. 142	42
1.3.	BL MS Harley 4203, f. 37	45
1.4.	BL MS Harley 4203, f. 39^v	46
1.5.	BL MS Harley 4197, f. 36	47
1.6.	BL MS Harley 1766, f. 98	47
2.1.	Bodleian MS Fairfax 16, f. 155	60
2.2.	Bodleian MS Fairfax 16, f. 211	74
3.1.	Cambridge, Trinity College MS O.3.12, f. 2^v	100
4.1.	Erasmus, *Moriae Encomium* (Cologne: E. Ceruicornus, 1526), 18	112
4.2.	Erasmus, *Moriae Encomium* (Cologne: E. Ceruicornus, 1526), 19	113
5.1.	William Baldwin, *A maruelous hystory intitulede, beware the cat* (London: Edward Allde, 1584), sig. Dvii^v	131
6.1.	Sir John Harington, *An Anatomie of the Metamorphosed Ajax* (London: Richard Field, 1596), sig. Lviii	168
6.2.	Sir John Harington, *An Anatomie of the Metamorphosed Ajax* (London: Richard Field, 1596), sig. Avi^v	171
7.1.	Thomas Nashe, *Pierce Penilesse his Supplication to the Diuell* (London: John Busby, 1592), f. 18^v	183
7.2.	Thomas Nashe, *Have with you to Saffron-walden* (London: J. Danter, 1596), title page	187
7.3.	Martin Marprelate, *Oh read ouer D. Iohn Bridges, for it is a worthy worke* (East Molesey, Surrey: Robert Waldegrave, 1588), 5	194

Introduction

This book owes its existence to an obscure sarcasm—or, to put it less cryptically, to a gloss in the margin of John Skelton's last surviving work, *A Replycacion* (1528). Printed in tidy alignment with an attack on heresy that was written to commission for Henry VIII's chief minister, Cardinal Wolsey, it reads simply 'Obscurus sarcasmos'.[1] It is a startlingly idiosyncratic note, grabbing the reader's attention with questions that have very little to do with the poem's ostensible subject. What and where is the sarcasm, and who is its object? Why is it obscure, and why does the gloss draw attention to it without giving us any further information? Who is responsible for this puzzle? The reader who pays attention to the gloss risks being diverted from the text to pursue something that may well prove to be a red herring.

In fact, of course, this particular puzzle was solved long ago. *A Replycacion* is an attack on two Cambridge scholars, Thomas Arthur and Thomas Bilney, who had been tried for preaching against idolatry, prayers to saints, pilgrimages, and miracles.[2] Throughout the poem, Skelton makes much of Arthur and Bilney's Cambridge education, and the poor use to which they have put it; the lines to which the 'obscurus sarcasmos' gloss is attached point out that Bilney had received a scholarship of ten pounds, and that this 'Employed . . . myght have be / Moche better other wayes' (ll. 149–50). Bilney, however, is not the only target of these lines. As William Nelson first demonstrated, his scholarship was granted by Wolsey: that is, by the very man who was now prosecuting him, and who was also Skelton's patron.[3] The text remains decently silent on this point, but the gloss rather ostentatiously draws attention to that silence. It thus provides

---

[1] *A replycacion agaynst certayne yong scolers, abiured of late* (London: Richard Pynson, 1528), STC 22609. The poem is also printed in glossed form in *The Poetical Works of John Skelton*, ed. Alexander Dyce, 2 vols. (London: T. Rodd, 1843), 1: 230–50. Unless otherwise specified, all quotations from Skelton's works will be taken from this edition, as the standard edition (*John Skelton: The Complete English Poems*, ed. John Scattergood (Harmondsworth: Penguin, 1983)) does not include the glosses.

[2] See further Greg Walker, 'Saint or Schemer: The 1527 Heresy Trial of Thomas Bilney Reconsidered', *Journal of Ecclesiastical History* 40 (1989), 219–38; and John F. Davis, 'The Trials of Thomas Bylney and the English Reformation', *Historical Journal* 24 (1981), 775–90.

[3] William Nelson, *John Skelton: Laureate* (New York: Columbia University Press, 1939), 217–19.

interesting evidence of Skelton's ambivalence towards Wolsey. Between 1520 and 1522 he had openly declared his antagonism to the Cardinal in a number of popular satires, and although they were ostensibly reconciled early in 1523, the sarcasm suggests that Skelton retained a degree of antagonism towards his former enemy.[4] At the same time, its obscurity suggests that he could not afford to have that antagonism too openly known. When the poem was published, the gloss would have made sense only to those readers who were aware of Wolsey's patronage of Bilney— including, of course, Wolsey himself. Skelton had once before used print to remind Wolsey of the embarrassing revelations he could make if he chose; one of the envoys to *A Garlande of Laurell* includes a veiled reference to Wolsey's promise to pay Skelton for his work, accompanied by the marginal comment 'Or els'.[5] It seems that Skelton makes use of a similar tactic in *A Replycacion*. The 'obscurus sarcasmos' gloss is a private aside, yet it gains its edge from the fact of being printed, and visible to all readers; it contains the implicit threat to publish less cryptic observations in future. For readers in the know it is dangerously provocative, while for others it intrigues and frustrates in equal measure, tantalizingly revealing that there is a meaning to which they are not privy. For both, in different ways, text and gloss are unfinished business.

Although there proves to be a reasonable explanation for this particular gloss, it is just one example of a phenomenon that raises larger questions. The 'obscurus sarcasmos' is far from the only instance of sixteenth-century glossing that stands in such an oblique relationship to the text that, regardless of whether the reader is the author's contemporary or our own, it is likely to distract his attention from the supposed matter at hand. Skelton is particularly fond of such glosses. In *Speke Parrot* (c. 1521) we find the teasingly cryptic 'Aphorismo, quia paranomasia certe incomprehensibilis' ('I say it in aphorism, because paranomasia is certainly incomprehensible'), and 'Notum adagium et exasperans' ('A well-known and exasperating proverb'), to give just two examples; in *A Garlande of Laurell* (1523), another of Skelton's own glosses, attached to a notoriously nonsensical piece of cod-Latin, observes: 'Cacosyntheton ex industria' ('Something badly put together on purpose').[6] Skelton is not alone in his fondness for

---

[4] For Skelton's apparent changes of allegiance in this period, see Greg Walker, *John Skelton and the Politics of the 1520s* (Cambridge: Cambridge University Press, 1988).

[5] See further Jane Griffiths, 'Text and Authority: John Stow's 1568 Edition of Skelton's Works', in *John Stow: Author, Editor and Reader*, ed. Ian Gadd and Alexandra Gillespie (London: British Library, 2004), 127–34.

[6] See further Jane Griffiths, *John Skelton and Poetic Authority: Defining the Liberty to Speak* (Oxford: Clarendon Press, 2006), 101–28; and John Scattergood, 'The Early Annotations to John Skelton's Poems', *Poetica* 35 (1992), 53–63.

such teasing glosses, however; other sixteenth-century authors whose margins threaten to divert their readers from the text include William Baldwin, William Bullein, George Gascoigne, John Harington, and Thomas Nashe. All incorporate within their works a version of the textual hide-and-seek of which E. K.'s commentary on Spenser's *Shepheardes Calendar* is the most famous instance.[7] Like Skelton's 'obscurus sarcasmos', their glosses pull the reader up short. Despite appearing in printed texts intended for wide dissemination, they are frequently obscure, self-referential, and elusive, seeming to assume that writer and readers share a set of reference points, or even a private language. In his seminal article on the marginal gloss, Lawrence Lipking draws a distinction between printed glosses, which 'respond to the need to spell everything out', and informal, handwritten marginalia: those incidental, often cryptic notes left in the margins by individual readers which 'are wayward in their very nature, [and] spring up spontaneously around a text unaware of their presence'.[8] Although sixteenth-century printed glosses are an integral part of the texts in which they occur, in tone and content a surprising number of them resemble readers' marginalia. They are like blank signposts: a contradiction in terms.

This study began with the urge to discover how and why the margins of so many early modern texts became the site of such strange, attention-seeking play. One specific question that it was intended to address was whether or not such glossing is peculiar to printed texts; another was how it might be related to ideas of authorship in the later fifteenth and sixteenth centuries. As William Slights demonstrated in his ground-breaking study of early modern printed glosses, glossing became an increasingly common feature of English texts over the course of the sixteenth century, coming to fulfil a number of distinct functions such as amplification, appropriation, correction, emphasis, exhortation, explication, organization, parody, pre-emption, simplification, and translation.[9] Of these, my initial interest was primarily in the category of 'parody'—but parody not so much of the content of the text as of reader expectations about how a gloss is

---

[7] E. K.'s commentary takes the form not of marginal glosses, but of endnotes to each of the eclogues, and is notorious for complicating rather than clarifying the text of the *Shepheardes Calendar*. See further Sherri Geller, 'You Can't Tell a Book by Its Contents: (Mis)Interpretation in/of Spenser's *The Shepheardes Calendar*', *Spenser Studies* 13 (1999), 23–64; James Kearney, 'Reformed Ventriloquism: *The Shepheardes Calendar* and the Craft of Commentary', *Spenser Studies* 26 (2011), 111–51; and Richard A. McCabe, 'Annotating Anonymity, or Putting a Gloss on *The Shepheardes Calendar*', in *Ma(r)king the Text: The Presentation of Meaning on the Literary Page*, ed. Joe Bray, Anne Henry, and Miriam Handley (Aldershot: Ashgate, 2000), 35–54.

[8] Lawrence Lipking, 'The Marginal Gloss', *Critical Inquiry* 3 (1977), 612.

[9] William W. E. Slights, *Managing Readers: Printed Marginalia in English Renaissance Books* (Ann Arbor: University of Michigan Press, 2002), 25–6.

'likely' to behave. As Slights has argued: 'While the announced and often achieved effect of the annotating procedure is to simplify, often by offering an epitome of the text, and sometimes by announcing one of the possible senses of the text as the authorized version, in other cases the annotations provide perspectives on the text that greatly complicate and in some cases radically destabilize it.'[10] The glosses I term 'diverting glosses' are those whose authors seem deliberately to invoke such a destabilizing effect. Like footnotes in fictional texts—which, as Shari Benstock argues, 'stem from a creative act rather than a critical one . . . [and are] an aberration, a highly unconventional use of a prescribed and specialized device'—these glosses draw attention to the artificiality of glossing conventions.[11] In consequence—like Skelton's—they both distract and entertain. It would clearly have been impossible, however, to consider them without reference to the context in which they were produced. Specifically, to consider whether print was a contributory factor in the emergence of 'diverting glossing' called for some discussion of self-glossing practices in works circulated in manuscript, of their subsequent printing, and of other contemporary printed glosses.

Extending the study to include manuscript as well as printed texts meant addressing two further questions: the feasibility of discussing self-glossing in manuscript, and the very definition of the term 'gloss'. These are closely connected. Although, as Slights has argued, even in a printed text it may be difficult to distinguish text from margin, it is nonetheless relatively straightforward to identify a gloss on grounds of its position on the page; it may also be assumed to be there in consequence of a decision by either the author or the printer.[12] With manuscript, however, matters are less clear-cut. Daniel Wakelin puts the case succinctly:

> Alongside authorial control of readers, there are several other possible sources for notes that appear in early copies: the notes might stem from the author's papers without his express will, say, as rough notes accidentally transferred to the circulating copies; they might stem from the earliest scribe, and get preserved by later scribes; they might stem from later scribes and get preserved by even later scribes; they might stem from readers adding marginalia to one copy and then get preserved by people transcribing that copy . . . The unsurveyable complexity is the point: there is no simple path to trace from instructive authors to passive readers.[13]

---

[10] Slights, *Managing Readers*, 19–20.
[11] Shari Benstock, 'At the Margin of Discourse: Footnotes in the Fictional Text', *PMLA* 98 (1983), 205.
[12] Slights, *Managing Readers*, 61–3.
[13] Daniel Wakelin, 'Instructing Readers in Fifteenth-Century Poetic Manuscripts', *Huntington Library Quarterly* 73 (2010), 446; and cf. Ardis Butterfield, 'Mise-en-page in

Even such a brief outline of the position clearly identifies both the difficulty of attributing the paratextual material found in manuscripts, and the sheer diversity of it. The latter comes about, at least in part, because of the remarkably complex history of glossing practices. Whereas early glosses were predominantly lexical ones, providing an interpretation of abstruse or foreign terms, this very basic grammatical function soon extended into much more substantive commentaries. Scripture and classical texts, in particular, were frequently accompanied by a standard commentary: the Bible by the *glossa ordinaria*, and classical texts by an academic *accessus* consisting of glosses on prosody, lexical glosses, grammatical glosses, syntactical glosses, and commentary glosses which interpreted, summarized, or indicated the text's background and sources.[14] Inclusion of such a wealth of material on the page necessitated the development of methods of strict visual organization to aid readers in their navigation and interpretation of complex subject matter; whereas early lexical glosses were frequently interlinear, with the development of a wider range of more complex functions, glosses were more frequently added in the margins. Such marginal glosses took their place alongside other means of clarifying the text, such as its division into books and chapters, indication of its topics by means of a rubric at the beginning of each chapter, and the use of running titles. From the twelfth century onwards, they acquired an increasingly important role in the organization of non-academic, non-Scriptural texts as well. Indeed, an *ordinatio* that clarified its structure came to be an expected part of a text; if it were not supplied by the author, it would be supplied by his scribes, and by the fourteenth century, a reader finding himself in possession of an earlier manuscript not so articulated might supply a rudimentary *ordinatio* himself.[15] In addition, of course, margins frequently attracted much

the *Troilus* Manuscripts: Chaucer and French Manuscript Culture', *Huntington Library Quarterly* 58 (1995), 49–51.

[14] For the *glossa ordinaria*, see Lesley Smith, *The Glossa Ordinaria: The Making of a Medieval Bible Commentary* (Leiden: Brill, 2009); and cf. Beryl Smalley, *The Study of the Bible in the Middle Ages* (Notre Dame: University of Notre Dame Press, 1964); Christopher Burdon, 'The Margin Is the Message: Commentary's Displacement of Canon', *Literature and Theology* 13 (1999), 222–34; and Evelyn B. Tribble, *Margins and Marginality: The Printed Page in Early Modern England* (Charlottesville: University Press of Virginia, 1993), 11–56. For the academic *accessus*, see A. J. Minnis, *Medieval Theory of Authorship: Scholastic Literary Attitudes in the Later Middle Ages*, 2nd ed. (Aldershot: Wildwood House, 1988).

[15] This summary is heavily indebted to M. B. Parkes, 'The Influence of the Concepts of *Ordinatio* and *Compilatio* on the Development of the Book', in *Medieval Learning and Literature: Essays Presented to Richard William Hunt*, ed. J. J. G. Alexander, M. T. Gibson, and R. W. Southern (Oxford: Clarendon Press, 1976), 115–41. Cf. also Martin Irvine, '"Bothe text and gloss": Manuscript Form, the Textuality of Commentary, and Chaucer's Dream Poems', in *The Uses of Manuscripts in Literary Studies: Essays in Memory of Judson Boyce Allen*, ed. Charlotte Cook Morse, Penelope Reed Doob, and Marjorie Curry Woods (Kalamazoo: Medieval Institute Publications, 1992), 87–90; and for vernacular texts specifically, see George R. Keiser, 'Serving the Needs of Readers: Textual Division in Some

less systematic responses from individual readers, including sporadic indications of points of interest and even annotations that have nothing to do with the text at all; in his exhaustive classification of marginal glosses in medieval literary manuscripts, Carl Grindley's first two categories are 'marginalia that are without any identifiable context' and 'marginalia that exist within a context associated with that of the manuscript itself', rather than with any of its texts.[16] He also provides detailed analysis of types of annotation that are more closely connected to the text they surround, distinguishing the categories of 'narrative reading aid', 'ethical pointers', 'polemical responses', 'literary responses', and 'graphical responses', each of which contains five or six subcategories.[17] Yet although his work takes scrupulous account of presentation, it nonetheless assumes that a gloss is invariably 'marginal', and thus cannot account for features such as summaries that appear sometimes in the margins, and sometimes in the text: those which we might now be inclined to define as 'headings' or 'rubrics' rather than 'glosses'.[18] Such migrations made it impossible to confine myself wholly to material that was 'marginal', while also suggesting that, for fourteenth- or fifteenth-century authors and readers, positioning on the page was not considered to affect the function of annotation, nor the function to determine where it should be placed on the page. I therefore chose to be similarly inclusive, taking 'gloss' to include any annotation that *may* be positioned in the margins, and that is in supplementary or dialogic relationship with the text, necessitating what Peter Stallybrass has called 'discontinuous reading'.[19]

Late-Medieval English Texts', in *New Science Out of Old Books: Studies in Honour of A. I. Doyle*, ed. Richard Beadle and A. J. Piper (Aldershot: Scolar Press, 1995), 207–26.

[16] Carl James Grindley, 'Reading *Piers Plowman* C-Text Annotations: Notes toward the Classification of Printed and Written Marginalia in Texts from the British Isles 1300–1641', in *The Medieval Professional Reader at Work: Evidence from Manuscripts of Chaucer, Langland, Kempe, and Gower*, ed. Kathryn Kerby-Fulton and Maidie Hilmo (Victoria: University of Victoria Press, 2001), 77.

[17] Grindley, 'Reading *Piers Plowman*', 81–91. For discussion of comparable responses by readers of printed texts, see William H. Sherman, *Used Books: Marking Readers in Renaissance England* (Philadelphia: University of Pennsylvania Press, 2008); and H. J. Jackson, *Marginalia: Readers Writing in Books* (New Haven: Yale University Press, 2001).

[18] See for example Julia Boffey's suggestion that what appear as 'headings' in some *Troilus and Criseyde* manuscripts may have migrated from the margins into the text-block ('Annotation in Some Manuscripts of *Troilus and Criseyde*', *English Manuscript Studies 1100–1700* 5 (1995), 13); and Wakelin's discussion of *Canterbury Tales* manuscript Bodleian MS Laud Misc. 600 ('Instructing Readers', 448); cf. also Aditi Nafde, 'Deciphering the Manuscript Page: The Mise-en-Page of Chaucer, Gower, and Hoccleve Manuscripts', unpublished DPhil. thesis, University of Oxford (2012), 203–4; and Siân Echard, 'Designs for Reading: Some Manuscripts of Gower's *Confessio Amantis*', *Trivium* 31 (1999), 59–72.

[19] Peter Stallybrass, 'Books and Scrolls: Navigating the Bible', in *Books and Readers in Early Modern England: Material Studies*, ed. Jennifer Anderson and Elizabeth Sauer (Philadelphia: University of Pennsylvania Press, 2002), 42–79; for the gloss as supplement, cf. Slights, *Managing Readers*, 62–9. For my inclusive use of the term 'gloss', cf. the decision made by C. David Benson and Barry A. Windeatt in their transcription of the glosses

But although this provides a working solution to the question of definition, it leaves unresolved the question of attribution. There is no doubt that self-glossing did occur in the late-medieval period; self-glossing in continental Europe can be traced back as far as Boccaccio's *Teseida* (c. 1340), while in England Gower's *Confessio Amantis* (1390), Hoccleve's *Regiment of Princes* (1410–11), and many of Lydgate's longer poems, including *The Siege of Thebes* (c. 1420–22) and *The Fall of Princes* (c. 1430–39), were all put into circulation with a more or less elaborate apparatus, and it is possible that some of Chaucer's works too were first disseminated in glossed form.[20] Of these, it is Gower's self-glossing that has attracted most attention, primarily because the elaborate apparatus to the *Confessio Amantis* is so demonstrably an integral part of the text that its attribution has never been in serious doubt, but in part also because it is easily accommodated to a narrative of self-authorization.[21] Glossing was not conventionally an authorial activity; Biblical and academic commentaries and textual *ordinatio* were traditionally supplied by a third person. In consequence, their presence implied that a text had been found worthy of detailed attention by someone other than the author. As Martin Irvine has argued: 'Only authoritative or canonical texts were presented in this format; in fact, the chief mark of a text's status, that it was received and read as a text, a privileged linguistic object in the cultural canon, is its presentation in this format.'[22] There is, then, a clear case for reading the glossing of the *Confessio* as a conspicuous way of challenging the assumption that literary authority is something inherent only in the work of an *auctor*: an established classical,

---

in manuscripts of *Troilus and Criseyde* ('The Manuscript Glosses to Chaucer's *Troilus and Criseyde*', *Chaucer Review* 25 (1990), 33).

[20] For other English vernacular examples, see Daniel Wakelin, 'Instructing Readers'. For Boccaccio, see Robert Hollander, 'The Validity of Boccaccio's Self-Exegesis in his *Teseida*', *Medievalia et Humanistica* n.s. 8 (1977), 163–83; Susan Noakes, *Timely Reading: Between Exegesis and Interpretation* (Ithaca: Cornell University Press, 1988), 87–97; and Jeffrey T. Schnapp, 'A Commentary on Commentary in Boccaccio', *South Atlantic Quarterly* 91 (1992), 813–34.

[21] See for example Ardis Butterfield, 'Articulating the Author: Gower and the French Vernacular Codex', *Yearbook of English Studies* 33 (2003), 80–96; A. J. Minnis, 'De vulgari auctoritate: Chaucer, Gower, and the Men of Great Authority', in *Chaucer and Gower: Difference, Mutuality, Exchange*, ed. R. F. Yeager (Victoria: University of Victoria, 1991), esp. 51–5; Derek Pearsall, 'Gower's Latin in the *Confessio Amantis*', in *Latin and the Vernacular: Studies in Late Medieval Texts and Manuscripts*, ed. A. J. Minnis (Cambridge: D.S. Brewer, 1989), 13–25; and Robert F. Yeager, 'English, Latin, and the Text as "Other": The Page as Sign in the Work of John Gower', *Text* 3 (1987), 251–67. For the relative rarity of commentary on English vernacular texts, see A. J. Minnis, *Translations of Authority in Medieval English Literature: Valuing the Vernacular* (Cambridge: Cambridge University Press, 2009), 17–37; and Andrew Galloway, 'Gower's *Confessio Amantis*, the *Prick of Conscience*, and the History of the Latin Gloss in Early English Literature', in *John Gower: Manuscripts, Readers, Contexts*, ed. Malte Urban (Turnhout: Brepols, 2009), 39–70.

[22] Irvine, ' "Bothe text and gloss" ', 90.

patristic, or Scriptural source.[23] Indeed, the appearance of the glosses and the Latin verses on the manuscript page, where they are almost invariably distinguished from the English text of the poem by being copied in red, does make a striking visual impact; Derek Pearsall has rightly described the poem as coming '"cased" or "boxed" in Latin'.[24]

The *Confessio*'s apparatus does not serve merely as an inert symbol of Gower's authoritative authorial status, however. Rather, it is one aspect of the larger phenomenon identified by Rita Copeland, whereby academic commentary—in principle the business of the grammarian—evolved into a rhetorical performance to rival the text it purported to serve.[25] Tracing such performances both in the margins and in the body of the texts of vernacular translations, which she identifies as a form of commentary, she argues that for authors including Chaucer and Gower 'translation comes to be perceived as a form of rhetorical *inventio*, which has in turn been redefined as exegetical performance on a text or textual topos'.[26] Her connection of academic exegesis with rhetoric and translation beautifully demonstrates that intrinsic commentary and its more visible counterpart, the gloss, are two sides of the same coin: both are sites of authorial invention, with the glosses serving as physical realization of the changes which the translator effects in turning an old text to new ends.[27] As Ralph Hanna has argued, when an annotator annotates 'he is in fact creating himself as a reader—and thus creating the reader of his work'.[28] With self-glossing, the author—in this case, Gower—creates himself as reader of his *own* work, and the glosses become a means of discovering, as well as asserting, the extent to which the 'sentence' of his material is affected by the process of writing.[29] This entails a radical rethinking of the *nature* as well as the *location* of literary authority, placing it not in inherited subject matter or a transposed 'sentence', but in the writerly business of re-creation. Gower's *Confessio* thus suggests the possibility of linking self-glossing to a theory of authorship that is grounded in practice.

It is not immediately clear, however, that it is feasible to trace comparable developments in the works of contemporary writers. Even to consider

---

[23] For this view of authority, see Minnis, *Medieval Theory of Authorship*, 1–12.
[24] Pearsall, 'Gower's Latin', 18.
[25] Rita Copeland, *Rhetoric, Hermeneutics and Translation in the Middle Ages: Academic Tradition and Vernacular Texts* (Cambridge: Cambridge University Press, 1991); for an introductory overview of her thesis, see esp. 1–8.
[26] Copeland, *Rhetoric, Hermeneutics and Translation*, 7.
[27] Copeland discusses the apparatus to the *Confessio* in precisely these terms (*Rhetoric, Hermeneutics and Invention*, 207).
[28] Ralph Hanna III, 'Annotation as Social Practice', in *Annotation and Its Texts*, ed. Stephen A. Barney (Oxford: Oxford University Press, 1991), 181.
[29] Cf. Wakelin, 'Instructing Readers', esp. 433–4.

self-glossing as, potentially, a distinct phenomenon gives rise to the questions succinctly formulated by Sylvia Huot in her study of the *Roman de la Rose*:

> Do we wish to study a historical process of creation, continuation, adaptation; or to reconstruct [a moment] of original poetic creation, to be preserved as such? Are we interested in a text as a reflection of its author or the circumstances of its composition; or are we more concerned with its subsequent reception by medieval readers?[30]

Although Huot concludes that 'there is, of course, no reason to view these possibilities as mutually exclusive', recent scholarship has tended increasingly to focus on reception and transmission rather than origination; the former is grounded in the evidence provided by material witnesses, whereas the latter risks reverting to some imaginary 'ideal' form of the text, whose existence must always remain a matter of speculation. Even critics with a strong interest in questions of authorship have necessarily remained wary; as Alexandra Gillespie writes: 'Certain circumstances may lead a writer to assert his or her authorship of a text, but... such assertions of "bibliographic ego" may or may not be preserved or promoted in the material forms of documents, usually books, which always present texts to readers.'[31] The risk of non-preservation is especially pronounced when it comes to glosses, which—as physically separate from the body of the text—are particularly susceptible to loss and alteration; moreover, as indicated by Wakelin, the strong likelihood that glosses of quite different origins will accrete around, fuse with, or supplant any authorial annotation means that there is a real difficulty in knowing what it is, in any given manuscript, that we are looking at.

Surviving Chaucer manuscripts provide a perfect illustration of the problem. Unlike Gower's, their glossing is fragmentary and inconsistent.[32] Various manuscripts of the *Canterbury Tales* include source and citation glosses to the Clerk's Tale, the Franklin's Tale, the Man of Law's Tale, the Merchant's Tale, the Pardoner's Tale, and the Wife of Bath's Prologue and Tale; while those of *Troilus and Criseyde* contain scribal glosses of widely divergent kinds, ranging from source glosses and explanatory glosses to lengthy summaries; and those of *The House of Fame* include just a handful of source glosses.[33] The source and citation glosses to the *Canterbury*

---

[30] Sylvia Huot, *The Roman de la Rose and Its Medieval Readers: Interpretation, Reception, Manuscript Transmission* (Cambridge: Cambridge University Press, 2007), 2.

[31] Alexandra Gillespie, 'Framing Lydgate's *Fall of Princes*: The Evidence of Book History', *Mediaevalia* 20 (2001), 154.

[32] Cf. Stephen Partridge, '"The Makere of this Boke": Chaucer's Retraction and the Author as Scribe and Compiler', in *Author, Reader, Book: Medieval Authorship in Theory and Practice*, ed. Stephen Partridge and Erik Kwakkel (Toronto: University of Toronto Press, 2012), 110–3.

[33] For a transcription of the *Troilus* glosses, see Benson and Windeatt, 'Manuscript Glosses'. 'Source' glosses are those that identify a literary source for the passage in the text

Tales, in particular, have been the subject of considerable critical debate, yet it has not been possible to demonstrate conclusively either whether they are authorial, or—if they are—whether they were intended for Chaucer's readers or for Chaucer himself.[34] Thus, critics including Daniel Silvia and Robert Lewis argue that at least some of the source and citation glosses should be considered as authorial working notes.[35] Others, including Graham Caie and Charles Owen, argue that they should not.[36] Slightly more recent articles focus not on the question of authorship, but on the significance of the glosses as early responses to the *Tales*.[37] Although the most detailed study of the *Canterbury Tales* glosses to date, that by Stephen Partridge, finds broadly in favour of the hypothesis that Chaucer was himself responsible for many of the source and citation glosses, he acknowledges that the evidence is not watertight. Partridge's work does, however, identify some important indicators for determining the matter of authorship: stressing the consistency of the manuscript evidence, the relative obscurity of several of the sources cited, and the fact that the later tales are the ones that are most heavily glossed, he argues that the glosses go back to a very early stage in the work's transmission, and that they are more likely to be evidence of Chaucer's own increasing interest in glossing than an attempt by an early scribe to give a coherently authoritative appearance to the *Tales* as a whole.[38] Recently, he has also made a compelling case

---

to which they are attached, but do not themselves quote from it; 'citation' glosses are those that quote, but do not provide a source. For an illuminating discussion of the effects these different kinds of gloss have in practice, see Wakelin, 'Instructing Readers', 445–6.

[34] For an overview and evaluation of criticism on the subject, see Stephen Bradford Partridge, 'Glosses in the Manuscripts of Chaucer's *Canterbury Tales*: An Edition and Commentary' (unpublished PhD thesis, Harvard University, 1992), 1.5–1.28.

[35] Daniel S. Silvia, 'Glosses to the *Canterbury Tales* from St Jerome's *Epistola Adversus Jovinianum*', *Studies in Philology* 62 (1965), 28–39; and Robert E. Lewis, 'Glosses to the *Man of Law's Tale* from Pope Innocent III's *De Miseria Humane Conditionis*', *Studies in Philology* 64 (1967), 1–16; cf. also three articles by Germaine Dempster: 'Chaucer at Work on the Complaint in the Franklin's Tale', *Modern Language Notes* 52 (1937), 16–23; 'A Further Note on Dorigen's Exempla', *Modern Language Notes* 54 (1939), 137–8; and 'Chaucer's Manuscript of Petrarch's Version of the Griselda Story', *Modern Philology* 41 (1943–44), 6–16.

[36] Graham D. Caie, 'The Significance of the Early Chaucer Manuscript Glosses (with Special Reference to the *Wife of Bath's Prologue*)', *Chaucer Review* 10 (1975–6), 350–60; and Charles A. Owen, Jr., 'The Alternative Reading of *The Canterbury Tales*: Chaucer's Text and the Early Manuscripts', *PMLA* 97 (1982), 237–50.

[37] See Susan Schibanoff, 'The New Reader and Female Textuality in Two Early Commentaries on Chaucer', *Studies in the Age of Chaucer* 10 (1988), 71–108; Christopher Baswell, 'Talking Back to the Text: Marginal Voices in Medieval Secular Literature', in *Uses of Manuscripts*, 121–60; Thomas J. Farrell, 'The Style of the "Clerk's Tale" and the Functions of Its Glosses', *Studies in Philology* 86 (1989), 286–309; and Theresa Tinkle, 'The Wife of Bath's Marginal Authority', *Studies in the Age of Chaucer* 32 (2010), 67–102.

[38] Partridge, 'Glosses', 2.1–2.24.

that the glosses to Chaucer's *Retraction* can be linked to the composition process, and should be considered authorial.[39] With many of the Chaucer glosses, however, it remains impossible to be certain; the probability is that the manuscripts witness a fusion of authorial glossing with a wide variety of different kinds of scribal and reader response.[40]

Despite these very real difficulties, Gower's example indicates that self-glossing is, at least in principle, a phenomenon worth considering. The case of Hoccleve's *Regiment of Princes* is particularly suggestive in this respect. Hoccleve has a demonstrable interest in questions of literary authority: notably in the physical form of the book, the composition process, and their relation to his own status as author.[41] The glosses to the *Regiment* form a clear extension of these interests: providing lengthy quotations from Hoccleve's source texts, those to the *Regiment* proper are visible proof of Hoccleve's extensive alterations to his sources, while those to the Prologue constitute an experiment in self-authorization along the lines of that in the *Confessio*; clustering around the Beggar's advisory speeches, they underwrite the sententious quality of his advice. As an exemplary work, the *Regiment* depends on analogies: the Beggar is a figure of the narrator (who in turn is a figure of Hoccleve), and his advice to the narrator is a displaced version of Hoccleve's advice to his patron. The glosses provide yet a further layer of exemplarity: an appeal to literary tradition and commonplace that makes the work's palimpsestic quality visible on the page.[42] Moreover, Partridge's suggestion that the glossing of the *Regiment* was a direct response to that of the Ellesmere manuscript of the *Canterbury Tales* reaffirms the hypothesis that glossing is potentially key to the development of an author's views *about* literary authority, as well as a means of conveying his pre-existing ideas on the subject.[43]

---

[39] Partridge, ' "The Makere of this Boke" '.

[40] See Partridge, 'Glosses', 2.24; Boffey, 'Annotation', 10; and cf. Butterfield, 'Mise-en-page'.

[41] See David Watt, ' "I This Book Shall Make": Thomas Hoccleve's Self-Publication and Book Production', *Leeds Studies in English* 34 (2003), 133–60; Sebastian Langdell, ' "What worlde is this? How vndirstande am I?" A Reappraisal of Poetic Authority in Thomas Hoccleve's *Series*', *Medium Aevum* 78 (2009), 281–99; and John Burrow, 'The Poet and the Book', in *Genres, Themes, and Images in English Literature*, ed. Piero Boitani and Anna Torti (Tübingen: Gunter Narr Verlag, 1988), esp. 242–5. For manuscripts of the *Regiment*, see Julia Boffey and A. S. G. Edwards, *A New Index of Middle English Verse* (London: The British Library, 2005); and for a more recent discovery, Linne R. Mooney, 'A Holograph Copy of Thomas Hoccleve's *Regiment of Princes*', *Studies in the Age of Chaucer* 33 (2011), 263–96.

[42] See further Marcia Smith Marzec, 'The Sources of Hoccleve's *Regiment* and the Use of Translations', *Équivalences* 13 (1982), 9–21; cf. also Nafde, 'Deciphering the Manuscript Page', 215–17; and Jane Griffiths, ' "In bookes thus I wryten fynde": Glossing Hoccleve's *Regiment of Princes*', forthcoming.

[43] Partridge, 'Glosses', 2.14.

As well as providing a framework for thinking about the implications of early self-glossing, Hoccleve's *Regiment* suggests a possible methodology, too. One significant reason for the attribution of its glosses to Hoccleve is the fact that almost all its extant manuscripts, including the holographs, are glossed near-identically; another is that their extensive citation from his sources indicates that the glossator had those sources to hand. The most economical hypothesis is, of course, that this was either Hoccleve, or a close associate of his. In the first two chapters I focus on texts whose glosses can similarly be shown to be connected to the composition of the poem to which they are attached: in the first chapter, Lydgate's *Siege of Thebes* and *Fall of Princes*; in the second, two poems from MS Fairfax 16: *Reson and Sensuallyte* and Chaucer's *House of Fame*.[44] This choice of texts was additionally governed by the opportunity they provide for examining the effect on their glosses of contrasting conditions of transmission.[45] Whereas the glossing of Lydgate's poems in manuscript can be compared with that of the early De Worde and Pynson prints and (for the *Siege of Thebes*) with that of the Stow and Speght editions of Chaucer as well, *Reson and Sensuallyte* survives in a single independent witness, where the contrast between its formal Latin apparatus and the less systematic glossing of other poems serves as a paradigm of heterogenous manuscript glossing practices.[46] The glosses to Lydgate's poems and *Reson and Sensuallyte* may thus be contextualized in two contrasting ways, providing an opportunity to consider both the different forms in which they might have been encountered and (with Lydgate's poems) how they are affected by appearing in print. The main focus of these chapters, however, is on the way in which the poems' glossing makes visible the writing process. As with Gower, their glosses can be shown to draw the writer's attention to his own powers of transformation, and thus to prompt further, more self-conscious consideration both of the writer's authority and of the potential of the gloss for conveying that authority to his readers. They represent a convergence of formal and theoretical experiment.

Whereas the first and second chapters are concerned almost entirely with vernacular glossing traditions, the third and fourth focus on works that explicitly position themselves in the academic commentary tradition. Erasmus' *Moriae Encomium* and Douglas' *Eneados* thus introduce a

---

[44] For the authorship of *Reson and Sensuallyte*, see Chapter 2, note 22.
[45] Hoccleve's *Regiment of Princes* would have been the obvious alternative to Lydgate's *Siege of Thebes* and *Fall of Princes*, but because it was not printed in the late fifteenth and sixteenth centuries, it would not have allowed for comparison of its glossing in manuscript and print.
[46] The second manuscript of *Reson and Sensuallyte*, BL MS 29729, is a sixteenth-century copy of MS Fairfax 16, and thus has no independent authority.

second important context for the development of subsequent self-glossing practices—but although they work within the same tradition, Douglas and Erasmus respond rather differently to the academic model. For Erasmus the fact that academic commentary is an established genre allows him to create a commentary that is both genuine exegesis and self-conscious performance, in which the layers of annotation around Moria's speech replicate its heterodox and unreliable qualities. In contrast, whereas Erasmus' commentary falls somewhere between imitation and parody of the commentary genre, Douglas' arises in response to what Jeffrey Schnapp has identified as the preconditions for the genre's development: that is, as 'a solution to and symptom of anxieties concerning temporal succession, present decline, and loss'.[47] Foregrounding the figure of the translator as a way of combatting such anxieties, Douglas emphasizes his own interventions in the text, repeatedly describing the process of making meaning whereby (in Schnapp's words) a text 'fundamentally at odds with the requirements of present readers and institutions, is made to speak in the voice of the present through the act of ventriloquism that is commentary'.[48] As with Lydgate's poems and *Reson and Sensuallyte*, vernacular authorial identity is *shaped by* the use of glosses, as well as expressed through them; like those earlier works, Douglas' *Eneados* shows formal experiment and theory to be inextricably linked.

With both the *Moria* and the *Eneados*, however, such experimental glossing is lost in transmission. William Copland's 1553 edition of the *Eneados* substitutes for Douglas' destabilizing glossing a series of ethical and preceptive pointers which imply that there is no essential difference between Virgil's original and Douglas' translation, and that either may be read as a storehouse of timeless wisdom. Sir Thomas Chaloner's 1549 translation of the *Moria* similarly appears with a much more restrictive set of glosses than that developed by Erasmus; far from allowing the proliferation of voices in the text to extend into the margins, they instead seek to contain potentially controversial elements of Folie's speech by stressing her fictionality. Thus, whereas Douglas' and Erasmus' commentaries contribute to the development of a style of glossing and a theory of authorship grounded in practice, the Copland print of the *Eneados* and Chaloner's *Praise of Folie* witness some of the contrary pressures arising from print publication: far from delighting in process, Copland's glosses respond to the commercial imperative to make the text useful (and thus attractive) to potential readers, while Chaloner's reflect contemporary anxieties around the widespread dissemination of printed texts.[49] In consequence,

---

[47] Schnapp, 'Commentary', 814.   [48] Schnapp, 'Commentary', 815.
[49] For such anxieties, see further David McKitterick, *Print, Manuscript, and the Search for Order* (Cambridge: Cambridge University Press, 2003), 8.

both texts simultaneously reflect and contribute to the sixteenth-century phenomenon identified by Andrew Taylor, whereby print, though not inherently stable, came to be associated with stability.[50] This is in large part because—despite numerous continuities between manuscript and print production, and despite the fact that print demonstrably did not, in any actual, physical sense, 'fix' a text—assertions of its stability nonetheless became something of a trope in the prefaces of early printed texts, as printers sought to advertise their editorial role.[51] One common tactic was to imply a qualitative difference between the single printed work and its numerous manuscript ancestors by claiming that the new edition had refined a wide variety of obscure and mutually contradictory manuscripts into a single, definitive, and readily available text.[52] In consequence, as Susan Noakes has argued, print came to serve as 'myth and emblem' for readers uncomfortable with textual instability, since:

> Printing was widely taken to circumvent. . . temporal loss: Gutenberg's press would seize an author's words just as written and transmit them, unchanged, to a reader anywhere, anytime. . . No matter that there were fifteenth-century scribes who produced copies far more accurate than those produced by presses of the era: a mechanism that would dissociate reading from temporal loss was what many wanted, and that is what some of them thought they got.[53]

With directive and moralizing glosses such as Copland's and Chaloner's, there is a strong analogy between the content of the glosses and the medium in which they appear; by indexing, summarizing, and extracting commonplaces, they reaffirm what is connoted by their appearance in print: that the text and its meaning are stable, timeless, and immutable. They are diametrically opposed to glosses such as Douglas', which recognize temporal

---

[50] Andrew Taylor, *Textual Situations: Three Medieval Manuscripts and their Readers* (Philadelphia: University of Pennsylvania Press, 2002), 15–18.

[51] For continuities between manuscript and print production, see C. F. Bühler, *The Fifteenth-Century Book: The Scribes, the Printers, the Decorators* (Philadelphia: University of Pennsylvania Press, 1960); Sandra Hindman and James Douglas Farquhar, *Pen to Press: Illustrated Manuscripts and Printed Books in the First Century of Printing* (College Park: University of Maryland and Baltimore and Johns Hopkins University, 1977); and Paul Saenger and Michael Heinlen, 'Incunable Description and its Implication for the Analysis of Fifteenth-Century Reading Habits', in *Printing the Written Word: The Social History of Books, circa 1450–1520*, ed. Sandra Hindman (Ithaca: Cornell University Press, 1991), 225–58. For the real instability of sixteenth-century printed texts, see Adrian Johns, *The Nature of the Book: Print and Knowledge in the Making* (Chicago: University of Chicago Press, 1998); and McKitterick, *Print, Manuscript*, esp. 97–165.

[52] See for example *The Canterbury Tales* (Westminster: William Caxton, 1483), STC 5083, sig. aii; *The fall of prynces* (London: John Wayland, 1554), STC 3177.5, sig. ✠i^v; *The woorkes of Geoffrey Chaucer, newly printed, with diuers addicions, whiche were neuer in printe before* (London: John White, 1561), STC 5076, sig. ii^v.

[53] Noakes, *Timely Reading*, 34–5.

loss and use it as a basis for a reinvention of authorship; to glosses such as Erasmus', which serve less to frame than to amplify the text; and to the very idea that the processes of writing and printing leave traces in a text and, in doing so, destabilize its 'sentence'.

They are diametrically opposed, as well, to diverting glossing. Yet it is precisely because glossing such as Copland's or Chaloner's seeks relentlessly to stabilize the text that it becomes a model against which diverting glossers react. Focusing on William Baldwin's *Beware the Cat* (1553; first edition 1570) and William Bullein's *Dialogue against the Fever Pestilence* (1564), the fifth chapter examines two such reactions, arguing that both texts exemplify the dangers of accepting the stability of the printed word at face value, and that they do so partly through the use of actively misleading glossing. Both authors locate their glossing in a variety of existing traditions: Baldwin's responds to academic commentary, but also to a tradition of vernacular writing on the subject of literary authority that goes back to Chaucer's *House of Fame*, as well as to evolving paratextual conventions in printed texts; the *Cat*'s glosses are only one in a series of framing devices that reveal Baldwin's familiarity with printing house practices. Bullein's *Dialogue* responds, among other things, to Baldwin's work, as well as to a tradition of advice writing with connections to both vernacular satire and a more Latinate, humanist conception of writing and reading as ethical activities. Both authors display a concern for the social health of their country that manifests itself through their linking of the questions of religious reform and the state of writing and publishing. Despite the clear Reformist sympathies of both writers, however, and despite the fact that Baldwin, in particular, explicitly associates Catholicism with oral culture, they do not grant unquestioning authority to the printed word, but rather demonstrate through the use of incongruously informal, partial, and diverting glosses that the printed text represents (in Irvine's words) 'an ongoing chain of supplements and interpretations'.[54] Their glossing is Reformist not in what it says, but in how it says it. It operates by the creation of what Wolfgang Iser has described as 'blanks'. Elaborating on this term, he writes that:

> Communication in literature . . . is a process set in motion and regulated, not by a given code, but by a mutually restrictive and magnifying interaction between the explicit and the implicit, between revelation and concealment. What is concealed spurs the reader into action, but this action is also controlled by what is revealed; the explicit in its turn is transformed when the

[54] Irvine, ' "Bothe text and gloss" ', 85.

implicit has been brought to light. Whenever the reader bridges the gaps, communication begins.[55]

Although Iser is talking purely about metaphorical blanks—gaps in the content of a work—in Baldwin's and Bullein's glossing the metaphorical is realized in the material. The literal blank—the white space—between text and gloss is an objective correlative, 'standing for' the oblique way in which the content of the diverting gloss relates to the text.[56] Their 'diversion' is both a form of entertainment and means of fostering responsible reading, shaping a commonwealth of active, morally engaged readers.

Baldwin's and Bullein's glossing thus depends on their thinking *through*—that is, by means of—the medium of print: on creating a discrepancy between the formality, stability, and atemporality which readers had been encouraged to associate with the medium, and the informal, destabilizing content of the glosses. By undermining the formal authority that the printed text confers on the author, their glosses re-authorize him on different terms: ones that allow for an element of the unpredictable and the improvised in writing, locating it not as the fixed communication of a timeless message, but as a form of improvisation. Such glosses are both an extension of the text and an acknowledgement that the business of writing must remain permanently unfinished.

A comparable consciousness of the impact of the medium of publication on the meaning of a text is found in the authors who are the subject of the two final chapters: George Gascoigne, Sir John Harington, and Thomas Nashe. For all of these, their understanding of authorship emerges from the intersection of their knowledge of the writing process with what Wendy Wall has called their 'experience with the book form', and from the discrepancy between the two.[57] By contrast to Baldwin's and Bullein's glosses, however, Gascoigne's, Harington's, and Nashe's do not

---

[55] Wolfgang Iser, 'Interaction between Text and Reader', in *The Reader in the Text: Essays on Audience and Interpretation*, ed. Susan R. Suleiman and Inge Crosman (Princeton: Princeton University Press, 1980), 111–2. For discussion of the active reader in an early modern English context, see Stephen B. Dobranski, *Readers and Authorship in Early Modern England* (Cambridge: Cambridge University Press, 2009), 21–62; and cf. Arthur F. Kinney, *The Cambridge Companion to English Literature, 1500–1600* (Cambridge: Cambridge University Press, 2000), 1–10; for an overview of reader-response theory, see Karin Littau, *Theories of Reading: Books, Bodies, and Bibliomania* (Cambridge: Polity Press, 2006), 103–24.

[56] For the way in which 'gaps' in the text act on the reader's imagination, see further Wolfgang Iser, 'The Reading Process: A Phenomenological Approach', in *The Implied Reader* (Baltimore: Johns Hopkins University Press, 1974), 274–94; Roland Barthes, *S/Z: An Essay*, tr. Richard Miller (London: Jonathan Cape, 1975); and Walter J. Ong, 'The Writer's Audience Is Always a Fiction', *PMLA* 90 (1975), 9–21.

[57] Wendy Wall, 'Authorship and the Material Conditions of Writing', in *Cambridge Companion to English Literature, 1500–1600*, 85.

seek to make print one of the subjects of their works, but rather to render it invisible. Recording what appear to be private words spoken in public—the writer's ostensibly spontaneous response to his own text—they eradicate the distinction between the moment of writing and the moment of reading, and thus create a brief illusion of the writer's real presence.[58] The fiction of intimacy is substituted for the trope of stability.

Such outlines over-simplify, of course. The glossing of Baldwin's *Beware the Cat* revels in collapsing distinctions between the spoken and the printed word, whereas that of Bullein's *Dialogue* ultimately attempts to reaffirm at least a potential textual stability. Gascoigne's is concerned almost entirely to further his creation of fictional self-representations in print, exploiting the real distance between himself and his readers, whereas Harington's seeks to replicate in print the conditions of manuscript transmission; Nashe's glossing responds not only to previous experimentation with printed glosses, but also to a specific tradition of radical Protestant glossing that extends through the Marprelate tracts back to Robert Crowley's 1550 edition of *Piers Plowman*. The very diversity of these broadly contemporary practices, and the confidence with which their authors assume a knowledge of more conventional glossing, suggest that the gloss was becoming established as what Irvine terms a 'macrogenre': 'A literary form embracing, and attached to, other genres, which was not only transcribed in the margins, outside the . . . space designed for texts (literary, legal, scientific, biblical) but . . . was also inscribed within many individual texts themselves, providing principles for composition and interpretation.'[59] It also gives an indication of the process by which such establishment comes about: namely through a diversity of responses to, and explorations of, the potential and the limitations of the relatively new medium of print.

In this respect diverting glossing is both consonant with and different from pre-print self-glossing. It would clearly be impossible to argue that there is a direct line of descent from, say, Lydgate's glossing through Skelton's to Nashe's. At most, it would be possible to suggest that glosses such as those to the *Siege of Thebes* and *Fall of Princes*, which found their way into print, became one of a diversity of possible influences on later self-glossing authors, and that the extreme variety of such influences prompted thought about the possible effects of glossing, thus encouraging further experiment with the form. Yet despite the very different relationships between author and readers enabled by the different media of

---

[58] Cf. Baswell, 'Talking Back to the Text', 123; Iser, 'The Reading Process'; and Barthes, *S/Z*. Glosses such as Gascoigne's and Harington's seem to anticipate in practice what Iser and Barthes have to say in theory about the importance of reader engagement.

[59] Irvine, ' "Bothe text and gloss" ', 87.

transmission, earlier self-glossing and diverting glossing are connected in the way they make visible the process of shaping the text—something that counters any notion that a text comes into being whole, or is univocal and atemporal—and use that visibility as a spur to re-examine questions of literary authority. In both cases, we find heterogenous influences, mediation of diverse material, and the use of the margins as a locus of experiment, whether with views concerning authorship or with the form in which they are expressed. Indeed, the two are inseparable; as Donald McKenzie says, 'Forms *effect* meaning'.[60] Diverting glossing and earlier self-glossing are linked by their authors' heightened awareness of such inseparability, and by their inscription of this awareness within the work. Each of these elements in turn helps shape the gloss as a means of making visible the resources available to the self-defining, self-fashioning author: that is, to a certain perennial *type* of author in his fifteenth- and sixteenth-century manifestations, whose interest is in the processes of writing, translation, or print publication rather than the finished work. Both enabling and making visible discoveries about authorial control of a text, the glossing examined here shows writers adapting their thinking about the business of writing according to the physical form of their texts, and in doing so catches late medieval and early modern authors in the very act of making meaning.

---

[60] Donald F. McKenzie, quoted in McKitterick, *Print, Manuscript*, 8.

1

Material Processes
The Glossing of Lydgate's *Siege of Thebes* and *Fall of Princes*

In Speght's editions of Chaucer's works (1598 and 1602), Lydgate's *Siege of Thebes* (c. 1420–22) is placed at the end of the volume, just as it had been in Stow's edition of 1561.[1] Both Stow and Speght are noted for their diligent searching out of previously unpublished works of Chaucer's, and also for including in their editions a number of works by other authors.[2] Unlike many of these additions, Lydgate's *Siege of Thebes* is correctly attributed; although in Speght's 1598 edition it is listed in the table of contents as Chaucer's, it is nonetheless preceded by its own title page that names Lydgate as its author.[3] In Speght's 1602 edition it is attributed to Lydgate on the part-title page, as well as being printed after the explicit 'Thus endeth the workes of Geffrey Chaucer', described as 'The Storie of Thebes Compiled by Iohn Lidgate, Monke of Bvrie'.[4]

The correct attribution of the *Siege* reflects the way Lydgate imagines himself as one of Chaucer's pilgrims in its Prologue, inscribing his authorship within the text of the poem. Whereas a number of fifteenth-century manuscripts present the *Siege* as a continuation of the *Tales*—not as a result of misattribution, but because of their closely related content—Stow's and Speght's separation of the two is indicative of how, by the mid- to late-sixteenth century, attribution to a named author had become the more common means of

---

[1] *The workes of our antient and learned English poet, Geffrey Chaucer* (London: George Bishop, 1598), STC 5077; *The workes of our ancient and learned English poet, Geffrey Chaucer* (London: Adam Islip, 1602), STC 5080 (henceforth cited as Chaucer, *Workes* (1598) and Chaucer, *Workes* (1602)). For the various issues of Stow's edition, see Joseph A. Dane, 'In Search of Stow's Chaucer', in *John Stow (1525–1605) and the Making of the English Past*, ed. Ian Gadd and Alexandra Gillespie (London: The British Library, 2004), 145–56.

[2] For Stow and Speght as editors, see Anne Hudson, 'John Stow (1525?–1605)' and Derek Pearsall, 'Thomas Speght (c. 1550–?)', both in *Editing Chaucer: The Great Tradition*, ed. Paul G. Ruggiers (Norman, OK: Pilgrim, 1984), 53–70 and 71–92.

[3] Chaucer, *Workes* (1598), sig. Aiii^v; f. 369.

[4] Chaucer, *Workes* (1602), f. 353; f. 352^v.

selecting and ordering texts.[5] Their editions of Chaucer's *Workes* witness two related effects of this phenomenon: on the one hand, the name 'Chaucer' becomes a magnet for previously unprinted material, with works by other authors being used to expand his canon; on the other hand, the inclusion among his works of poems attributed to others implicitly canonizes him on grounds of influence as well as output.

This project of canonization is nowhere more apparent than in Speght's extensive prefatory material. Like previous editors before him, Speght makes much of the labour he has expended in preparing the text. In a prefatory epistle to his patron Cecil, he declares:

> That both by old written Copies, and by Ma. William Thynne's praise-worthy labours, I haue reformed the whole Worke, whereby Chaucer for the most part is restored to his owne Antiquitie, and noted withall most of his Sentences and Prouerbes; hauing also with some Additions reduced into due place those former Notes and Collections; as likewise proued the significations of most of the old and obscure words, by the tongues and dialects, from whence they are deriued; translated also into English all the Latine and French by him vsed; and lastly, added to his Workes some things of his own doing, as the treatise of Iacke Vpland against Friers, and his A.B.C.[6]

His labour, he suggests, has been both backward-looking and forward-facing. On the one hand, he claims to have built on the work of at least one previous editor, and consulted a number of older manuscripts alongside it, in order to restore Chaucer's works to something as close as possible to what—he asserts—was their original form. On the other hand, however, he emphasizes the additions he has made for his readers' convenience: the glossing of difficult words, the translation of foreign terms, the provision of etymologies, and the identification of sententious matter and commonplaces. His apparatus reflects the concern that is apparent in so much of the prefatory matter: to elevate Chaucer's works above merely

---

[5] Manuscripts that copy the *Siege* continuously with the *Canterbury Tales* include BL MSS Egerton 2864 and Additional 5140; Oxford, Christ Church MS 152; Longleat MS 257; and University of Texas MS 143. For further discussion of material frequently paired with the *Siege*, see A. S. G. Edwards, 'Beinecke MS 661 and Early Fifteenth-Century English Manuscript Production', *Yale University Library Gazette* 66 (supp.) (1991), 181–2. For the increasing use of the author as an organizing principle in printed texts, see Siobhan Bly, 'From Text to Man: Re-creating Chaucer in Sixteenth-Century Print Editions', *Comitatus* 30 (1999), 131–66; and A. S. G. Edwards, 'Chaucer from Manuscript to Print: The Social Text and the Critical Text', *Mosaic* 28 (1995), 1–12; cf. also Cynthia J. Brown, *Poets, Patrons, and Printers: Crisis of Authority in Late-Medieval France* (Ithaca: Cornell University Press, 1995), 61–195.

[6] Chaucer, *Workes* (1602), sig. Aiii. I cite this edition because it witnesses the fullest form of Speght's apparatus. For details of the differences between the 1598 and 1602 editions, see Pearsall, 'Speght', 85–8.

vernacular status. A second prefatory epistle, from Francis Beaumont to Speght, makes explicit this endeavour. Beaumont enquires:

> And now (M. Speght) seeing not onely all Greeke and Latine Poets haue had their interpretours, and the most of them translated into our tongue, but the French also and Italian, as Guillaume de Sallust, that most diuine French Poet; Petrarke and Ariosto, those two excellent Italians (wherof the last, instructed by M. Iohn Harington doth now speake as good English, as he did Italian before,) shall onely Chaucer, our ancient Poet, nothing inferiour to the best, amongst all the Poets of the world, remaine alwaies neglected, and neuer be so well vnderstood of his owne countrie men, as Strangers are?[7]

Whereas Beaumont's letter supplements Speght's own earlier assertion that Chaucer's work deserves a commentary because of its resemblance to classical literature, it also shows explicit nationalism in its emphasis on Harington's 'naturalization' of Ariosto, and implies the emergence of a community of literary excellence from which Chaucer threatens to be excluded. Other parts of the prefatory matter state with equal confidence that he deserves attention not just on literary, but on social grounds. As Tim Machan has argued, Speght's edition not only 'canonizes' Chaucer as the father of English literature, but does so by elevating him socially.[8] The title page that describes Chaucer as 'our antient and learned poet' is followed not by a list of his works, but by a family tree under the heading 'The Progenie of Geffrey Chaucer'. Exploiting to the full the fact that Chaucer's wife's sister was John of Gaunt's third wife, and that his son married the daughter of a knight, this shows a woodcut portrait of Chaucer flanked on the left by the royal family tree from John of Gaunt to Henry V and, on the right, by that of his daughter-in-law and grandchildren. Titles and coats of arms abound. Moreover, although the woodcut figure at the centre is clearly based on the famous Chaucer portrait in BL MS Harley 4866, the position of the right hand has tellingly been altered.[9] Whereas in the surviving manuscript versions it points to the text where Chaucer is mentioned, here it points to his own breast, as if to indicate that he is defined by this glorious genealogy. Social status takes precedence over literary achievement.

---

[7] Chaucer, *Workes* (1602), sig. Aviii.

[8] Tim W. Machan, 'Speght's *Works* and the Invention of Chaucer', *Text* 8 (1995), 145–70; and cf. Derek Pearsall, 'John Stow and Thomas Speght as Editors of Chaucer: A Question of Class', in *John Stow and the Making of the English Past*, 119–25.

[9] For the portrait, see further Michael Seymour, 'Manuscript Portraits of Chaucer and Hoccleve', *Burlington Magazine* 124, no. 955 (October, 1982), 618–23; and David R. Carlson, 'Thomas Hoccleve and the Chaucer Portrait', *Huntington Library Quarterly* 54 (1991), 283–300; cf. also Jeanne E. Krochalis, 'Hoccleve's Chaucer Portrait', *Chaucer Review* 21 (1986), 234–45.

The marginal glosses to Speght's prefatory matter serve a comparable end. Although their primary purpose is to furnish the reader with additional information about the places and the persons mentioned in the biography of Chaucer, their almost exclusive focus on English history serves both to reinforce the impression that Chaucer was at the very centre of the life of his time, and to educate readers in their national heritage. Assuming an intimate and casually informative tone, they seek to forge a community of Englishmen united by a common knowledge of their common history, while at the same time drawing on that idea of community as proof of Chaucer's importance. Each of the figures they discuss is introduced with a demonstrative article—'This Sir Richard Dangle', or 'This Iohn Burghershe'—in a way that draws them out of the historical past into the reader's present. Moreover, the glosses frequently give more information than is strictly necessary, and they are not above reproducing hearsay; thus, alongside the text's assertion that it was at John of Gaunt's instigation that Chaucer 'made the Treatise Of the alliance betwixt Mars and Venus', the gloss comments:

> Some say hee did but translate it: and that it was made by sir Otes de Grantsome Knight, in French: of my lady of Yorke daughter to the K. of Spaine, representing Venus, & my Lord of Huntingdon sometime Duke of Excester. This lady was younger sister to Constance Iohn of Gaunts second wife. This Lord of Huntingdon was called Iohn Holland, halfe brother to Richard the second: hee married Elizabeth the daughter of Iohn of Gaunt Duke of Lancaster.[10]

Almost all of this is (strictly speaking) otiose. It does, however, present the editor-glossator as a well-informed and helpful guide, able to grant insights into family connections at the highest level of society. His frequent use of the first person further implies that he has privileged knowledge, as when he comments on the assumption that the presence of 'the Armes of the Merchants of the Staple' in the windows of a house belonging to Chaucer's ancestors is evidence of their profession: 'This coinecture is of small force: for the Merchants of the Staple had not any Armes graunted to them, as I haue been informed, before the time of Henry the sixt, or much thereabout.'[11] Speaking man to man or man to woman, such comments imply that the book is the gateway for the reader to join this elevated community. Like the 'arguments' that preface each of the poems and sometimes include quite detailed information about the circumstances of their making, the glosses are at once knowledgeable and companionable.[12] They are the reader's friend.

---

[10] Chaucer, *Workes* (1602), sig. Bviii[v].   [11] Chaucer, *Workes* (1602), sig. Biii.
[12] See for example the arguments attached to *La Belle Dame sans Merci* and Hoccleve's *Letter of Cupid*, in Chaucer, *Workes* (1602), f. 238[v]; f. 310[v].

Although Speght is so confident in presenting biographical and historical information to his readers, he conspicuously does not annotate the poems themselves; with the exception of the prefatory arguments and (in his 1602 edition) the provision of numerous small marginal hands, or 'manicules', whose extended index fingers indicate sententiae in the text, the supplementary material that he prints is inherited from Stow's edition.[13] Such material is relatively rare; it includes the speech markers in *La Belle Dame sans Merci*, the headings in *The Treatise of the Astrolabe*, the Latin verses in *Boece*, a passage from the *Thebaid* inserted into Cassandra's interpretation of Troilus' dream in *Troilus and Criseyde*, and of course the glosses in Lydgate's *Siege*. Their inclusion suggests that, where such supplementary material was available, Speght—like Stow before him—considered it to be significant.[14] Precisely what he considered its significance to be is less clear, however. The mise-en-page of the *Workes* indicates that he did not consider it equivalent in kind to his own glosses to the prefatory matter: whereas the latter appear in the margins in italic, those to the *Siege* are printed within the text-block in Roman. Yet one feature of his 1602 edition suggests that this inherited matter did influence the presentation of part of Speght's own apparatus. In the 1598 edition the arguments Speght provides for each of the *Canterbury Tales* and the other major poems in the volume are grouped together as part of the prefatory matter. By contrast, in the 1602 edition, each appears at the head of the poem to which it relates, printed in identical format to the inherited paratextual material in a typeface that contrasts strongly with the black letter of the text, and surrounded by a large amount of white space.[15] This visual punctuation is most emphatic in the *Canterbury Tales* (which contains numerous arguments) and the *Siege of Thebes* (which contains numerous glosses). The effect is to create a striking visual consonance between the two poems: one that mirrors their closely related contents. The resemblance suggests that the *Siege* glosses served as Speght's model in his ongoing attempt to establish an authoritative presentation of Chaucer's *Canterbury Tales*.[16]

---

[13] See Clare R. Kinney, 'Thomas Speght's Renaissance Chaucer and the Solaas of Sentence in *Troilus and Criseyde*', in *Refiguring Chaucer in the Renaissance*, ed. Theresa Krier (Gainesville: University of Florida Press, 1998), 66–84; and for the definition of 'manicules', see William H. Sherman, *Used Books: Marking Readers in Renaissance England* (Philadelphia: University of Pennsylvania Press, 2008), 25–52.

[14] Stow used the 1550 edition of Thynne's Chaucer (STC 5071–74) as copy-text for by far the greater part of his edition (see Bradford Y. Fletcher, 'Printer's Copy for Stow's Chaucer', *Studies in Bibliography* 31 (1978), 184–201; and Hudson, 'Stow', 58).

[15] Speght adopts the arrangement of the inherited paratextual material from Stow, who similarly places any paratextual material in the text-block, in a variety of distinct typefaces, frequently (though not quite consistently) Roman for Latin material, Italic for French, and Black Letter for English.

[16] In the 1598 edition a comparable visual connection is established by using the same border for the title page of the *Siege* as for that of the *Canterbury Tales*.

How, though, do the glosses of the *Siege* relate to the text? Despite the prominence he gives them, Speght's alignment of the *Siege* glosses with his own narrative summaries does not do justice to their complexity. Although many of them function as a form of running index, this chapter will argue that they also register a clear interest in questions of authorship and authority, and that—like those to the later *Fall of Princes* (c. 1430–9)—they witness Lydgate's discovery of the extent of his impact on the 'sentence' of the text he translates. Lisa Cooper and Andrea Denny-Brown's discussion of the significance of the frequently repeated term 'matere' in Lydgate's writing is relevant here. Arguing that it is used both of his subject-matter and of 'physical matter, especially the mortal body and its worldly attachments', they state that:

> 'Matter' for Lydgate . . . is a term that stretches to encompass not only the details of many and varied poetic projects but also the body that weighs us down and holds us back; the objects, both necessary and less so, with which we furnish our everyday lives; and the intellectual and spiritual illumination that we urgently seek to find and strive toward.[17]

A term associated with 'matere' that is also common in Lydgate's writing is 'process'. He uses the word in a number of different senses; frequently, it appears as a synonym for 'story', 'writing', or 'part of a book'. Thus, early in the *Fall of Princes*, he refers to both Laurent de Premierfait's prologue and Boccaccio's entire work as 'processe' (Prol. I. 42; 127), addresses women who 'beholde & see/this chapitle and the process reede' (I. 6707–8), and writes in lines only three stanzas apart that readers of his previous work, the *Troy Book*, may 'see' its 'processe' and 'beholde' its 'materis' (I. 5993; I. 6014); here, the two terms seem to be used almost interchangeably.[18] Elsewhere Lydgate uses 'process' to refer to the passage of time, sometimes with the connotation of cause and effect, or inevitable sequence of events, as when he writes that 'Afftir gret age, bi processe deth in cam' (I. 773), states of a pregnant woman that 'bi processe foorth a child she brought' (I. 4124), or refers to 'processe off yeris' (I. 1504). In theory, as the *Middle English Dictionary* entry makes clear, these are quite separate senses of the word.[19] In practice, however, their

---

[17] Lisa H. Cooper and Andrea Denny-Brown (eds), *Lydgate Matters: Poetry and Material Culture in the Fifteenth Century* (Basingstoke: Palgrave MacMillan, 2008), 2–3.

[18] Unless otherwise specified, all quotations from the *Fall* will be taken from John Lydgate, *The Fall of Princes*, ed. Henry Bergen, 4 vols., Early English Text Society, e.s. 121–4 (London, 1924–7).

[19] *Middle English Dictionary*, s.v. proces, *n*. 'Processe' and 'matere' are terms commonly linked in prologues to dramatic interludes of the period; see for example 'The Killing of the Children', ll. 20, 30, 49, and 559, in *The Late Medieval Religious Plays of Bodleian MS Digby 133 and e. Musaeo 160*, ed. Donald C. Baker, John L. Murphy, and Louis B. Hall, EETS e.s. 183 (London, 1982).

frequent juxtaposition allows for a degree of 'bleed' between the two: one that is encouraged by Lydgate's almost equally frequent use of the cognate verb 'proceed' in the sense 'continue to write', as when he states that 'Iohn Bochas procedyng in his book . . . Gan for to write' (II. 127; 129) or that:

> Anon afftir, I off entencioun,
> With penne in hande faste gan me speede,
> As I koude, in my translacioun,
> In this laboure ferthere to proceede.
>
> (II. 141–4)

'Proceeding', or the making of 'process', is here described specifically as both mental and physical endeavour, connected with the poet's 'entencioun' but also with the physical activity of writing.[20] Moreover, it is clear that Lydgate associates 'processe' specifically with amplification of his source. Early in his prologue he writes that:

> A story which is nat pleynli told,
> But constreyned vndir woordes fewe
> For lak off trouthe, wher thei be newe or old,
> Men bi report kan nat the mater shewe;
> These ookis grete be nat doun ihewe
> First at a stroke, but bi long processe,
> Nor longe stories a woord may not expresse.
>
> (Prol. I. 92–8)

'Processe' here refers to the expenditure of effort over a passage of time necessary to bring down an oak tree, but because the oak is used as a simile for the 'story' in the first line of the stanza, the juxtaposition of the two words raises the ghost of the literary sense of 'process'. The association is reaffirmed when Lydgate writes at the end of the prologue that he attempted 'my processe pleynli for to leede' (Prol. I. 453): in both cases the 'matter' of the story is plainly inseparable from the style, or the process of making meaning. As a result—unlike 'matere', which emphasizes the substance of the text—'process' emphasizes the labour expended by the poet, over a period of time, in order to bring that substance into being.[21] It thus conveys a view of text of which glossing is a natural

---

[20] For the connection with mental effort, cf. Thiestes' declaration that his brother: 'Bi long processe in his entencioun /. . . ymagined my destruccioun' (I. 3926–7).
[21] For Lydgate's development of a vocabulary that reflects his view of writing as a craftsmanlike reworking of his material, see Lois Ebin, *Illuminator, Makar, Vates: Visions of Poetry in the Fifteenth Century* (Lincoln, NE: University of Nebraska Press, 1988), 19–48. For two more recent arguments that confirm that both his style and translation practices were genuinely experimental, see Phillipa Hardman, 'Lydgate's "Uneasy Style"', in *John Lydgate: Poetry, Culture, and Lancastrian England*, ed. Larry Scanlon and James Simpson (Notre

counterpart, since glosses stand as material signs of the different stages of composition: that is, of the text itself as 'process'. As we shall see, whereas Speght's glossing is part of a considered strategy to strengthen Chaucer's reputation as the father of English literature, that of the *Siege* bears witness to the writer's realization of his own transformation of a text in translation. It is less an attempt to authorize the text for its readers than it is a cause of this essentially private discovery, but it nonetheless represents an early instance of experimentation with a form of writing 'beside the text' to which Speght's confident, rhetorical glossing is one of many heirs.

A THEORY OF EXPERIMENT: GLOSSING LYDGATE'S *SIEGE OF THEBES* AND *FALL OF PRINCES*

To date, the glossing of Lydgate's poems has not received much critical attention. It thus stands in striking contrast to that of Gower's *Confessio Amantis*, whose Latin verses and marginal glosses have both been subject to extensive analysis as an integral part of the play of meaning in the poem and a conscious attempt at self-authorization.[22] The difference is almost certainly due to the rather haphazard appearance of the glosses to Lydgate's poems. Far from forming a coherent apparatus, they consist primarily of short phrases that indicate the main subjects of the text, but also include occasional source and citation glosses, proverbial phrases, single word indications of characters, and simple 'nota' glosses.[23] The fact that not all glosses occur in all manuscripts makes it still less surprising that they have not been considered as, potentially, part of the design of the

---

Dame: University of Notre Dame Press, 2006), 12–35; and Ardis Butterfield, 'Rough Translation: Charles d'Orléans, Lydgate and Hoccleve', in *Rethinking Medieval Translation: Ethics, Politics, Theory*, ed. Emma Campbell and Robert Mills (Cambridge: D.S. Brewer, 2012), 204–25; cf. also the editors' introduction to the latter for usefully contextualizing discussion.

[22] For discussions of the apparatus to the *Confessio*, see for example Siân Echard, 'With Carmen's Help: Latin Authorities in the *Confessio Amantis*', *Studies in Philology* 95 (1998), 1–40; Derek Pearsall, 'Gower's Latin in the *Confessio Amantis*', in *Latin and Vernacular: Studies in Late-Medieval Texts and Manuscripts*, ed. A. J. Minnis (Cambridge: D. S. Brewer, 1989), 13–25; Winthrop Wetherbee, 'Latin Structure and Vernacular Space: Gower, Chaucer, and the Boethian Tradition', in *Chaucer and Gower: Difference, Mutuality, Exchange*, ed. R. F. Yeager (Victoria: University of Victoria, 1991), 7–35; and R. F. Yeager, 'English, Latin, and the Text as "Other": The Page as Sign in the Work of John Gower', *Text* 3 (1987), 251–67.

[23] As with Gower manuscripts, the position of the glosses in relation to the text also varies; in most manuscripts they appear in the text-block, but in some they are copied in the margins, and in others they are divided between the two.

poems.[24] With both the *Siege of Thebes* and the *Fall of Princes*, however, the extant manuscripts do suggest that at least some of the glosses may be traced back to the poems' composition, and that they are significant for our understanding of Lydgate's views of authorship.[25]

With the *Siege of Thebes*, despite complex relations between the thirty-one surviving manuscripts, there are strong resemblances—both of content and position—between the glosses of manuscripts that belong to different branches of the stemma.[26] The phrasing of these glosses varies slightly from manuscript to manuscript and the fact that not all glosses occur in all manuscripts complicates things further. Yet the consistency with which identical points in the text are emphasized is remarkable nonetheless.[27] Even when, as in MS Rawlinson C.48, the language of the glosses changes from English to Latin, their content corresponds to that of the glosses in other manuscripts, and they are attached to the same lines. The implication is that the *Siege* glosses are one element of an *ordinatio* that goes back to a very early stage in the transmission of the poem. With the *Fall of Princes*, the case is comparable. Despite the extreme complexity of the textual evidence, the majority of manuscripts contain traces of a single *ordinatio*, using oversize decorated or illuminated initials to emphasize the

---

[24] One exception is Daniel Wakelin's cautious suggestion that some of the glosses to the *Fall* may be authorial (*Humanism, Reading, and English Literature 1430–1530* (Oxford: Oxford University Press, 2007), 39–43.

[25] Stephen Partridge has recently made an analogous argument with reference to the glossing of Chaucer's *Retraction* (' "The Makere of this Boke": Chaucer's Retraction and the Author as Scribe and Compiler', in *Author, Reader, Book: Medieval Authorship in Theory and Practice*, ed. Stephen Partridge and Erik Kwakkel (Toronto: University of Toronto Press, 2012), 106–53).

[26] For the extant manuscripts, see Julia Boffey and A. S. G. Edwards, *A New Index of Middle English Verse* (London: The British Library, 2005); and cf. John Lydgate, *The Siege of Thebes*, ed. Robert R. Edwards (Kalamazoo: Medieval Institute, 2001), 16–18. For the stemma, see *Lydgate's Siege of Thebes*, ed. Axel Erdmann and Eilert Ekwall, 2 vols., EETS e.s. 108 and 125 (London, 1911 and 1930), 2: 36–61 and 62–94.

[27] The glosses in BL MSS Arundel 119; Bodleian MSS Laud Misc. 557 and Bodley 776; Oxford, St John's College MS 266; Oxford, Christ Church MS 152; CUL MS Additional 3137; Cambridge, Magdalene College MS Pepys 2011; Cambridge, Trinity College MSS R.4.20 and O.5.2; Durham UL MS Cosin V.ii.14; Coventry City Record Office MS Acc. 325/1; and PML MS Morgan 4 are closely related, as are those in Book III of Lambeth Palace MS 742 (whose first two books are unglossed). A. S. G. Edwards' descriptions show that Beinecke MS 661 and Boston Public Library MS f. med. 94 also contain a version of these glosses ('Beinecke MS 661 and Early Fifteenth-Century English Manuscript Production', *Yale University Library Gazette* 66 (supp.) (1991), 181–96); Erdmann and Ekwall say that the glosses in the manuscript that was formerly at Old Buckenham Hall, and is now lost, closely resembled those in Arundel 119. Bodleian MSS Digby 230 and Rawlinson C.48 also share many glosses with the other manuscripts, although Digby includes a large number of additional ones, while in Rawlinson the language of the glosses changes from English to Latin part-way through. BL MS Royal 18 D.ii and Bodleian MS Laud Misc. 416 are very sparsely glossed, but those glosses they do include are shared with the other manuscripts.

same stanzas; in a number of manuscripts several of these stanzas are also accompanied by glosses that index the subjects of the text or identify the envoys and their speakers.[28] Although with both poems, these points of emphasis tend to mark 'natural' divisions in the text, such as a new stage in the narrative, or the appearance of a new character, their recurrence in so many different manuscripts is too consistent for them to have been arrived at independently by different scribes or readers. The *Siege of Thebes* manuscript BL MS Additional 18632, whose glosses differ entirely from the glosses that are found elsewhere, is the exception that proves the rule, demonstrating that the *ordinatio* shared by the majority of the manuscripts is by no means an inevitable one.[29]

Just as the recurring glosses and points of emphasis suggest, in general terms, that the *ordinatio* of both poems goes back to a very early stage in their transmission, the content of some glosses indicates specifically that these may have originated as part of the process of translation. In both poems, the indexing glosses are closely related to those in some manuscripts of their respective source texts: for the *Fall of Princes*, Laurent

---

[28] Manuscripts with oversized and/or illuminated initials on many of the same stanzas include BL MSS Harley 1245; Harley 3486; Harley 4197; Harley 4203; Royal 18.D.iv; Royal 18.D.v; Sloane 4031; Additional 21410; and Additional 39659; Bodleian MSS Bodley 263; Hatton 2; e. Musaeo 1; and Rawlinson C.448; Glasgow University Library MS Hunter 5; Princeton MSS Taylor 2 and Garrett 139; PML MS Morgan 124; Rosenbach MS 439/16; and the fragments of the poem preserved as Columbia University Library MS Plimpton 255. Manchester MS Rylands English 2 is the most fully glossed manuscript. Reduced versions of the same set of glosses appear in BL MSS Harley 3486; Harley 4203; Additional 39659; and Bodleian MS Bodley 263. In BL MS Royal 18.D.v space has been left for them, but with one exception—where the scribe mistook gloss for text and began copying it as verse—they have not been supplied. Although it contains a different version of the text of the poem, some glosses in BL MS Harley 1766 do correspond to those in the above manuscripts. I have not seen Longleat MS 254; Chicago University Library MS 565; Chicago, Newbery Library MS 33.3; Berkeley, University of California MS 75; Huntington MS 268; or Tokyo, MS Takamiya 40. The correspondences are by no means complete; not all manuscripts that include decorated or illuminated initials emphasize all of the same stanzas, and BL MS Royal 18.B.xxxi is a notable exception; although it emphasizes some of the same stanzas as other manuscripts with oversized initials, it also contains a unique series of Latin indexing glosses. Despite such variations, however, there is a 'hard core' of emphases that recurs, including on stanzas that do not obviously mark major divisions in the text.

[29] In principle it is possible that in some manuscripts the glosses were copied from a different exemplar than the text; Erdmann and Ekwall argue that there is conflation of exemplars even within the text in MS Royal 18 D.ii and MS Lambeth 742—something which is confirmed, in the Lambeth manuscript, by the sudden introduction of the standard glosses in Book III (*Lydgate's Siege of Thebes*, 2: 62, 85, 88). It is unlikely, however, that this could account for the correspondences between so many different manuscripts. Cf. Stephen Partridge's discussion of Marcia Smith Marzec's discovery, in her work on Hoccleve, that 'most often the variants in the marginalia confirmed the manuscript groups established by collating the English text of the poem itself' ('Designing the Page', in *The Production of Books in England 1350–1500*, ed. Alexandra Gillespie and Daniel Wakelin (Cambridge: Cambridge University Press, 2011), 85–9).

de Premierfait's *De Ruine des nobles hommes et femmes* (1409), and for the *Siege of Thebes*, two thirteenth-century prose redactions of the verse *Roman de Thèbes*, the *Ystoire de Thebes* and the *Roman de Edipus*.[30] Many of the *Fall* glosses correspond closely to Laurent's chapter headings. More significantly, they also include versions of glosses that, in several Laurent manuscripts, mark less obvious developments in the narrative, and do not appear in their tables of contents: in Book I, for example, including 'De Oggigus Roy de thebes et du deluge deaue qui en son temps adiunt'; 'De Grisiton de Thessalie et de la grant famme qui adiunt en son temps'; 'De Narcisus'; 'De Biblis'; and 'De Mirra'.[31] Whereas those that mark major structural divisions might have been added to Lydgate's work without reference to Laurent, this is not true of the latter type of gloss. The fact that the latter nonetheless single out the same episodes as those marked by Laurent's 'secondary' glosses suggests that the glossing of the *Fall* was carried out by someone with a Laurent manuscript to hand, and the most economical hypothesis is that this was the translator, or someone working in close association with him.[32]

With the *Siege of Thebes*, correspondences between its glosses and those of its source-texts are slighter; although both provide a running index to the narrative, they do not necessarily mark the same episodes, and in the *Siege* they are much less frequent than in either of the French texts.[33] Nonetheless, there is one gloss that does imply a close relationship between the glossing of the *Siege* and that of its sources. This is the one that

---

[30] For Laurent, and Lydgate as translator of Laurent, see Laurent de Premierfait's *Des Cas des Nobles Hommes et Femmes, Book I*, ed. P. M. Gathercole (Chapel Hill: University of North Carolina Press, 1968), 34–8. For the sources of the *Siege of Thebes*, see Alain Renoir, 'The Immediate Source of Lydgate's *Siege of Thebes*', *Studia Neophilologica* 33 (1961), 86–95; and cf. Paul M. Clogan, 'Imaging the City of Thebes in Fifteenth-Century England', in *Acta Conventus Neo-Latini Hafniensis* (Binghamton, NY: Medieval and Renaissance Texts and Studies, 1994), 157.

[31] Quoted from MS Bodley 265, ff. 12ᵛ, 13, 42ᵛ, 43. Laurent MSS Paris, BN fr. 226; Bodleian Bodley 265; and BL Royal 14.E.v; Royal 18.D.vii; Royal 20.C.iv; and Additional 18750 contain the chapter headings. With the exception of the last two they also contain the secondary glosses.

[32] By no means all 'secondary' Laurent glosses have counterparts in the apparatus to the *Fall of Princes*, but although this suggests that the glosses to the *Fall* are not translations in the strictest sense, it does appear that the Laurent glosses served as a *model* (and occasionally as a direct source). For a comparable instance of a French model for experimental English glossing, see Stephen Bradford Partridge, 'Glosses in the Manuscripts of the Canterbury Tales: An Edition and Commentary', unpublished PhD thesis (Harvard University: 1992), 2.19–2.24.

[33] I have based this on a comparison of the glosses of the *Siege* with those in *Le Roman de Edipus. . . Nouuellement imprime a Paris*. [S.l., n.d.]; and *Lystoire de Thebes*, in *Prose, Verse, and Truthtelling in the Thirteenth Century: An Essay on Form and Function in Selected Texts, Accompanied by an Edition of the Prose Thèbes as found in the Histoire ancienne jusqu'a César*, ed. Molly Lynde-Recchia (Lexington, KT: French Forum, 2000).

notes: 'Here bigynneth þe storie of Thebes.' Appearing in at least eleven of the surviving manuscripts, with the variant 'Here beginneth the lamentable storye of Thebes & þe destruxion', in a twelfth, it does not occur at the obvious place, at the end of Lydgate's prologue and the beginning of the *Siege* proper; instead, in each of these manuscripts, it appears after a lengthy passage on the foundation of the city which Lydgate added to his source (see Plate 1.1).[34] Although this looks like a simple indexing error, it may be explained by the fact that the position of the gloss corresponds exactly to that of the first rubric in the prose Thebes: 'Ci comence de Thebes'.[35] While it is not conclusive evidence, it does raise the possibility that the glosses in Lydgate's *Siege*, like those in the *Fall*, go back to the process of composition.

Support for this hypothesis is found in the glossing of the first two parts of the *Siege*, which have no counterpart in Lydgate's source: Lydgate's Prologue, which frames the narrative of Thebes as one of the tales told on the road to Canterbury, and a substantial passage on the foundation of the city. The fact that this new material is also glossed is significant in itself, since these glosses could clearly not have been translated from a pre-existing source. Their presence therefore suggests that glossing was perceived as an important feature of the text. In principle the glossator could, of course, have been either the scribe or a reader with an interest in both the content of the poem and its visual appearance. However, the relatively complex relationship between the glosses and the text, as well as the glosses' rather idiosyncratic interest in questions of authorship, again suggests that they mark a stage in the composition of the poem.

We should consider the latter point further. As A. C. Spearing has argued, Lydgate's choice of the story of Thebes as his retrospective contribution to the *Canterbury Tales* constitutes an act of literary rivalry.[36] This is signalled early on, when the Host enquires of Lydgate's narrator who he is, and the narrator tells us how he replied that: 'My name was Lydgate,

---

[34] The gloss is found in Bodleian MSS Bodley 776 and Digby 230; Christ Church MS 152, MS Pepys 2011; Trinity MSS R.4.20 and O.5.2; Coventry City Record Office MS 325/1; PML MS M 4, Boston PL MS f. med. 91; and Beinecke MS 661. The variant is found in BL MS Royal 18.D.ii. At this point CUL MS Additional 3137 and Durham UL MS Cosin V.ii.14 are defective and Lambeth MS 742 and Longleat MS 257 are unglossed. I am extremely grateful to A. S. G. Edwards for confirming the occurrence of the gloss in the Boston and Beinecke manuscripts. I have not seen University of Texas MS 143.

[35] Lynde-Recchia, *Prose, Verse*, 135.

[36] A. C. Spearing, 'Lydgate's Canterbury Tale: *The Siege of Thebes* and Fifteenth-Century Chaucerianism', in *Fifteenth-Century Studies: Recent Essays*, ed. R. F. Yeager (Hamden, CT: Archon, 1984), 338; and cf. James Simpson, 'Dysemol daies and fatal houres': Lydgate's *Destruction of Thebes* and Chaucer's *Knight's Tale*', in *The Long Fifteenth Century: Essays for Douglas Gray*, ed. Helen Cooper and Sally Mapstone (Oxford: Clarendon Press, 1997),

Sich sparseth rickely for the nones
The cite Thebes of myghty sixe stones
As I was tolde a litel here to forn
And Cadmus was hath his Thebes corn
Scept & crosse & his power roial
Wose haue I tolde was ye spouse of al
That ye wel knowe by informacioun
Clerly the pith and the exposicioun
Of this mater as clerkes can wos telle
It were but veyn lenger for to dwelle
To tarie was as in this mater
Sith my tale that ye shal here
Upon your day sal cast a loke shal se
The space in sope as I suppose of an myle
And now ye knowe the firste house amphioun
Bitte began his cite and this toun
And went there long after as I rede
Of hym no more for I wol procede
To my purpos that I furste be gan
Wel tellinge here house ye lyne ran
Lo se the lyne of amphioun by
Siscent was conneted to kyng Layus
Fro kyng to kyng by successioun
Conveynge doun to ye stocke of Amphioun
Derionsly by lyneal discent
But leve al this plenly of entent
To telle forthe in bookes as I rede
Lo se Layus by processe gan procede
Here bigynneth ye story of Thebes
To bere the crowne in this mighty londe
Holdinge ye sceptre of Thebes in his honde
Manly and wysly during al his lyf
And Jocasta called was his wyf
Of kyng Layus & Jocasta his Quene
Ful soomanly the story serth certeyn
For a tyme yong she were bareyn
Til Layus in ful humble wise
To haue a childe he dise sacrifice
Furste to Apollo in his chare so bright
And to Jubiter that hap so grete myght
Besechinge he sith denoute reuence
To graunte only youre heuen influence
That his request may execute be
And specially to the goddesse thre
He besoughte pallas and Juno

And to Diane for to helpen also
That she be not agreued of his bone
And his praier accepted was ful sone
That finally youre his rites colde
Euene like as his herte wolde
The Quene Jocasta hap anon conceyued
Sich shriue ye kyng fully hay pcernes
He made in haste hym list not to abide
Shortly his kyng sent messagers to ride
Lo se the kyng sente oute messagers
For Synynos to telle the fate of Edypus
Fro coste to coste ye sonde can anse
For Synynos and philosophres wise
For sich as wern fam? physiciens
And experte Astronomiens
To come in haste on to his presence
To finden oute shortly in sentence
By crafte conys of calculacioun
The childes fate and exposicioun
Lo se the astronomers called
oute the fate of Edypus
And ther vpon to se a iuggement
The roote taken at the ascendent
The ech souzte oute by minute & degre
The silf oure of his Natiuite
That forzete the heuenly mansions
Clerly cereded by finale fraccions
First by secondes ters & the quars
On augrym stones & on Slate
I proued out by dilligent labour
In tables correct & no ise of al errour
Iustly souzte and sonde oute bope tho
The zeues collect and expanse also
Considres eke by goode inspeccioun
Euy houre and constellacioun
And ech aspect and lokes ek others
Sich were good & sich also euers
There ye were to sad & or at desbat
Happy helful other infortunat
The sides constellacioun of heuene
in the Burthe of Edypus
And finally in conclusioun
They fonde Saturne in ye Scorpion
Heuy cheres malencolik and loth
And was wars furious and swyth

Plate 1.1 Bodleian MS Digby 230, f. 2. Reproduced courtesy of The Bodleian Libraries, The University of Oxford.

// Monk of Bery / Ny3 fyfty 3ere of age' (ll. 92–3). As Robert Meyer-Lee has pointed out, this bold declaration contrasts markedly with Chaucer's own, more oblique self-inscriptions in the *Canterbury Tales*, and it has frequently been read as clumsiness on Lydgate's part.[37] The lines play havoc with common-sense chronology: John Lydgate, aged 49¾, allows himself to participate in a pilgrimage that is not only fictional, but which—had it been real—would have taken place when he was less than 30 years old. On a logical level this simply does not work. On a literary level, however, it does. By joining Chaucer's pilgrims, Lydgate places himself inside a work that had a formative influence on him; without being 'realistic', his appearance there attests an imaginative reality, in which association is privileged over chronology. It thus accurately represents the position of the new poet in relation to his source, as he simultaneously internalizes it, and is internalized by it. By portraying Lydgate as one of the pilgrims on the road to Canterbury, the prologue jokingly implies that he is one of Chaucer's creations, yet because this fictional Lydgate speaks of Thebes, and thus provides the back-story for Chaucer's *Knight's Tale*, it also symbolically presents Lydgate as Chaucer's source.

The glosses to Lydgate's Prologue reflect this ambivalent relationship. As Ralph Hanna and A. S. G. Edwards have argued, their format recalls that of those to the General Prologue in the Ellesmere manuscript of the *Canterbury Tales*; most—like those in Ellesmere—identify the pilgrims by name, while the first of the *Siege* glosses—'Phebus in ariete'—is a close echo of the gloss '*id est sol in ariete*' in the General Prologue in Ellesmere.[38] Like the text of Lydgate's own Prologue, such resemblances both posit Lydgate's poem as an imitation of Chaucer's and, by tacitly claiming a status for Lydgate's work equivalent to that of his master, develop further the text's theme of literary rivalry. There is something odd about this, however. The resemblances would have been visible only to those readers familiar with the Ellesmere *Canterbury Tales* (or any direct descendants that replicated its glosses) and these are likely to have been in a distinct minority. Although the glosses imply that the form as well as the content of the *Siege* asserts Lydgate's status as Chaucer's natural successor and potential surpasser, the claim they make is a relatively private one.

15–34; and Karen Smyth, *Imaginings of Time in Lydgate and Hoccleve's Verse* (Farnham: Ashgate, 2011), 95–114. For the Theban tradition and its significance, see Lee Patterson, *Chaucer and the Subject of History* (London: Routledge, 1991), 1–230.

[37] Robert J. Meyer-Lee, *Poets and Power from Chaucer to Wyatt* (Cambridge: Cambridge University Press, 2007), 38–9.

[38] Ralph Hanna III and A. S. G. Edwards, 'Rotheley, the De Vere Circle, and the Ellesmere Chaucer', *Huntington Library Quarterly* 58 (1995), 17–19.

This, then, suggests that the glosses may be genuinely experimental: that they show Lydgate (or a glossator intimately associated with him) trying out, in practice, the effect of form on content. The same is true of the glosses to his description of the founding of Thebes, which is where the glossator's idiosyncratic interest in authorship becomes apparent. Unlike those to the Prologue, these glosses take the form of summaries; they are very comparable to those which Lydgate inherited from his source texts. This suggests either that they were the work of a different glossator, or that they represent a different type of emulation: a concern to keep the layout of the text self-consistent, rather than the desire that was apparent in the Prologue's glosses to imitate a Chaucerian precedent. Yet because they summarize key points in the text, they inevitably reflect its theme of poetic authority, and thus—despite their different forms—share the concerns of the glosses to the Prologue.

As Lois Ebin has argued, the way in which Lydgate describes the foundation of Thebes has radical implications. Although he alludes briefly to the standard account of its founding by Cadmus, he does so only to reject this in favour of an alternative myth: that Thebes was founded by the poet Amphion. By privileging Amphion over Cadmus, Lydgate presents the poet as the force that civilizes society: not just an advisor to princes, but a symbolic ruler in his own right.[39] In his own words:

> This kyng / thys prudent Amphyoun,
> With the swetnesse / and melodious soun
> And armonye / of his swete song
> The Cyte bylt / that whilom was so strong,
> Be vertue only / of the werbles sharpe
> That he made / in Mercuries harpe.
>
> (ll. 201–7)

As Ebin argues, Lydgate here presents Amphion as 'a symbol of the relation between the poet and the state fully realized—the poet, orator, and statesman, who through his golden language brings harmony and order to the realm'.[40] In characteristic style, Lydgate goes on to provide an explication of this symbol, stating that:

---

[39] Lois Ebin, 'Lydgate's Views on Poetry', *Annuale Mediaevale* 18 (1977), esp. 96–104; and cf. Robert R. Edwards, 'Translating Thebes: Lydgate's *Siege of Thebes* and Stow's Chaucer', *ELH* 70 (2003), 325–9. In contrast, Scott Morgan-Straker argues that Lydgate's poem shows rhetoric and counsel to be futile, and that this undermines the claims he makes for them at the outset ('Deference and Difference: Lydgate, Chaucer, and the *Siege of Thebes*', *Review of English Studies* 52 (2001), 1–21).

[40] Ebin, 'Lydgate's Views', 97.

> To hem that ben prudent,
> The Musycal / the lusty instrument,
> I mene the harpe / most melodious,
> yove to this kynge / be Mercurius,
> And his song/ this auctour can ʒow teche,
> was no thyng / but the crafty speche
> Of this kyng / ycalled Amphioun.
>
> (ll. 221–7)

One of the glosses, 'The exposicioun of Iohn Bochas vpon þis derk poysie', reinforces the reference in the text to Lydgate's source for this material, and the significant authority it grants to poets:

> As Bochas / list to specifie,
> Cler expownyng / this poysye,
> Seith Mercurye / god of Eloquence,
> ʒaf, be the myght / of heuenly influence,
> Vnto this kyng [*sc.* Amphion] / as His natiuitie
> Thurgh glade aspectes / that he shulde be
> Most excellent / be craft of Rhethorik.
>
> (ll. 213–19)

Whereas Lydgate focuses on the connection between poetry and good governance, Boccaccio's argument is a more radical one; he not only argues that the poet is necessary to civilization but, in an assertion which was not matched in English until Skelton's *Replycacion* (1528), attributes his authority to the fact that he is divinely inspired.[41] Although Lydgate does not repeat what Boccaccio says about inspiration, the high status Boccaccio accords to poets is clearly reflected not only in the text of this part of the *Siege*, but in its glosses too. These recapitulate the main points of the narrative: 'How kyng Amphyoun was þe first þat bilt the Cyte of Thebes be þe swetnesse of his soune'; 'The significacioun of þe harpe of Mercure'; 'How kyng Amphion be mediacion of his soft spech, wan þe loue and þe hertes of the puple'; 'What availeþ to a kyng or to a prince to ben goodly and benynge of his port to his puple'; 'How the powre people supportith þe state of a kynge'; and 'What the goodlihed of a kynge avaylith to wynne the hertis of the people'.[42]

---

[41] See Boccaccio, 'De Genealogiae Deorum Gentilium', ed. Vittorio Zaccaria, in *Tutte le opere di Giovanni Boccaccio*, gen. ed. Vittore Branca (Milan: Arnoldo Mondadori, 1998), 8: 1398 and 1410–18; for a translation, see *Boccaccio on Poetry*, ed. Charles G. Osgood (Princeton: Princeton University Press, 1930), 39 and 47–51. For Skelton's use of Boccaccio, see Jane Griffiths, *John Skelton and Poetic Authority: Defining the Liberty to Speak* (Oxford: Clarendon Press, 2006), 33–6 and 131–2.

[42] Quoted from BL MS Arundel 119, ff. 4–5ᵛ. All glosses are also found in Laud Misc. 557 and Christ Church MS 152. The first and second, and the Bochas gloss, also appear (in

Although their primary function is a summarizing or indexing one, these glosses also enact the fusion of the roles of poet and king which they describe: in the ideal world of the newly founded Thebes, the king is a rhetorician and his rhetorical ability both justifies and enables his rule. Yet the fact that this inextricable connection between rhetoric, rule, and justice is expressed through myth implies that, in Lydgate's own, fallen world, the roles of ruler and rhetorician have become separated. The implicit consequence is that a king needs a poet in his service to rule effectively. This, of course, was a commonplace, but in making his case indirectly, through the story of Amphion, Lydgate does not just repeat a well-rehearsed argument; he also gives a practical demonstration of how he, as a poet, is able to use fiction as a means of persuasion.[43] Considered in this light, the glosses do more than repeat the message of the text. For Lydgate, the power of fiction lies not in the story itself, but in the way the poet amplifies and explicates it. This emerges with striking clarity from his discussion, in the Prologue to the *Fall of Princes*, of Laurent de Premierfait's habit of altering the text he translates:

> Artificeres hauyng exercise
> May chaunge and turne bi good discrecioun
> Shappis, formys, and newli hem deuyse,
> Make and unmake in many sondry wyse,
> As potteres, which to that craft entende,
> Breke and renewe ther vesselis to a-mende.
> . . .
> Thyng that was maad of auctours hem beforn,
> Thei may off newe fynde and fantasie,
> Out of old chaff trie out ful cleene corn,
> Make it more fressh and lusti to the eie.
>
> (Prol. Bk. I, 9–14; 22–5)

Despite these rather mixed metaphors, the licence he claims 'Fro good to bettir for to chaunge a thyng' (l. 20) is also implicit throughout his own translations, which are notorious for exceeding the length of their originals several times over, as Lydgate incorporates elucidation, moralization, and instruction

some cases with minor differences in phrasing) in MSS Bodley 776; Pepys 2011; Rawlinson C.48; St John's College 266; Trinity R.4.20 and O.5.2; Coventry Acc. 325/1; and PML M 4. The third, fifth, and sixth appear in all of these except Trinity O.5.2 and Coventry; the fourth in all but Rawlinson and Coventry. At this point MS Cosin V.ii.14 is defective, and Lambeth MS 742 and Longleat MS 257 are unglossed.

[43] See further Daniel Wakelin, 'Hoccleve and Lydgate', in *A Companion to Medieval Poetry*, ed. Corinne Saunders (Oxford: Wiley-Blackwell, 2010), 557–74, esp. 558–61. For Lydgate's persuasive techniques, see also Meyer-Lee, *Poets and Power*, 49–87; and for a more general discussion of the poet as advisor, see Richard Firth Green, *Poets and Princepleasers: Literature and the English Court in the Late Middle Ages* (Toronto: University of Toronto Press, 1980).

within his text. Ebin has convincingly demonstrated that, although Lydgate left no formal poetics, his habit of amplification and the terms he coins to describe the effect of that practice do in fact constitute an entirely coherent poetic theory.[44] The glossing of the new parts of the *Siege of Thebes* fulfils an analogous elucidatory role, and a remarkably *visible* one. Amplification within the body of the text does not meet the eye, whereas glossing stands as a material witness of Lydgate's alteration of his source. Making visible not only the work's 'sentence', but the means by which it is created, these glosses are thus far less neutral than they initially appear. They both constitute a discovery of their own potential to shape the meaning of a text by shaping its form, and function as metonym for that same ability in the writer. Although it is not possible to link them to the composition process on the basis of external evidence, as it is with some of the glosses to the translated parts of the *Siege*, these glosses nonetheless manifest an awareness of the writer's shaping power within the form of the text. They suggest that Lydgate's poetic practice does not merely imply his theories of authorship, but prompts their explicit formulation.

A comparable interplay of theory and practice occurs with one particular kind of glossing in the *Fall of Princes*. Here, of course, Lydgate was translating a work that was itself a translation—Laurent de Premierfait's 1409 French version of Boccaccio's *De casibus virorum illustrium* (1353)— and that contained explicit reflection on what the process of translation entailed. Laurent had previously translated *De casibus* in 1400, and in his second attempt he not only treats Boccaccio's text with much greater freedom, but also reflects explicitly on the changes he introduces, arguing that: 'de tant . . . sera plus cler & plus ouuert en sentences & en parolles, de tant Il delectera a lire & a escouter plusieurs hommes & femmes'.[45] As we have seen, Lydgate clearly approves of Laurent's procedure, and his own practice is equally interventionist, as he amplifies and edits the text, adding new envoys that explicitly moralize the tragedies for the benefit of princes and nobles, and—significantly—choosing not to write in the person of 'Bochas', but instead to refer to him in the third person.[46] By

---

[44] Lois Ebin, *Illuminator, Makar, Vates*, 19–48. Cf. also Robert O. Payne, *The Key of Remembrance: A Study of Chaucer's Poetics* (New Haven: Yale University Press, 1963) for a study of analogously 'informal' poetics.

[45] Laurent de Premierfait, 'Le prologue du translateur', in Lydgate's *Fall of Princes*, 1: p. liii. 'The clearer and plainer [it] is in meaning and expression, the more it will delight many men and women to read it or to hear it read.'

[46] For Laurent's changes, see further Gathercole (ed.), *Des Cas des Nobles Hommes*, 17–22; and Nigel Mortimer, *John Lydgate's Fall of Princes: Narrative Tragedy in Its Literary and Political Contexts* (Oxford: Clarendon Press, 2005), 37 and 40–1; cf. also Stephanie A. Viereck Gibbs Kamath, *Authorship and First-Person Allegory in Late Medieval France and England* (Cambridge: D. S. Brewer, 2012), 142 and 164–72; and Jennifer Summit, ' "Stable

indicating so clearly that he and 'Bochas' are separate entities, this last alteration in particular allows Lydgate to emphasize his own responsibility for the work. The change of grammatical person means that the poem is presented not as a record of the narrator's own visions and visitations, but as the reworking of an 'old book'. Yet this substitution of literary authority for the authority of experience paradoxically emphasizes the translator's role by constantly invoking him: even as his frequent mentions of 'myn auctor' authorize Lydgate's work by reference to an external source, they also draw attention to Lydgate's own distinct presence in the text.[47]

In the majority of manuscripts, the same is true of the poem's *ordinatio*. Lydgate's added envoys are among the kinds of passage most consistently emphasized; in Alexandra Gillespie's words: 'Each of Lydgate's interpolations into his material is visually realized, attended by white space, filled with professional rubrics and headings, and marked by illuminated initials.'[48] This confirms that glosses identifying the envoys—like those marking minor divisions in the text which replicate those in Laurent manuscripts—were produced by someone with an intimate knowledge of the source text, able to state with confidence where 'Bochas' ends and Lydgate begins. This is by no means always clear from the text of the *Fall*. Although Lydgate's new envoys differ from Laurent's moralizations by being addressed specifically to princes and other nobles, it is only occasionally that there is an explicit change from the third to the first person to indicate that they are of his own making.[49] Moreover, a number of individual glosses, such as 'Lenvoye direct to wydowys off the translatoure'

in study": Lydgate's *Fall of Princes* and Duke Humfrey's Library', in *John Lydgate: Poetry, Culture, and Lancastrian England*, ed. Larry Scanlon and James Simpson (Notre Dame: University of Notre Dame Press, 2006), 221.

[47] In one manuscript, Rosenbach MS 439/16, the miniatures consistently depict the author-figure as a cleric in the black habit of Lydgate's Benedictine order, ignoring what is stated explicitly in the text about the authorship of the work and responding instead to Lydgate's *de facto* control. For the decoration of this manuscript, and reproductions of some of its miniatures, see Victoria Kirkham, 'Decoration and Iconography of Lydgate's *Fall of Princes* (De Casibus) at the Philadelphia Rosenbach', *Studi sul Boccaccio* 25 (1997), 297–310; and for discussion of a comparable portrait in Huntington Library MS HM 268, see Seth Lerer, *Chaucer and his Readers: Imagining the Author in Late-Medieval England* (Princeton: Princeton University Press, 1996), 40–4.

[48] Alexandra Gillespie, 'Framing Lydgate's *Fall of Princes*: The Evidence of Book History', *Mediaevalia* 20 (2001), 159. For the layout of the page as an integral part of the meaning of a text, see Mary Carruthers, *The Book of Memory: A Study of Memory in Medieval Culture*, 2nd ed. (Cambridge: Cambridge University Press, 2008), 274–337; for a specific case study of fifteenth-century material, see Siân Echard, 'Designs for Reading: Some Manuscripts of Gower's "Confessio Amantis"', *Trivium* 31 (1999), 59–72.

[49] At one of the points where such a change does occur, a unique gloss in MS Rylands 2 seeks to disambiguate the 'I' speaker by glossing the line 'For I had oonys in commaundement': '.i. The monke of Bury' (f. 31).

and 'Thexcuse of Bochas for his writyng ageyn misgouerned women instede of lenvoie', confirm the need for inside knowledge on the glossator's part; the identification of the translator's contribution speaks for itself, while Lydgate's inconsistency in adding envoys means that only a glossator involved in the translation process would be in a position to comment on the decision not to include one.[50]

What, then, do these glosses have to say about the connection between Lydgate's theory and practice? As with the *Siege of Thebes*, the 'envoy' glosses to the *Fall of Princes* are consonant with the themes of the text. By articulating its structure, they clearly assist the reader in navigating an extremely long and complex work. However, they also emphasize those points where Lydgate most decisively departs from his source, adding material that functions as practical political advice to princes rather than stressing the need to be reconciled to the unforeseeable vicissitudes of Fortune.[51] In addition, by emphasizing those points where Lydgate adds entirely new passages to his source, and drawing attention to his presence in the text, they assert his independence of literary as well as social sources of authorization. Far from being a neutral channel through which the innate 'sentence' of the work is conveyed intact, both the glosses and the narrative technique of Lydgate's *Fall* present the translator as someone who devises the work anew, the better to bring out its meaning. Just as the glosses to the early stages of the *Siege of Thebes* reflect the text's concern with the authority of the poet, the 'envoy' glosses to the *Fall* reflect that work's concern with the process of translation.

As with the *Siege of Thebes*, however, the full effect of the poem's apparatus depends on a level of knowledge not available to the majority of readers. Although Lydgate's contributions to the text are consistently emphasized, in the majority of cases it is not clear that they *are* his contributions. Even in the most fully glossed manuscript, MS Rylands 2, there are very few glosses that identify Lydgate by name or by role. One rare exception is the 'Lenvoye addressed to wydowys off the translatoure', and another is the first, which gives a full description of the work: 'Here begynneth the book callyd J. Bochas descriuyng the falle of Pryncis pryncessys

---

[50] Quoted from MS Rylands 2, f. 47ᵛ and f. 35; cf. Lydgate, *Fall of Princes*, at I. 6706–7 and II. 2198–9. Versions of these glosses are also found in MS Bodley 263 and in BL MSS Harley 3486; Harley 4203; Additional 21410; and Additional 39659. In BL MS Royal.18.D.v space has been left for them, but they have not been supplied.

[51] For Lydgate's treatment of the questions of Fortune and personal responsibility, see Mortimer, *Lydgate's Fall of Princes*, 133–218. For the radical potential of the *de casibus* genre, see Paul Strohm, *Politique: Languages of Statecraft between Chaucer and Shakespeare* (Notre Dame: University of Notre Dame Press, 2005), 87–104.

and othir nobles translatid in to Inglissh bi John Ludgate monke of the monastery of seynt Edmundes Bury atte commaundement of the worthi pryncessys humfrey duk of Gloucester begynnyng at Adam & endyng w^t Kung John take prisoner in France bi Prince Edward.'[52] A third appears shortly afterwards in Book I: 'Off Priamus kyng of Troye and how the monke of Bury translator of this book wroot a boke of the siege of Troye callid Troye book.'[53] Although many of the other glosses in the Rylands manuscript draw attention to Lydgate's additions, they do not specify that these *are* additions; they identify 'Lenvoy' rather than 'Lydgate's envoy' or 'Lenvoy of the translator'. Given that their ability to draw attention to Lydgate's alterations depends on comparison of his poem with Laurent's, they do not constitute an overt assertion of his authority. For the translator himself, however, they are physical signs of the way in which he has made the text his own. Like those to the early parts of the *Siege of Thebes*, then, these *Fall* glosses constitute, in part, the translator's discovery of his own power of invention.

PRACTICAL CONFUSION: THE TRANSMISSION OF THE *SIEGE OF THEBES* AND *FALL OF PRINCES*

There is of course a caveat to this hypothesis of authorial glossing. Although aspects of the glossing of both the *Siege* and the *Fall* do clearly suggest that they were composed as an integral part of the poems, with the *Fall* in particular there is a great deal which cannot be so explained; a comparison of the manuscripts reveals more inconsistencies than consistencies in the glossing. As Paul Zumthor puts it:

> Any work, in its manuscript tradition, appears as a constellation of elements, each of which may be the object of variations in the course of time or across space. The notion of *mouvance* implies that the work has no authentic text properly speaking, but that it is constituted by an abstract scheme, materialized in an unstable way from manuscript to manuscript, from performance to performance.[54]

Such disparate performances are created not just by diverse scribal representations of any original apparatus, but by the addition of reader annotation as well. Surviving manuscripts of the *Siege* and *Fall* suggest a relatively

---

[52] MS Rylands 2, f. 1.   [53] MS Rylands 2, f. 31.
[54] Paul Zumthor, *Essai de poétique médiévale*, quoted in Martin Irvine, '"Bothe text and gloss": Manuscript Form, the Textuality of Commentary, and Chaucer's Dream Poems', in *The Uses of Manuscripts in Literary Studies: Essays in Memory of Judson Boyce*

high level of engagement; in several cases readers have added tables of contents, marks of emphasis, and summary glosses that show a purposeful appropriation of the text for their own use and moral edification.[55] On occasion, their interests are at odds with those encouraged by the existing apparatus. Thus, in BL MS Harley 1245, one reader has provided a running index to the first few folios of Book I by noting the characters of each tragedy in the margins. Far from recognizing the stanzas privileged by the scribe, however, it picks out quite other points of emphasis, marking up the text in a highly personal way.[56] The annotator of CUL MS Additional 6864 treats the *Siege* still more cavalierly; although he supplements the scribe's gloss 'Thebes' with the additional comment 'founded by kyng Amphion' and observes 'laus clementie', at the point where Lydgate stresses the need for a prince to be just, he also spots something in the text that can be lifted entirely out of its literary context when he marks 'To auoyd the Collyc' against the Host's advice to Lydgate 'toward nyght ete some fenel rede / Annys commyng or colyaunder sede'.[57]

Whereas all of these annotations are instantly recognizable as the additions of various readers of the manuscripts, there are also cases where reader annotation is recopied by the scribe of a subsequent manuscript, and thus becomes visually indistinguishable from the formal apparatus. An unusually striking example occurs in BL MS Harley 2251, whose glosses actively challenge the text to which they are attached.[58] Unlike the *Fall* manuscripts mentioned so far, Harley 2251 does not contain a complete text of the poem, but a series of extracts, presented as part of a collection of works by or attributed to Lydgate.[59] The manuscript is glossed throughout, predominantly in the hand of the scribe. In the extracts from the

Allen, ed. Charlotte Cook Morse, Penelope Reed Doob, and Marjorie Curry Woods (Kalamazoo: Medieval Institute Publications, 1992), 85.

[55] In MS Pepys 2011, for example, one reader has supplied a detailed table at the beginning of the poem and a number of glosses in the margins; MS Rawlinson C.448 and MS Rylands 2 also contain tables (that in Rylands 2 based on the pre-existing glosses); and in Rosenbach MS 439/16 an early reader has added 'nota' to a large number of the most explicitly moralizing stanzas.

[56] This reader also includes cross-references between tales, for example on ff. 113^v and 114^v.

[57] CUL MS Additional 6864, ff. 4, 5, 3.

[58] The scribe of this manuscript has been identified as the 'Hammond-scribe', a copyist with links to John Shirley. See further Alexandra Gillespie, *Print Culture and the Medieval Author: Chaucer, Lydgate, and their Books, 1473–1557* (Oxford: Oxford University Press, 2006), 49; and Linne Mooney, 'A New Manuscript by the Hammond Scribe Discovered by Jeremy Griffiths', in *The English Medieval Book: Studies in Memory of Jeremy Griffiths*, ed. A. S. G. Edwards, Vincent Gillespie, and Ralph Hanna (London: The British Library, 2000), 113–23.

[59] For this and other fifteenth-century manuscripts containing excerpts from the *Fall*, see Mortimer, *Lydgate's Fall of Princes*, 224–44.

Fall, the majority of these glosses are indexing ones, identifying the main characters of the various tragedies and envoys, as for example 'The tragedye of Duk Theseus and parotheus', and 'Lenvoy of þe story of Lucresse and false tarquine'.[60] Interspersed among these narrative summaries, however, are others that take the form of ethical precepts. Some mark points of particular moral interest, for example 'A comendacioun of humylite' or 'Off the gret stedefastenesse of vertu', while others address the reader directly: 'Consyder this ye wise'; 'Beware ye conquerours'; 'Take hede ye rewlers of princis'.[61] And at one point they become highly combative in tone. Alongside an extract that consists of various antifeminist stanzas from Book I of the *Fall* edited together into a continuous passage, the glosses repeatedly attack the text with exclamations such as: 'Ye haue no cause to say so'; 'Ye wilbe shent'; 'Be pees i bidde yow'.[62] The openly feminist antagonism and the tendency to personify (and gender) the text are remarkable enough in themselves, yet they seem still more so both because these glosses are identical in appearance to the narrative summaries and because the two kinds of gloss are intermingled. Thus the margin of one folio records 'Nisus of magarence and Scilla his doughtir', and shortly after 'So shul ye be pese'; elsewhere, the gloss 'Of myghti Sampson' is followed by 'be my trowth ye wilbe shent' and then (in an echo of Janekin and the Wife of Bath): 'Be pees or i wil rende this leef out of your booke' (see Plate 1.2).[63] Giving a positively schizophrenic impression, the juxtaposition of such exclamatory, highly personal glosses with plain indexing glosses provides a striking instance of a scribal practice that also affects many other manuscripts in less apparent ways, and contributes significantly to the development of distinct textual traditions.[64]

---

[60] MS Harley 2251, ff. 87, 91ᵛ.   [61] MS Harley 2251, ff. 84, 84ᵛ, 86ᵛ.

[62] MS Harley 2251, ff. 138, 138ᵛ, f. 139. For a transcription and discussion of the contentious glosses, see A. S. G. Edwards, 'Lydgate, Medieval Antifeminism and Harley 2251', *Annuale Medievale* 13 (1972), 32–44. For the reception of the *Fall* more generally, see A. S. G. Edwards, 'The Influence of Lydgate's *Fall of Princes* c.1440–1559: A Survey', *Mediaeval Studies* 39 (1977), 424–39; and Mortimer, *Lydgate's Fall of Princes*, 219–77.

[63] BL MS Harley 2251, ff. 137ᵛ and 142. The general impression of chaos is only enhanced by further annotations in the hand of a sixteenth-century reader, who marks passages of particular interest to him with variations on the phrase 'read this', and frequently reaffirms the text against a gloss that takes issue with it; for example, the sarcastic aside 'There is no goode wommann that wilbe wroth no take no querell agenst this booke as I suppose' is followed only a few lines later by the note 'Reade thys oftyn' in the sixteenth-century hand (f. 143). Occasionally, the text becomes too much for this later reader too, as when he comments 'Do not reade thys, but hyde your eye' (f. 149ᵛ). The British Library online catalogue identifies the later hand as that of John Stow.

[64] For an exemplary attempt to tease out the different layers of annotation in the manuscripts of a near-contemporary work, see Julia Boffey, 'Annotation in Some Manuscripts of *Troilus and Criseyde*', *English Manuscript Studies 1100–1700* 5 (1995), 1–17.

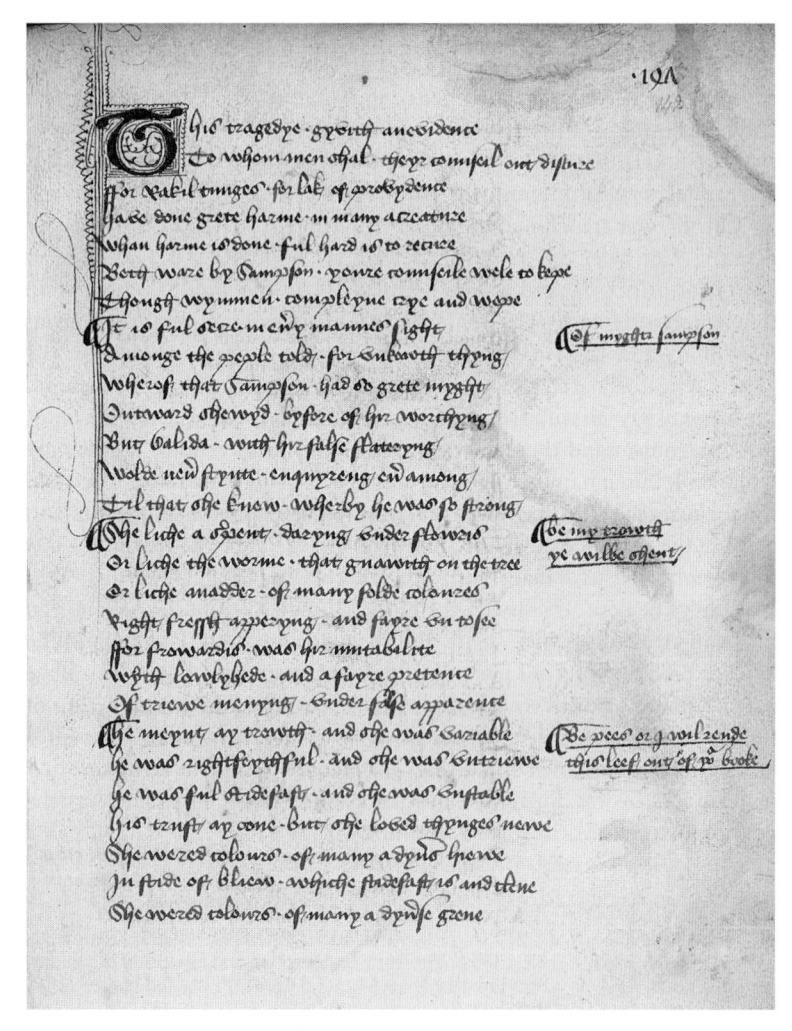

Plate 1.2 MS Harley 2251, f. 142. © The British Library Board.

To complicate matters further, any consideration of the origin and purpose of the *Fall* glosses has to negotiate not only reader annotations (whether or not these are scribally homogenized), but also manuscripts with a non-standard apparatus, and manuscripts (notably MS Harley 1766) that witness an entirely different *text* of the poem. These differences are infinitely greater than can be accounted for by a simple narrative of loss and accretion; on the contrary, it is clear that the sum total of all surviving glossing is the product of multiple hands and multiple stages of annotation. A comparison with the *Siege of Thebes* may be helpful here. Even with its relatively straightforward stemma, there are witnesses to strikingly different sets of glosses: not just BL MS Additional 18632, but the intriguing variations on a familiar theme found in MSS Digby 230 and Rawlinson C.48. The Digby manuscript contains all the glosses that recur in the majority of the *Siege* manuscripts, but also a large number of additional glosses which closely resemble them in kind; some, though not all, of these are also found in MS Royal 18.D.ii. The Rawlinson manuscript presents a different kind of complication: here, the first glosses are in English, and correspond (almost) word for word with those in other manuscripts, but the later stages of the poem are glossed in Latin, even though the content of the glosses continues to correspond to those that are found elsewhere. Odd though it sounds, such variation may confirm, rather than conflict with, the hypothesis that the early glossing of the poem was experimental. With the Digby manuscript, the fact that a number of the additional glosses are shared by MS Royal.18.D.ii, which is from an entirely different branch of the stemma, suggests that they *are* early, and it is possible that they witness the trying out of different kinds of glossing for effect. The switch from English to Latin in the Rawlinson glosses is most likely to be due to a change of exemplar during the copying process, and suggests that a Latin as well as an English version of the apparatus may have been in circulation, as if both of these, too, were being tried out.[65] The switch may thus imply that experimentation in the glossing of the *Siege of Thebes* was not entirely a private authorial concern, but was being considered for rhetorical effect as well.

With the *Fall of Princes*, too, some of the inconsistencies in glossing are suggestive of deliberate experiment. This applies particularly to a series of glosses that are different in kind from the majority of glosses shared by multiple manuscripts, but nonetheless appear in several manuscripts which the poem's first editor, Henry Bergen, found to be unconnected with one another.[66] All occur in BL MS Harley 4203. But whereas the majority of the glosses that this manuscript shares with others are attached to stanzas highlighted by decorated or illuminated initials, these annotations appear at points in the text that are not otherwise emphasized. The most obvious hypothesis to account for this difference would be that the scribe of Harley 4203, like the scribe of Harley 2251, copied across reader annotations from his exemplar. But in that case these glosses should appear only in Harley 4203 and in the manuscripts that derive from it, whereas

---

[65] Cf. Stephen Partridge, 'Designing the Page', in *Production of Books*, 98.
[66] Lydgate, *Fall of Princes*, 4: 3–9.

in fact they are neither unique to Harley 4203, nor shared exclusively with its nearest relations. The most idiosyncratic of them, which display a sudden interest in Saul, also occur in Glasgow UL MS Hunter 5; in both manuscripts his name appears in the margin five times in just two folios.[67] In addition, Harley 4203 contains four sententious glosses: 'ars mutat naturam', 'demonstrat fructus de quo sit stipite ductus', 'pauper virtuosus est generosus', and 'Cum malis operibus principium corrumpitur conuersacionem subiectorum'. The first two of these also appear in MS Rylands 2, and the last three are shared with MS Harley 4197.[68] Moreover, the 'demonstrat fructus' gloss also occurs in PML MS M 124, and the 'cum malis operibus' one in MS Harley 1766; Harley 1766 additionally shares the adjacent gloss 'virtutem superuit & ominem religionem' with Harley 4203, but not with Harley 4197 (see Plates 1.3, 1.4, 1.5, and 1.6).[69] This rather odd set of partial correspondences is in addition to a series of shared source glosses identified by Daniel Wakelin, which similarly links MSS Harley 1766, Harley 4203, and Harley 4197.[70]

Although in themselves such connections imply nothing more than that these glosses go back to an early stage in the transmission of the text, the fact that one of the manuscripts in the case is Harley 1766 may indicate (as Wakelin has cautiously suggested) that they are Lydgate's. Harley 1766 was long held to be a corrupt manuscript, but it has recently been argued that it witnesses a variant text prepared on Lydgate's instruction as a presentation copy.[71] If this is the case, its variant apparatus implies serious authorial experimentation with the layout of the text. And if *this* is the case, these glosses—like the altered form of the text in Harley 1766—may be a sign that different versions of apparatus were being tried out, and that they reflected not only Lydgate's private discovery of his powers, but his discovery that glosses have the potential to make those powers public, and become a fully fledged rhetorical strategy.

Such a hypothesis is not conclusive, of course. What can be said, however, is that—with both poems—there is evidence going back to a very early stage in their transmission that glossing and mise-en-page are considered a significant part of the work, that there is some evidence that

---

[67] MS Harley 4203, ff. 37ᵛ–39; MS Hunter 5, ff. 42–4.
[68] MS Harley 4203, ff. 24, 37, 39ᵛ; MS Rylands 2 f. 25; MS Harley 4197 ff. 36, 38. 'Art alters nature'; 'the fruit reveals from which branch it fell'; 'the virtuous poor man is generous'; 'by evil deeds a prince corrupts the behaviour of his subjects'.
[69] PML MS M 124, f. 25; MS Harley 1766, f. 98; MS Harley 4203, f. 39ᵛ.
[70] Wakelin, *Humanism, Reading, and English Literature*, 39–43.
[71] See further A. S. G. Edwards, 'The McGill Fragment of Lydgate's *Fall of Princes*', *Scriptorium* 28 (1974), 75–7.

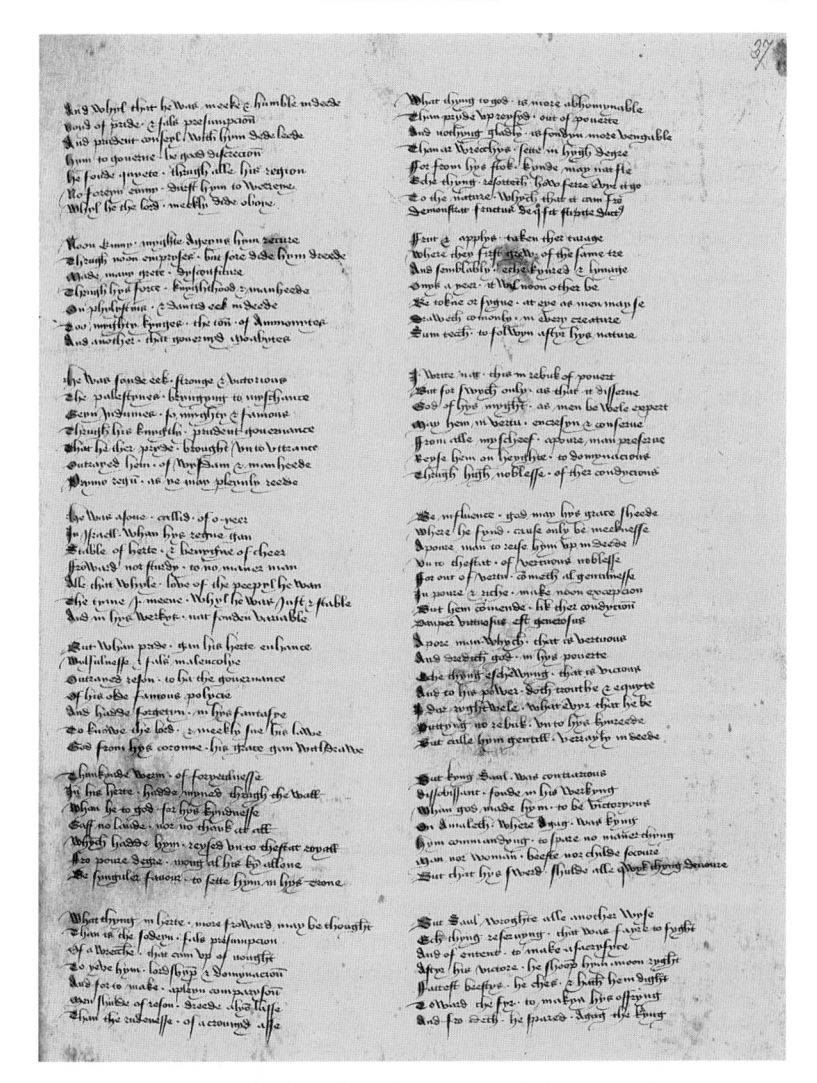

Plate 1.3 BL MS Harley 4203, f. 37. © The British Library Board.

such interest begins with the translator, and that much of that interest is centered around the translator's presence in the text. There is at least a possibility that Lydgate's poems manifest a fusion of the roles of author and exegete or translator analogous to that which Rita Copeland has identified in Gower's *Confessio Amantis* and Chaucer's Prologue to the *Legend of Good Women*, which:

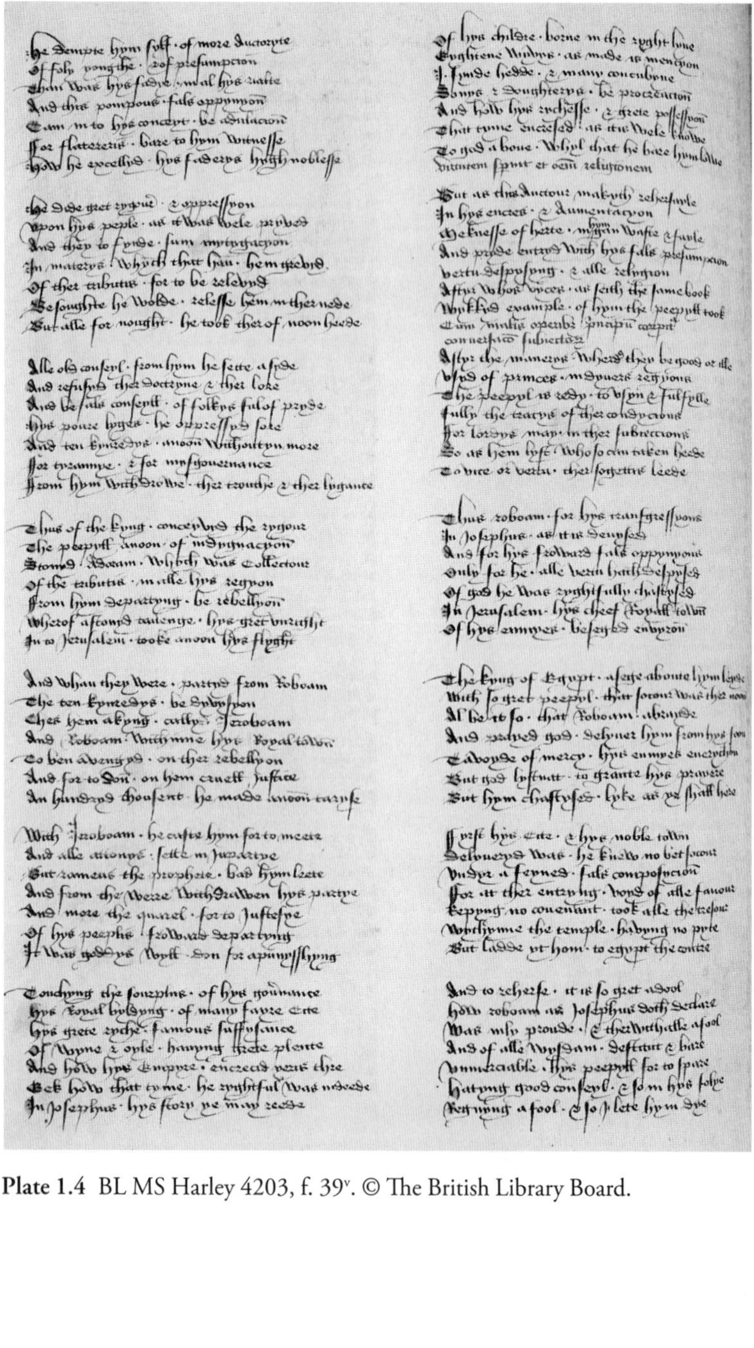

Plate 1.4 BL MS Harley 4203, f. 39ᵛ. © The British Library Board.

Plate 1.5 BL MS Harley 4197, f. 36. © The British Library Board.

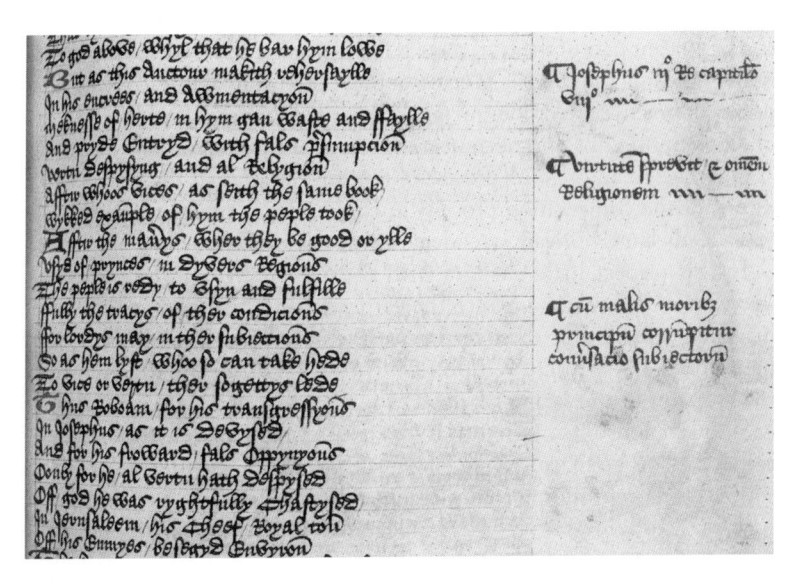

Plate 1.6 BL MS Harley 1766, f. 98. © The British Library Board.

Turn the techniques of exegesis into techniques of topical invention . . . [and thereby] redefine the terms of vernacular translation itself: they use the techniques of exegetical translation to produce, not a supplement to the original, but a vernacular substitute for that original.[72]

In the *Confessio*, that substitution is signalled by Gower's provision of an exegetical apparatus for his own text. In parts of the *Fall* and the *Siege* too, translation that is itself a form of interpretation is provided with a rudimentary interpretative apparatus of its own: although the glosses to these poems are less comprehensive and less ambitious than the apparatus of the *Confessio*, they may nonetheless have functioned as a locus for discovering and exploring the translator's ownership of his work.

ENVOY: FROM MANUSCRIPT TO PRINT

Two main themes emerge from the examination of these glosses: on the one hand, the way in which they reflect an interest in the process of making meaning and its representation on the page; on the other hand the *mouvance* which the texts undergo in the process of transmission. Although the extent of scribal glossing suggests that any existing annotations tended to be treated as a significant part of the text, there is little sign that there are fixed conventions governing the glossing process, or the relationship of text to gloss; what occurs in practice are various juxtapositions of glosses of different kinds and of different origins. This, of course, encourages a view of each copy of a text as one stage in an ongoing process of transmission, rather than as a partial record of the composition process; in consequence, experimentation that was already largely private is rendered effectively invisible.

In this respect little changes with the passage of the *Siege of Thebes* and *Fall of Princes* into print. The earliest editions of both poems replicate the glossing of their respective exemplars just as a scribe might have done. Those in De Worde's 1497 *Storye of Thebes* include not only that version of the standard glosses found in Oxford St John's College MS 266, but also its numerous 'Nota' glosses, which are without counterpart in other manuscripts, suggesting that the printer (like many scribes) was reproducing all elements of the text that were available to him.[73] Indeed, De Worde replicates not only the wording of the

---

[72] Rita Copeland, *Rhetoric, Hermeneutics and Translation in the Middle Ages: Academic Tradition and Vernacular Texts* (Cambridge: Cambridge University Press, 1991), 179; and cf. A. J. Minnis, *Medieval Theory of Authorship*, 2nd ed. (Aldershot: Wildwood House, 1988), 160–210.
[73] John Lydgate, *The Storye of Thebes* (Westminster: Wynkyn de Worde, 1497). For the relationship between the De Worde print and St John's College MS 266, see Alexandra

glosses from his copy-text, but its layout as well; the St John's College manuscript is unusual among glossed *Siege* manuscripts in having the glosses copied in the margins and, despite the obvious technical difficulty of printing marginal material, the De Worde edition does the same.[74] Similarly, although Stow's copy-text for the *Siege* has not been conclusively identified, the glosses in his edition are a version of those found in the majority of manuscripts and, as we have seen, Speght's are derived from Stow's.[75]

Yet although printers—like scribes before them—made use of what was available in their copy-text, because their products—unlike those of scribes—were disseminated in multiple copies, a continuity of practice brings about a different effect: the privileging of a single, chance set of glosses. Moreover, as Gillespie has argued: 'Despite similarities, the printed text is framed differently from its manuscript copy—by woodcut illustrations . . . by the printer's colophon and device, by the new marks made by type.'[76] With the *Siege of Thebes*, the woodcut on the title page has a particularly pronounced impact. As Robert Edwards has shown, by combining a representation of Amphion founding the city with a portrayal, in the background, of its other putative founder, Cadmus, the woodcut and its caption 'This is the Royall Cyte of Thebes' emblematize 'Theban doubleness and the contending sources of origin, authority and legitimacy', while at the same time dramatizing 'the effort to obscure one myth of origin with another'.[77]

With the *Fall of Princes*, the reframing of the work also creates a kind of doubleness—but in terms of the presentation of its author, rather than in terms of its content. Here too, we find that in the printing of the poem a chance manifestation of the glosses is captured and passed down: Richard Pynson's 1494 edition of the *Fall* takes as its copy-text MS Rylands 2 and

---

Gillespie, '"Folowynge the trace of mayster Caxton": Some Histories of Fifteenth-Century Printed Books', in *Caxton's Trace: Studies in the History of English Printing*, ed. William Kuskin (Notre Dame: University of Notre Dame Press, 2005), 167–95; for De Worde's interest in layout, see Martha Driver, 'Ideas of Order: Wynkyn de Worde and the Title Page', in *Texts and their Contexts*, ed. John Scattergood and Julia Boffey (Dublin: Four Courts Press, 1997), 87.

[74] It may thus witness a phenomenon common at the time: the attempt to make print resemble manuscript (see further Introduction, note 51).

[75] Although Stow's owner inscription, dated 1558, appears in BL MS Additional 29729, this was not his copy-text; he appears to have used Wynkyn de Worde's edition for the first 400 lines of the poem and thereafter a manuscript closely related to MS Pepys 2011, Lambeth MS 742, Trinity College MS O.5.2, and Christ Church MS 152. See further Edwards, 'Translating Thebes', 339; and cf. Hudson, 'Stow', 55–6.

[76] Gillespie, 'Framing Lydgate's *Fall of Princes*', 161; she also makes the point that 'the circulation of this version of the text in multiple copies' significantly affects its meaning.

[77] Edwards, 'Translating Thebes', 325–6.

replicates the glosses found there.[78] As Gillespie argues, however, this is not unthinking duplication, but part of a considered strategy 'to promote an idea of the author, Lydgate' in such a way as to facilitate Pynson's marketing of his book:

> The new framework Pynson provides for Lydgate's *Fall of Princes* [is] not merely . . . the corollary of the shift to print, but . . . the result of a shift from a trade in which books were typically, though not exclusively, owner or author-initiated products, to one in which books were made by producers for a speculative market.[79]

In Pynson's 1527 edition of the *Fall* the promotion of Lydgate as author is still more pronounced. Whereas the woodcuts in his earlier edition illustrate the subjects of the tales, in that of 1527 the first, most prominent one is the frontispiece that shows a figure in clerical dress seated at a lectern and holding up a finished book in such a way as to display it both to the reader and to the first of a long line of nobles who are queuing up to view it.[80] As Gillespie has argued, the woodcut represents a variation on a presentation scene, with the seated figure representing the printer's patron, Wolsey, rather than the author's patron, Duke Humfrey. Wolsey's power is nonetheless qualified in a number of ways. As Gillespie says, with hindsight the image of the cardinal furnishes an example of the instability of fortune as powerful as any of those provided by Lydgate.[81] The way in which the book in the woodcut is held to face the actual book's readers marks a further shift in the balance of power: the recognition that the relevant relationship is no longer between author and patron, nor even exclusively between printer and patron, but between printer and reader. Moreover, as with the frontispiece to John Skelton's *A Garlande of Laurell* (1523), there is a possibility that the seated figure may represent the author rather than the patron.[82] Although he is not seated at a writing desk, as the figure in the Skelton frontispiece is, the form of the lectern recalls that of the kind of desk represented not only in the *Garlande* woodcut, but in Pynson's own title page to Lydgate's *Testament* (1520), where the seated

---

[78] To judge by the phrasing of the glosses and a number of shared errors, the copy-text of his 1527 edition is either the 1494 Pynson print or MS Rylands 2.
[79] Gillespie, 'Framing Lydgate's *Fall of Princes*', 161–2. For the pressures of speculative publishing at the time, see David R. Carlson, 'A Theory of the Early English Printing Firm: Jobbing, Book Publishing, and the Productive Capacity in Caxton's Work', in *Caxton's Trace: Studies in the History of English Printing*, ed. William Kuskin (Notre Dame: University of Notre Dame Press, 2006), 35–68.
[80] For the 1494 woodcuts, see Gillespie, 'Framing Lydgate's *Fall of Princes*', 163–4.
[81] Gillespie, *Print Culture and the Medieval Author*, 170–6.
[82] For the Skelton frontispiece, see Gillespie, *Print Culture and the Medieval Author*, 170–2; and cf. Jane Griffiths, 'What's in a Name? The Transmission of "John Skelton, Laureate" in Manuscript and Print', *Huntington Library Quarterly* 67 (2004), 231.

figure is unambiguously a writer.[83] The precedent of the *Testament*, in particular, suggests that readers would have *expected* to find a representation of the author at this point in the text. Although the clerical dress of the figure in the 1527 frontispiece is considerably more formal than that of the diligently scribbling monk of 1520, in this context it evokes the ghost of the author even as it shows the patron. But although the frontispiece hints at Lydgate's presence, it also stresses the importance of his readers as substitute patrons, and indeed something of the power wielded by the printer who frames the text in this way.

Pynson's priorities, then, both anticipate those that are apparent in Speght's elaborate framing of Chaucer, and also seem to develop Lydgate's own interest in the writer's or translator's authority as expressed in his text. In one respect they differ strikingly from Lydgate's, however, as appears (among other things) from the way Pynson treats the glosses to the *Fall*. These are privileged by being made the basis of a prefatory table of contents, yet despite this prominence, their significance within the text itself is diminished. Appearing in the text-block, they are not visually dominant; despite being prefaced by a paraph sign, they are printed in the same typeface as the text, and many of the shorter ones are printed as if they were the first line of the following stanza, without a distinguishing border of white space. Whereas the table of contents is both practically useful and indicative of the substance of the work (in both senses), the glosses within the text become subordinate to the prefatory table rather than a significant part of the text in their own right. Adding chapter numbers to those which mark major divisions in the text, and running together glosses that occur at too short an interval to function convincingly as chapter headings, Pynson ensures that they serve purely as a practical finding aid.

This suggests that the kind of authority that Pynson invests in the author figure differs markedly from the kind of authority explored through the marginal glosses to Lydgate's *Siege* and *Fall*. Because Pynson bases his table of contents on glosses that cluster around Lydgate's interventions in his translated text, there is inevitably some consonance, as Pynson inherits Lydgate's emphases. But whereas the significance of the experimental early glossing of the *Siege* and the *Fall* was for the most part private and exploratory, Pynson deploys his apparatus for rhetorical effect, as a counterpart of the author portrait. And there is a further difference. The dissemination

---

[83] *Here begynneth the testament of Iohn Lydgate monke of Berry which he made hymselfe* (London: Richard Pynson [1520]), STC 17035. This figure too is seated at a writing desk, and is represented in the act of writing. The same woodcut appears in six other of Pynson's publications (see Edward Hodnett, *English Woodcuts, 1480–1535* (London: The Bibliographical Society, 1935), no. 1510).

of a text in multiple copies is only one effect of mechanized production. Equally significant in thinking about the relationship between print and glossing is the fact that the printed page eradicates traces of process in the making of the text. Despite the many consonances between manuscript and print production, and the fact that print does not definitively 'fix' a text, there is nonetheless a significant difference between a page produced line by line, by a hand that is physically incapable of writing two things at once, and a page produced in a single impression.[84] Although the setting of type is very time-consuming indeed, the printed page shows no sign of the stages of composition that went into its making. Thus, not only does each edition formalize one possible relation between text and gloss, it also does so in a way that visually eradicates both kinds of process that are apparent in manuscript glossing.[85] The text is no longer visibly something that was created in stages, over a period of time; composition and production are framed as distinct procedures.

As with Speght's printing of the glosses to the *Siege*, then, the treatment of both *Siege* and *Fall* glosses in the earliest prints of the poems substitutes printer experiment for authorial experiment. Whereas the first glosses captured—or even influenced—the discovery that the writing process and the writer's invention are inextricably connected, the printed glosses seem to affirm—however inaccurately—that meaning is something predetermined before the production of the text begins: that it is reasserted, rather than newly achieved. At the same time, however, dissemination of a work in print rather than in manuscript increases the chances that glosses and apparatus will circulate relatively widely in a given form. Both these things will affect later writers with an interest in the gloss. As we shall see in subsequent chapters, writing specifically for print prompts a move from experiment with glossing as a reflection of the composition process to experiment with the *rhetorical* potential of the form: its capacity to influence its readers. After examining in more detail the importance of translatorial and compositional practices to emerging ideas of poetic authority, we shall turn to a variety of authors whose interest in print publication shapes the form of their texts: who

---

[84] For the many ways in which individual copies of a single edition may differ from one another, see David McKitterick, *Print, Manuscript, and the Search for Order* (Cambridge: Cambridge University Press, 2003), 97–138. For a rather more polemical assertion of a similar position, which sets itself up in opposition to Elizabeth Eisenstein's discussion in *The Printing Press as an Agent of Change: Communications and Cultural Transformations in Early Modern Europe* (Cambridge: Cambridge University Press, 1980), see Adrian Johns, *The Nature of the Book: Print and Knowledge in the Making* (Chicago: University of Chicago Press, 1998), 1–57.

[85] Cf. Daniel Wakelin, 'Writing the Words', in *Production of Books in England*, 34–8.

build on printers' experiments with rhetorical glossing, but who are also visibly concerned to find a means of reflecting the writing process within a printed text. For such authors, as for Lydgate, theories of authorship are grounded in practice, or process: but a process that includes the use of print, and reflection on the way in which the fact of being printed affects the meaning of a text.

2
Authors, Translators, and Commentators
Glossing Practices in Bodleian MS Fairfax 16

This chapter will consider two further instances of self-glossing that serve as a means of reflecting on questions of authorship, arguing that these show particularly acutely how the process of *translatio* affects the form of the text. Both are found in Bodleian MS Fairfax 16. This manuscript, compiled in the 1440s, gathers together vernacular poems loosely connected by the theme of love, and predominantly Chaucerian in nature; as well as Chaucer's *Book of the Duchess, Parliament of Fowls, Legend of Good Women,* and *House of Fame,* it includes works by Clanvowe, Lydgate, and Hoccleve, *Reson and Sensuallyte,* and a number of anonymous love lyrics.[1] It is far from being the only such compilation of thematically related Chaucerian material of the fifteenth century; it has particularly strong links with MS Bodley 638 and MS Tanner 346, but also shares some material with MS Pepys 2006 and MS Arch. Selden B. 24.[2] A number of its poems are glossed, and two of these—*Reson and Sensuallyte* and Chaucer's

---

[1] For a full description of the manuscript, see *MS Fairfax 16: A Facsimile,* ed. John Norton-Smith (London: Scolar Press, 1979); and cf. Julia Boffey and A. S. G. Edwards, 'Bodleian MS Arch. Selden B.24 and the "Scotticization" of Middle English Verse', in *Rewriting Chaucer: Culture, Authority and the Idea of the Authentic Text,* ed. Thomas A. Prendergast and Barbara Kline (Columbus: Ohio State University Press, 1999), 166–85; A. S. G. Edwards, 'Bodleian MS Arch. Selden B.24: A "Transitional" Manuscript', in *The Whole Book: Cultural Perspectives on the Medieval Miscellany,* ed. Stephen G. Nichols and Siegfried Wenzel (Ann Arbor: University of Michigan Press, 1996), 53–67; J. P. M. Jansen, 'Charles d'Orléans and the Fairfax Poems', *English Studies* 70 (1989), 206–24; and Theresa Tinkle, 'The Imagined Chaucerian Community of Bodleian MS Fairfax 16', in *Chaucer and the Challenges of Medievalism: Studies in Honor of H. A. Kelly,* ed. Donka Minkova and Theresa Tinkle (Frankfurt-am-Main: Peter Lang, 2003), 157–74.

[2] For the relationships between these manuscripts, see *MS Bodley 638: A Facsimile,* ed. Pamela Robinson (Woodbridge: Boydell & Brewer, 1982), pp. xxxv–xxxvii. For manuscript compilation as instrumental in the shaping of vernacular literary identity, see Julia Boffey, 'The Reputation and Circulation of Chaucer's Lyrics in the Fifteenth Century', *Chaucer Review* 28 (1993), 23–40; and A. S. G. Edwards, 'Chaucer from Manuscript to Print: The Social Text and the Critical Text', *Mosaic* 28 (1995), 1–12; for a comparable argument with reference to early prints of Chaucer, see Stephanie Trigg, 'Discourses of Affinity in the Reading Communities of Geoffrey Chaucer', in *Rewriting Chaucer,* 270–91.

House of Fame—provide evidence of practices comparable to those found in Lydgate's *Fall of Princes* and *Siege of Thebes*. As with the *Fall* and the *Siege*, their glosses make visible the stages of composition, becoming a kind of objective correlative for the transformation which a translator effects within the text proper. There is nonetheless a significant contrast between the glossing of the two poems: whereas the relatively sporadic glosses to *The House of Fame* seem most likely to be working notes—traces of an essentially private process—those to *Reson and Sensuallyte* constitute an extensive Latin apparatus that mirrors the glossing of its source text, *Les Echecs Amoureux*.[3] Like the marginal glosses to *Les Echecs*, those to *Reson and Sensuallyte* are in Latin, and they frequently replicate the former verbatim.[4] In addition, however, they also show the influence of a separate vernacular prose commentary on *Les Echecs*, which was composed by the physician and courtier Évrart de Conty at a later date than the poem, and circulated independently of it. This fusion of two distinct sources suggests that the translator of *Reson and Sensuallyte* was attempting to confer the status of a classical text on a vernacular work—and that, unlike those to *The House of Fame*, its glosses represent a sustained and public experiment.

Within Fairfax 16, however, the elaborate apparatus of *Reson and Sensuallyte* is juxtaposed not only with the less demonstrative glosses to *The House of Fame*, but with a variety of other glosses of widely differing kinds and origins. These include literal glosses that interpret difficult words, exhortatory comments, and glosses that emphasize proverbial phrases, identify speakers, or index narrative development. Such heterogeneity is unexceptional; indeed, the way in which the Fairfax glosses variously preserve traces of the composition of a poem, comment on that process, provide practical indexes and authorizing frameworks, and record miscellaneous later responses might be considered as paradigmatic of the glossing of contemporary manuscripts. Viewed in their entirety, its glosses show how considered explication that mediates a work for its readers or that reflects authorial discoveries about the writing process may co-exist with ephemera whose survival is a matter of chance rather than design.[5] But although the Fairfax manuscript is typical of

---

[3] For the dating of the poem, see *Les Eschéz d'Amours: A Critical Edition of the Poem and Its Latin Glosses*, ed. Gregory Heyworth and Daniel E. O'Sullivan (Leiden: Brill, 2013), 7–9; for the editors' unconventional titling of the poem, see 21–9.

[4] *Les Echecs* survives in two manuscripts: Venice, Bibliotheca Marziana Fr. App. 23 (a substantial fragment of over 13,000 lines, datable to the first decade of the fifteenth century) and Dresden Oc. 66 (an almost complete copy of over 30,000 lines, c. 1478). The Venice manuscript contains the Latin glosses; the Dresden one does not. See further *Eschéz d'Amours*, 81–4 (for a description of the manuscripts) and 95–104 (for the glosses).

[5] For lack of authorial control over transmission, see Ardis Butterfield, 'Mise-en-page in the *Troilus* Manuscripts: Chaucer and French Manuscript Culture', *Huntington Library Quarterly* 58 (1995), 49–51.

many others of the period, in which texts accompanied by their own more or less formal apparatus acquire a range of subsequent annotations, it is less typical in having been copied by a single meticulous scribe. Presenting all its glosses in a uniform format, set off from the text with a blue paraph and copied in red ink, he renders readers' responses to the text visually indistinguishable from more formal commentary.[6] The scribe's concern to establish a single consistent *ordinatio* reflects the relatively high status of the manuscript; originally owned by the Stanley family, it has been described by John Norton-Smith as 'a nearly perfectly preserved example of a manuscript produced to order . . . for a single owner belonging to the landed gentry'.[7] Its striking homogenization of diverse material makes more than usually visible the three different sets of requirements that might be reflected in the glossing of a text: those of the author, those of various subsequent readers, and those of the scribe or scribes who were charged with making visual sense of heterogenous texts, heterogenously arranged and annotated in their exemplars. Each of these types of gloss individually has some bearing on the subsequent development of glossing practices, but in the Fairfax manuscript they are more than the sum of their parts: their diversity in unity itself becomes a potential model for later, self-consciously self-glossing authors.

ALLEGING *AUCTORES*: GLOSSING *THE HOUSE OF FAME*

The vast majority of the glosses to *The House of Fame* are citation glosses drawn from the *Aeneid* and the *Metamorphoses*. They are not unique to the copy of the poem in the Fairfax manuscript; they are also found, along with several additional glosses, in MS Bodley 638, and a smaller number of them appear in MS Tanner 346 and MS Pepys 2006. The first three of these manuscripts are closely related, but Pepys 2006 is less so, implying that the glosses go back to an early copy of the poem. Their purpose is

---

[6] The scribe was so scrupulous that he replicated the shape of a page of damaged text in one of his exemplars (f. 197ᵛ). See further *Fairfax 16*, p. xi; and for the ways in which the copying process might affect a text, see Stephen Partridge, 'Designing the Page', in *The Production of Books in England 1350–1500*, ed. Alexandra Gillespie and Daniel Wakelin (Cambridge: Cambridge University Press, 2011), 82–90; and cf. Daniel Wakelin, 'Instructing Readers in Fifteenth-Century Poetic Manuscripts', *Huntington Library Quarterly* 73 (2010), 446–8.

[7] *Fairfax 16*, p. vii. Norton-Smith assumes that such a manuscript would have been produced in a scriptorium; for a more recent reassessment of this view, see Linne R. Mooney, 'Locating Scribal Activity in Late-Medieval London', in *Design and Distribution of Late Medieval Manuscripts in England*, ed. Margaret Connolly and Linne R. Mooney (Woodbridge: York Medieval Press, 2008), 183–204.

not immediately obvious, however. Unlike those in the Fairfax copies of *The Temple of Glass* and *La Belle Dame sans Merci*, they do not mark rhetorical set pieces or identify speakers or stages in the development of the narrative; the most that can be said is that several of them occur at points where the text makes clear that an authority is being cited, and others at points where characters are said to speak. Thus, when the narrator begins his invocation to Morpheus, two glosses cite from the description of that god and his domain in Book XI of Ovid's *Metamorphoses*; and when he encounters the inscription 'I wol now singe, if that I can, / The armes, and also the man', the gloss quotes the opening lines of the *Aeneid*.[8] But although these glosses occur at points where the source texts particularly obtrude themselves, this is not a consistent principle; other passages that are equally indebted to Virgil or Ovid are not glossed.

One explanation for such sporadic annotation would be that the glosses were added by a reader who was interested enough to note the passages and phrases on which Chaucer was drawing at those points where he happened to recognize them. An alternative explanation is that they represent the accidental survival of Chaucer's own working notes. Although Lawrence Warner has recently cautioned against considering as authorial anything that is 'detachable' from the text, the latter possibility is consonant both with the textual evidence and with what has been hypothesized about Chaucer's compositional practices in the *Canterbury Tales*.[9] Here, as critics including Daniel S. Silvia and Robert E. Lewis have argued, the glosses that occur in a number of manuscripts appear to represent just such survivals: either recording points of reference for the author which would allow him to paraphrase his sources accurately, or serving as notes of additional material that might be incorporated.[10] It is clear that the *House of Fame* glosses, too, *could* have functioned in this way; indeed, this hypothesis would account for some of their inconsistencies. A number of glosses serve primarily to identify the analogous passage in Virgil: for example, that to the lines where Venus appears to Aeneas disguised as a huntress is the first line of Virgil's description of the goddess ('Namque humeris de more habilem suspenderat arcum venatrix dederatque'), and when Aeneas' dead wife Creusa appears to him and exhorts him to take good care of their son, the gloss records a version of her words alongside

---

[8] *Fairfax 16*, ff. 155 and 156. As Wakelin has argued, the juxtaposition of Virgil's confident opening lines with Chaucer's tentative paraphrase creates a distinctly comic effect ('Instructing Readers', 440).

[9] Lawrence Warner, 'Langland's Collaborators and the Quick Brown Fox', paper delivered to the Medieval Research Seminar, University of Oxford, 24 April 2013.

[10] For Silvia, Lewis, and other critics who have addressed the glossing of the *Canterbury Tales*, see Introduction, notes 34–7.

Chaucer's paraphrase: 'Verba Creuse. Iam que vale et nati seruacionis [*sic*] amorem'.[11] In contrast, a gloss such as that which appears at the point where the narrator mentions the death of Priam provides much greater detail than Chaucer's text.[12] The latter states simply that 'Ilyon assayled was / And wonne, and kyng Priam yslayn' (ll. 158–9), whereas the gloss is considerably more circumstantial: 'Vnde virgilius // Ecce autem elapsus Pirri de cede polites vnus natorum priami per tela per hostes porticibus longis fugit, etc'.[13] The gloss to Dido's cursing of Fame is more complicated still; unlike the others, it is not taken from the corresponding passage in the *Aeneid*, but from an earlier passage that treats the consummation of Dido and Aeneas' relationship. Moreover, it does not consist solely of a Virgilian quotation, but combines Virgil's words with a line from the Gospel of St Matthew: 'Virgilius. ffama malum quo non velocius vllum / Nichil occultum quod non reueletur'.[14] The same juxtaposition is found in the text, where Dido exclaims:

> O wikke Fame! for ther nys
> Nothing so swift, lo, as she is!
> O, soth ys, every thing ys wyst,
> Though hit be kevered with the myst.
>
> (ll. 349–52)

Although the gloss here—like all the glosses—*could* be following the text, the combination is idiosyncratic enough to make it possible that the gloss effectively came first: that it provided a reminder of which passages to use and how to 'moralize' Virgil in a way consistent with the poem's wider concern with reputation.

The hypothesis that these glosses represent working notes is supported by their positioning. Not only are they clustered around the narrator's retelling of the *Aeneid* but, even within this cluster, they tend to occur in groups of two or three; as with the glosses of several *Canterbury Tales*, it is as if they marked points in the text that needed particularly careful

---

[11] *Fairfax 16*, f. 157. 'For from her shoulders in huntress fashion she had slung the ready bow'; 'And now farewell, and guard thy love for our common child.' Cf. *Aeneid* I. 318–19 and II. 789. The translations are from *Virgil*, tr. H. Rushton Fairclough, 2 vols., rev. ed. (Cambridge, MA: Harvard University Press, 1935).

[12] Unless otherwise specified, all quotations from *The House of Fame* will be taken from *The Riverside Chaucer*, ed. Larry D. Benson (Oxford: Oxford University Press, 1988).

[13] *Fairfax 16*, f. 156ᵛ. 'But lo! escaping from the sword of Pyrrhus, through darts, through foes, Polites, one of Priam's sons, flees down the long colonnades.' Cf. *Aeneid*, II. 526–8. The translation is from Fairclough, *Virgil*.

[14] *Fairfax 16*, f. 159. 'Rumour of all evils the most swift'; 'There is nothing hidden which will not be revealed.' Cf. *Aeneid*, IV. 174 and Matthew X. 26. The translation of the former is from Fairclough, *Virgil*.

construction. This is not conclusive, of course: the fact that a gloss would have made an effective working note does not mean that it was one. The two glosses that occur at the point where the narrator invokes Morpheus are nonetheless particularly suggestive. Both are quotations from the episode in which the same figure appears in Ovid's *Metamorphoses*—'Ouidius tamen exit ab imo riuus aque lethes' and 'Vnde Ouidius libro xj. Est prope Cimereos longo spelunca recessu, etc'—and they are copied almost back to back (see Plate 2.1).[15] The use of two glosses so very close together suggests not only that the passage was of particular interest to the glossator, but that their content as well as the visual emphasis they provide is significant; if their purpose were purely to authorize Chaucer's work by linking his text to its source, a single gloss would have sufficed. It is suggestive, too, that the glosses are taken from that episode of the *Metamorphoses* that also features in Chaucer's earlier *Book of the Duchess*, as his treatment of Morpheus there reflects on the processes of *translatio* and imitation with which he is engaged in the writing of the poem. As A. J. Minnis has demonstrated, *The Book of the Duchess* both draws on and significantly alters a number of sources, including not only the *Metamorphoses*, but also Machaut's *Jugement dou Roy de Behaigne* and *Remede de Fortune*.[16] This reworking has an equivalent within the poem in the narrator's thought-processes: not only is his dream prompted by his reading of Ovid's *Metamorphoses*, but it begins in a room whose walls and windows reflect fragmented versions of the matter of Troy and the *Romance of the Rose*; the contents of his head form a kind of compendium of contemporary reading.[17] Although the narrator is not explicitly identified as a writer, what Mann says of his reading process proposes it as the internal equivalent of the creation of a new text:

> Although Chaucer's first response to the story of Ceyx and Alcyone is . . . both contingent and tangential, the story nevertheless . . . expands within the reader's mind, taking on its own life and fashioning itself into new shapes, realizing its effects obliquely and over time.[18]

What occurs in the narrator's mind represents the transformation effected on the page by Chaucer's own reworking of his models.

---

[15] *Fairfax 16*, f. 155. 'But from the bottom of the cave there flows the stream of Lethe'; 'Near the land of the Cimmerians there is a deep recess'. Cf. *Metamorphoses*, XI. 592 and XI. 602–3.

[16] A. J. Minnis, *The Shorter Poems,* Oxford Guides to Chaucer (Oxford: Clarendon Press, 1995), 91–112.

[17] For the dreamer as reader, see Jill Mann, 'The Authority of the Audience in Chaucer', in *Poetics: Theory and Practice in Medieval English Literature*, ed. Piero Boitani and Anna Torti (Cambridge: D.S. Brewer, 1991), 1–12.

[18] Mann, 'Authority of the Audience', 11.

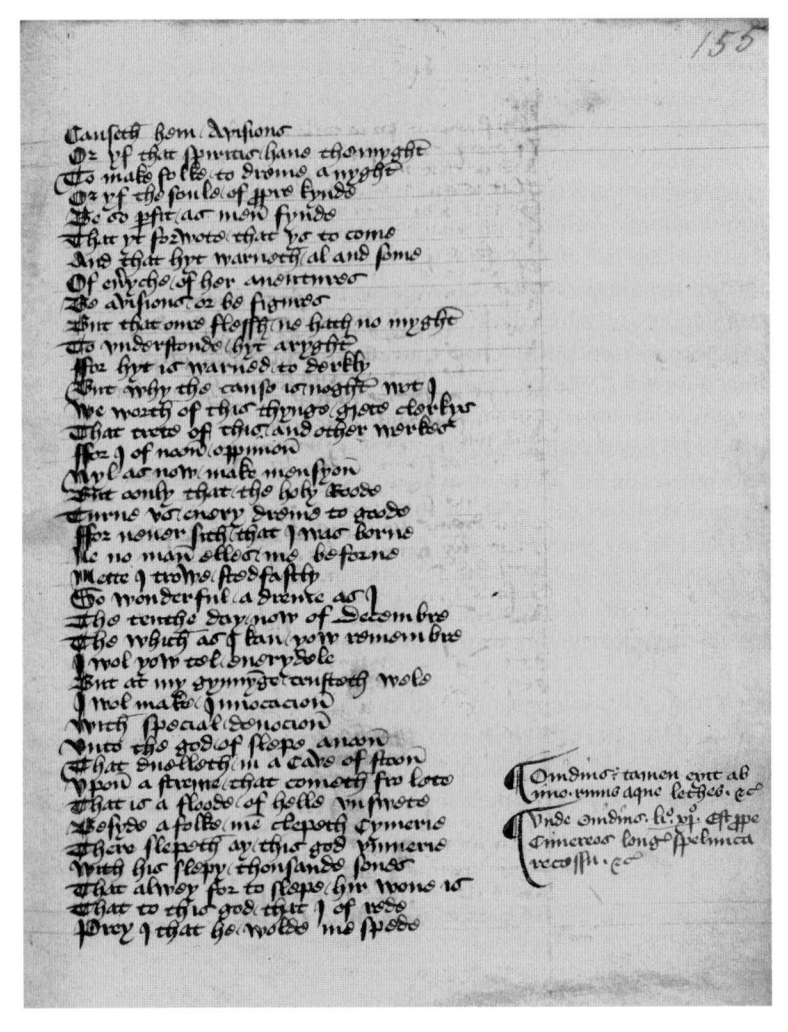

Plate 2.1 Bodleian MS Fairfax 16, f. 155. Reproduced courtesy of The Bodleian Libraries, The University of Oxford.

In the context of the poem's concern with *translatio*, the Morpheus episode takes on a particular significance. As Colin Burrow has argued, Ovid used it as a means of reflecting on literary imitation:

> [Morpheus'] ability to make constructive use of his unlikeness to his original is what makes him a great imitator . . . a great mutator and reviver of the dead. The episode could be read as a defence of the imitative: mere imitations

of reality or other texts may be evidently false or secondary, but they carry as much or greater emotional charge than their originals . . . Being a little unlike your original, the passage intimates, is the best way to affect the emotions of your audience.[19]

Ovid's version of the Morpheus story thus reflects both the anxiety surrounding literary imitation (will it live up to the original?) and the potential benefits of it. In Chaucer's retelling of Ovid, the story may at first appear to function differently. As Mann has pointed out, his narrator is initially interested in Morpheus not because of what he symbolizes, but for the prosaic reason that he himself is unable to sleep, while Burrow himself argues that, whereas Ovid's Morpheus creates a likeness of Ceyx, Chaucer's Morpheus enters into the real Ceyx's dead body, and therefore does not engage in literal imitation. In his reading, although Ovid's 'energetic defence of the imitative arts positively welcomes imitators', Chaucer's *Book of the Duchess* is not such an imitation.[20] Yet the very clumsiness with which Chaucer's Morpheus lifts the dead weight of Ceyx's body is analogous to the difficulty that the Black Knight experiences in expressing the reality of his lady Blanche, and the reality of her death, by means of the conventional literary modes of allegory and complaint; both reflect a poet's effortful reanimation of existing literary material. Although the narrator's interest in Morpheus is a purely practical one, *Chaucer* is able to allude, through it, to Ovid's symbolic use of him, and to reflect on his own relation to his sources by means of that allusion. His version of the story seems both gently to mock Ovid's anxiety and to imply, however comically, that there are good grounds for it.

The two Morpheus glosses in *The House of Fame* similarly suggest a reconsideration of the poet's relation to his sources, in part in consequence of Chaucer's previous use of Morpheus, in part due to the fact that they *are* glosses. Both thematically and materially *The House of Fame* is more overtly concerned with literary tradition than *The Book of the Duchess*. Unlike the narrator of the earlier poem, that of *The House of Fame* is explicitly identified as a would-be poet who is unable to identify a single, stable source for his own writing either in life or in art, and his concerns have a physical counterpart in the glosses to the poem.[21] The narrator is

---

[19] Colin Burrow, ' "Full of the Maker's Guile": Ovid on Imitating and the Imitation of Ovid', in *Ovidian Transformations: Essays on the Metamorphoses and Its Reception*, ed. Philip Hardie, Alessandro Barchiesi, and Stephen Hinds (Cambridge: Cambridge Philological Society, 1999), 278–9.
[20] Mann, 'Authority of the Audience', 10; Burrow, ' "Full of the Maker's Guile" ', 279–80.
[21] For readings of *The House of Fame* which emphasize the importance of the narrator's quest for source material, see Piero Boitani, *Chaucer and the Imaginary World of Fame* (Cambridge: D.S. Brewer, 1984); Jesse M. Gellrich, *The Idea of the Book in the Middle*

first confronted with the absence of a stable source when, dreaming that he is viewing a pictorial version of the story of Aeneas on the walls of a temple, he remembers that Virgil's treatment of Dido differs from that of Ovid: that is, that two equally authoritative versions of the same story are incompatible. By quoting both Virgil's and Ovid's words, the source glosses make manifest on the manuscript page the problem confronted by the narrator. Moreover, a number of them—specifically those that refer to the death of Priam and Aeneas' encounter with his mother, Venus—draw attention to Chaucer's own divergence from as well as dependence on his sources.[22] When his narrator tells of Priam's death before he recounts Aeneas' meeting with the disguised Venus, he reverses the order in which the episodes occur in the *Aeneid*, creating a smooth transition from Venus' first mention of Dido to that part of the Aeneas story that is concerned with her.[23] The reversal anticipates his focus on Dido later in his dream, when he is distracted from the *Aeneid* entirely by remembering Ovid's version of the same story. The glosses identifying the parallel passages in Virgil are thus a material sign of the process of *translatio*, drawing attention to both Chaucer's sources and his own poem as parts of a continuous chain of writing, reading, interpretation, and—thus, significantly—alteration. They serve as a visual reminder of the process by which the poem came into being, providing physical evidence of the distance between Chaucer's new text and its source, as well as of the close correlation between the two.

The glosses to *The House of Fame* thus show Chaucer as author negotiating precisely the same terrain as his narrators do when (in their dreaming state) they reconstruct a narrative from metamorphosed elements of diverse classical texts. Just as the poem's narrator is repeatedly confronted with conflicts between supposedly authoritative sources and with the impossibility of separating tale from teller, or truth from falsehood, the juxtaposition of the glosses with Chaucer's text similarly draws attention to the conflict between the authority of old books and that of the new writer. Although, at first glance, they seem to confirm the viability of a process of transmission whereby books breed books and writers begin where their predecessors end, on reflection the juxtaposition of the new text with its

---

Ages: Language Theory, Mythology, and Fiction (Ithaca: Cornell University Press, 1985), 167–201; Pamela M. King, 'Chaucer, Chaucerians, and the Theme of Poetry', in *Chaucer and Fifteenth-Century Poetry*, ed. Julia Boffey and Janet Cowan (London: King's College, 1991), 1–14; and Christiania Whitehead, *Castles of the Mind: A Study of Medieval Architectural Allegory* (Cardiff: University of Wales Press, 2003), 178–84; cf. also Minnis, *Shorter Poems*, 74–251.

[22] Cf. Wakelin, 'Instructing Readers', 440.

[23] *The House of Fame*, I. 159 and I. 225. In the *Aeneid*, Venus appears at I. 314; Priam's death occurs at II. 526–8.

source can be seen to function in the opposite way: as a means of laying bare the discrepancies between the two. Neither supplementary to the text, nor intended for the guidance of subsequent readers, they instead reveal something of the process of the text's creation. Even as they support the argument that Speght makes in his 1602 edition of Chaucer's works, that Chaucer is a 'learned' poet, they reveal that Chaucer's writing is very far from the straightforward inheritance that Speght implies; rather, they contribute to that redefinition of vernacular translation identified by Rita Copeland, in which 'the techniques of exegetical translation [are used] to produce, not a supplement to the original, but a vernacular substitute for that original'.[24] Although their authorship must ultimately remain a matter of speculation, the way in which they make visible the writer's shaping of his work nonetheless indicates how effectively they might serve as a locus for the discovery of his innate authority. In this, they anticipate not only Lydgate's glossing, but also the more self-conscious experimentation with a formal Latin apparatus which is found in *Reson and Sensuallyte*.

'VERBA EXPOSITORIS ET VERBA TRANSLATORIS': THE GLOSSING OF *RESON AND SENSUALLYTE*

The glossing of the early fifteenth-century poem *Reson and Sensuallyte* differs from that of *The House of Fame* both in being demonstrably an integral part of the work, and in being rhetorical as well as practical in effect. The poem itself, which survives only in the Fairfax manuscript and in a later copy of it, is relatively little known.[25] An anonymous translation of an anonymous French text, *Les Echecs Amoureux* (c. 1370), which is itself a response to the *Roman de la Rose*, *Reson and Sensuallyte* is a didactic poem in the guise of a romance with the theme of man's self-governance.[26]

---

[24] Rita Copeland, *Rhetoric, Hermeneutics and Translation in the Middle Ages: Academic Traditions and Vernacular Texts* (Cambridge: Cambridge University Press, 1991), 179.

[25] The poem appears on ff. 202–300 of the Fairfax manuscript. The only other extant copy of the poem is that in BL MS Additional 29729, a manuscript of works by or attributed to Lydgate, compiled by the sixteenth-century antiquarian John Stow; its copy of the poem derives from that in the Fairfax manuscript. The poem has been edited as *Lydgate's Reson and Sensuallyte*, ed. Ernst Sieper, 2 vols., EETS e.s. 84 and 89 (London, 1901 and 1903). For ease of reference, all quotations will be from this edition unless otherwise specified.

[26] Although *Reson and Sensuallyte* was traditionally attributed to Lydgate, A. S. G. Edwards has challenged the attribution on the grounds that there is no evidence for Lydgate's authorship other than Stow's attribution of the poem in BL MS Additional 29729 ('Lydgate Manuscripts: Some Directions for Future Research', in *Manuscripts and Readers in Fifteenth-Century England: The Literary Implications of Manuscript Study*, ed. Derek Pearsall (Cambridge: D.S. Brewer, 1983), 24–5). This is not entirely the case, however; in his survey

Waking early on a spring morning, the narrator is advised in turn by Nature, Venus, and Diana as to how best to conduct himself in the world. Rejecting Nature's and Diana's advice to follow the path of reason, he enters a garden of pleasure, where he encounters Venus' son, Deduit, and plays chess with a beautiful maiden. *Reson and Sensuallyte* is incomplete, breaking off in the middle of the description of the chess game, but in *Les Echecs* the narrator is defeated by the maiden and instructed by Amor in new tactics of seduction; before he can challenge the maiden to a repeat match, however, he is intercepted by Pallas. Her lengthy speech gradually leads away from the narrator's immediate situation to the praise of marriage, divinely approved methods of child-rearing, and a disquisition on the proper regulation of each order of society. At this point, both surviving manuscripts of *Les Echecs* also break off, leaving it, too, incomplete, but (as Alastair Minnis says): 'To judge by what we have . . . the text's pedagogic objective was clear in view throughout. Indeed, it could be argued that the frisson of the *ars amatoria* is designed to entice the young aristocrat into the moral centre of the text, where unimpeachable doctrine holds sway.'[27] Adopting a number of tropes and images from the *Roman de la Rose*, most notably the garden of pleasure and the game of chess, *Les Echecs* is engaged in a conscious process of 'correcting' or 'moralizing' its source. To borrow Minnis' term, it 'prunes' and trains the *Rose* to a single model of instruction, in which courtship is the means by which the protagonist will become a useful member of society.[28]

As a translation of an adaptation, *Reson and Sensuallyte* has a complex literary heritage that raises acute questions both about the relation of new

---

of the Lydgate canon, H. N. MacCracken not only follows Stow's attribution but selects the opening lines of *Reson and Sensuallyte* as a particularly good example of Lydgate's use of stock phrases as rhymes (John Lydgate, *The Minor Poems*, Vol. I, ed. H. N. MacCracken, EETS e.s. 107 (London: 1911), pp. xxiv and x). The spectacular amplification of the poem's source text, the detailed explication of allusions, the addition of explicitly moral passages, and the heightened misogyny of the poem—in particular perhaps the ironic passages in praise of women—are also consonant with Lydgate's practice elsewhere. Although I do not refer to the translator as 'Lydgate', I am inclined to believe that Stow's attribution is correct. For an overview of the authorship question, see further James Simpson, 'The Economy of Involucrum: Idleness in *Reason and Sensuality*', in *Through a Classical Eye: Transcultural and Transhistorical Visions in Medieval English, Italian, and Latin Literature in Honour of Winthrop Wetherbee*, ed. Andrew Galloway and R. F. Yeager (Toronto: University of Toronto Press, 2009), 392.

[27] A. J. Minnis, *Magister Amoris: The Roman de la Rose and Vernacular Hermeneutics* (Oxford: Oxford University Press, 2001), 261. For a fuller summary of the poem, see *Les Eschéz d'Amours*, 105–14 and, for its historical and literary context, 11–20 and 49–80. Cf. also Ernst Sieper, *Les Echecs Amoureux: Eine Altfranzösische Nachahmung des Rosenromans und Ihre Englische Übertragung* (Weimar: Verlag von Emil Felber, 1898), 5–94; and *Lydgate's Reson and Sensualltye*, 2: 59–76.

[28] Minnis, *Magister Amoris*, 257.

writing to existing texts and, by extension, about the extent of a writer's control over the transmission of his work.[29] The translator's treatment of his source and his use of glosses suggest a clear awareness of these matters, and also imply that he used the form of the text, in particular its glosses, to explore them further. In striking contrast to the other poems in Fairfax 16, *Reson and Sensuallyte* is provided with an uneven but extensive Latin apparatus. This corresponds closely to an almost identical apparatus in one of the surviving manuscripts of *Les Echecs*, that in the Biblioteca Nazionale Marciana in Venice. It also shows the influence of a further work: an extensive and popular French prose commentary on *Les Echecs* composed by Évrart de Conty (c. 1330–1405), the physician of Charles V.[30] Though it is concerned with a vernacular text, the latter is modelled on academic commentary. Évrart conceives of his role as very much in line with the grammarian's traditional office of *enarratio*, or textual explication: that is, not just commenting on, but 'placing' a text, by providing the framework within which it should be understood.[31] Although, as Minnis points out, he does not replicate the standard structure of an academic *accessus*, he does use terms that clearly reflect its influence, such as 'la fin de son livre': a phrase that clearly echoes the 'causa finalis'.[32] Moreover, he explains his aims in light of those of academic commentators, arguing that the author of *Les Echecs*:

> Semble aux poetes anciens qui en leurs faiz et en leurs escriptures quierent tousjours profit ou delectacion, car le delit et la plaisance que on a en lire ou en oyr les anciennes escriptures recree moult et resjoist nature, dont grandement vault mielx la corporele disposicion; et le profit aussi que on en raporte parfait l'ame et amende. Finablement l'entente principal de l'acteur dessusdit et la fin de son livre, c'est de tendre a vertu et a bonne oeuvre, et de fouir tout mal et toute fole oyseuse.
>
> Il resemble aux poetes anciens en tant qu'il parle aucunefoiz aussi come en faignant et fabuleusement, en disant moult de choses qui ne sont pas du tout a entendre a la lectre.[33]

---

[29] For significant alterations which the translator makes to his source, see Stephanie A. Viereck Gibbs Kamath, 'John Lydgate and the Curse of Genius', *Chaucer Review* 45 (2010), esp. 37–54.

[30] The commentary has been edited as Évrart de Conty, *Le Livre des Eschez Amoureux Moralisés*, ed. Francoise Guichard-Tesson et Bruno Roy (Montreal: CERES, 1993); its popularity appears from the fact that complete copies survive in six manuscripts, with a further extract in a seventh: significantly more than survive of *Les Echecs* itself.

[31] For academic commentary, see Judson Boyce Allen, *The Ethical Poetic of the Later Middle Ages: A Decorum of Convenient Distinction* (Toronto: University of Toronto Press, 1982), 3–66; and A. J. Minnis, *Medieval Theory of Authorship*, 2nd ed. (Aldershot: Wildwood House, 1988), 1–39.

[32] Minnis, *Magister Amoris*, 281–3.

[33] *Eschez Amoureux Moralisés*, 2–3. The poet 'resembles classical poets who, in their creations and their writings always sought profit or delight, because the delight and pleasure one

In Évrart's understanding, then, *Les Echecs* is intended to delight and instruct, just as the works of classical authors are, and it achieves these ends by means of a fictional narrative whose true purpose remains to be unveiled.[34] Taking upon himself the process of unveiling, he performs for *Les Echecs* a service comparable to that which earlier scholars provided for classical texts, ensuring that the work fulfils its instructive purpose by supplying a detailed interpretation of those things which should not be understood literally. By doing so, he implicitly ascribes the status of *auctor* to the anonymous author of the vernacular *Echecs*.[35]

Évrart's commentary differs strikingly from the marginal glosses that accompany *Les Echecs*. The latter adduce parallel passages from classical and medieval works, provide detailed allegorical interpretations of the chess pieces used by the narrator and his opponent, and supply quotations from Ovid's *Remedia Amoris* alongside the part of *Les Echecs* that is based on that poem.[36] The allegorical glosses, in particular, provide essential information; they alone contain the key to the text's moral allegory. A clear example of the interdependence of text and gloss is found in the description of the game of chess between the narrator and the maiden. Introducing the game, the narrator speaks of the 'mistere' of the pieces, indicating that they should be read allegorically.[37] Yet although he goes on to state of which stone each of the pieces is made, and what kind of emblem it bears, he gives no indication in the text as to how these should be interpreted; this information is contained exclusively in the glosses. For example, the description of the narrator's first pawn states merely that:

> Li premiers, qui assis estoit
> Devers sa main destre, portoit
> Un croissant de lune nouvelle,
> Pourtrait par maniere moult belle.[38]

has in reading or hearing the old writings greatly revives and revivifies one's inner nature, which greatly improves the bodily disposition. And in addition, the profit which one derives from it perfects and amends the soul. Finally, the main intention of the author, and the purpose of his book, is to encourage the reader to virtue and good deeds, and to cause him to flee all evil and all idle follies.

He also resembles classical poets in so far as he sometimes speaks feigningly, by fabling, saying many things that should absolutely not be interpreted literally'.

[34] See further Minnis, *Magister Amoris*, 282–96.
[35] For discussion and dismissal of the possibility that Évrart was the author of the poem as well as the commentary, see *Eschéz d'Amours*, 35–9.
[36] See further *Eschéz d'Amours*, 95–7; here F. Coulson points out that the glosses are written in three different hands, with the third appearing exclusively in those that quote the *Remedia Amoris*.
[37] Coulson argues that the glosses should not be considered as an integral part of the poem (*Eschéz d'Amours*, 97), but the reference in the text to an otherwise unexplained 'mistere', which the glosses elucidate, suggests that the allegorical glosses at least are part of its design.
[38] *Eschéz d'Amours*, ll. 4771–4. 'The first, which was placed on his right hand, carried a crescent new moon, depicted very beautifully.'

Information concerning its allegorical significance appears in the Latin glosses alone:

> Primus ergo pedes in bello mulieris ponitur hic Jonesche, quia, licet in facto amoris conveniat et viro et mulieri, convenientius tamen est quod ponitur in bello mulieris, quia illa conditio in muliere multum movet amantem. Et significatur convenientissime per lunam novam, quia crescit, quia in suo lumine multipliciter variatur, et quia recipit lumen a sole. Et ita iuventus crescit et tendit continue ad augmentum, multis etiam figuris et multis motibus agitator; ista etas similiter sequitur communiter impetus et influentiam cordis, qui est in humano corpore sicut sol in maiori mundo, unde iuvenes sunt passionum insequetores, ut dicit Philosophus. Item, sicut luna in modico tempore peragrat multa signa—multa monstra—ita iuventus pertransit multa pericula, etc.[39]

This gloss reveals the thought-process that lies behind the finished allegory. Relating each symbol to a human faculty, which is in turn described in terms of the opportunity or the threat it poses to the lover, it allows the reader to trace the process of allegorical encryption in reverse, from fiction back to underlying meaning. Only with all of this information can the reader grasp the poem's warning to beware of being led astray by the senses; without it, the chess game stands as a slightly cryptic romantic diversion from the main, didactic business of the work.[40] Although the fact that the French text is glossed in Latin suggests that it is possible to read it on two separate levels—just the text for entertainment, or text and gloss together for instruction—the glosses are nonetheless integral to the work.

What, then, does the author of *Reson and Sensuallyte* make of his two-part inheritance of glossed vernacular text and separate commentary? The most striking change he introduces is to the relationship between text and gloss, and thereby to the function of the glosses. Although it is incomplete, the extant part of *Reson and Sensuallyte* runs to 7042 lines, representing only 4873 lines in the French text. Its length is in large part attributable to the translator's habit of incorporating material from the

---

[39] *Eschéz d'Amours*, gloss to l. 4749. 'So the first pawn in the woman's army is said here to be Youth because, although in the deed of love it is fitting for both man and woman, it is more fitting that it is placed in the woman's army, because this condition in a woman has a great effect on the lover. And it is represented most fittingly by the new moon, because it grows, because in its own light it varies in multiple ways, and because it gets its light from the sun. So too youth grows and tends always to increase, and is set in motion by many figures and movements. This age likewise usually follows the onslaughts and influence of the heart, which in the human body is just like the sun in the larger world; hence young men are followers of passions, as the Philosopher says (Aristotle, Rhetoric 2.12). Also just as the moon in a moderate time period travels through many signs—many monsters—thus youth travels through many dangers, etc.' The translation is Heyworth and O'Sullivan's.

[40] Cf. *Echecs Amoureux Moralisés*, p. lxi.

glosses to *Les Echecs* within the body of the text.[41] As a general rule, he departs from 'word for word' translation of the French poem in order to include the 'sentence' provided by the glosses and fully to bring out their instructive message. Thus, whereas in *Les Echecs* the meaning of the action is declared only in the glosses, the text of *Reson and Sensuallyte* states directly that each of the chess pieces represents a means of seduction or defence. The increased transparency of *Reson and Sensuallyte* suggests that the translator was fully in sympathy with his source's didacticism; by including its allegorical material in English, as well as in Latin, he makes it available to all readers of the poem.

The case of the narrator's second pawn provides a good example of the translator's methods. As with the other chess pieces, the reader of the French poem is dependent on the gloss to learn what the significance of the pawn is. The text makes a bare mention of the fact that his shield bears the cognisance of a key (l. 4871), and it is the gloss that elucidates:

> Secundus est Regars, qui per clavem intelligitur, quia sicut per clavem aperitur porta domus, ita per visum aperitur introitus et porta amoris; visus enim primo praesentat delectabilia que sunt in muliere.[42]

In contrast, *Reson and Sensuallyte* fuses the information contained in the French text with that contained in its gloss:

> The secounde povne of grete might
> In ordre next was callyd syght,
> Which in his shelde, shortely to y-sey,
> Bare y-grave a large key,
> To specify erly and late:
> That, as a key vndooth a yate,
> Ryght so the syght, who kan se,
> To vices alle yiveth entre
> Throgh hys wyket as porter,
> And ys the hertys messager;
> And of tresour and Rychesse,
> Of golde and siluer, in sothenesse,
> Of semelynesse, and of beaute,

---

[41] For the translator's habit of amplification, see *Lydgate's Reson and Sensualltye*, 2: 59 and 2: 40–59. For other examples of a translator taking 'the entire page, both center and margin' as his text, see Christopher Baswell, 'Talking Back to the Text: Marginal Voices in Medieval Secular Literature', in *The Uses of Manuscripts in Literary Studies: Essays in Memory of Judson Boyce Allen*, ed. Charlotte Cook Morse, Penelope Reed Doob, and Marjorie Currie Woods (Kalamazoo: Medieval Institute, 1992), 135.

[42] *Eschéz d'Amours*, gloss to l. 4867. 'The second pawn is Regars, which is represented by a key, because just as by a key the door of the house is opened, so by a look is opened up the entrance and doorway of love. For a look shows the delights which are in a woman.' The translation is Heyworth and O'Sullivan's.

>   And of al worldly vanyte:
>   The eye, by fals collusion,
>   Ys Rote and chefe occasion.
>
>   (ll. 6953–68)

In addition to incorporating an interpretation of the pawn's symbol of the key within the text, these lines are characteristic of the translator's practice in the way they subtly alter the tone of his source. Although the *Les Echecs* gloss to this passage refers to 'delectabilia qui sunt in muliere', acknowledging grounds for the narrator's attraction to the maiden even as it warns against following his example, these delights do not appear in the translation; on the contrary, female beauty becomes just one of a number of vices which seduce the sight, encouraging it, in turn, to seduce the reason. The translator introduces these changes even at the risk of undermining both narrative continuity and allegorical consistency: although this is a game of courtship, the pawn Beauty is not allowed simply to stand for the beauty of the woman, but the beauty of the woman is 'moralized' as just one of many worldly vanities, or false objects of desire.

The translator, then, does not merely depart from the text of his source in order to incorporate the sense present in its glosses, but departs from both text and gloss in order to bring out *his own understanding* of the sense. Whereas *Les Echecs* keeps its narrative formally and linguistically separate from its allegorical interpretations, and thus posits two different levels of reader and two different levels of understanding, *Reson and Sensuallyte* collapses this distinction by incorporating the allegorical sense within the literal narrative. The translator thus effects a fundamental change in the mode of the work. *Les Echecs* is an exercise in the kind of dark allegory advocated by Boccaccio in his *De Genealogiae Deorum Gentilium* (c. 1360–74), in which the true meaning of a text is concealed from all but those readers who have the learning requisite to uncover it.[43] In contrast, *Reson and Sensuallyte* exemplifies the theory which Lydgate expressed in the *Fall of Princes*: that the poet's role is to elucidate his material, the better to educate and guide. Like Lydgate, and like Chaucer in *The House of Fame*, the translator understands his role as an interventionist one.[44] While his habit of altering his source in order to bring out his own reading of it reflects the conventional wisdom that a translator should translate not word for word, but sense for sense, this commonplace

---

[43] Boccaccio, 'De Genealogiae Deorum Gentilium', ed. Vittorio Zaccaria, in *Tutte le opere di Giovanni Boccaccio*, gen. ed. Vittore Branca (Milan: Arnoldo Mondadori, 1998), Vols. 7–8.

[44] For Lydgate, see Chapter 1 above; and cf. Jennifer Summit, ' "Stable in study": Lydgate's *Fall of Princes* and Duke Humfrey's Library', in *John Lydgate: Poetry, Culture, and Lancastrian England*, ed. Larry Scanlon and James Simpson (Notre Dame: University of Notre Dame Press, 2006), 207–31.

had long been used as a prompt to or cover for a complex renegotiation of literary authority—and this is precisely what happens in *Reson and Sensuallyte*.[45]

Given the incorporation of the content of the glosses in the text of the poem, it might seem surprising that they are also replicated in its margins. The correspondences between the glosses to *Les Echecs* and those to its translation are generally very close indeed. For example, returning to the second pawn, we find that although *Reson and Sensuallyte* gives a full description of the chess piece in the text, it also includes the gloss:

> Secundus pedinus in bello amoris ex parte viri vocatur in gallico Regars / qui pro claue intelligitur. Et merito quia sicut per clauem aperitur introitus domus ita per visum introitus et porta amoris aperitur / visus enim primo presentat cordi delectabilia que sunt in muliere.[46]

The differences between this and the corresponding gloss in *Les Echecs* are minimal, but because the gloss to the French text provides new information, while that to the English text duplicates what the reader has already read, they are entirely different in effect: the glosses to *Les Echecs* are its key to all mythologies, while those to *Reson and Sensuallyte* are tautologous. From a practical point of view, then, it is not entirely clear what purpose the latter serve. Other than in the game of chess, where they usefully indicate which of the chess pieces is under discussion, the information they provide is too diffuse for them to function as an effective index. And despite the fact that the glosses derive from *Reson and Sensuallyte*'s source text, they do not include any information about that derivation. Therefore, they do not function as a self-authorizing strategy in the way that (for example) Hoccleve's source glosses do in his *Regiment of Princes*, validating the new work by explicitly anchoring it to previous writing, nor do they obviously invite comparison between the English poem and its source.[47]

What then is their function? It has become a commonplace that Latin glosses to a vernacular text serve as an authorizing device, both by underwriting the content of the text, and on a purely visual level, whereby the mere presence of the Latin lends weight to the vernacular work.[48] Here, the fact that the translator reproduces the glosses from *Les Echecs*, despite the resulting duplication of information, certainly does suggest that the visual consideration is a significant one. In *Les Echecs*, the use of Latin for the glosses ensures that the moral 'sentence' of the poem is withheld from

---

[45] See Copeland, *Rhetoric, Hermeneutics and Translation*, 9–62.
[46] *Lydgate's Reson and Sensualltye*, gloss to l. 6953.
[47] For the glossing of Hoccleve's *Regiment*, see the Introduction.
[48] For versions of this argument, especially in relation to Gower's *Confessio Amantis*, see the Introduction.

those who can read only the vernacular. In *Reson and Sensuallyte*, however, their Latinity has a purely symbolic function, not just for readers who do not know Latin and therefore respond simply to its presence, but also for those readers who are able to compare text with gloss. Since neither kind of reader gains any additional information from the glosses, they are less useful than iconographic. Siân Echard has explored the possibility that the *ordinatio* of Gower's *Confessio Amantis* represents a memory system—a visual means of committing the text to memory—and although the layout of *Reson and Sensuallyte* is not systematic enough to lend itself to such a reading, the glosses nonetheless imply a concern with another kind of memorialization.[49] Preserving visual traces of the old text within the new, they do not so much prompt the reader to commit the poem to memory as reveal it to be part of a continuum of writing. Although only a reader with a glossed copy of *Les Echecs* to hand would know that they replicate, almost verbatim, elements of their source text, their presence nonetheless draws attention to the fact that the text is part of an ongoing process of reading and interpretation: if they do not reflect a source for, then they must represent a response to *Reson and Sensuallyte*, and whether they are backward-looking or forward-facing, they are signs of process. For a reader who (like the translator) *does* have such a copy of *Les Echecs* to hand, they make strikingly visible the translator's amplification, as he seeks to bring out the sense of what was previously concealed; they not only verify his accuracy, but also affirm his powers of transformation. Like the references to 'Bochas' in the margins of Lydgate's *Fall of Princes*, and like the source glosses in Chaucer's *House of Fame*, these glosses have the potential to make visible the process of *translatio* to their authors, as well as prompting subsequent readers to become aware of their reading too as a process of active mediation and reinvention.

Signs that the translator was aware of his transformative ability are found in his use of Évrart's commentary as a source of additional material for his glosses. Although this is very much a secondary source, it nonetheless accounts for several pieces of information that are not found in the glosses to *Les Echecs*. For example, when the translator writes in his description of the maiden's bishops that heliotrope, the stone of which they are made, has as one of its many virtues that it 'also, yif yt be credible / Maketh a man Invisible' (ll. 6783–4), he is using material that is not found

---

[49] Siân Echard, 'Designs for Reading: Some Manuscripts of Gower's *Confessio Amantis*', *Trivium* 31 (1999), 59–72; cf. also her 'Dialogues and Monologues: Representations of the Conversations of the *Confessio Amantis*', in *Middle English Poetry: Texts and Traditions in Honour of Derek Pearsall*, ed. A. J. Minnis (York: York Medieval Press, 2001), 57–75; and Mary Carruthers, *The Book of Memory: A Study of Memory in Medieval Culture*, 2nd ed. (Cambridge: Cambridge University Press, 2008), 276–8.

in either the text or the gloss of *Les Echecs*, but which does appear in Évrart's commentary, where Évrart speaks of: 'Les grans merveilles . . . que les anciens dient de ceste pierre, qui sont fortes a croire et sembleroient mielx selon la verité estre fables ou fictions que vertus natureles.'[50] Évrart and the *Reson and Sensuallyte* gloss share not only the information, but also the sceptical tone in which it is presented. A comparable correspondence is found in the translator's discussion of the emblem borne by the maiden's first rook, the 'calaundre'. This, he says, is:

> A bridde of merveylous nature,
> The whiche kan, as clerkys seye,
> Shewe a man yif he shal deye;
> Yif he withdrawe and torne away,
> Of deth ther ys no more delay,
> And yif he look vpon hys face,
> Of lyf he shal haue lenger space.
> Ryght so, in sooth, doth Doulz Regarde:
> Whan a womman hath no rewarde
> With her eyen of pite
> Vpon hir servant for to se
> Ther ys vnto hys maladye
> But deth with-oute remedye.
>
> (ll. 6740–52)

The gloss to the equivalent line of *Les Echecs* (l. 4823) states merely that the bird 'etiam de morte vel de vita certificat egrotantis' ['makes a determination about the death or life of the sick man'], but in Évrart's commentary we find a precedent for the elaborate description in *Reson and Sensuallyte*:

> Nous povons tiercement dire encore oultre que doulx regard, a la similitude de la kalendre dessusdite, ses yeulx adresce et tourne devers la face du malade d'amours et, s'il s'y tient voulentiers et arreste, que c'est signe certain qu'il garira, car par les doulx regars pluseurs fois repetés que celle ly envoie qui peut ses maulx garir, cely prend en ly sy bonne ymaginacion, sy bon confort et sy bonne esperance qu'il se sent tout finablement gary.[51]

---

[50] *Eschez Amoureux Moralisés*, 671–2. 'The most wonderful stories which our ancestors told about this stone, which are difficult to believe and, in truth, seem more likely to be fables or fictions than actual characteristics.'

[51] *Eschez Amoureux Moralisés*, 664. 'Thirdly, we may say once more that Gentle Gaze, like the aforementioned bird, directs and turns her eyes towards the face of the sick man and, if she pauses and rests her gaze there voluntarily, that that is a sure sign that he will recover, because by the frequently repeated kind looks which she sends him, who is able to cure his ills, he is so encouraged, comforted, and given hope, that he feels fully recovered.' Heyworth argues (*Eschéz d'Amours*, 95) that the glosses to *Les Echecs* influenced Évrart's commentary, so that his influence on those to *Reson and Sensallyte* comes full circle.

Here, in a series of shifts in the mode of signification, 'doulx regard' is likened to the bird and then (once personified) described as the literal soft looks of the lady. In the equivalent passage in *Reson and Sensuallyte*, too, there is a strange double simile: the personified 'Doulz Regarde' is said to act in the same way as the marvellous bird, but is then instantly described as one of the attributes of a woman. Such an idiosyncratic and rather indistinct fusion of tenor and vehicle, in which a personification is likened to a bird before both together are revealed to be a metaphor, is unlikely to have been arrived at by two writers working independently. Its occurrence in *Reson and Sensuallyte* indicates that the translator was not slavishly adopting the glosses from *Les Echecs*, but that—despite their apparent redundancy—they form a considered part of his moralizing of his material.

The use of Évrart's commentary not only leaves traces in the content of the glosses to *Reson and Sensuallyte*, but may also provide a context for the translator's thinking about his own role. By incorporating material from both the *Les Echecs* glosses and Évrart's commentary, the translator of *Reson and Sensuallyte* includes within the text of the poem a version of Évrart's service to the reader. But he also internalizes Évrart's valorization of the work, providing a prompt to consider the English poem too as an academic, glossed, and moralized text of equivalent standing, and thus to consider himself as *auctor*. His realization of this transfer of authority is evident in a number of glosses that are unique to *Reson and Sensuallyte*, and that comment explicitly on the translator's practice. The first of these occurs at the point where Nature describes the two paths between which the narrator may choose: that which begins in the 'orient' and that which begins in the 'occident'. Here Fairfax 16 includes a gloss explaining that the 'orient' stands for celestial things, the 'occident' for sensual ones (see Plate 2.2). The path of the orient 'a consideracione celestium et eternorum et leuiter transeundo per ista terrena semper redit et finaliter se conuertit ad eterna / Alia vero via que incipit ab occidente significat viam sensus qui adheret communiter magis temporalibus et terrenis.'[52] As is the translator's standard practice, the information contained in the gloss is duplicated in the body of the text, where Nature has the lines:

> Of hem thys ys the difference:
> Thorient, which ys so bryght
> And casteth forth so clere a lyght
> Betokeneth in especiall
> Thinges that be celestiall
> . . .
> This is the wey[e] of Reson
> . . .

---

[52] *Lydgate's Reson and Sensuallyte*, gloss to l. 653. The orient 'is to be considered heavenly and eternal, and passing lightly through this world always tends towards and finally arrives

> But the tother of the west
> Ys, who that kan beholde and se,
> The wey of sensualyte,
> Which set his entente in al
> To thinges that be temporal,
> Passynge and transytorie,
> And fulfylled of veyn glorie.
>
> (ll. 664–8, 672, 676–82)

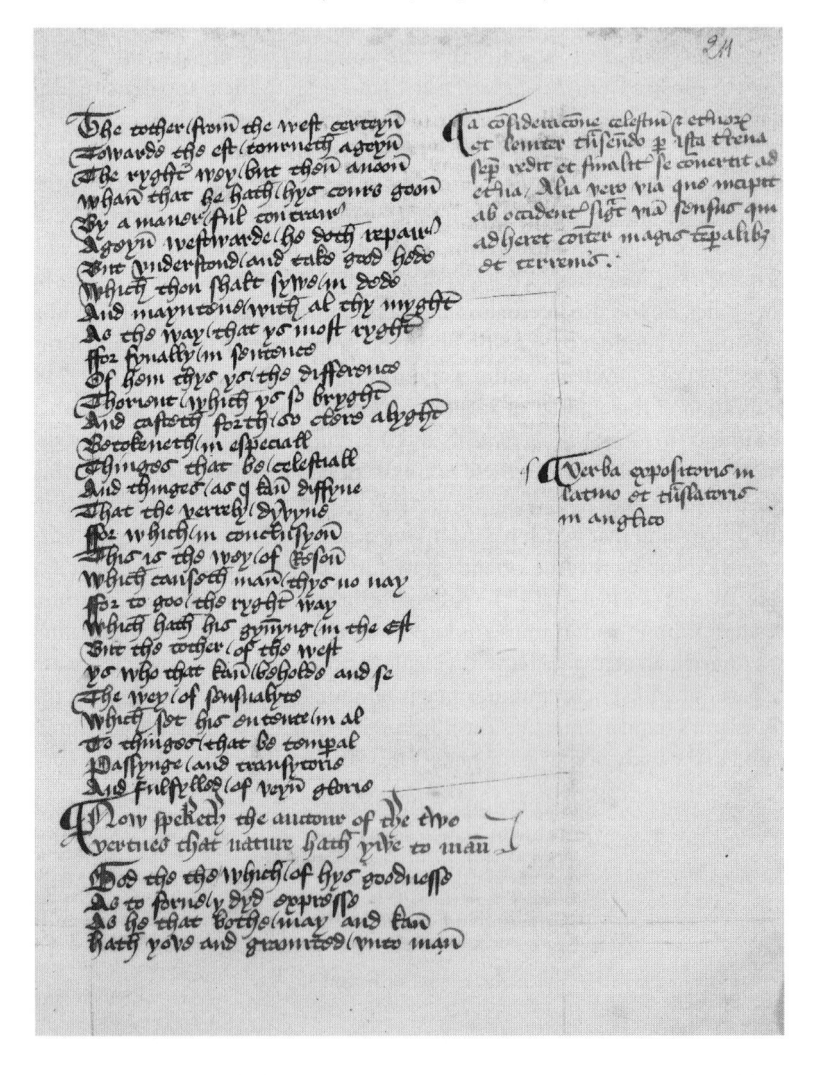

Plate 2.2 Bodleian MS Fairfax 16, f. 211. Reproduced courtesy of The Bodleian Libraries, The University of Oxford.

Alongside this speech, Fairfax 16 contains the marginal comment: 'Verba expositoris in latino et translatoris in anglico.'[53] Similarly, when the translator describes the cygnets that circle the goddess Pallas' head, commenting that '[This] thing to my fantasye / Of wisdom may signyfye' (ll. 1245–6), a marginal note declares: 'Ista sunt verba translatoris'.[54] A third instance of such a gloss occurs after the lengthy description of Pallas, when the translator provides some conventional lines of transition:

> Now no more of thys matere,
> But first, so as I vndertook,
> To the processe of my book
> I will retourne.
>
> (ll. 1278–81)

Here the gloss comments: 'Huc vsque verba translatoris.'[55] Such attributions are self-evidently different in kind from the glosses that replicate those in *Les Echecs*. Unlike those inherited glosses, they comment not on the content of the text, but on the process of creating it. On the one hand, they emphasize the resemblance between translator and commentator, both of whom have the task of serving the source text by expounding its 'sentence'. On the other hand, they draw attention to the text as a made object, and thus to the translator's role in its making, thereby rendering the margin a means of exploring both the relationship between source and translation and, by extension, the nature of the writer's or translator's authority.[56] As Stephanie Kamath has argued with reference to some almost identical glosses in *The Pilgrimage of the Life of Man*: 'The marginal notes that isolate particular contributions to the text made by the translator . . . lend emphasis to the passages in which the translator assumes the authority to expand the text with interpretative commentary, *emulating the author's composition process.*'[57] Indeed, as with the glosses to *The House of Fame*, it is even possible that there is a mutual influence between practice and theory: that the translator's use of material from the glosses to *Les Echecs* for the text of his translation prompts

---

in eternity. The other path, however, which begins in the occident, signifies the way of sensuality, which is generally more focused on temporal and earthly things.'

[53] *Fairfax 16*, f. 211. See Plate 2.2; and cf. Minnis, *Magister Amoris*, 290–1.

[54] *Fairfax 16*, f. 219. For this gloss, and the translator's possible misinterpretation at this point in the text, see Stephanie A. Viereck Gibbs Kamath, 'Periphery and Purpose: The Fifteenth-Century Rubrication of the *Pilgrimage of Human Life*', *Glossator* 1 (2009), 45.

[55] *Fairfax 16*, f. 219ᵛ.

[56] Cf. Simpson, 'Economy of Involucrum', 409–10.

[57] Kamath, 'Periphery and Purpose', 34 (italics mine); she also notes the occurrence of the 'verba auctoris' and 'verba translatoris' glosses in *Reson and Sensuallyte* (45–6). As she

thought about his own contribution to the new work, and that this in turn prompts a more experimental use of the glosses, as he begins to use the margins explicitly to draw attention to his own shaping presence.[58] Viewed in this light, the replication of the glosses from *Les Echecs* in the margins of *Reson and Sensuallyte*, redundant though they are in terms of content, becomes part of a sustained reflection by the translator on the processes of creating and presenting a text, and on the relationship between the two. Practice and theory become inseparable; the glosses stand as an early example of the emergence of glossing as a means of thinking about the writing process and, by making such thought visible, become rhetorical: intended for effect.

'PER CONTRARIUM': SCRIBAL EDITING AND ANOMALOUS GLOSSING IN MS FAIRFAX 16

Experimental though they may be, it is impossible to consider these Latin glosses in *Reson and Sensuallyte* in isolation. Even within *Reson and Sensuallyte* itself, the Latin apparatus is juxtaposed with some very different kinds of gloss: the poem also contains numerous English indexing glosses, which are distinguished from the Latin ones by being copied in the text-block, and is accompanied by a number of 'Nota' glosses, as well as a handful of glosses that identify instances of irony. Each of these types of gloss has a different relationship to the text. The English indexing glosses—like the Latin apparatus—have counterparts

---

points out, almost identical glosses occur in a number of manuscripts of works whose attribution to Lydgate is undisputed, which means that their occurrence in *Reson and Sensuallyte* may support the argument that Lydgate was its author. If so, Nigel Mortimer's suggestion that *Reson and Sensuallyte* was a product of Lydgate's 'French period' (1422–6) becomes especially interesting. Such a dating would make it broadly contemporary with both the *Siege of Thebes* and the *Fall of Princes*, and would suggest that the glossing of the three works was part of an ongoing process of experimentation (see *John Lydgate's Fall of Princes: Narrative Tragedy in its Literary and Political Contexts* (Oxford: Clarendon Press, 2005), 49).

[58] Intriguingly, there are two equivalent glosses in *La Belle Dame Sans Merci*: those that note 'Verba auctoris' when the lengthy dialogue between Lamant and La Dame ends, and 'Verba translatoris' at the point of transition from translation to translator's envoy (ff. 61ᵛ and 62). These differ from those in *Reson and Sensuallyte* in that the text of *La Belle Dame* clearly indicates the change of authorship (indeed, the 'verba auctoris' gloss may have been prompted by the speech markers on so many of the preceding stanzas), whereas only someone with both *Les Echecs* and *Reson and Sensuallyte* to hand would be able to comment so accurately on the way in which the translator incorporates in his text material from the gloss in *Les Echecs*. The *Belle Dame* glosses may nonetheless signal that the *Reson and Sensuallyte* translator was working in a context where such attributions were increasingly of interest. They are not unique to the Fairfax manuscript, but also appear in the copy of the poem in BL MS Harley 372.

in *Les Echecs*, and are demonstrably part of the translation. Indeed, although the majority speak of the poem's narrator in the third person (for example, 'Here spekyth thauctour of the beaute of Nature'), one of them anomalously declares 'Now, after descripcioun of hir beaute, *I* shall declare the maner of hir clothyng', in a slip that indicates the intensity of the translator's engagement with his work, and may suggest something of the mindset that gave rise to the 'verba translatoris' glosses.[59]

The 'nota' glosses are entirely different. These occur not only in *Reson and Sensuallyte*, but throughout the manuscript, and—unlike all other marginal material—they are not emphasized with paraphs and underlining, but copied tightly against the text-block. Although the hand in which they are copied strongly resembles that of the scribe, and their neatness and uniformity demonstrate a concern with orderliness that matches the scribe's own, it is possible that they are not scribal, but represent the additions of an early reader.[60] If they are scribal, however, the way in which they are treated reflects a very definite decision to subordinate them to all other glosses in the manuscript: unlike those other glosses, at first glance they are barely noticeable.[61] Once they have been noticed, however, they contribute to the impression that *Reson and Sensuallyte* is an exceptionally well-mediated text: articulated by its English glosses, framed by its Latin ones, and with preceptive pointers already in place. But although *Reson and Sensuallyte* represents the high point of the scribe's systematic presentation, something comparable is apparent in the less heavily glossed poems in Fairfax 16: he is entirely consistent in attempting to impose visual coherence on diverse material. In terms of presentation, there is no distinction between the citation glosses and preceptive pointers in *The House of Fame*; the Latin and English glosses that mark the beginning and the end of the major rhetorical set pieces in *The Complaint of Mars* and *The Temple of Glass*; the

---

[59] These glosses follow ll. 314 and 345 respectively. The italic is mine.
[60] Although the lines highlighted in this way are extremely diverse, they frequently include sententious and anti-clerical material; in *The Temple of Glass*, for example, the lines 'Remembreþ eke, how neuer ʒit no wiʒt / Ne came to wirship withoute some debate' (ll. 398–9) are marked, as is Venus' comment on those who 'al her life cannot but complein, / In wide copis perfeccion to feine' (ll. 203–4). The 'nota' glosses appear to be unique to the copy of *The Temple of Glass* in Fairfax 16.
[61] For the scribe as editor, see note 6 above; and cf. Barbara Kline, 'Scribal Agendas and the Text of Chaucer's Tales in British Library MS Harley 7333', in *Rewriting Chaucer*, 116–44; Seth Lerer, 'Rewriting Chaucer: Two Fifteenth-Century Readings of *The Canterbury Tales*', *Viator* 19 (1988), 311–26; and Susan Schibanoff, 'The New Reader and Female Textuality in Two Early Commentaries on Chaucer', *Studies in the Age of Chaucer* 10 (1988), 71–108.

French glosses that attribute alternate stanzas to each of the two speakers (Lamant and La Dame) in *La Belle Dame Sans Merci*; a stray Latin interpolation in *Anelida and Arcite*; and the two anomalous preceptive pointers in *The House of Fame*. Indeed, the last of these, 'Nota of many untrewe lovers', is copied in such close juxtaposition with a citation gloss from Ovid's *Heroides* that, despite the scribe's careful use of two separate paraphs, at first glance it is difficult even to determine that there are two glosses, let alone to see that they are of different kinds.[62]

This 'nota of many untrewe lovers' is thus a particularly striking instance of the way in which the scribe's attempt at clarity creates ambiguity. As Christopher Baswell has argued:

> The margin provides a space where voices or preoccupations (and the textual communities implicit behind them) relatively ignored or suppressed in the primary text are able to enter into conflict with it—to talk back to the text. This can happen in very simple ways, and arguably without specific intention on the part of the glossators, as when an early manuscript receives successive but inconsistent layers of annotation. The result is a manuscript that proposes to its readers varying versions of the auctor. But it can happen in much more intriguing ways, as when voices from the central text quite literally leak out into the margin in a sort of textual diastole or centrifugal action.[63]

In Fairfax 16, due to the meticulousness of its scribe, there is no immediate way of telling which of these two situations we are dealing with. The identification in the margin of the names of the speakers in *La Belle Dame*, for example, is not unique to the Fairfax manuscript, and may represent a very early *ordinatio*; the glosses marking rhetorical set pieces in *The Temple of Glass*, on the other hand, are found only in Fairfax and the manuscript mostly closely associated with it.[64] The impossibility of determining the origin of the glosses is especially tantalizing when it comes to those

---

[62] *Fairfax 16*, f. 159ᵛ. The other preceptive pointer, 'Cavete vos innocentes mulieres', appears on f. 158ᵛ.
[63] Baswell, 'Talking Back', 122–3.
[64] There are equivalents of the Fairfax *Temple of Glass* glosses in MS Bodley 638, but MS Tanner 346 and MS Pepys 2006 are unglossed, while CUL MS Gg.4.27 and BL MS Additional 16165 each contain different glosses. I have not seen Longleat MS 258. There are equivalents of the Fairfax glosses to *La Belle Dame* in BL MS Harley 372. CUL MSFf. 1.6 contains the identification of the speakers, but not the indications of 'verba auctoris' and 'verba translatoris'; Cambridge, Trinity College MS R.3.19 contains neither. BL MS Sloane 1710 does not contain the identification of the speakers and is defective at the point where the 'verba auctoris' gloss might have appeared. For the representation of speech in medieval manuscripts, see further Colette Moore, *Quoting Speech in Early English* (Cambridge: Cambridge University Press, 2011).

glosses in *Reson and Sensuallyte* which draw attention to irony in the text by means of phrases such as 'per contrarium', 'Cuius contrarium est verum', or, in one instance, the more elaborate: 'Sed absit quod aliqua variacio foret reperta in sexu muliebri qui non habet aliquam influenciam variacionis a luna / per Antifrasim.'[65] Attached to passages that are ostensibly in praise of women, these glosses reaffirm the anti-feminism that characterizes the poem. Yet in identifying a rhetorical trope they are noticeably different from its other glosses, and they differ, too, in their implicit directiveness: their manifest anxiety to avoid any risk that the praise of women might be interpreted literally. In this respect they are consonant with the translator's desire to spell things out, which is so abundantly apparent in his inclusion of the subject-matter of the *Echecs* glosses within the text of his translation. Given this, and given the translator's evident interest in glossing, it is not inconceivable that he is responsible for these glosses, too. If so, that would suggest that the discoveries about his own control over the text resulting from his use of the formal apparatus have found expression in direct attempts to influence his readers: not just in the 'verba translatoris' glosses that draw attention to his presence, but in others that extend his mediation of the text from the body of the translation to the margins.

Although this must remain speculation, the significance of the Fairfax copy of *Reson and Sensuallyte* for a discussion of early self-glossing practices is clear. Surrounded by many different kinds of annotation, it is a particularly acute example of the way differing interpretations—translator's, scribe's, reader's—may be inscribed and transmitted within a text. Like many of the manuscripts of Lydgate's poems, it witnesses the emergence of the gloss as a locus for discoveries about and reflections on the writing process, but by presenting such glosses in the context of heterogenous, unsystematic annotation, it provides a reminder of how unusual and how fragile such experimentation is, and thus how easily it may become invisible. The scribe's homogenizing practice is especially significant here. The fact that there is no visual distinction between those glosses that are supplementary to the text and those with origins in the translation process, nor between those that respond, however casually, to the text, and those that link it to its sources, means that the glosses in the Fairfax manuscript eradicate any trace of sequential composition or accretion. In giving the text and margins a timeless appearance that

---

[65] *Fairfax 16*, ff. 288ᵛ, 290ᵛ. 'On the contrary'; 'Which is contrary to the truth'; 'But it is not the case that any kind of changeability is found in the female sex, which isn't at all influenced by the moon in its changeability. Said ironically.'

belies their content, and in giving the most throwaway comment an incongruously formal appearance, the Fairfax manuscript anticipates an effect that will be exploited to diverting ends by later authors who write for print. In its appearance, as well as its record of experimental glossing, it witnesses phenomena that will be important for the subsequent development of the gloss.

3

Exhortations to the Reader
The Double Glossing of Douglas' *Eneados*

Examining self-glossing as part of the business of translation, the previous chapters demonstrated how it might reflect and develop a writer's thinking about his control over his material: specifically, by making visible the possibility that his authority derives not from any inherited 'sentence', but from changes introduced in the course of the writing process itself. Whereas in Lydgate's *Siege of Thebes* and *Fall of Princes* such glossing appeared to be genuinely experimental, in *Reson and Sensuallyte* it serves a more self-consciously self-authorizing purpose, as part of an extended moral interpretation of the text influenced by the academic commentary tradition. Such a transition from essentially private discovery to public strategy is still more apparent in Gavin Douglas' glosses to his translation of the *Aeneid* (1513). With their explicit references to academic commentaries on Virgil, these simultaneously cast Douglas as the latest in a series of interpreters and draw attention to the historical particularity of his work. Despite (or perhaps because of) their quite radical rethinking of poetic authority, Douglas' glosses did not achieve widespread circulation; they survive only in Cambridge, Trinity College MS O.3.12. The glosses that most sixteenth-century readers of Douglas' work would have encountered were those that appear in its first printed edition, published by William Copland in 1553, and these have different priorities entirely.[1] Douglas' glosses provide information designed to bridge the cultural gap between Virgil and the sixteenth century and, in doing so, become potentially destabilizing, demonstrating that even the 'sentence' of an established *auctor* such as Virgil is subject to change. In contrast, the glosses to Copland's edition interpret the text in such a way as to suggest that it functions as a storehouse of moral commonplaces with timeless applicability.

---

[1] *The xiii. Bukes of Eneados of the famose Poete Virgill Translatet out of Latyne verses into the Scottish metir bi the Reverend Father in God Mayster Gawin Douglas Bishop of Dunkel and vnkil to the Erle of Angus* (London: William Copland, 1553), STC 24797.

It would be tempting to attribute this difference to the demands of the market for which Copland produced his edition: to argue that, unlike Douglas', his glosses constitute a response to a commercial imperative to make his book attractive and accessible to a potentially large and diverse readership. The distinction between manuscript and print glossing is less complete than this would imply, however. On the first few leaves of the Trinity manuscript, Douglas' glosses have been supplemented by four of Copland's, which momentarily counter Douglas' destabilizing tendencies with an alternative, less challenging form of glossing. The manuscript thus bears witness to a brief struggle over the interpretation of the text, making startlingly visible the extent to which glossing might not only reflect but also shape consideration of the way in which a text means.

AUTHORITY AND INNOVATION IN DOUGLAS' 'COMMENT'

The Trinity manuscript of the *Eneados*, in which Douglas' glosses appear, has considerable textual authority. The author of the text is circumstantially identified as 'Master Gawyn Dowglas provest of Sanct Gylys Kyrk in Edinburgh and person of Lyntoun in Louthiane quilk eftyr was bischop of Dunkeld', and the colophon asserts the scribe's close connection with him: 'Heir endis the thretteyn and final buke of Eneados quhilk is the first correk coppy nixt efter the translation Wrytin be Master Mattho Geddes scribe or writar to the translator.'[2] The majority of the glosses in the manuscript are copied in Geddes' hand, and—unlike those to Lydgate's *Fall of Princes* and *Siege of Thebes*—they have long been accepted as an integral part of Douglas' translation. Douglas himself draws attention to them in the 'Direction' of the book, where he writes that he has compiled 'a schort comment . . . to expon strange histouris and termys wild' (ll. 141–2); the layout of the manuscript, in which ample space has been allowed for the glosses, confirms that they 'belong'.[3]

This tells us a great deal about the way in which Douglas viewed his work. His description of the glosses is suggestive in itself; the use of the term 'comment' and the elucidatory purpose that he attributes to it imply that he viewed it as a vernacular counterpart to Latin academic commentaries on

---

[2] Gavin Douglas, *Virgil's Aeneid*, ed. David F. C. Coldwell, 4 vols. (Edinburgh: Scottish Text Society, 1957–64), 2: 1 and 4: 187. For ease of reference, all quotations will be taken from this edition unless otherwise specified.

[3] Only the Prologue and the first seven 'chapters' of Book I are consistently glossed, but the layout of the manuscript suggests that the comment was originally intended to accompany the whole of Douglas' translation.

the *Aeneid*. Both in manuscript and in print, these had long been a standard part of the work's transmission. One of the earliest and most popular was that by the fifth-century grammarian Servius, and this forms an important part of the edition of the *Aeneid* which Douglas used in preparing his translation: that published by Johannes Badius Ascencius in 1501.[4] Here it appears alongside a further commentary by Ascencius himself, and extracts from three others attributed to Beroaldus, Donatus, and Dathus. These academic commentaries had clearly defined functions; their purpose was the provision, first, of an introduction to Virgil and his works (the *accessus*); second, of the phrase-by-phrase analysis of Virgil's text, discussing grammar and style, identifying allusions, conveying linguistic information, and providing additional information about Roman mythology, customs, and place names.[5] Ascensius' edition thus presents a heavily mediated text; on many folios the commentary is so dense that only a few lines of Virgil appear, and in some cases none at all. Nor are the multiple commentaries the only paratext. There is an alphabetical table of contents, an introductory life of Virgil, a preface to the text, and a set of twelve 'monosticha' (single lines summarizing the contents of each book); the edition also includes the apocryphal 'Book XIII' of the *Aeneid*, originally composed by Mapheus Vegius in 1428.[6] Virgil's work is therefore approached through, and dominated by, multiple layers of *accessus*; although Douglas asserts in the Prologue to Book I that '[I] dyd my best, as the wyt mycht atteyn, / Virgillis versys to follow and no thing feyn' (ll. 265–6), the form in which he encountered Virgil was very far from providing a naked text.

Douglas' translation too is heavily framed by an apparatus that includes not only his own 'comment' and prologues to each book, but paratexts

---

[4] For identification of this edition as that used by Douglas, see Priscilla Bawcutt, *Gavin Douglas* (Edinburgh: Edinburgh University Press, 1976), 98–102. Over 100 editions of the *Aeneid* were printed in Europe between 1469–1512; the first edition to include Servius' commentary appeared in 1475, and the first to include multiple commentaries in 1484 (see Bawcutt, *Douglas*, 95). For the commentary tradition in manuscript, see Christopher Baswell, *Virgil in Medieval England: Figuring the Aeneid from the Twelfth Century to Chaucer* (Cambridge: Cambridge University Press, 1995).

[5] For academic prologues, see further A. J. Minnis, *Medieval Theory of Authorship: Scholastic Literary Attitudes in the Later Middle Ages*, 2nd ed. (Aldershot, 1988); and cf. Judson Boyce Allen, *The Ethical Poetic of the Middle Ages: A Decorum of Convenient Distinction* (Toronto: University of Toronto Press, 1982).

[6] For Mapheus, see *Maphaeus Vegius and his Thirteenth Book of the Aeneid*, ed. Anna Cox Brinton (Bristol: Bristol Classical, 2002); Robert Cummings, ' "To Cart the Fift Quheill": Gavin Douglas' Humanist Supplement to the *Eneados*', *Translation and Literature* 4 (1995), 133–56; and Kantik Ghosh, ' "The Fift Quheill": Gavin Douglas' Maffeo Vegio', *Scottish Literary Journal* 22 (1995), 5–21. In Ascensius' edition, his authorship is acknowledged in the heading 'Maphi Veggii Laudensis Poetae clarrissimi Liber Tertiusdecimus Additius duodecim Aeneidos libris' (f. ccclxxxxxiii), but the change of authorship is not discussed in the commentary.

inherited from his source: rhyming couplets giving an overview of the contents of the work, and headings to each of its chapters. Yet Douglas does not simply replicate those elements of paratext that appear in Ascensius' edition; rather, he takes on board the implications of Ascensius' very visible mediation of Virgil by reflecting explicitly on the process of transmission. In consequence, Douglas' glosses and prologues manifest the same tension between authorizing and destabilizing tendencies that we saw in the glosses to *Reson and Sensuallyte*, but—perhaps because he is responding directly to a classical model of commentary, rather than a pre-mediated version of it—they do so in a more self-evidently self-conscious form. Just as the layout of Ascensius' edition emphasizes the importance of both commentator and printer as creators of new meaning in the work, Douglas' translation emphasizes that he, as translator and commentator, has joined the ranks of these creative interpreters. What is only implied in *Reson and Sensuallyte* about the translator's impact on the translated work is here made explicit.

Douglas' interest in his own contribution to the text is most fully expressed in his prologues, many of which focus on the business of translating rather than on Virgil's work. Those to Books VII and VIII, in particular, are concerned not with the monumental quality of the finished book, but with the labour of producing it in 'real', human time. A recurrent theme throughout is the inevitability of difference between his translation and Virgil's original.[7] In the Prologue to Book I Douglas presents the problem as a linguistic one. Explaining that 'sum history, subtell word or the ryme' may cause him 'to mak digressioun sum tyme' (ll. 305–6), he goes on to give specific instances of the problem. Virgil's *oppetere*, for example, has obliged him to make three words of one, while *animal, homo, genus, sexus*, and *species* are adduced as examples of words that simply have no exact equivalent in the vernacular, and thus compel circumlocution (I. Prol. 359–72).[8]

However, the glosses to these lines reveal that Douglas' departures from Virgil's exact 'sentence' are not due exclusively to differences between English and Latin, but arise from the process of interpretation itself; arguably, they are due precisely to Douglas' scrupulous attempts at accuracy. The gloss to his discussion of the term *oppetere* elaborates on the difficulty he alludes to in the text: 'Oppetere is alsmekil to say as ore terram petere,

---

[7] For Douglas' Prologues and their relation to his translation, see A. E. C. Canitz, 'The Prologue to the *Eneados*: Gavin Douglas' Directions for Reading', *Studies in Scottish Literature* 25 (1990), 1–22; and Lois Ebin, 'The Role of the Narrator in the Prologues to Gavin Douglas' *Eneados*', *Chaucer Review* 14 (1980), 353–65.

[8] For Douglas' fidelity in the detail of his translation, see A. E. C. Canitz, 'From *Aeneid* to *Eneados*: Theory and Practice of Gavin Douglas' Translation', *Medievalia et Humanistica* 19 (1991), 81–100.

lyke as Seruius exponys the sammyn term, quhilk to translate in our tung is, with mowth to seik or byte the erd. And lo, that is ane hail sentens for ane of Virgillis wordis.'[9] The gloss discussing the words *animal* and *homo* elaborates further on the difficulty of word-for-word translation, forming one of Douglas' best-known statements on the subject of translation:

> As for animal and homo in our langage is nocht a propir term, and thai be bot bestis that exponys animal for a beste. Ane beste is callit in Latyn bestia and pecus, and animal betakynnys all corporall substans that haβ ane saull quhilk felis payn, ioy, or ennoy. And vndyr animal beyn contenyt all mankynd, beist, byrd, fowll, fisch, serpent, and all other sik thingis at lyfis and steris, that haβ a body, for al sik and euery ane of thame, may be properly callit animal. And thus animal is ane general name for al sik maner thingis quhatsumeuer. Homo betakynnys baith a man and a woman, and we haue na term correspondent tharto, nor ʒit that signifyis baith twa in a term alanerly.[10]

Like many of Douglas' glosses, these manage to be at once conventional and idiosyncratic. Although they are clearly modelled on the academic commentary glosses that surround Ascensius' edition of the *Aeneid*, and fulfil the traditional function of conveying linguistic information that may help to bridge the gap between modern reader and classical author, they do not comment on Virgil's lines, but on Douglas'. They thus frame Douglas' own framing of Virgil, and thereby contribute to a discussion of the business of translation which has no source in the *Aeneid*, but is peculiar to the *Eneados*. The *animal* gloss in particular makes visible Douglas' thought-processes, as the margin is used to pursue a detailed proof of a case made in outline in the text. Even in the more succinct *oppetere* gloss, Douglas does not stop at the canonical provision of an etymology for the Latin word, but goes on to reflect on his own translation of Servius' phrase; his own words become the subject of what appears an almost spontaneous discussion, prompted by the translation process itself. Rather than providing the 'last word' on the text, these glosses imply that there is no such thing. They do not just express, but emblematize the view that the process of translation generates a surplus: a series of possible interpretations, and reflections upon them, which cannot be contained within the finished text. The presence of the glosses on the page, separate from the main body of the text, is the visible correlative of that position. While translation itself had long been viewed as a form of commentary (something that Douglas himself reflects when he identifies one of the problems of translation as

---

[9] Gloss to I. Prol. 350. The reference is to Servius' gloss to *Aeneid*, I. 96.
[10] Gloss to I. Prol. 367.

the need to give 'ane expositioun' of the text), the way he splits his discussion between text and gloss gives visual representation to the difficulty of conveying the meaning of the original. The glosses make visible Douglas' continued process of reflection on the text, and the unfinished nature of the 'finished' work.

Douglas' interest in the process of making meaning, and in making that process visible to the reader, is also apparent from the inconsistent ways in which he treats his academic sources. At times he adheres closely to one or more of the earlier commentaries. Servius is particularly important to him; his commentary provides material not only for the *oppetere* gloss, but for glosses discussing the etymology of the city of Latium, identifying Samo as 'an ile in Trace, quhar Juno was weddit and born, as sais Servius', and explaining the confusion as to whether Antenor or Aeneas arrived first in Italy, among many others.[11] Douglas also makes extensive use of the later commentary of Ascensius, on one occasion even disrupting his own text in order to do so. His gloss to the lines 'And as the Troianis frakkis our the fluide, / Scars from the syght of Sicillie the land ...' is an unusually lengthy one, recapitulating the action of the beginning of the book and anticipating its development from this point onwards:

> First abuyf the poete proponis his entent, sayand, 'The batellis and the man, &c.'; nyxt makis he inuocation, calland on his muse to tech hym thar, 'O thou my Muse &c'; and ther, lyke as his muse spak to hym, declaris the caussis of the feid of Juno, sayand, 'There was ane anchient Cyte, hecht Cartage.' Now heir thridly proceidis he furth on his narration and history, and begynnys at the sevint ȝeir of Eneas departyng of Troy, as ȝe may se in the end of this first buyk, and efter the deceß by hir self, tretis scho with Eolus, the neddyr part of raison, quhilk sendis the storm of his fadir Anchises, quham he erdit in Sycill at Drepanon, as ȝe haf in the end of the thrid buyk. The remanent of his auenturis beyn reseruyt, be craft of poetry, to the banket of Queyn Dido, quhar thai be then lenth rehersit by Eneas in the secund and thryd.[12]

The position of this discussion is curious; it appears in what seems to be a random position towards the end of the first chapter of Book I. There is no obvious reason why it is here precisely that Douglas chooses to elaborate on Virgil's technique in such general terms, rather than providing information directly relevant to the glossed lines. In Ascensius' edition, however, the lines to which this gloss is attached are the opening lines of Book II, and thus form a natural place to recapitulate what has gone before and reflect on Virgil's ordering of his material. Douglas places the beginning of his second chapter twenty-five lines later, at the point where Juno departs

---

[11] Glosses to I.i.8, I.i.28, and I.v.29. [12] Gloss to I.i.62.

in search of Eolus, but although he alters the arrangement of the text, his 'comment' continues to reflect the *divisio* of his source. Such extreme fidelity is rare, however. Douglas often displays a striking independence in the treatment of his sources, not least in his selective acknowledgement of them. As Priscilla Bawcutt has demonstrated, he frequently omits to mention the commentary from which he has drawn a reference, instead citing the more authoritative writer who is quoted in his source.[13] Thus, even as the glosses give the impression that the *Eneados* is grounded in a remarkably wide range of previous writing, Douglas' selective citation gives rise to a suspicion that he is concerned not only to elucidate Virgil's work, but also to enhance the status of his own translation.

This is confirmed by a number of glosses that juggle sources in such a way as to draw attention quite explicitly to Douglas' own mediation of Virgil's work. Douglas' frequent use of Servius and Ascensius places his translation in a tradition of commentary that, in Christopher Baswell's words, 'approaches classical Latin texts grammatically and rhetorically, and attempts to read them in a fashion that in some ways acknowledges and restores their historical and religious difference'.[14] On occasion, however, Douglas draws not only on these pedagogical commentaries, but also on commentaries whose concerns are with the figurative rather than the literal sense of Virgil's text: that is, what Baswell classifies as 'allegorizing' commentaries.[15] Douglas thus incorporates two very different critical traditions within a single work, and sometimes even within a single gloss. Whereas pedagogical commentary conveys information that will allow the reader to bridge the gap between Virgil's time and his own, allegorizing commentary effectively denies the existence of such a gap. In the *Eneados*, we find an example of the latter approach in Douglas' glossing of the description of the storm that drives Aeneas and his fleet to the coast of Libya, where he follows the elaborately allegorizing readings of the fifteenth-century Italian Cristoforo Landino:

> Eneas purposis to Italy, his land of promyssion; that is to say, a iust perfyte man entendis to mast soueran bonte and gudnes, quhilk . . . is situate in contemplation of godly thyngis or dyvyn warkis. His onmeysabill ennymy Iuno . . . entendis to dryve him from Italle to Cartage; that is Avesion, or concupissence to ryng or haf warldly honouris, wald draw him fra contemplation to the actyve lyve; quhilk, quhen scho falis of mony warldly consalis in the iust manis mynd. Bot, quhoubeyt the mynd lang flowis and delitis heirintyll, fynaly by the fre wyll and raison predomynent, that is, ondirstand, by Neptun, the storm is cessit, and . . . arryvit in sond havin, quhilk is

---

[13] Bawcutt, *Douglas*, 108–9.   [14] Baswell, *Virgil*, 12.
[15] Baswell, *Virgil*, 10–11.

> tranquilitie of consciens; and fynaly Venus . . . schawis Ene his feris recouerit again, quhilk is, fervent lufe and cherite schawis the iust man his swete meditationys and feruour of deuotion, quham he tynt by warldly curis, restorit to hym again, and all his schippis bot on, be quham I ondyrstand the tyme lost.[16]

The contrast with the kinds of interpretation that Douglas draws from Servius is extreme. In this gloss not only gods and mythological characters such as Juno and Eolus, but also incidents and features of the story (such as 'sond havin' and the single lost ship) are subjected to an allegorized reading that renders Aeneas' journey less an individual enterprise than an allegory of the journey of life—specifically, and anachronistically, the journey of a *Christian* life.

Read in isolation, this interpretation is consistent with one of Douglas' main concerns in the *Eneados*. Although he reveals a strong awareness of the difference between Virgil's time and his own, he also presents Aeneas as an exemplary figure for the sixteenth century, a model of the ideal ruler; thus, he declares in the Prologue to Book I that Eneas 'perfytely blasonis . . . All wirschep, manhed and nobilite' (ll. 329–30). The Christian emphasis of glosses such as the one derived from Landino contributes to that exemplarity.[17] Yet the juxtaposition of a gloss that reads the narrative allegorically with the more factual ones derived from Servius' and Ascencius' commentaries not only reflects a strong awareness that both interpretations of the text are provisional, but also conveys that awareness to the reader. It makes visible the concerns about change of meaning which Douglas expresses in the Prologue to Book I. Like the glosses to that Prologue, however, it does so in such a way as to draw attention to his own role in overseeing and contributing to that change.

This effect is still more apparent when Douglas juxtaposes divergent readings within a single gloss. For example, in the long gloss to the first mention of 'Jove, or Jupiter', Douglas gives a summary of various ways in which the deity has been viewed.[18] He first explains that, for the pagans, Jove 'was clepit the mast soueran god, fader of goddis and men, and all

---

[16] Gloss to I.iii.100. See further Charles Blyth, *'The Knychtlyke Stile': A Study of Gavin Douglas' Aeneid* (London: Garland, 1987), 29–30.

[17] Opinion differs as to the extent to which Douglas presents Eneas as exemplary, and the kind of example he might be. Coldwell reads Douglas' prince as a political figure (*Virgil's Aeneid*, 1: 32–7); cf. also Bruce Dearing, 'Gavin Douglas' *Eneados*: A Reinterpretation', *PMLA* 67 (1952), 845–62. Bawcutt, however, argues that Douglas' treatment of Eneas is designed to bring out his moral and ethical qualities rather than his political ones (*Douglas*, 82–5 and 124–7); while Douglas Gray argues that Douglas' hero is as varied as Virgil's was ('Gavin Douglas and "the gret prynce Eneas" ', *Essays in Criticism* 51 (2001), 18–34).

[18] Gloss to I.v.2.

the otheris war bot haldyn as poweris dyuerß of this Iupiter', but then refers to both St Augustine's and his own refutations of that position before going on to declare, with reference to Boccaccio's *De Genealogiae Deorum Gentilium*, that there were three Jupiters: two kings, and a planet. Focusing on the last of these, he suggests that when Virgil writes of Venus' complaint to Jupiter, this is a way of describing the conjoining of the planets Jupiter and Venus. Finally, this astrological reading is given unexpected prominence, yet at the same time rendered metaphorical, when Douglas concludes that the planet Jupiter: 'Completis his curß in xii ȝeris; and by this constylation betwix him and Venus, Seruius ondirstandis felicite to cum be a woman, as followis be Dido. And that Venus was sorofull, that is to knaw, discendent, and nocht in hir strength, signifeis the sorofull departyng and myschans of Dido.' Douglas thus amalgamates two very different kinds of interpretation. First he argues that the gods Jupiter and Venus signify the planets that bear their names, then that the planets and their aspects prefigure the action of the poem. Combining elements of the pedagogical and allegorizing commentary traditions, the gloss both provides scholarly and historical information to assist with the literal interpretation of the text and emphasizes the difference between that literal sense and the kind of significance that can be attributed to it in a Christian society.

It is not only different ways of reading Virgil that are made visible in the gloss, however. Due to the sheer amount and diversity of information it contains, there is an implicit first person present, marshalling the elaborate sequence of shifts by which the vehicle of one metaphor becomes the tenor of the next. As Daniel J. Pinti has argued, such a presence is inevitable in a translated text:

> Translated discourse is at once reported and responsive discourse, recounted by the translator in reply to the source text—a relation of the original in relation to the original. In other words, at its core a translation is the work of a writer interpreting and reporting to us a text that we, at the moment of reading the translation, are not directly 'witnessing' for ourselves.[19]

In the *Eneados*, however, such 'interpreting and reporting' appear twice over, not only in the text of Douglas' translation, but also in its glosses. On occasion this is made explicit by Douglas' references to himself in the first person. He once goes so far as to provide a cross-reference to his own *Palice of Honour*, but even less conspicuously self-conscious glosses make very clear that his is the controlling intelligence in the work.[20] As the single stable presence that orders the various, potentially contradictory

---

[19] Daniel J. Pinti, 'The Vernacular Gloss(ed) in Gavin Douglas' *Eneados*', *Exemplaria* 7 (1995), 443.

[20] See gloss to I.i.13.

interpretations, the translator emerges clearly as the figure that shapes the text. In the terms of the academic *accessus*, he becomes the work's dominant 'cause'.[21]

Douglas' glosses thus serve a double purpose. It would be difficult not to read them as, to some extent, a self-authorizing strategy. The very presence of the 'comment' ensures that his translation appears on the page in a way that visually recalls the presentation of Virgil's own, untranslated work; although they show Douglas' readings of Virgil's text to be well grounded, the glosses implicitly allow him to claim the status of *auctor* as well as that of commentator or translator.[22] Douglas' recurrent emphasis on his own contribution to the work further supports the idea that these glosses are a demand for recognition, but his glosses are by no means solely the emblem of an authority which he himself is already convinced that he possesses. Rather, they represent his discovery of his ability to shape his work, and reveal that his claim to authority entails the acknowledgement that his own work too is unstable. Thus, although they draw attention to the way in which he shapes the text, Douglas' glosses also encourage the reader to continue his process of interpretation.

A clear example of such encouragement is found in the gloss where Douglas refutes the commonly held belief, derived from Guido de Colonne's history of Troy, that Antenor was a traitor to the city, and then adduces Virgil's, Livy's, and Landino's authority against Guido:

> Becauβ ther is mention of Anthenor, quham many, followand Gwydo De Columnis, haldis tratour, sum thing of him will I speyk, thocht it may suffis for his purgation that Virgil heir hayth namyt him, and almaste comparit him to the mast soueran Eneas, quhilk comparison na wyβ wald he haf maid for lak of Eneas, gif he had bein tratour. Bot to schaw his innocens, let vs induce the mast nobill and famus historian and mylky flud of eloquens, gret Tytus Lyuius . . . Now I beseik ȝow, curteβ redaris . . . wey the excellent awtorite of Virgill and Tytus Lyuius wyth ȝour pevach and corrupt Gwido.[23]

The immediate effect of these citations is to buttress Douglas' own title to be believed; the gloss draws attention to the amount of thought and learning that underlies his decisions as translator, while by citing Virgil as an authority in a gloss apparently intended to defend Virgil's own work, Douglas effectively shifts his focus from defence of Virgil to defence of his own translation. Yet when he continues 'Now I beseik ȝow, curteβ redaris . . . wey the excellent awtorite of Virgill and Tytus Lyuius with ȝour pevach and corrupt Gwido', it is the readers, rather than Douglas,

---

[21] For the terminology of academic commentary, see Minnis, *Medieval Theory of Authorship*, 9–72.
[22] See further Bawcutt, *Douglas*, 70–8 and 102–27. [23] Gloss to I.v.28.

who are given ultimate responsibility for the interpretation of the work. The gloss thus implies Douglas' recognition that reading and interpretation of all kinds are what Susan Noakes has defined as 'timely': that is, 'constituted, motivated, and defined' by their temporal situation. Even as the gloss attempts what Noakes terms 'exegesis'—'a form of reading that emphasizes the words' temporal distance from the reader'—it shifts into 'interpretation': a form of reading that is concerned with the glossator's own 'historical character and position'.[24] By their very presence, Douglas' glosses are emblematic of that shift. Whereas academic commentaries such as those of Servius and Ascensius attempt to bridge an actual gap in time between writer and reader, Douglas' self-conscious glosses create other, smaller lacunae that provoke an awareness of the reading process itself as something that takes place in time and alters the meaning of the text.

Douglas' glosses, then, are genuinely experimental: they reflect not only the discovery of his own status of author, but also the realization, visible in the form as well as the content of his text, that his translation itself is far from definitive. Although Douglas' glossing shows clear influence of the academic commentary tradition, his use of the gloss as a vehicle for discovering how a text signifies suggests that he also continues the vernacular tradition of experimentation with the gloss, considering the implications of glossing a text, rather than using glosses simply as a means to a predetermined end. By implying that the reader's activity is a continuation of that of the translator, Douglas' glosses also reveal a shift from the assumption that poetry is a means of instruction towards a view of reading itself as an ethical activity.[25] They function as implicit exhortations to the reader to play his part in a continued effort to understand the difficult, particular text.

GLOSSING OVER THE GAP: COPLAND'S EDITION OF THE *ENEADOS*

Despite—or perhaps because of—the pronounced interest in reading and interpretation apparent in Douglas' comment, the surviving evidence suggests that it was not widely known. Even in the Trinity manuscript, it peters out part-way through Book I, while of the remaining

---

[24] Susan Noakes, *Timely Reading: Between Exegesis and Interpretation* (Ithaca: Cornell University Press, 1988), 11–12.

[25] For the view of poetry as direct instruction, see Allen, *Ethical Poetic*; for the view that readers themselves were responsible for extracting meaning from the text, see Eugene R. Kintgen, *Reading in Tudor England* (Pittsburgh: University of Pittsburgh Press, 1996).

sixteenth-century witnesses, only the Longleat manuscript and Lambeth Palace MS 117 contain any of the comment glosses—and then just a very few.[26] The majority of sixteenth-century readers would have encountered the *Eneados* with the very different and more extensive set of glosses published in William Copland's edition of 1553.

It seems that the Copland glosses reflect commercial imperatives rather than authorial ones. Copland's output indicates that he regularly published popular items, and had a particular interest in medieval works.[27] His edition of the *Eneados* shows a characteristic concern to present the 'old' author Douglas in a form that would be accessible and attractive to potential purchasers of printed books. The fact that it was published simultaneously with, and in the same format as, Douglas' *Palice of Honour* suggests that Copland intended both to assert Douglas' importance as author and to use that assertion as a marketing strategy. The appearance of the books confirms this inference. Their format is a relatively modest octavo, but the margins are wide, and the layout is orderly: the various parts of the text are neatly articulated, and the text is set in a larger type size than the glosses. Although the typesetting was careless enough to introduce a number of errors into the text, these are attractive books; they give the impression that considerable thought has been given to the reader's pleasure and convenience.[28]

The glosses to the *Eneados* also seem intended to make the work accessible to the reader. Identifying key moments in the text, their most obvious function is that of an index. For example, the beginning of Douglas' fulmination against Caxton's rival translation of the *Aeneid* is glossed 'Caxton's faultes', while Juno's expression of anger at the Trojans takes the gloss 'The occasione and counsal of Juno to reuenge hir self on the Troyanis'; when Eneas encounters Venus disguised as a huntress, the gloss helpfully declares: 'The commonyng betwixe eneas and hys mother venus whom at the fyrst he dyd not knawe.'[29] Other glosses identify stylistic features, such as 'A comparison', or highlight certain speeches or addresses, such as 'A protestacion to the Reader', and an 'Inuocacion to God'.[30] Their neutrality

---

[26] The Ruthven and Elphynstoun manuscripts (now Edinburgh University Library MSS Dc.1.43 and Dk.7.49) contain a very few sporadic glosses, not connected to those of Douglas' comment, and although two of the extracts from the *Eneados* in the Bannatyne manuscript are quite heavily glossed, it is again with glosses quite distinct from Douglas'.

[27] See Mary C. Erler, 'Copland, William', in *The Oxford Dictionary of National Biography*, <http://www.oxforddnb.com/view/article/6266>; and A. S. G. Edwards, 'William Copland and the Identity of Printed Middle English Romance', in *The Matter of Identity in Medieval Romance*, ed. Phillipa Hardman (Cambridge: D.S. Brewer, 2002), 139–48.

[28] For the errors in Copland's edition, see Coldwell, *Virgil's Aeneid*, 1: 101–2.

[29] Copland's *Eneados*, f. iii, ff. ix^v–x, ff. xvi^v–xvii.

[30] Copland's *Eneados*, f. i, f. ii^v, f. vii^v.

itself colours the reader's apprehension of the text; they serve as a verbal counterpart to the spacious layout, emphasizing the work's transparency and accessibility by echoing the text in a minor key.

On occasion, however, the Copland glosses seek to influence the reader's interpretation of the text more directly. For example, at the point where Aeneas is reminded by the gods that it is his duty to leave Carthage (and Dido), the gloss reads: 'Gods wyl and commaundement shuld euer be prefered and haue the first place in all mens actions and doynges', and in the Prologue to Book III, where Douglas expresses his contempt for those readers who would criticize either his translation or Virgil's work, the gloss declares stoutly: 'Inuyus personnys can do nothynge against good men but bark and chyd and with that schaw ther awine fulyshnes. Good men with wysdom tempereth theyr tonges.'[31] Rather than draw attention to the precise circumstances described in the text, these glosses focus on universally applicable morals. Whereas the glosses of Douglas' comment in the Trinity manuscript implied that reading itself was an ethical process, these revert to the less challenging idea that reading is the means of receiving explicit moral instruction.

They also risk significant misinterpretation of the text. Of the glosses quoted above, the first in particular reveals a marvellously universalizing, anti-historical sleight of thought. Douglas' reference is clearly to 'the goddes', in the plural, who commanded Eneas to leave, yet the Copland glossator sees no difficulty in interpreting Eneas' action as a model of that behaviour to be expected from a devout Christian: glossing over the historical and religious differences between Virgil's Rome and sixteenth-century Britain, his instinct is to find the universal moral. The Copland gloss thus stands in stark contrast to Douglas' own consciousness of the differences between the two, as witnessed in his very deliberate invocation of the Christian God and the Virgin to aid his work, and his eschewal of 'Calliope [and] payane goddis wild'.[32] In Copland's edition these lines too are glossed in a way that suppresses difference: 'The werk that beginnes not of God can neuer haue prosperyus success.'[33] The gloss thus elides differences between Christian and pagan, focusing instead on the generic commonplaces that may be extracted from the text.

This kind of 'glossing over' occurs repeatedly. When Douglas addresses Virgil directly, declaring that 'na lovingis ma do incres thi fame, / Nor na reproche diminew thi guid name', the gloss extrapolates: 'He is happye, whose fame nother prayse reproufe or enuye can distayne', substituting the general for the particular.[34] Similarly, when

---

[31] Copland's *Eneados*, f. vii, f. l.
[32] *Virgil's Aeneid*, I. Prol. 460.
[33] Copland's *Eneados*, f. vii^v.
[34] Copland's *Eneados*, f. ii.

Douglas challenges those of his readers who believe they can outdo him in translation 'Quha can do bettir, say furth in Goddis name', the gloss states that: 'It is more easy to reproue a good worke then to make or do a good worke.'[35] Interpretation of a highly specific example in general terms is found even in the context of Douglas' discussions of the difficulties inherent in translation, where the views expressed are inimical to such approximate readings. A striking instance occurs when Douglas writes in the Prologue to Book I that his intention was not to translate word for word, 'bot sentence follow algait' (I. Prol. 396). This phrase is of course a commonplace of translation theory: one that had been made familiar by repetition in authors from Horace onwards. It is so familiar, in fact, that in Copland's edition it is used as a gloss not to the lines where Douglas alludes to it, but forty lines earlier, where Douglas writes of the difficulties of translation:

> Sum tyme the text mon haue ane expositioun,
> Sum tyme the collour will causs a litill additioun,
> And sum tyme of a word I mon mak thre.
>
> (I. Prol. 347–9)

Here the glossator adds the comment 'Vyrgil is so sentencious that he cannot be translated worde by worde', but although his echo of Horace is accurate, it is peculiarly misplaced.[36] The decision whether to translate verbatim, or with respect to the meaning, is very far from Douglas' argument at this point in the Prologue: it is here that he goes on to discuss the term *oppetere*, and the troubling fact that he cannot render it without resorting to an entire sentence in English. Here Douglas is less concerned with Virgil's particular skill than he is with the wider differences between Latin and English; it is only later that he makes the connection between his own (professed) difficulties and Virgil's eloquence. By stressing Virgil's sententiousness, however, the gloss discourages thought about the way in which language works (that is, how the available linguistic resources shape what it is possible to say) in favour of generic praise of an acknowledged *auctor*, thus stressing the accessibility rather than the difficulty of the text. The implication is that text and gloss illustrate the same universally acknowledged truth, whereas Douglas suggests the opposite: that such truths cannot exist.

Elsewhere the Copland glosses' moralizing tendency results not so much in a slant reading as in a seriously mistaken one. A notable instance occurs in the gloss to the very end of the first Prologue, at the point where

---

[35] Copland's *Eneados*, f. viii. [36] Copland's *Eneados*, f. vi.

Douglas translates the lines which Ascensius (like many others before him) gives as the first of the *Aeneid*:

> I the ylk vmquhile that in the small ait reid
> Tonyt my sang, syne fra the woddis ʒeid,
> And feildis about taucht to be obesand,
> (Thocht he war gredy) to the bissy husband,
> Ane thankfull werk maid for the plewchmanis art,
> Bot now the horribill sterne dedys of Mart,
> The batalys and the man I will discryve.
> (I. Prol. 505–11)

Douglas is here performing a subtle act of textual criticism. By separating these lines from the body of the text and rendering them at the end of his Prologue, prefaced by the line 'Me thocht Virgill begouth on this maner', he both allows the lines to stand and draws attention to a possible doubt as to their authenticity. He thus again (as in his comments on the difficulty of translation) emphasizes the way in which the transmission of a text can affect its meaning. Yet the gloss—'A good counsel for euery man to do as they wolde be done vnto'—recognizes none of this.[37] Moreover, the interpretation it puts on the text wholly ignores the greater part of the passage. Rather than focusing on the declaration that the poet who previously worked in a pastoral vein will now turn to sterner stuff, it instead takes its cue purely from the phrase 'thankfull werk', and in a way that bears no relation at all to the sense or the subject of the text. The effect is of an almost random response to fragments of phrases rather than a digest of a sustained effort of reading.

It seems, then, that whereas Douglas' glosses emphasize difference, those in Copland's edition homogenize. Their different responses to the text reflect very different types of reading current in sixteenth-century Britain, both of which may ultimately derive from the increasing influence of humanist reading practices and teaching methods. Douglas' position is consonant with the theories of fifteenth-century, Continental humanist writers such as Lorenzo Valla and Poggio Bracciolini, with their acknowledgement of the gaps between classical and contemporary culture, classical and medieval Latin.[38] The glosses in Copland's edition, on the other hand, reflect the more usual effect of humanist influence in practice, as mediated through the grammar schools. They might be viewed as a response to the contemporary practice of gathering and framing, the popular

---

[37] Copland's *Eneados*, f. viii[v].
[38] For Douglas' familiarity with Poggio and Valla, see *The Palis of Honoure*, ed. David Parkinson (Kalamazoo: Medieval Institute Publications, 1992), ll. 1232–3.

sixteenth-century educational technique whereby students were encouraged to view any text they studied as a storehouse of universally applicable sententious wisdom: that is, as a collection of interchangeable parts, rather than as a unique whole.[39]

The latter habit of mind is betrayed even by those relatively neutral glosses that identify the presence or the parts of an oration, or are as innocuously indexing as 'A discription of the tempest'.[40] Like the glosses in Copland's edition of *The Palice of Honour*, those in his *Eneados* place a consistent emphasis on the efficacy of rhetoric, as for example when they note 'By Neptun's oratione the tempest cesed' at the point where Neptune begins to calm the seas, and 'The frute of eloquence' when he ends.[41] They draw attention to exactly the kind of performance which gathering and framing were intended to facilitate: just as those processes treat the text as a store of possible examples of good rhetorical or poetic practice as well as of material to be used, the glosses in Copland's edition are concerned with the form of speech, not with what it conveys. Reflecting the interests of a reader who mines the text for immediate moral instruction or for help with his own compositions, they focus on the practical usefulness of eloquent speech in the present, not on its historical significance. Whereas Douglas' glosses draw attention to difficulties of interpretation, those in Copland's edition gloss over them. In doing so, however, they inadvertently create lacunae of their own: disjunctions between text and gloss which require new interpretative efforts.

Of course, such selective interest on the part of an individual glossator was nothing new. As Daniel Wakelin has argued with reference to the annotation of fifteenth-century manuscripts, for a reader to leave traces of what appear to be relatively narrow interests is not necessarily a sign of careless or disengaged reading; the annotations may be outward signs of much more elaborate inner thought-processes.[42] What *is* relatively new, however, is the appearance of this kind of glossing in print. For glosses that identify commonplaces and mine the text for future use to be formalized in the medium of print means that they no longer signal one stage in an individual's thought-process, but form a fixed part of the text. In consequence, as Noakes puts it, they allow the reader to 'evade awareness of the temporal nature of reading'; divorced from their originator and from the

---

[39] See Mary Thomas Crane, *Framing Authority: Sayings, Self and Society in Sixteenth Century England* (Princeton: Princeton University Press, 1993); and Ann Moss, *Printed Commonplace Books and the Structure of Renaissance Thought* (Oxford: Clarendon Press, 1996).
[40] Copland's *Eneados*, f. ix.   [41] Copland's *Eneados*, f. x, f. x^v.
[42] Daniel Wakelin, *Humanism, Reading, and English Literature 1430–1530* (Oxford: Oxford University Press, 2007), 16–19.

originating thought-process, they denote the end rather than the beginning of interpretation.[43]

There are exceptions, of course. Just occasionally, the strain of interpreting the text in a suitable way becomes visible, as the quietly authoritative voice declaring the subject of the text slips into more discursive discussions that seem to catch the annotator in the act of working out his interpretation. In Book X, for example, the long gloss to the Duke Pallas' encouragement of his army moves from summary gloss ('Pallas wyse and stout exhortacion to the troyanys') to advice on the conduct of battles, and finally to a rather awkward invocation of Pallas' rhetorical skills: 'wysdom fortytude and stoutnes with a litil tarying [is] the caus of wynnyng of the battell, as be his awin exempil he schawis to them.'[44] Here, as in the discursive introductory gloss to the Prologue to Book X ('In thys prolog he schawis gods workes to be incomprehensybil be mannis wit or reason and that he preuis be the creacyon and mystery of the trinitie'), it appears as if the annotator were recording his thought-process, rather than making available the finished thought for public instruction.[45] But despite such aberrations, the consistent identification of moral commonplaces in the Copland glosses implies the opposite of Douglas' discovery of the translator's determining influence over a text: that meaning is not fluid, but innately stable. By suggesting that such *sententiae* can be detached from the text in which they are embedded, the Copland glosses minimize the importance of context, implicitly de-authorizing a writer or translator who derives his perception of his own status from the way in which he shapes the text he works on.

CROSS-REFERENCES AND CROSSED PURPOSES: COPLAND'S GLOSSES IN THE TRINITY MANUSCRIPT

A comparison of the Trinity and the Copland glosses thus reveals a striking contrast between Douglas' own interest in the processes of translation and transmission and the publisher's interest in creating a marketable, 'profitable' text. Nonetheless, a renewed examination of the Trinity manuscript reveals an unexpected connection between the Copland glosses and those of Douglas' comment. As appears from various additions and alterations, the Trinity *Eneados* is a work in progress. At several points the margins contain notes of possible variants for words in the text, such as 'payntit'

---

[43] Noakes, *Timely Reading*, 34.   [44] Copland's *Eneados*, ff. cclxiii–cclxiii^v.
[45] Copland's *Eneados*, f. ccxlvii.

for 'carvyt', 'breistis' for 'pappys', 'schap' for 'presence', and 'braid' for 'stalwart'.[46] These appear to be authorial revisions, or suggestions for possible revisions. Although they resemble literal glosses that clarify the meaning of unfamiliar words, most of the words thus glossed are common enough to need no clarification. Moreover, several of the glosses have a distinct look of authorial second thoughts; for example, where 'breistis' appears as an alternative for 'pappys', 'pappys' has already been used two lines earlier, so that the proposed substitution avoids repetition, while the proposed substitutions of 'schap' for 'presence' in the line 'Terribill of port and schamful hir presence' and 'braid' for 'stalwart' in 'Throw gyrdis baith hys stalwart schulder banys' suggest attempts to improve the alliteration. The fact that, in subsequent manuscripts, at least some of these alternatives have been incorporated in the text also suggests that they are notes of possible revisions, and thus that the text of the *Eneados* was not wholly determined at the point when Geddes copied it.[47]

There are signs of alterations to the comment as well. One of the most notable curiosities, the presence of two glosses that are formally indistinguishable from those of Douglas' comment, but which take issue with the text, has been convincingly explained by Priscilla Bawcutt; she argues that these glosses record the reactions of Douglas' scribe, Geddes, to what he was copying.[48] Like the rest of the comment, the glosses are in Geddes' hand, but unlike the comment glosses that refer to Douglas, they do so in the third person. The first of them is particularly argumentative,

---

[46] MS O.3.12, f. 225ᵛ (X.viii.147), f. 259ᵛ (XI.xi.88), f. 111 (VI.iiii.84), f. 261 (XI. xii.105).

[47] Although these corrections are not part of the original copying of the text, they are clearly very early additions: they were made before the manuscript was rubricated, as they are keyed to the text in red, and the 'or' which introduces them is also added in red ink. The manuscript contains other traces of revisions. Although the comment breaks off well before the end of Book I, there are nonetheless sporadic glosses in the later stages of the text, including the note 'Her fyrst namys Virgill Eneas' at the beginning of the third chapter of Book I; the citation 'de duplis amori vide augustinus de civitate dei Cap li.xv c. xxij.' in Book IV; and the observation 'comparatio non virgiliana' in Book XII, at the point where Douglas writes of Turnus and Eneas that they went about the battle-field 'Lyke as befor the hund wiskis the hair'. Although the ink in which they were copied shows that these glosses were not added at the same time as the comment glosses to Book I and its Prologue, the fact that (like some of the glosses suggesting alternative words for Douglas' translation) they recur in a number of later witnesses implies that they do belong to an early stage in the life of the manuscript. They also show a level of attention to the text equivalent to that in the comment glosses; although two of them differ from those glosses in being in Latin rather than English, and all three lack the discursive character of Douglas' commentary, it is possible that, like the glosses in Chaucer's *House of Fame*, they were intended as authorial 'notes to self': that is, not as glosses for general circulation, but (like the record of alternative word choices) as memoranda to reflect upon in subsequent work on the text.

[48] Bawcutt, *Douglas*, 108.

appearing at the point in the Prologue to Book I where Douglas defends Aeneas against Chaucer's charge that he betrayed Dido on the grounds that: 'Certis Virgill schawys Enee dyd na thing / From Dydo of Cartage at his departyng, /Bot quhilk the goddis commandit him beforn' (I. Prol. 425–7). To this the gloss opposes a detailed argument, complete with citation from an earlier part of Douglas' translation:

> This argument excusis nocht the tratory of Eneas na his maynsweryng, considering quhat is said heir afoir, in the ii. c. of this prolog, that is,
>
> > Iuno nor Venus goddes neuer war,
> > Mercur, Neptun, Mars nor Iupiter
> > Of Forton eik, nor his necessite,
> > Sic thingis nocht attentik ar, wait we.
>
> It follows than, that Eneas vroucht not be command of ony goddis, bot of his awyn fre wyl, be the permission of God, quhilk sufferis al thing, and stoppis nocht, na puttis nocht necessite to fre wyll. He falit than gretly to the sueit Dido; quhilk falt reprefit nocht the godessis diuinite, for thai had na diuinite, as said is befoir.

Shortly afterwards, at the point where Douglas argues that in the fourth book 'Ene maid nevir aith, / Promyt nor band with hir for till abyde' (I. Prol. 438–9), the gloss comments succinctly: 'Heir he argouis better than befoir.' The effect is thus comparable to the homogenization of glosses of diverse origins found in MS Fairfax 16, or indeed the *Fall of Princes* manuscript MS Harley 2251.

These are not the only anomalous glosses, however. Early in the Prologue to Book I, four glosses appear in a hand different from that of the scribe, and in darker ink. These too are very different in kind from the comment glosses. Rather than providing additional information or interpreting the text, three of them have an indexing function, identifying the subject under discussion, while one attempts a summary of the 'message' of the lines to which it is attached. Noting 'Caxton faltes', 'Vnder derk Poetrye is hid great wisdome and lerning', 'Exhortacioun to the Reder', and 'Admonicioun vnto vnlerned peopill, quhose rudnes cannot onderstand Vyrgill', they not only resemble the glosses in Copland's edition, but prove to have exact counterparts there (see Plate 3.1).[49]

This is distinctly peculiar. The editor most thoroughly to have examined the relation between the surviving sixteenth-century witnesses to

---

[49] MS O.3.12, f. 2ᵛ, f. 3, and f. 4ᵛ. Cf. Copland's *Eneados*, f. iii, f. iiiᵛ, f. iiiiᵛ, and f. v. In Coldwell's edition, the four glosses are printed as if they were part of the comment, with no acknowledgement that they are in a different hand and a different ink.

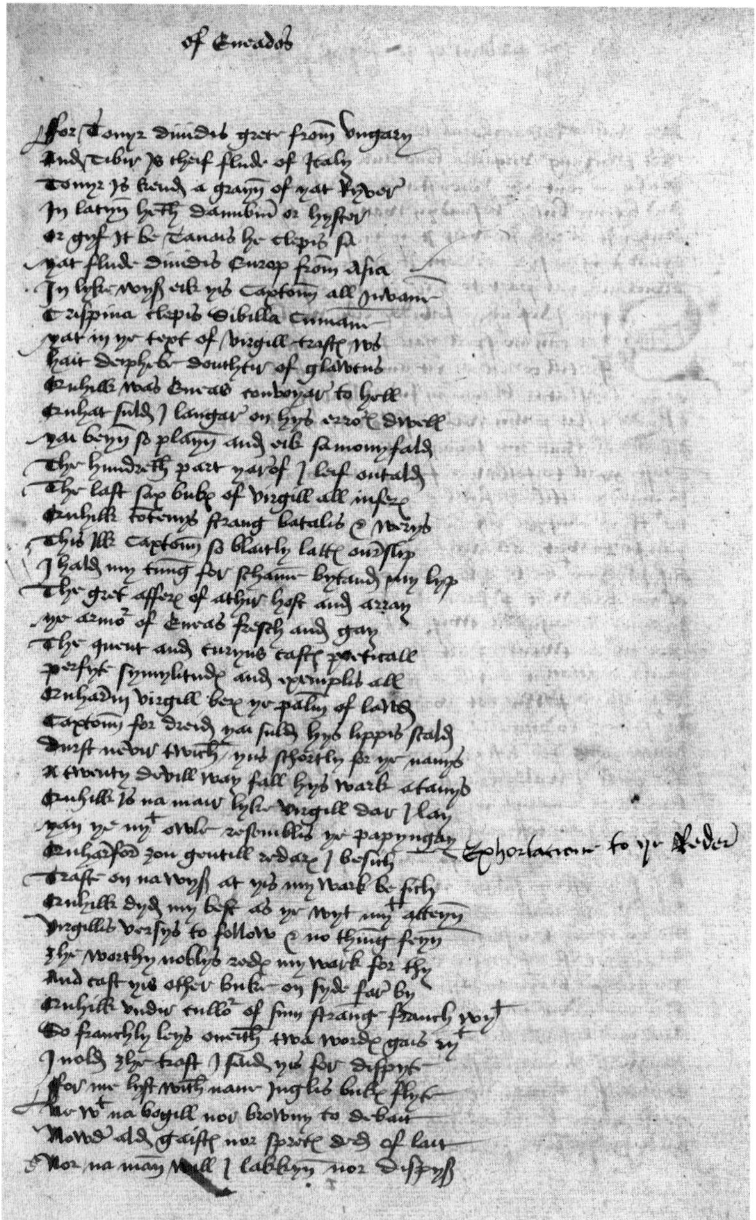

Plate 3.1 Cambridge, Trinity College MS O.3.12, f. 2ᵛ. Reproduced by kind permission of the Master and Fellows of Trinity College.

the *Eneados*, David Coldwell, finds no connection between the Trinity manuscript and Copland's edition; he believes each ultimately to derive from a different exemplar.[50] Yet the reappearance of these four glosses from Copland's edition in the manuscript suggests that there is a connection nonetheless. Two of the four shared glosses, 'Exhortacioun to the Reder' and 'Caxton faltes', might arguably have been supplied by two annotators independently, but the phrasing of the other two glosses is too complex for that to be likely. But although the probability is that these glosses derive from a single source, it is not clear how they came to be shared by the Trinity manuscript and the Copland edition. One possibility is that an interested reader of the manuscript began copying across the glosses from the Copland print. Another is that the Copland glosses were not created specifically for his edition, but derive from those of a lost manuscript which was at some point in contact with the Trinity manuscript. In the latter case, either the four anomalous glosses in the Trinity manuscript were copied from the one that is now lost, or they represent an early attempt to develop a set of glosses as an alternative to those of the comment. Interestingly, although the glosses appear near the beginning of the text, they are not the first of Copland's glosses, making it less likely that a reader began copying the printed glosses into the manuscript before losing interest. It is thus just possible that Douglas himself was responsible for them.[51]

This must remain speculation, of course.[52] What can be said with certainty is that the duplication of the Copland glosses in the manuscript suggests a degree of resistance to the kind of reading proposed by Douglas' comment. The comment's examination of the way the process of

[50] *Virgil's Aeneid*, 1: 105. Coldwell argues that Copland's edition derives ultimately from the lost manuscript α – which, like the Trinity manuscript, would have been a copy of Douglas' holograph.

[51] The presence in the Bannatyne manuscript of glosses that resemble those in the Copland edition, but are not identical to them, suggests that the *Eneados* was circulated with a number of different sets of glosses, and may support this hypothesis. For a related discussion, see Denton Fox, 'Manuscripts and Prints of Scots Poetry in the Sixteenth Century', in *Bards and Makars. Scottish Language and Literature: Medieval and Renaissance*, ed. Adam J. Aitken, Matthew P. McDiarmid, and Derick S. Thomson (Glasgow: Glasgow University Press, 1977), 156–71. His argument that the Bannatyne extracts were copied from a now lost print of the *Eneados* and Bawcutt's suggestion that the Copland gloss 'Ane singular lernit Prologue' derives from a manuscript gloss such as Trinity's 'explicit scitus prologus' (*Douglas*, 176) both suggest a history of exchange between manuscript and print witnesses.

[52] Palaeographic evidence is inconclusive; the hand in which the four anomalous glosses are added is a Secretary hand of a kind common in sixteenth-century Scotland. Comparison with a letter in Douglas' hand (reproduced as the frontispiece to *The Poetical Works of Gavin Douglas*, ed. John Small, 4 vols. (Edinburgh: William Patterson, 1874), Vol. I) shows that it is not unlike Douglas', but there is insufficient evidence to demonstrate either that it is definitely his, or that it is definitely not.

translation or rewriting alters the meaning of a translator's material reflects concerns that are emphatically those of a *writer*. By contrast, the four glosses in dark ink represent a different and less challenging form of glossing: one that draws attention to the text's universally applicable morals rather than emphasizing the difficulty of interpretation, and that emphasizes Virgil's immediate relevance to his readers, rather than calling it into question. Stressing the timeless sententious wisdom that can be extracted from the text, rather than the process by which the work comes into being, they make the translator's mediation of the text less visible (even as they themselves significantly alter the way in which the text means) and thereby misleadingly imply that its meaning is immutable. Their effect is thus to reinforce what Noakes has described as the sixteenth-century 'mythology' that printing was 'a mechanism that would dissociate reading from temporal loss'.[53] The coexistence of two such different sets of glosses to a single text—and particularly their juxtaposition in the Trinity manuscript—reveals just how protean glossing practices were in the first half of the sixteenth century. Incompatible though they are, both kinds of glossing will prove to be significant in the subsequent development of the gloss. Visible attempts to tame the (printed) text become grounds for further experiment with the form of a kind that revisits, develops further, and extends those discoveries of the writer's shaping authority witnessed in the glosses of translators including Douglas and Lydgate.

---

[53] Noakes, *Timely Reading*, 35.

4

Glossing the Spoken Word
Erasmus' *Moriae Encomium* and Chaloner's *Praise of Folie*

Like the two sets of glosses to the *Eneados,* the glossing of Erasmus' *Moriae Encomium* (1511) and that of its first English translation, Sir Thomas Chaloner's *Praise of Folie* (1549), prompt very different kinds of reading. The former consists of two discrete levels of glossing: the commentary attributed to Gerardus Listrius and a series of shorter glosses that annotate this commentary as well as Folly's speech. The commentary visually dominates the text, just as academic commentaries do. Providing a dense frame for Folly's oration, it demands a constant effort of cross-reference and interpretation on the part of its readers, and its juxtaposition with an outer ring of glosses further emphasizes the extent to which reading is an active process of learning and judging. By contrast, Chaloner's glossing is relatively restricted and restrictive in scope. As part of his translation of a demanding and potentially heterodox work, his glosses attempt to limit the ways in which the text might be interpreted even as he makes it available to a relatively wide audience. Whereas the glossing of the *Moria* is performative, replicating the shifts in tone that are also found in Folly's oration, Chaloner's seeks to define and fix her protean speech. A comparison of these different kinds of glossing reveals two strikingly opposed views of how and what a text communicates. It also gives an indication of the complex of humanist and vernacular models out of which later sixteenth-century glossing practices evolved, and how artless, as well as artful, glossing strategies contributed to their development.

THE *MORIAE ENCOMIUM*: TRUTH AND PARADOX

Even without its glosses, the *Moria* is a notoriously slippery work. As an elaborate instance of the paradoxical encomium, in which something commonly held to be undeserving of praise is praised nonetheless, its very genre is a contradiction in terms.[1] To complicate matters further, it is spoken by its own subject, the innately paradoxical figure of Folly. Erasmus makes full use of the inherent contradictions in her character.[2] In the first part of Folly's oration, she presents herself as a fool in the most literal sense of the word: a figure of fun whose pronouncements may, by their sheer perversity, challenge normative social and moral assumptions, but which certainly cannot be taken at face value. Arguing that she is the source of all that is enjoyable in life, and even of life itself, Folly engages in a thorough-going exercise in turning the world upside-down. In the second part of her oration, however, she shifts her emphasis from folly as a cause of pleasure to folly as a source of delusion, dropping her playful tone to attack all those who are foolish enough to believe themselves wise, most notably those theologians so engrossed in their own dialectic that they have lost all sense of Christ's teaching. Yet although here she appears to be speaking plainly, in the third part she praises Christian folly—the abandonment of self-interest and all things of this world—in such exaggerated terms that it has proved impossible to determine whether her advocacy of worldly renunciation and spiritual ecstasy should be taken at face value, or whether she has reverted to the shock tactics of the early stages of her speech.[3] Her argument reflects Erasmus' internalization of a broad range of both Christian and classical (notably Platonic) teaching, but it is framed in such a way as to provide continual reminders that she is by no means to be trusted.[4]

Folly's oration thus repeatedly raises the question whether the character of a speaker has any bearing on the value of what he or she says. It is this, too, which she chooses to emphasize in her final lines:

---

[1] For the paradoxical encomium, see Rosalie L. Colie, *Paradoxia Epidemica* (Princeton: Princeton University Press, 1966), esp. 3–40. For the *Moria* as a demonstration of 'the power of humanist oratory and the skill and ingenuity available to the humanist rhetorician', see A. F. Kinney, *Humanist Poetics: Thought, Rhetoric, and Fiction in Sixteenth-Century England* (Amherst: University of Massachusetts Press, 1986), 41–56 (41).

[2] For the different levels of irony in the figure of Folly, see Walter Kaiser, *Praisers of Folly: Erasmus, Rabelais, Shakespeare* (London: Victor Gollancz, 1964), 19–100. For a sustained Bakhtinian reading of Folly which links her both to folk figures such as *mère sotte* and to Christian renewal, see Donald Gwynn Watson, 'Erasmus' *Praise of Folly* and the Spirit of Carnival', *Renaissance Quarterly* 32 (1979), 333–53.

[3] For the view that the third part of Folly's oration should be taken as Erasmus' expression of his own views, see M. A. Screech, *Ecstasy and The Praise of Folly* (London: Duckworth, 1980). For dissenting voices, see Clarence H. Miller, 'Styles and Mixed Genres in Erasmus' *Praise of Folly*', in *Acta Conventus Neo-Latini Guelpherbytani*, ed. Stella P. Revard, Fidel Rädle, and Mario A. Di Cesare (Binghamton: Medieval & Renaissance Texts & Studies, 1988), 277–87; and Peter Ruditsky, 'Ironic Textuality in *The Praise of Folly* and *Gargantua and Pantagruel*', *Erasmus of Rotterdam Society Yearbook* 3 (1983), 56–103.

[4] For the *Moria*'s synthesis of Christian and Platonic teaching, see Screech, *Ecstasy and the Praise of Folly*.

Verum ego iamdudum oblita mei ὑπέρ τα ἐσκαμμένα πηδῶ. Quanquam si quid petulantius aut loquacius a me dictum videbitur, cogitate et Stulticiam et mulierem dixisse. Sed interim tamen memineritis illius Graecanici prouerbii, πολλάκι τοι καὶ μωρὸς ἀνὴρ κατακαίριον εἶπεν, nisi forte putatis hoc ad mulieres nihil attinere.[5]

Rather than directing our attention to her subject matter, Folly ends by reminding us who she is, in lines that give a lively demonstration of her untrustworthiness. After declaring that she is unreliable because she is both Folly and a woman, she promptly reminds us that fools are proverbially wise, but then retracts her retraction by suggesting that female fools may be the exception to that rule. Throughout her oration, such self-contradictions arise from Folly's extemporizing habits. As she tells us repeatedly, she speaks whatever springs to mind, ostentatiously digressing, interrupting herself, and adding parenthetical asides. Her motto might be the one delivered by the apocryphal old woman who asked: 'How do I know what I think until I see what I say?'

Folly's habit of improvisation draws attention to the complicated relationship she has with her maker. The ability to extemporize is one mark of the skilled orator; Quintilian argues in his *Institutio Oratoria* that: 'si calor ac spiritus tulit, frequenter accidit ut successum extemporalem consequi cura non possit.'[6] Quintilian's reference to inspiration suggests that the successful improviser experiences a genuine internal alchemy that results in heightened eloquence. Yet, as Quintilian acknowledges, and as Erasmus himself argues in *De copia*, this apparently natural phenomenon is itself an acquired rhetorical technique; in Erasmus' words, a training in copiousness of speech: 'Neque vero mediocriter contulerit . . . ad extemporalem vel dicendi vel scribendi facultatem praestabitque, ne subinde vel haesitemus attoniti vel turpiter intersileamus.'[7] Erasmus' artful creation of the artless persona of Folly

---

[5] Erasmus, *Moriae Encomium*, ed. Clarence H. Miller, *Opera Omnia*, Vol. IV: 3 (Amsterdam: Koninklijke Nederlandse Akademie van Wetenschappen, 1979), 194. 'I've long been forgetting who I am, and I've overshot the mark. If anything I've said seems rather impudent or garrulous, you must remember it's Folly and a woman who's been speaking. At the same time, don't forget the Greek proverb "Often a foolish man speaks a word in season", though of course you may think this doesn't apply to women.' Translation from Erasmus, *The Praise of Folly*, tr. Betty Radice, *Collected Works of Erasmus*, Vol. 27, *Literary and Educational Writings* 5 (Toronto: University of Toronto Press, 1986), 153.

[6] *Institutio Oratoria*, 10: 7: 13–14; and cf. 8:3:67–70. 'Once the heat of inspiration takes over, it often happens that deliberate effort cannot rival the success of an improvisation.' Translation from *De Institutio Oratoria*, tr. Donald A. Russell (Cambridge, MA: Harvard University Press, 2001).

[7] Erasmus, *De copia verborum ac rerum*, ed. Betty I. Knott, *Opera Omnia*, Vol. I: 6 (Amsterdam: Koninklijke Nederlandse Akademie van Wetenschappen, 1988), 34. 'Will make no insignificant contribution to the ability to speak or write extempore, and will prevent us from standing there stammering and dumbfounded, or from disgracing ourselves by drying up in the middle.' The translation is from Erasmus, *De copia*, tr. Betty I. Knott,

brilliantly articulates this paradox, splitting it into its constituent parts. Folly's self-contradictions break all the formal rules of oratory, allowing her to present herself, by studied informality, as her audience's friend and accomplice. Yet readers remain aware that Folly, her speech, and her spontaneity are all Erasmus' fictions. The effect is comparable to that in More's *Utopia*, where the presence of the fictional 'Thomas More' provides a constant reminder that the well-travelled Raphael Hythlodaye is also More's creation, and that his first-person narrative is at the service of More's satirical ends as much as his own self-aggrandizing ones. As A. F. Kinney has argued, this divided perspective puts a considerable weight of responsibility on the works' readers, who can neither wholly trust Folly or Hythlodaye, nor wholly ignore the abuses which they satirize:

> If we must develop a third viewpoint in an act of triangulation, that is not the viewpoint of the narrator, for another Erasmian strategy is to place the narrator squarely within the narrative and make him or her, Hythlodaye or Folly, a subject of the argument the narrative is meant to provide. The reader is left, then, to judge by contextual standards within the work as well as by exterior traditions . . . The end of such a dynamics of fiction is not merely to entertain or challenge the reader but to instruct him.[8]

In the *Moria*, as in the *Utopia*, the glossing of the text is a renewed means of contributing to this instruction.[9] The play of voice within Folly's encomium is replicated in that between text and gloss. As one—or several—of the many voices in the work, the glosses are the printed counterpart of Folly's constantly shifting perspective, making visible what Rosalie Colie has called its 'mocking [of] formal limitation' and thus further encouraging the reader to an independent effort of interpretation.[10]

A TWO-PART INVENTION: GLOSSING THE *MORIAE ENCOMIUM*

When the *Moriae Encomium* was first published in 1511, it was prefaced by a letter from Erasmus to Thomas More in which he makes much of the

---

Collected Works of Erasmus, Vol. 24, *Literary and Educational Writings* 2 (Toronto: University of Toronto Press, 1978), 302.

[8] Kinney, *Humanist Poetics*, 55.

[9] For the glossing of the *Utopia*, see Dana McKinnon, 'The Marginal Glosses in More's *Utopia*: The Character of the Commentator', *Renaissance Papers* (1970), 11–19; and cf. Warren W. Wooden, 'A Reconsideration of the Parerga of Thomas More's *Utopia*', in *Quincentennial Essays on St Thomas More: Selected Papers from the Thomas More College Conference*, ed. Michael J. Moore (Boone, NC: Albion, 1978), 151–60.

[10] Colie, *Paradoxia Epidemica*, 21.

circumstances of its composition, claiming that he made it up while journeying on horseback from Italy to England, and that it is, consequently, entirely improvised.[11] Erasmus' insistence that he is extemporizing anticipates Folly's own. So too does the fondness for paradox he reveals in arguments such as 'nugae seria ducant' and 'nihil festiuius quam ita tractare nugas, vt nihil minus quam nugatus fuisse videaris'.[12] The introductory epistle thus gives an early indication that the boundary between author and character will be a permeable one, and that the paratext may be only a partially reliable guide to the work. Yet despite its playful opening, the glosses to the first edition of the *Moria* are fairly straightforward, consisting almost exclusively of Latin translations of Greek phrases in the text, identifications of tropes or allusions, and glosses that index the text. The translations in particular show a scrupulous concern for the reader, making accessible the relatively unfamiliar language of Greek. The purpose of the identifications and the indexing glosses is less clear, however. They do not constitute a sustained interpretative performance, but record what appear to be a series of incidental responses to the text; despite being printed as an integral part of it, they frequently resemble annotations by diverse hands in the margins of manuscripts such as those of Lydgate's *Fall of Princes*.[13]

The *Moria* was reprinted several times between 1511 and 1513, and a substantially revised and expanded edition was published by Matthew Scheurer in 1514.[14] Yet despite its evident popularity, the work also attracted much criticism, most notably from the grammarian Martin Dorp, who in 1515 published an open letter to Erasmus in which he argued that it threatened to undermine both the Christian faith and Erasmus' own reputation. Subsequent editions of the *Moria* show just how seriously Erasmus took these criticisms. They include not only a letter replying directly to Dorp, but also a further response in the form of a substantial commentary by 'Gerardus Listrius'.[15] The latter was clearly modelled on academic commentaries; using words and phrases from the text as lemmas, it provides information as to sources, stylistic analysis, and extensive historical and contextual information.[16] For example, the very first gloss gives detailed

---

[11] *Moriae Encomium*, 67; *Praise of Folly*, 27.
[12] *Moriae Encomium*, 68. 'Trifling may lead to something more serious'; 'nothing is more entertaining than treating trivialities in such a way as to make clear you are doing anything but trifle with them' (*Praise of Folly*, 84).
[13] For reader annotation in manuscripts of the *Fall of Princes*, see Chapter 1 above.
[14] For the early publication history of the *Moria*, see Screech, *Ecstasy and The Praise of Folly*, 1–6.
[15] See Screech, *Ecstasy and The Praise of Folly*, 4; and cf. Genevieve Stenger, '*The Praise of Folly* and Its Parerga', *Medievalia et Humanistica* 2 (1971), 97–117.
[16] See further J. Austin Gavin and Thomas M. Walsh, '*The Praise of Folly* in Context: The Commentary of Gerardus Listrius', *Renaissance Quarterly* 24 (1971), 193–209.

definitions that will ground the reader's interpretation of the work that is to follow:

> Μωρίας ἐνκώμιου, id est, Morias encomium μωρία stulticiam significat, & ἐνκώμϊου scriptum aliquod, in alicuis laudem compositum, ut Lucianus scripsit encomium Demosthenis. Et laudatorium genus Graeci uocant encomiasticum. Et ἐνκωμιάζειν, est laudes alicuius oratione prosequi. Differt autem encomium ab hymno, ut scribit Hammonius: Hymnus namque est deorum: Encomium autem hominum.[17]

As well as proclaiming the genre to which the *Moria* belongs, this gloss gives a strong indication of the function of the commentary itself, clearly recalling the type of comment found at the beginning of an academic *accessus*.[18] The signal is strategically important. Not only does the use of commentary for Erasmus' self-defence allow for a detailed, phrase-by-phrase refutation of Dorp's attack, but the connotations of the form themselves authorize Erasmus' work. It is not only what is said that matters, but also the form in which it appears.

Despite the attribution of the commentary to Listrius, it is largely an exercise in self-glossing. As Erasmus explained in a letter to Martin Bucer, although Listrius had indeed been commissioned to write it, he procrastinated to such an extent that Erasmus himself was obliged to take over.[19] This intervention indicates a degree of urgency on Erasmus' part; it suggests that he took Dorp's criticisms seriously enough to want to refute them immediately, and to prevent further attacks along the same lines. This is confirmed by a recurrent note of defensiveness in the commentary, for example when he writes:

> Nullus igitur opinor erit tam iniquus, ut si quid dictum uidebitur in principes, aut sacerdotes, aut in alios offendatur, cum non taxentur ulli, nisi leniter & iucunde magis quamque acriter . . . Postremo cum stulticiae personam loquentem fecerit, non conueniet imaginari personam authoris, id dicere, quod sub persona Moriae dictum est.[20]

---

[17] Erasmus, *Moriae Encomium* (Basel: Joannes Froben, 1516), sig. A1ᵛ. 'Μωρίας ἐνκώμιου: that is, the praise of folly. μωρία means folly, and ἐνκώμϊου means a particular kind of writing composed in praise of someone, as Lucian wrote an 'encomium' of Demosthenes. And the Greeks called the 'encomium' a form of eulogy. And ἐνκωμιάζειν is to give a eulogy of someone. However, an 'encomium' differs from a hymn, as Hammon writes: for a hymn pertains to the gods, whereas an encomium pertains to men.'
[18] For the *accessus*, see A. J. Minnis, *Medieval Theory of Authorship*, 2nd ed. (Aldershot: Scolar Press, 1984), 9–39.
[19] See Gavin and Walsh, '*Praise of Folly* in Context', 195–6; and Joseph A. Gavin and Clarence H. Miller, 'Erasmus' Additions to Listrius' Commentary on *The Praise of Folly*', *Erasmus in English* 11 (1981–2), 19–20.
[20] *Moria* (1516), sig. A4. 'Therefore I consider nothing to be so unjust, as when something that has been said is considered to give offence to rulers, or priests, or others, when

The gloss does not just offer the sophistical defence that the work will offend only those who are guilty of the abuses it describes, but also introduces a theme that will recur throughout the commentary: the fact that the *Moria* takes the form of an oration spoken by Folly, and should not be held to express Erasmus' own views. This is a point that was made with increasing frequency when the commentary was revised for subsequent editions; Erasmus' additions to the Listrius commentary for the edition of the *Moria* printed later in 1516 insist still more emphatically that Folly is fictional and entirely distinct from the author of the work.[21]

The Listrius commentary is more than just defensive, however. It also forms a practical illustration of the reading methods advocated by Erasmus in *De ratione studii*.[22] Describing the method that a grammar school teacher should use to introduce a new text to his students, Erasmus advises that:

> Deinde, si qua insignis elegantia, si quid prisca dictum, si quid novatum, si quid graecanicum, si quid obscurius aut longius redditum, si durior aut perturbatior ordo, si qua etymologia, si qua deriuatio aut compositio scitu digna, si qua orthographia, si qua figura, si qui loci rhetorici, si qua exornatio, si quid deprauatum, diligenter admoneat. Tum loci similia ex auctoribus conferat, si quid diuersum, si quid affine, si quid imitatum, si quid allusum, si quid aliunde translatum aut mutuo sumptum . . . Postremo ad philosophiam veniat, et poetarum fabulas apte trahat ad mores, vel tanquam exempla, vt Pyladis et Orestis ad amicitiae commendationem, Tantali fabulam ad auaritiae detestationem.[23]

Ideally, then, Erasmus advocates an extremely active form of reading: not a form of rote learning, but a thorough analysis of the various elements of the text by which the student draws connections between it and other works

they were not judged, or only in moderation and in jest rather than harshly. . . Besides, when the persona of Folly speaks, it is wrong to presume that the person of the author says those things which are spoken by Moria.'

[21] For these glosses and their attribution, see Gavin and Miller, 'Erasmus' Additions to Listrius'. Erasmus' additions to the commentary in the 1532 edition change tactics, stressing Folly's orthodoxy rather than her fictionality.

[22] Cf. Gavin and Walsh, '*Praise of Folly* in Context', 199–201.

[23] Erasmus, *De ratione studii*, ed. Jean-Claude Margolin, *Opera Omnia*, Vol. I: 2 (Amsterdam: Koninklijke Nederlandse Akademie van Wetenschappen, 1971), 137–9. 'He should carefully draw [the students'] attention to any purple passage, archaism, neologism, Graecism, any obscure or verbose expression, any abrupt or confused order, any etymology, derivation, or composition worth knowing, any point of orthography, figure of speech, or rhetorical passages, or embellishment or corruption. Next he should compare parallel passages in authors, bringing out differences and similarities—what has been imitated, what merely echoed, where the source is different, where common. . . Finally he should turn to philosophy and skillfully bring out the moral implication of the poets' stories, or employ them as patterns, for example, the story of Pylades and Orestes to show the excellence of friendship; that of Tantalus the curse of avarice.' The translation is from Erasmus, *De ratione*

with which he is already familiar; *De ratione studii* gives theoretical expression to the kind of reading encouraged by Douglas' glossing practices too.[24] The Listrius commentary not only exemplifies this kind of reading, but shapes its readers in its own image, in the first instance by the model of active reading which it provides, and secondarily by complicating the reading process sufficiently to prompt the reader to engage still more closely with the text.[25]

Like earlier instances of self-glossing, including Douglas', the Listrius commentary includes an experimental element. While much of it is informative and elucidatory, it also includes a number of glosses that replicate the slippery, shifting perspectives of Folly's speech. For example, when Folly attacks writers who assume pseudo-classical pseudonyms, Listrius claims that her use of the names Telemachus, Stenelus, and Laertes is a kind of discretion: 'Vide ut data opera cauerit, ne alicuius famam laederet. Hic poterat nominare quosdam & locus requirebat, tamen de industria posuit nomina, quae nullus adhuc scriptorum huius temporis, usurpauit.'[26] Even as the gloss asserts how discreet Folly (or Erasmus) has been, the very fact that it reminds its readers that actual names could have been named entices them to engage in a game of identification and thus subversively extends the satire of the text into the margins. There is a still more striking instance of such complicity when Folly quotes St Paul's statement that 'I speak as a fool, I am more' and, in expounding it, refers to the interpretation of 'quidam gloriosus Theologus, cuius ego nomen prudens supprimo, ne graculi nostri continuo graecum in illum scomma iaciant ὄνος λύσας'. Here the gloss spells out what Folly just barely withholds: the name 'Nicholas de Lyra'.[27] While ostensibly helpful, providing its readers with additional information, the gloss also prevents them from

---

studii, trans. and ed. Brian McGregor, *Collected Works of Erasmus*, Vol. 24, *Literary and Educational Writings* 2 (Toronto: University of Toronto Press, 1978), 683.

[24] For education by this method, see Rebecca W. Bushnell, *A Culture of Teaching: Early Modern Humanism in Theory and Practice* (Ithaca: Cornell University Press, 1996), 117–43; Anthony and Lisa Jardine, *From Humanism to the Humanities* (London: Duckworth, 1986), esp. 122–60; and Eugene R. Kintgen, *Reading in Tudor England* (Pittsburgh: University of Pittsburgh Press, 1996), 18–57.

[25] For discussion of the Listrius commentary as a reflection of Erasmus' scholarly interests, see Gavin and Walsh, '*Praise of Folly* in Context', 196–205; for contemporary English views of reading as a process of active engagement, see Daniel Wakelin, *Humanism, Reading, and English Literature* (Oxford: Oxford University Press, 2007), 199–211.

[26] *Moria* (1516), sig. O–O^v: 'Look how careful he has been not to injure anyone's reputation. He could have named certain names here, and the place required it, but with great care he chose names which none of the writers of our times has yet adopted.' The translation is from Gavin and Walsh, '*Praise of Folly* in Context', 198.

[27] *Moria* (1516), sig. U2^v. 'A certain renowned theologian (renowned perhaps in his own eyes?) whose name I have the sense to suppress, lest some of our jackdaws are quick off the mark with the Greek taunt of the "ass playing the lyre"' (*Praise of Folly*, 145).

resting in a clear understanding of its relation to the text. Rather than taking the form of primary text and supplement, text and gloss appear as two linked performances.

The extent to which the glossing of the *Moria* is experimental appears even from those conservative revisions and additions which urge the reader to distinguish between the author Erasmus and the persona of Folly. Thus, when Folly reels off a list of pagan gods who do not form part of her genealogy before claiming Plato as her father, one of the 1532 glosses queries:

> Qui in opere ex professo ludicro ac ridiculo inquirunt articulos haereticos, quin hunc criminantur locum, qui toties deos ac deas commemorat: cuiusmodi loci sunt alii quoque complures. Quod si illic agnoscunt iocum et stulticiae personam, quur non idem faciunt in caeteris? Quum plures nominantur dii pro ioco ducunt: quum tribus uerbis attingitur monachorum maiestas, nutat universa ecclesia.[28]

Although this gloss makes the text 'safe' by reasserting Folly's fictionality, it is also disingenuous; Folly's discussion here is not 'heretical' precisely because it *does* deal with multiple—that is, pagan—gods. Moreover, the gloss is not neutral, but (in its final comment on the monks) makes explicit the satire that is only implicit in the text; like the Nicholas de Lyra gloss, it suggests that there is a degree of collusion between Folly and the commentator. This is confirmed by resemblances of style and tone. The gloss poses a rhetorical question in an apparently innocent voice that strongly recalls Folly's own, suggesting that she is speaking from the margins as well as from the pulpit. It not only encourages the reader to distinguish 'fact' from 'fiction' and author from persona, but also mirrors Folly's own shift from earnest to game.

The layout of the text further encourages us to understand the Listrius commentary as a performance equivalent to Folly's own. When the commentary was added to the *Moria*, the short, predominantly indexing glosses that predated its composition were not simply superseded. Rather, they went through a series of revisions over the course of several subsequent editions. At first, in the 1516 edition, they replicate those of earlier editions, continuing to index Folly's oration from the outer margins, but by the edition of 1526 they also index Listrius' commentary. For example, when Folly suggests that her audience is drunk on 'nectare

---

[28] 'Why do not those who search out articles of heresy in a work professedly playful and humorous indict this passage which makes such frequent mention of gods and goddesses? And there are many other places just like it. But if they understand the humour and the mask of Folly there, why don't they do so in other places? When many gods are named, they take it as a joke. When the majesty of the monks is very lightly touched on, the whole church totters.' Text and translation from Gavin and Miller, 'Erasmus' Additions to Listrius', 20–21.

> ito frontem exporrexiftis, *Frontem ex-*
> fic læto quodam & amabi- *porrexift.) Fron-*
> li applaufiftis rifu, ut mihi *tem exporrigi-*
> profecto quotquot undiq; *mus, cum hilare*
> præfentes intueor, pariter *fcimus : contra,*
> deorum Homericorū ne- *moefti fronte co*
> &are non fine nepenthe te *trahimus.quære*
> mu- *fmi.* Deorum
> *Homericorū.) Facete uocat Homericos, qui cū nō fint ul-*
> *li in rerum natura, tamen ab Homero finguntur eiufmo-*
> *di.* Nepēthes. *Non fine nepenthe.) Nepenthes herba, cuius memi-*
> *nit &*

Plate 4.1 Erasmus, *Moriae Encomium* (Cologne: E. Ceruicornus, 1526), 18. 8° E.3 Art. BS. Reproduced courtesy of The Bodleian Libraries, The University of Oxford.

non sine nepenthe' ['nectar with the addition of Nepenthes'], the Listrius gloss gives an extensive discussion of the unfamiliar term, referring to Penelope's use of it in the *Odessey*, quoting from Homer, and then elaborating further on the word πένθος which appears in the quotation.[29] Of the two outer glosses to this passage, the first, 'Nepenthes', identifies the topic that Listrius has chosen to discuss, giving further prominence to something which is only incidental in Folly's speech, while the second, πένθος, picks up a word that appears exclusively in the commentary (see Plates 4.1 and 4.2).[30]

Such double glossing has good academic precedents; many of the late-fifteenth and early sixteenth-century printed editions of Virgil, for example, contained just such a ring of indexing glosses surrounding both text and commentary. Indeed, by inviting a comparison with classical texts, the continued presence of the outer ring of glosses confirms that one of their purposes is the visual authorization of Erasmus' work. They also serve as a genuine aid to the reader in navigating the text, something that becomes especially important with the addition of the commentary and

---

[29] According to the gloss, Nepenthes is a herb with the power to banish melancholy.
[30] *Moriae Encomium* (Cologne: E. Ceruicornus, 1526), 18–19.

> **STVLTITIAE LAVS.** 19
>
> *nit & Plinius. Apud Homerum Penelope, huius succo addito poculis, discutit tristitiam conuiuij. Vnde illud Odyssex quarto:*
>
> ἔνθεν ἔπινον
> νηπευθές τ' ἄχολόν τε κακῶν ἐπίληθες ἁπάντων
>
> *Id est, Vnde bibebant
>   Irae, nepenthes, omnisq; obliuia curae.
> Nam hanc uim habere traditur, & hinc nomen habet.
> Nam* πένθος *Graece, luctus est: ne, priuandi uim ha-* πένθος
> *bet. Sunt qui putant esse buglossam, de qua Gale. scribit:*
>
> ὅτι οἴνοις ἐμβαλλομένη εὐφροσύνης αἰτία γίνε
> ται, *Id est, quod uino immissa, laetitiae causa fit.*

Plate 4.2 Erasmus, *Moriae Encomium* (Cologne: E. Ceruicornus, 1526), 19. 8° E.3 Art. BS. Reproduced courtesy of The Bodleian Libraries, The University of Oxford.

the resulting complexity of the page layout. Yet, at the same time, the outer ring of glosses reinforces the impression that the commentary, just as much as Folly's oration, is a performance: an exercise in the *genre* of commentary just as Folly's speech is an exercise in the genre of encomium. This impression is further strengthened by the addition of an index, at the end of the volume, which refers exclusively to the words and phrases discussed by Listrius. As an exercise, the commentary cannot be regarded as a transparent or an objective guide to the text; instead, it raises the same questions about objectivity and sincerity as Folly's extemporizing does. Like Folly's speech, it can be read in two ways: either as a serious attempt to assist the reader in extracting sense from paradox and providing a model of how to do so, or as a way of 'putting the case' with no necessary truth value. The glossing of the *Moria* thus becomes as inalienable a part of its 'sentence' as the choice of Folly as persona; indeed, they are natural counterparts of one another. The double-voiced, dialogic quality of Folly's own speech might even be said to be reflected in the paradox of glossing Folly at all—which, by implying a want of discrimination on the part of the glossator, places the onus of interpretation on the reader just as Folly's own instability does.

THE GLOSSING OF CHALONER'S
PRAISE OF FOLIE

By contrast to the complex glossing of the *Moria*, Chaloner's glossing seeks quite unequivocally to direct its readers' interpretation of the text. The contrast between the two is comparable to that between Douglas' and Copland's glossing, and similarly encourages different kinds of reading. Chaloner's glossing is not the result of a lack of awareness of that of his source, however. The 1526 edition of the *Moria* which Chaloner used for his translation contains both the Listrius commentary and the 'outer ring' of glosses, and it is clear that Chaloner was in principle willing to use material from Listrius. As Clarence Miller has demonstrated, there are numerous instances where Chaloner's translation follows the phrasing of the commentary rather than the text, or includes information contained only in the commentary.[31] Thus, like Douglas in his translation of the *Eneados*, Chaloner treats the commentary on his source-text as an integral part of it, and the selection of material from it for inclusion in his own text as part of the business of translation. Yet with the exception of those glosses where Chaloner stresses Folie's fictionality, Chaloner uses information from the Listrius commentary only in his text. In both form and content, his glosses bear a much closer relation to those of the 'outer ring' in the *Moria*; indeed, they seem to have begun as direct translations. Chaloner's 'oratours and poetes' corresponds to 'Poetae & rhetores'; 'Folie dissembled' to 'Dissimulata stultitia'; 'Obscuritie and affectacion of writers' to 'Affectata obscuritas'; 'Folies nourses' and 'Folies handmaides' to 'Nutrices stultitiae' and 'Comites Moriae'; 'Folies diuine operacion' to 'Diuinitas Moriae'; and 'Mariage, to procede of Folie' to 'Matrimonium a stultitia'.[32] Thus (although it is notable that Chaloner omits the gloss immediately before this last, 'Pudenda membra sine risu non nominantur' ['the private parts may not be mentioned without laughing']), at first it appears that Chaloner's glosses simply replicate those available to him, perhaps with the aim of providing summaries to aid navigation of the text.[33]

---

[31] Sir Thomas Chaloner, *The Praise of Folie*, ed. Clarence H. Miller, EETS o.s. 257 (London, 1965), pp. xxiv–xxvii. For ease of reference I have used this edition throughout, except when the layout of the 1549 edition has a bearing on the argument.

[32] Chaloner, *Praise of Folie*, 8, 10, 13, 14; *Moria* (1526), 22, 26, 28, 35, 36–7. Chaloner's omission of Listrius' etymological glosses may be attributable to the difficulty of printing Greek letters; despite his known proficiency in the language, as a student of Sir John Cheke's at Cambridge, and his translation of a number of works that derive ultimately from Greek sources, none of Chaloner's texts printed in his lifetime includes Greek quotations. The omission of etymological glosses is far from the most significant change that Chaloner makes to the apparatus of the *Moria*, however; his treatment of it represents a more radical simplification of both its form and its content.

[33] Chaloner, *Praise of Folie*, 15; *Moria* (1526), 39.

Even among these relatively straightforward glosses, however, some have a significantly different effect from their counterparts in the *Moria*. One of these is the gloss 'A fooles presence sterreth laughter', translating 'risus stultorum' ['the laughter of fools'] in Chaloner's source. In the lines to which this gloss is attached, Folie describes the reaction of her audience to her first appearance:

> As soone as I came forth to saie my mynd afore this your so notable assemblie, by and by all your lokes began to clear vp: vnbendyng the frounyng of your browes, and laughyng vpon me with so merie a countinaunce, as by my trouth me semeth euin, that all ye (whom I see here present) doe fare as if ye were well whitled.[34]

The gloss in the *Moria* echoes Folly in identifying the audience as fools, but Chaloner's gloss inverts the sense of the text; it merely identifies the presence of Folie herself as that which causes laughter, and passes no comment on the nature of her audience. Folie's tactic as an orator is to shape her auditors in her own image: by describing them as delighted, she predisposes them to find her delightful, and then coaxes them into a shared conspiracy of laughter against the serious world. Yet where the *Moria* gloss 'risus stultorum' recognizes the likeness between Folie and her audience (and so arguably shares in Folie's project), Chaloner's gloss invites the readers of the work to maintain a critical distance, viewing Folie coolly from the outside as 'a fool', and by implication being no fools themselves. In Chaloner's version, the readers are invited to take a clear-cut position towards text and speaker: precisely the kind which the *Moria* makes impossible.

At first it seems that such differences may be accidental. As his translation progresses, however, Chaloner's use of glosses increasingly diverges from that of his source. He not only omits all those outer glosses in his source which refer exclusively to Listrius' commentary, but also those that are inappropriate to the religious climate of the 1540s. Thus, the glosses 'Etiam in sacramentis aliud alio sanctius' ['There is something more sacred even than the sacraments'] and 'Festiua fabella de theologo' ['A merry tale about a theologian'] have no counterpart in Chaloner's work.[35] The first of these affirms the value of the Mass, while the 'merry story' to which the second refers is a debate as to whether or not heretics should be burned. The joke hinges on one theologian's insistence on reading the single word 'deuita' as two, but although the story is told against such Catholic

---

[34] Chaloner, *Praise of Folie*, 7.
[35] *Moria* (1526), 302 and 325. The equivalent (unglossed) passages in Chaloner's *Praise of Folie* appear on pp. 114 and 125.

hair-splitting, Chaloner nonetheless appears to have considered it transgressive in a context where heresy had become a matter for the state as much as the church. Several of Chaloner's new glosses, such as 'Inuentors of oldwyues tales and feigned miracles' and 'Supersticious worshipping of sainctes', as well as his translation of the Erasmian outer gloss 'summi pontificales' as 'Bishops of Rome', similarly place a distinctly 1540s interpretation on Erasmus' work.[36] Although they do not strictly misrepresent Folly's subject matter, and have approximate counterparts in the outer ring of *Moria* glosses, in the first the 'miracles' are of Chaloner's own invention, giving a specifically anti-Catholic slant to a passage that was originally directed merely against superstition, while the second contrasts strikingly with the insistence in the Listrius commentary that Folly does not condemn the worship of saints per se, but only the habit of praying to them as a means of avoiding personal responsibility.

Yet not all of Chaloner's additions are attached to passages or phrases that had become potentially contentious by the time he was writing. He also contributes large numbers of indexing glosses at points where these are wanting in his source, such as 'Folie the guide vnto Sapience' and 'The difference between a Foole and a wyseman', as well as several interpretative and moralizing glosses, including the gloss 'The force of money' to the passage where Folly declares the power of her father Pluto, the god of riches, and the severely moral gloss 'Hereby is ment that those whiche ar born to moste wealth proue many times most fooles' attached to Folly's eloquent description of the delights of her birthplace, the Fortunate Isles.[37] Chaloner's provision of such a large number of new glosses, especially at those points where the glossing of his source is sporadic, indicates that he viewed them as an important part of his mediation of Erasmus' work. Like the Copland glosses to the *Eneados*, Chaloner's attempt both to aid the reader and to circumscribe or direct his or her response to the text.

Chaloner's directive tendencies become particularly apparent in the glossing of the later stages of Folly's speech. At the point where Folly argues that the best Christians are the greatest fools, the glosses repeatedly seek to draw a firm distinction between Folly and the author of the work, asserting that: 'These arguments must be taken as spoken by Folie, not that Erasmus ment so in deede'; 'By Folie in these places is ment godly symplicitee and by wysedome a worldly politikenesse'; 'These wordes muste

---

[36] Chaloner, *Praise of Folie*, 56, 57, 97. In the *Moria* (1526) the equivalent glosses read: 'Preces superstitione' ['A form of superstition'] and 'Sacerdotes abutuntur superstitione uulgi ad suum quaestum' ['priests abuse the superstition of the people for their own profit'] (153).

[37] Chaloner, *Praise of Folie*, 39, 11, 13.

not be wrested to any euill sense otherwise than the autour ment'; 'Take these woordes to be spoken vnder the person of Folie'; 'Foly speaketh'.[38] Chaloner even explicitly urges the reader to take responsibility for stabilizing an ambiguous text: 'Marke how Folie dalieth in hir wordes whiche are to be construed to a good sense or els to be but as a talke of Folie'.[39] As we have seen, the Listrius commentary can be equally defensive, as when Folly's phrase 'mea quidem sententia' is glossed: 'Festiuiter adiecit, Mea quidem sententia, quasi diceret, stultorum iudicio. Nam mea, ad stulticiae personam refertur'.[40] Naming Erasmus as author and Folly as speaker, with a gender of her own, this clearly insists on the distinction between them. So too does the following observation: 'non conueniat stulticiam de rebus tam arcanis loqui', or that lengthier defensive gloss added to the 1532 edition, in which Erasmus insists: 'Vide, ut hoc opus declamationem appellat, hoc est argumentum fictum, atque ingenii duntaxat exercendi gratia tractatum. Proinde uehementer ineptiunt, qui non secus excutiunt hic uerba, quam si serio tractaret de rebus theologicis.'[41] Despite such resemblances, the effect of exhortations to distinguish carefully between Folly and Erasmus is very different in the *Moria* than it is in Chaloner's translation. In the Listrius commentary they form only a small part of a comprehensive analysis of the text, whereas in Chaloner's version they stand out prominently in the margins, catching the reader's eye before he turns to the text, and pre-empting his reading. Moreover, in Listrius, they are part of a discursive commentary that contains multiple voices, ranging from the informative to the opinionated. In Chaloner's glossing there is no such slippage. Rather than match Folly's performance, they remind us that it *is* one. In order to do so, they maintain a tone of studied neutrality; even as they insist that 'Folie speaketh', the pretence is that no one 'speaks' the glosses. They simply exist.

In their ostentatious transparency, Chaloner's glosses very neatly reflect the views he sets out in the prefatory letter to his readers. Although he writes appreciatively of Erasmus' style, he nonetheless focuses primarily on the moral usefulness of his subject matter, asserting that: 'a profite also

---

[38] Chaloner, *Praise of Folie*, 116–17, 120–1.
[39] Chaloner, *Praise of Folie*, 126.
[40] *Moria* (1526), 326: 'He humorously interjected the phrase "in my opinion" as if to mean "in the opinion of fools," because "my" refers to Folly herself.' Translation from Gavin and Miller, 'Erasmus' Additions', 23.
[41] *Moria* (1526), 330: 'It is not fitting that Folly speak about such mysteries'; *Moria* (1532): 'Notice that he calls this work a declamation, that is, fictional subject matter which is treated merely as an intellectual exercise. Therefore, those who scrutinize the words in this work as if the author were writing a serious theological treatise are hopelessly wide of the mark'. Both translations and the text of the second quotation are from Gavin and Miller, 'Erasmus' Additions to Listrius', 23, 20.

maie arise therethrough to the readers, besides the delectation, beyng so pithilie pleasaunt as it is.'[42] A similar interest in content rather than style is apparent in his discussion of his own translation methods, where he states that: 'In all my translacion I haue not peined my selfe to render worde for woorde, nor prouerbe for prouerbe . . . but rather markyng the sence, I applied it to the phrase of our englishe.' Yet despite this, he continues: 'And where the prouerbes woulde take no englishe, I aduentured to put englisshe prouerbes of like waight in their places.'[43] Here, although Chaloner declares that his translation privileges the sense rather than the exact phrasing of Erasmus' Latin, he reveals that he attaches considerable importance to replicating the form of its proverbs, if not their content. We see what this means in practice at the beginning of Folly's oration, where she rattles off a startling string of Greek proverbs in her scathing description of those who pay other men to sing their praises:

> Tamen verecundus interim ille pauonis in morem pennas tollit, cristas erigit, cum impudens assentator nihili hominem diis aequiparat, cum absolutum omnium virtutem exemplar proponit, a quo sciat ille se plus quam δὶς διὰ πασῶν abesse, cum corniculam alienis conuestit plumis, cum τὸν αἰθίοπα λευκαίνει, denique cum ἐκ μυίας τὸν ἐλέφαντα ποιεῖ. Postremo sequor tritum illud vulgi prouerbium, quo dicitur is recte laudare sese, cui nemo alius contigit laudator.[44]

In his translation of this passage Chaloner scrupulously matches its proverbs and similes:

> And yet shall one of those shamefast, maidenly men not sticke than to displaie his pecockes fethers, and rowse hym selfe, whyles such shameles flaterers dooe goe about to make him, being a man lesse worth than naught, coequall yet vnto the Gods, in blasonnyng hym for a paragonne, and absolute example of all maner vertues, from which he knoweth hym selfe to be as farre wyde, as from hence to the man in the moone. Namely whiles those glorious glosers would decke the crow with other burds fethers, or peyne theim to washe awaie a Morions blackenesse, or labour of a sely fly to make an Elephant. For shorte, I folowe in this poincte the common prouerbe, whiche saieth, that he maie rightly praise hym selfe, whom none other body will.[45]

---

[42] Chaloner, *Praise of Folie*, 5.   [43] Chaloner, *Praise of Folie*, 6.

[44] *Moriae Encomium*, 72, 74: 'The bashful listener spreads his tail-feathers like a peacock and carries his head high, while the brazen flatterer rates this worthless individual with the gods and sets him up as the perfect model of all the virtues—though the man himself knows he is nowhere near that; infinity doubled would not be too far away. Thus the wretched crow is decked out in borrowed plumage, the Ethiopian washed white, an elephant created out of a gnat. Finally, I follow that well-worn popular proverb which says that a man does right to praise himself if he can't find anyone else to praise him' (*Praise of Folly*, 86–7).

[45] Chaloner, *Praise of Folie*, 9.

But despite what appears to be a quite literal translation, Chaloner's emphasis is in fact very different from Erasmus'. Folly's troping is excessive. Her proverbs are offered not as alternatives, but as if they described simultaneous effects of the flattery; they thus create a kind of menagerie of incompatible exotics which both dazzles and confuses the listener. Her compilation raises the question whether, if all of these proverbs are applicable, any one of them is truly so, and thus draws attention to the dangers of being persuaded by style rather than substance. She even re-emphasizes these dangers by ending on the proverb 'to make an elephant of a gnat', which might be applied to her own belabouring of the point as much as to the flattery she condemns, and by her throwaway change of tone in the final line, where she effectively confesses that she will use any supporting evidence that comes to hand, so long as it is familiar. Proceeding by symbolic logic, her heedless conflation of proverbs is startling enough to engage the reader's attention, and thus foster the kind of engaged reading which Erasmus advocates in *De ratione studii*, though by means very different from his correct and detailed analysis of the text. As Miller puts it: 'Proverbs tend to be unqualified, categorical, and extreme: they gain their intensity by narrowness of focus. So too does Folly, who loves to deal in extremities. But Erasmus . . . managed Folly's presentation of extremities in such a way as to leave his audience intensely aware of the need for some tertium quid.'[46] In Chaloner's translation, by contrast, the focus is genuinely narrow. The various proverbs are offered as alternatives, linked by 'or'. They thus become examples of a number of slightly different activities, rather than an exuberantly copious redescription of a single phenomenon. And this sets Chaloner a little at odds with his source. Whereas Folly's fluid juxtaposition of multiple proverbs calls into question their universal applicability, demonstrating just how contingent their meaning is, Chaloner's proverbs provide both a neat turn of phrase and a general truth; in both respects, they are exemplary.

To the extent that they seek general truths in a particular text, Chaloner's glosses are the marginal counterpart to his proverbs. His summary glosses frequently shade into sententiousness, as for example in 'This world a stage play of Folie', or 'All the worlde a temple to Folie'.[47] Although these accurately reflect the subject of the text, by taking the form of truisms they cross the line from summary to interpretation and direction. Elsewhere, Chaloner's glosses take an almost explicitly proverbial form, as for example

---

[46] Clarence H. Miller, 'The Logic and Rhetoric of Proverbs in Erasmus' *Praise of Folly*', in *Essays on the Work of Erasmus*, ed. Richard L. De Molen (New Haven: Yale University Press, 1978), 94.

[47] Chaloner, *Praise of Folie*, 38, 67.

'To trifuls better eare geuen, then to grauer matters'. This too is an accurate reflection of Folie's speech, as she exhorts her audience to 'bestowe on me your eares . . . not those eares that ye carie with you to sermons, but those ye giue to plaiers, to iesters, and to fooles'.[48] Yet its sententious form nonetheless distorts her meaning. Folie is very far from condemning the fact that players and jesters receive more attentive hearings than preachers; rather, she delights in it and exploits it. Chaloner's gloss fails to recognize the tone of her remarks. Instead, as in his translation of her proverbs, it extrapolates a dubiously applicable 'kernel' of truth from Folie's highly particular speech. On occasion such extrapolation brings the glosses' reliability into question, as when Folie's argument that flattery is a virtue in men because it is one in dogs is glossed: 'Flaterie a most requisite and commodious thyng to mans conuersacion'.[49] The inappropriateness of such glosses reveals Chaloner's neutrality to be as much a performance as Folie's flamboyant paradoxes.

The same is true of those of Chaloner's glosses that are accidentally comic in effect. Among the most prominent of these is the gloss 'Saincte Bernard dranke oyle in stede of wyne'. Although an equivalent is found among the outer ring of glosses in the 1526 *Moria*, its effect is very different in Chaloner's translation. This is due partly to the form and partly to the content of the two glosses. In the *Moria*, the gloss is juxtaposed with a full explanation, in the Listrius commentary, of the circumstances in which Bernard came to mistake oil for wine:

> Nam cum quodam tempore intentissime in diuinis scripturis (ut ei mos erat) meditaretur sitiensque, cantharum plenum olei, forte fortuna astantem uidisset ex eo bibit, non sentiens oleum esse. Deinde cum quidam frater eum accessisset, rogassetque, cur nam os (nam adhuc nonnihil olei ori mentoque adhaesit) oleo oblitum haberet, illique cum iamdiu admiratur esset, unde nam oleo inquinatus esset tandem in mentem uenit, quod ex canthoro bibisset. Itaque cum cantharum inspexisset, uidit eum plenum esse, non uini, ut putarat, sed olei.[50]

In the Listrius version, the commentary satisfies the reader's curiosity, piqued by the cryptic gloss, as to what circumstances could have led to Bernard's bizarre behaviour. By contrast, in Chaloner's version, there is no

---

[48] Chaloner, *Praise of Folie*, 8.   [49] Chaloner, *Praise of Folie*, 62.
[50] *Moria* (1526), pp. 323–4. 'For once when he had studied the scriptures very intently (as was his habit) and was thirsty, by chance he saw a carafe full of oil standing there and drank from it, not noticing that it was oil. Later, when a certain friar approached him and asked why he had covered his face in oil (for a great deal of oil remained on his mouth and chin), he was the more amazed, because he had wondered when he drank from the carafe how it came to be contaminated with oil. And when he looked properly at the carafe, he saw that it was full, not of wine (as he had imagined) but of oil.'

such contextualization; the gloss' snippet of information is quite literally left hanging. It is thus paradigmatic of one of the problems latent in his summary glosses: due to their succinct phrasing and visually prominent position, they can appear to reduce the text to an almost random selection of disconnected observations. For example, the gloss immediately following that which identifies Nicholas of Lyra reads simply 'Holy writ likened to a Cheverel skin', while even those that are less startling in their own right read as a bizarre collection of topics when taken together; thus, consecutive glosses on just three folios of *The Praise of Folie* read: 'Euery error is not madnesse', 'No man voyde of madnesse', 'Folie of hunters', 'Builders', 'Multipliers', 'Dyse plaiers', 'Inuentors of oldwyues tales and feigned miracles', 'Perdones', 'Rosaries'.[51] Individually they are unexceptionable. Cumulatively they suggest an absurd want of discrimination on the part of either the author or the glossator.

Erasmus' and Chaloner's respective practices might stand as paradigms of two entirely different kinds of glossing. By the highly self-conscious double glossing of the *Moria*, Erasmus draws attention to the performative nature of commentary, making his interpretations an extension of Folly's own rhetorical display. It appears that Chaloner sets out to do quite the opposite. Providing glosses that do their best to render themselves transparent, he implies that the readings they provide are wholly objective, and thus also 'true'. Chaloner's glosses evince a strong awareness that, by translating Erasmus' complex work into English, he is making it available to the less well educated; they imply that part of the translator's project is to minimize the resulting dangers. Whereas Erasmus' glossing contributes a further layer to the play in Folly's own speech, Chaloner's seeks to eradicate uncertainty as to her meaning; whereas Erasmus' glossing makes visible the various stages in the reading process, Chaloner focuses on the 'sentence' of the text as if it were the same for all readers, regardless of the time and place of reading. Chaloner's sententiousness and his emphasis on the fictional nature of the persona of Folie are different ways of achieving the single end of translating playfulness into profit. Distinguishing the 'peculiar' from the 'general', his glosses—like those in Copland's *Eneados*—aim to separate what cannot safely be taken from the text from the rest, which can be tidily, universally, and non-controversially abstracted.

Despite their very different priorities, Erasmus' and Chaloner's glossing practices both respond, among other things, to the fact of writing specifically for print. Chaloner's cautious glossing may be understood as a response to fears about the potentially limitless readership of *vernacular*

---

[51] Chaloner, *The Praise of Folie* (London: Thomas Berthelet, 1549), sigs. Hi–Hiii.

printed texts in particular, and as an attempt to resist an equivalently extreme proliferation of interpretations. In Erasmus' provision of the Listrius commentary, however, what we see is not simply a reaction to the potentially wide circulation of a printed text. The commentary also witnesses an emerging interest in the way its printing affects what and how a work communicates. Specifically, the glossing of a speech whose speaker insists on the extemporary and unpredictable quality of her own utterance provides a constant visual reminder to the reader that he is dealing with a *book*, not a speech, and thus draws attention to the gap between Folly's insistence on her own unpredictability, and the definitive representation of her voice on the printed page. The distinction, of course, is not a real one; Erasmus invented Folly's oration with the sole purpose of writing it down. The implicit oxymoron of 'printed speech' is one that will exercise writers throughout the sixteenth century, and one of the ways in which their interest finds expression is an experimental use of glossing. Using glosses as a means of conveying apparently impromptu asides, writers including Baldwin, Bullein, Gascoigne, Harington, and Nashe will treat the form as a means of counteracting the implicit finality of the printed text. Implying that they are speaking off the record to each reader individually, their glosses become the locus of 'extemporary' and hence persuasive speech, creating a fiction of intimacy in a public text. In its blurring of the boundaries between author and persona, and between truth and fiction, the glossing of the *Moria* clearly anticipates such techniques. Yet although Chaloner's glossing is entirely different in aim, seeking to close down interpretation rather than open it up, it too invites thought about the exact nature of the relationship between text and gloss. Still more than the Copland glosses to the *Eneados*, Chaloner's are apprentice work; he is not fluent in the use of the form. Yet his intensely serious and sometimes inadvertently comic glossing is characteristic of a style that will be adopted as a purposeful rhetorical strategy by later self-glossing authors. As we shall see in the following chapters, Chaloner's slightly awkward glossing practices are representative of a style of glossing that will have as much bearing as Erasmus' confident performance on the subsequent development of the form.

5

A Broil of Voices
The Printed Word in Baldwin's *Beware the Cat* and Bullein's *Dialogue against the Fever Pestilence*

Whereas the previous two chapters examined sententious glossing in printed texts of the mid-century, this chapter considers two instances of glossing that react against such overt direction of the reader, instead inviting consideration of the level of authority that should be accorded to the printed word. Focusing on William Baldwin's *Beware the Cat* (1553, first published 1570) and William Bullein's *Dialogue against the Fever Pestilence* (1564), it argues that their glossing reflects both the contemporary controversy over the translation, printing, and glossing of the Bible, and a wider curiosity about the impact of print on the way in which a text means. Both the *Cat* and the *Dialogue* are strongly anti-Catholic, and both reflect Protestant insistence on the plain word of God as sole spiritual authority. Yet at a time when the glossing of the Bible was a subject of contention, Baldwin's and Bullein's wayward glosses did not simply underwrite the Reformist message of their works. Recording in printed form a series of responses to the text which have a strong element of the unauthorized and improvised about them, their glosses blur the boundaries between speech and writing. Although the orality they ostensibly record is a *fictional* orality—like that of Erasmus' *Moriae Encomium*, invented precisely in order that it should be printed—they nonetheless call into question the assumption that the printed word has an authority distinct from that of its contents. As a concomitant, they propose that the educational potential of a text lies less in its own innate 'sentence' than in provoking the reader into independent interpretation. But although their emphasis on reading as an ethical activity recalls that of Latin humanist texts such as Erasmus' *Moria* and More's *Utopia*, the glossing of both the *Cat* and the *Dialogue* draws heavily on vernacular precedents as well. Adapting a wide variety of glossing traditions for use in a very specific context—one that is informed by both contemporary religious debates and emerging print conventions—Baldwin's and Bullein's works bear witness to the development of diverting glossing as an identifiable genre, characterized by studied unpredictability and play.

BALDWIN'S *BEWARE THE CAT*: PROTESTANT PRINT AND CATHOLIC ORALITY?

Despite recent critical interest, Baldwin's *Beware the Cat* remains less well known than his near-contemporary work, *A Mirror for Magistrates*.[1] Written circa 1553, but not published until 1570, it is a fantastical concoction: a textual cacophony in which a debate as to whether animals have the powers of speech and reason forms a transparent pretext for satirizing the Catholic faith. The narrator, Baldwin's alter ego G. B. (or Gulielmus Baldwin), explains the work as the transcript of 'one of the stories which Master Streamer told the last Christmas', when he and Streamer debated whether animals have the ability to speak.[2] In the three-part 'oration' that forms the main part of the text, Streamer first revisits a comparable dispute, which itself encompasses many tales of speaking cats; then explains how, after observing a colloquium of cats beneath his window, he concocted a variety of lotions, pills, and potions to enable him to understand what they said; and finally records what he overheard of the cat Mouseslayer's confession while he was eavesdropping on them. Following the transcription of this lengthy speech and its numerous embedded tales, G. B. adds a line or two declaring that the moral of the whole is that men should live so 'that neither thine own nor the Devil's cat . . . find anything therein whereof to accuse thee to thy shame'.[3] Like the prefatory epistle, 'T.K. to the Reader', that was added to the 1584 edition, this epigraph encourages the reader to treat the work as a compendium of Catholic abuses, and as a warning to avoid these themselves.

In its combination of an elaborate fictional framework and a strong anti-Catholic slant, *Beware the Cat* is characteristic of Baldwin's writings. The dedication of his *Treatise of Moral Philosophy* (1547/8) to the Protector Somerset's son and of his translation of the *Canticles of Solomon* (1549) to Edward VI indicate a strong desire to align himself with the Reforming court, while his translation of the bitingly satirical *Wonderful News of the Death of Paul III* (1552) similarly demonstrates his Protestant credentials.[4]

---

[1] For the *Mirror*, see Scott Lucas, *A Mirror for Magistrates and the Politics of the English Reformation* (Amherst: University of Massachusetts Press, 2009); and Paul Budra, *A Mirror for Magistrates and the De Casibus Tradition* (Toronto: University of Toronto Press, 2000); cf. also Jessica Winston, 'A Mirror for Magistrates and Public Political Discourse in Elizabethan England', *Studies in Philology* 101 (2004), 381–400.
[2] William Baldwin, *Beware the Cat*, ed. William Ringler and Michael Flachmann (San Marino: Huntington Library, 1988), 3. For ease of reference, all further quotations will be from this edition unless otherwise specified.
[3] Baldwin, *Cat*, 55.
[4] For these earlier works of Baldwin's, see John N. King, *English Reformation Literature: The Tudor Origins of the Protestant Tradition* (Princeton: Princeton University Press, 1982),

In this last work, Baldwin experimented with a technique he would use again in *Beware the Cat* and *A Mirror for Magistrates*. Presenting himself as the compiler or editor of a feigned narrative, he creates a framework for the text which both emphasizes its fictionality and stresses its relevance to Baldwin's own times.[5] In each case, Baldwin claims to be merely a facilitator, the means of making a written record of other men's spoken words available to the public, yet his framing of their narratives is itself an integral part of the text.[6] Thus, in *Beware the Cat*, the way in which G. B. makes Streamer's oration 'book-like' by providing prefatory material, a moralizing epigraph, and a set of marginal glosses creates an emphasis on the process of making the book which allows Baldwin to explore the very different kinds of authority inherent in the spoken and the written word, and thereby the way in which print affects the meaning of the texts it transmits.[7]

In *Beware the Cat* the contrast that is drawn between orality and print has a clear polemical purpose. In the early stages of the work, G. B. makes much of the need to ground all arguments in written authority, most explicitly when he criticizes a play in which actors took the part of birds on the grounds that 'it was uncomely . . . and without example of any author, to bring [birds] in lively personages to speak, do, reason, and allege authorities out of authors'.[8] For G. B. it is evidently impermissible to think that which has not been written before. Not only does he object to writing that is 'without example of any author', but he appears so to have internalized the theory of authorship according to which 'authority' was necessarily borrowed from a source outside the text that he considers 'alleging authorities' to be a defining human characteristic, just as speech

358–406; and cf. R. W. Maslen, 'William Baldwin and the Tudor Imagination', in *The Oxford Handbook of Tudor Literature, 1485–1603*, ed. Mike Pincombe and Cathy Shrank (Oxford: Oxford University Press, 2009), 291–306.

[5] This blurring of the boundary between fact and fiction may in part be attributable to a self-protective instinct on Baldwin's part. The *Cat* was written towards the very end of the reign of Edward VI, when the king was already known to be ill, while Baldwin's work on the *Mirror* spans the end of Edward's reign and the beginning of Mary's. However, the delayed publication of both works suggests Baldwin's strategy was only partially successful (see further Baldwin, *Cat*, pp. xxix–xxx; *A Mirror for Magistrates*, ed. Lily B. Campbell, 2 vols. (Cambridge: Cambridge University Press, 1938), 1: 5–20; and Budra, *Mirror*, 3–13).

[6] For the importance of the fictional framework in *A Mirror for Magistrates*, see Sherri Geller, 'What History Really Teaches: Historical Pyrrhonism in William Baldwin's *A Mirror for Magistrates*', in *Opening the Borders: Inclusivity in Early Modern Studies*, ed. Peter C. Herman (Newark: Associated University Presses, 1999), 150–84; and Winston, '*Mirror*'.

[7] Baldwin, *Cat*, 3. See further Edward T. Bonahue, '"I Know the Place and the Persons": The Play of Textual Frames in Baldwin's *Beware the Cat*', *Studies in Philology* 91 (1994), 283–300.

[8] Baldwin, *Cat*, 5.

and reason are. While his provision of a framework for Streamer's oration is a clear attempt to present this teller of tall tales as an *auctor*, G. B. also invites us to consider his faith in the written word as a reflection of Protestant belief in the Bible as the sole doctrinal authority. For example, when one of Streamer's interlocutors explains how witchcraft runs in families, with mothers passing on their secrets to their daughters, G. B.'s gloss comments: 'Witchcraft is kin to unwritten verities, for both go by traditions.'[9] This clearly alludes to Reformist attacks on Catholic doctrines such as the veneration of images, the celibacy of the clergy, sacraments other than baptism and the Eucharist, the efficacy of prayers for the dead, good works as a means to salvation, and the doctrine of transubstantiation. Reformers asserted that these had no basis in Scripture, and therefore had no place in Christian faith; Tyndale, for example, exhorted the readers of *The Obedience of a Christian Man* to 'get thee to God's word, and thereby try all doctrine, and against that receive nothing'.[10] Baldwin expresses the same view in a less serious vein, by means of an insulting analogy.

Although it seems at first that G. B.'s faith in the written word is intended as a corrective to Catholic oral traditions, *Beware the Cat* proves not to satirize Catholicism by straightforward assertion of the superiority of the written over the spoken word.[11] Rather, it presents a significant challenge to the authority of the written word itself, revealing G. B.'s faith in its immutability to be seriously misplaced.[12] Despite G. B.'s elaborate

---

[9] Baldwin, *Cat*, 19. For the anti-Catholicism of *Beware the Cat*, and its reflection in G. B.'s self-conscious production of a printed book, see Robert Maslen, '"The Cat Got Your Tongue": Pseudo-Translation, Conversion, and Control in William Baldwin's *Beware the Cat*', *Translation and Literature* 8 (1999), 3–27. For a discussion of other anti-Catholic aspects of *Beware the Cat*, see King, *English Reformation Literature*, 401–3; and for a reading of the *Cat* in the context of the historical association of cats and Catholics, see Bruce Thomas Boehrer, *Animal Characters: Non-Human Beings in Early Modern Literature* (Philadelphia: University of Pennsylvania Press, 2010), 110–30.

[10] Quoted in Stephen Greenblatt, *Renaissance Self-Fashioning: From More to Shakespeare* (Chicago: University of Chicago Press, 1980), 93–4. For the importance Protestants attributed to the Bible, see David Ginsberg, 'Ploughboys versus Prelates: Tyndale and More and the Politics of Biblical Translation', *Sixteenth Century Journal* 19 (1988), esp. 46–49. For a detailed discussion of contrasting Catholic and Protestant practices in the mid-sixteenth century, see Susan Brigden, *London and the Reformation* (Oxford: Clarendon Press, 1989), 255–98 and 378–422; and Eamon Duffy, *The Stripping of the Altars: Traditional Religion in England, c1400–c1580*, 2nd ed. (Harvard: Yale University Press, 2005), 377–477; for a succinct overview, see Jamey Hecht, 'Limitations of Textuality in Thomas More's *Confutation of Tyndale's Answer*', *Sixteenth Century Journal* 26 (1995), 823–8.

[11] See further Terence Bowers, 'The Production and Communication of Knowledge in William Baldwin's *Beware the Cat*: Towards a Typographic Culture', *Criticism* 33 (1991), 1–29.

[12] See further Clare R. Kinney, 'Clamorous Voices, Incontinent Fictions: Orality, Oratory, and Gender in William Baldwin's *Beware the Cat*', in *Oral Traditions and Gender in Early Modern Literary Texts*, ed. Mary Ellen Lamb and Karen Bamford (Burlington,

apparatus, Streamer's voice dominates the book, and Streamer is far from sharing G. B.'s respect for written sources. He asserts that he will speak 'not only what by hearsay of some philosophers I know, but what I myself have proved', thus explicitly equating the written word with rumour. He neglects his books in order to muse on a conversation he has just had; and, when making his potion and philter to understand the speech of animals, he ignores the instructions he finds in the *Booke of Secretes of Albertus Magnus*, introducing his own whimsical variations.[13] Worse, he is conspicuously in love with the sound of his own voice, agreeing to recount his experiences only if his auditors promise not to interrupt. Even without any interruptions, however, he is quite unable to control his narrative, digressing and diverging until the point of the narrative is lost in a mass of accretions.[14] G. B.'s printed apparatus merely invests Streamer's monologue with an authoritative appearance at odds with its content, creating a discrepancy so striking that it becomes one of the main means by which Baldwin encourages his readers to take responsibility for their own interpretation of the text.

The problematic relationship between speech and writing which Baldwin addresses is one previously explored by Chaucer in his *House of Fame*, which is a significant pre-text for Baldwin's work. When Streamer describes the cacophony that assaulted his ears when he purged them in preparation for eavesdropping on the cats, he draws attention to the connection, declaring:

> While I harkened to this broil, laboring to discern both voices and noises asunder, I heard such a mixture as I think was never in Chaucer's House of Fame; for there was nothing within an hundred mile of me done on any side (for from so far, but no farther, the air may come because of obliquation) but I heard it as well as if I had been by it.[15]

Diligently noting the allusion to 'Chaucer's House of Fame', the gloss to this passage constitutes a kind of oxymoron. Its confident citation implies the immutability of the text it refers to, yet *The House of Fame* itself repeatedly calls textual permanence and stability into question, as Chaucer's narrator discovers that there is no clear distinction to be drawn between spoken rumour and the supposedly stable and authoritative written word.

VT: Ashgate, 2008), 195–207; and cf. Trudy Ko, 'The Hybrid Text: Transformation of the Vernacular in *Beware the Cat*', in *The Transformation of Vernacular Expression in Early Modern Arts*, ed. Joost Keizer and Todd M. Richardson (Leiden: Brill, 2011), 207–27.

[13] Baldwin, *Cat*, 6, 24–7, 22. For the status of Albertus Magnus, see King, *English Reformation Literature*, 392; and for Streamer's unreliability, see further Kinney, 'Clamorous Voices, Incontinent Fictions', 199–200; and Maslen, '"Cat Got Your Tongue"', esp. 10–15.

[14] Baldwin, *Cat*, 6–7.   [15] Baldwin, *Cat*, 31–2.

So too does Baldwin's work—and its glosses are key to this process. As the most prominent element of the apparatus, in which G. B. records diverse (and often strikingly inept) interpretations of the text, they are the printed equivalent of the spoken interruptions that Streamer refuses to countenance. Just as Chaucer's eagle discusses the endless outward ripple effect of 'air ybroke', in which every word spoken acts like a stone dropped in water, 'Euery sercle causynge other / Wydder than hymselfe was . . . And multiplyinge ever moo', G. B.'s own glossing amplifies and distorts without clarifying, appearing on the page as the outermost ring of air.[16] An effect that, in the glossing of *The House of Fame* itself, was almost certainly accidental, here becomes strategic. Baldwin's diversionary tactics nonetheless prove to be a means of instruction, as they educate his readers in good, self-reliant, interpretative practice by demonstrating that the reliability of the printed word is not to be taken for granted.

WRITTEN AND UNWRITTEN VERITIES: GLOSSING *BEWARE THE CAT*

As an associate of the radical Protestant printer Edward Whitchurch, Baldwin was intimately familiar with paratextual conventions, and the apparatus G. B. provides for Streamer's oration clearly reflects that knowledge; his glosses take their place alongside his dedicatory epistle and moral epigraph as part of the apparatus properly belonging to a printed book.[17] In function too, the glosses initially appear quite conventional; they include quotations from other works, summaries of G. B.'s own text, and preceptive or sententious comments that extrapolate general morals from specific incidents in the narrative. Yet although they seem to exemplify a diligent printer's attempt to make his text accessible to the reader, in practice they are very far from providing straightforward mediation.[18] Their shifts in tone and the frequently questionable interpretations they place upon the text mean that the voice of the glossator obtrudes and, by

---

[16] Chaucer, *The House of Fame*, in *The Riverside Chaucer*, ed. Larry D. Benson (Oxford: Oxford University Press, 1988), ll. 796–7, 801.

[17] For Baldwin's life, see John N. King, 'Baldwin, William', in *The Oxford Dictionary of National Biography*, <http://www.oxforddnb.com/view/article/1171?docPos=1>. For the role of the printer in preparing a book for the press, see *The Cambridge History of the Book in Britain*, Vol. 3, 1400–1557, ed. Lotte Hellinga and J. B. Trapp (Cambridge: Cambridge University Press, 1999), 82–91. For analysis of the real instability of printed texts in this period, which Baldwin would have been intimately aware of, and which *Beware the Cat* makes so very visible, see David McKitterick, *Print, Manuscript, and the Search for Order* (Cambridge: Cambridge University Press, 2003), 97–138.

[18] Cf. Bonahue, '"I Know the Place and the Persons"', 292–7.

revealing itself to be the voice of an unreliable individual, invites the reader to contest its readings.

G. B.'s limitations as a glossator are apparent from the very first. At the beginning of Streamer's oration he carefully indicates the points where Streamer gives the etymology of each of the various gates of London: 'Why Aldersgate was so named', 'Bishops built Bishopsgate', 'Why Moorgate', 'Why Newgate', 'Why Ludgate', and so on. The text that is so scrupulously glossed is very far from deserving this level of attention, however. Streamer's discussion of etymologies is an early indication of his inability to control his material, leading him to digress before he has even begun:

> Being lodged (as, I thank him, I have been often) at a friend's house of mine, which, more roomish within than garish without, standeth at Saint Martin's Lane end and hangeth partly upon the town wall that is called Aldersgate (either of one Aldrich, or else of Elders, that is to say ancient men of the city which among them built it—as bishops did Bishopsgate; or else of eldern trees, which perchance as they do in the gardens now thereabout, so while the common there was vacant grew abundantly in the same place where the gate was after builded, and called thereof Elderngate—as Moorgate took the name of the field without it, which hath been a very moor; or else, because it is the most ancient gate of the City, was thereof in respect of the other, as Newgate, called the Eldergate; or else . . .[19]

Streamer's narrative style is a debased version of the copious speech advocated by Erasmus in *De copia*.[20] His words breed words, and he speaks without hesitation, but his is a spurious fluency. Rather than displaying a fertile mind that is able to illuminate its subject from various angles, it reveals only his inability to discriminate. This has serious consequences for his authority as narrator. As Martin Elsky has argued, whereas medieval scholastic thought had considered language to be referential, the verbal reflection of a non-verbal reality, in the fifteenth and sixteeth centuries this view was largely superseded by the belief that language is conventional: that is, that words do not refer to an objective reality outside themselves, but create their own field of reference through repeated use.[21] In this context copia, or abundant expression, assumes a moral significance. If language does not refer to an external reality, copious speech not only reflects but creates meaning; it is at once the mirror of the speaker's mind

---

[19] Baldwin, *Cat*, 9.
[20] Erasmus, *De copia*, tr. Betty I. Knott, *Collected Works of Erasmus*, Vol. 24, *Literary and Educational Writings* 2 (Toronto: University of Toronto Press, 1978). For the considerable significance of copia as a trope, see Terence Cave, *The Cornucopian Text: Problems of Writing in the French Renaissance* (Oxford: Oxford University Press, 1979), 3–34.
[21] Martin Elsky, *Authorizing Words: Speech, Writing and Print in the English Renaissance* (Ithaca: Cornell University Press, 1989), 35–69.

and his means of improving it. Thus, Streamer's chaotic narrative reveals him to be morally and spiritually disordered.[22]

G. B.'s glosses signally fail to recognize either Streamer's shortcomings or the incompatibility between his ungoverned sentences and their own neatly compartmentalizing summaries. They are at once entirely accurate and entirely useless; for a reader who attempts to use them to determine the point of Streamer's meandering speech, their main effect is to reveal its essential incoherence. Just occasionally, G. B. does show himself capable of clear judgement; for example, when Streamer lists the cacophony of sounds that assailed him as he prepared to eavesdrop on the cats, itemizing the 'barking of dogs, grunting of hogs, wawling of cats, rumbling of rats, gaggling of geese, humming of bees . . . ringing of pans, crowing of cocks, sewing of socks . . . with such a sort of commixed noises as would a-deaf anybody to have heard', G. B. remarks wrily: 'Here the poetical fury came upon him'.[23] On occasion, too, G. B.'s naïve readings serve Baldwin's anti-Catholic ends, as when the cat Mouseslayer describes how one of her mistresses would light candles before praying to an image of the Virgin and G. B. comments that 'images cannot see to hear except they have much [1584: 'without'] light' (see Plate 5.1), or when Streamer asserts at the very end of his oration that he has 'told you . . . a wonderful matter, and yet as incredible as it is wonderful', and the gloss affirms that 'wonders are incredible'.[24]

More frequently, however, G. B.'s glosses record alarmingly undiscriminating responses to the text. This is especially apparent when they seek to provide moral commonplaces for which the text provides no adequate foundation.[25] Thus, when Streamer observes that 'I was straight caught with such a desire to know what [the cat] had said that I could not sleep of all that night', G. B. notes that 'Earnest desire banisheth sleep', seeming not to notice that his moral places more weight on an inconsequential remark than it can possibly bear.[26] When Streamer describes how 'I whipped into my chamber quickly and, finding my lamp still burning, I set me down upon my bed and devised upon the doings of these cats', G. B.'s sententiousness is still more disproportionate to its object; his gloss 'The good housewife's candle never goeth out' is almost entirely unrelated to the text.[27] Extrapolating a general moral from a particular occasion, and giving excessive importance to the metaphorical lamp which it substitutes for Streamer's physical one, it mirrors Streamer's absurd self-importance. Such glosses render preposterous the habit of mind that seeks commonplaces in overly dark corners, and

---

[22] Cf. Elsky, *Authorizing Words*, 76.
[23] Baldwin, *Cat*, 32.
[24] Baldwin, *Cat*, 40, 52..
[25] Cf. Kinney, 'Clamorous Voices', 201.
[26] Baldwin, *Cat*, 24.
[27] Baldwin, *Cat*, 24.

Beware the Cat.

whores
ganing
and good
hostices,
make ma-
ny gentle-
mē make
shamefull
shifts.

Allis fish
that come
to net.

A catho-
lik quean.

Images cā
not see to
hear with
out light.

rous, as deceitful. For when she had so-
ked from yung Gentlemen all that they
had: then would she cast them of except
they fell to cheting. Wherfore many of
thē in the night time would goe abrode,
and bring the next morning home with
them sometimes money, sometime Ie-
wels, as ringes or chaines, somtime apparel, and somtime they would come a-
gain cursing their il fortune, with no
thing saue per aduenture drye blowes or
wet woūds, but whatsoeuer they broght
my dame would take it, and finde the
meanes either so to gage it ȳ she would
neuer fetch it again: or els melt it & sel it
to ȳ Goldesmithes. And not withstāding
that she vsed these wicked practises: yet
was she very holy and religious, & ther-
fore although that all Images were for-
bidden; yet kept she one of our Lady in
her cofer and euery night when euery bo
dy were gone to bed, & none in her chaū
ber but she and I, then would she fetch
her out, and set her vpon her Cupborde
and light vp two or three wax candels be
fore her, and then knæle down to her,
sometime an hole houre saying ouer
her bedes, and praying her to be good vn
to her, and to saue her and all her geasts
bothe

records them in the margins for all to see; they serve as a warning against placing undue trust in the printed word simply because it is printed.

Just as G. B.'s faith in the printed word has Protestant overtones, the way his glosses call into question the innate authority of the printed word has a particular resonance in the context of contemporary debates over the translation, printing, and glossing of the Bible. As Evelyn Tribble has demonstrated, early advocates of Biblical translation argued not just that the word of God should be made available in the vernacular, but also that translation would provide the opportunity to strip away the *Glossa ordinaria*: the marginal commentary that had become a standard part of the Bible, and which—like the use of Latin—was considered by Reformers to obscure the word of God.[28] The very presence of glosses in *Beware the Cat* might thus be read as satirical: a marginal counterpart to the work's nesting of narratives which parodies Catholic privileging of unwritten verities over Scripture. They are not simply a form of anti-Catholic satire, however. By the time Baldwin was writing, Biblical glossing was no longer associated with the Catholic faith alone. In the ongoing struggle to determine the meaning of the work, many of the vernacular translations published in the first half of the sixteenth century had been glossed as well; in several cases, such as the 1549 Matthew Bible, they contained glosses that drew explicit and detailed attention to contested points of doctrine.[29]

Thus, although it is tempting to read G. B.'s faith in the authority of print as analogous to Reformist faith in Scripture, the glosses' failure to provide a single reliable perspective means that the onus is placed on the reader to make sense of the work. In a text in which much is made of the innate authority of both the main speaker and the printed word, but in which these claims to authority are unsupported by the content of either text or gloss, there is no one 'sentence' for the reader to take on trust; rather, he himself is made responsible for establishing a more satisfactory interpretation. The inadequacy of G. B.'s glosses thus aligns *Beware the Cat* with what Nancy A. Gutierrez has identified as 'one of humanism's most demanding theories . . . [according to which] a text was not merely a product crafted by the author, but an experience—the experience of reading—through which process the reader would be persuaded to ethical activity that would irrevocably change his moral life'.[30] It is clear from Baldwin's *Treatise of Moral Philosophy* that

[28] Evelyn B. Tribble, *Margins and Marginality: The Printed Page in Early Modern England* (Charlottesville: University of Virginia Press, 1993), 11–17.

[29] Tribble, *Margins and Marginality*, 18–31; and cf. William W. E. Slights, *Managing Readers: Printed Marginalia in English Renaissance Books* (Ann Arbor: University of Michigan Press, 2001), 101–27. For the extensive use of the printing press by early Protestant writers, see William Clebsch, *England's Earliest Protestants, 1520–1535* (New Haven: Yale University Press, 1964), 252–70; and King, *English Reformation Literature*, esp. 76–121.

[30] Nancy A. Gutierrez, '*Beware the Cat*: Mimesis in a Skin of Oratory', *Style* 23 (1989), 49. For the 'active conception of reading' in the sixteenth century, see further Victoria

he was strongly influenced by Erasmus' *Adages*, and there is an identifiable Erasmian influence on the glossing of *Beware the Cat* too. Even in the most general terms, Baldwin's concern with engaged reading seems to reflect the views Erasmus expressed in *De ratione studii*, which were echoed by English educational reformers such as William Lily and John Colet.[31] More specifically, the oxymoron of a printed oration owes a debt to Erasmus' *Moria*, while G. B.'s studious determination to make Streamer's tale 'book-like' similarly reflects that work's double-glossing and the frequent discrepancies in tone between the various parts of the text that occur as a result. Yet as well as representing a vernacular adaptation of Latin humanist practice, Baldwin's text responds to previous attempts to make humanist works available to a wide vernacular audience—most notably to Chaloner's *Praise of Folie*.[32] Chaloner was one of Baldwin's collaborators on *A Mirror for Magistrates* at about the time that his translation of the *Moria* was published, and the glossing of *Beware the Cat* seems to parody the conspicuously partial interpretations with which the glosses to *The Praise of Folie* seek to tame a potentially controversial, even heretical text. Rather than drawing a straightforward contrast between Catholic orality and Protestant scripture, Baldwin contrasts passive with active reception. By glossing in a way that makes the written word as unreliable as the spoken one, he spurs his readers to approach the text with an independent mind. If they are to learn to read critically rather than Catholically, they must begin by identifying Baldwin's own elaborate fiction for what it is.[33]

ETHICAL READING IN BULLEIN'S *DIALOGUE AGAINST THE FEVER PESTILENCE*

Baldwin is not the only Reformist writer concerned to promote ethical reading. In William Bullein's *Dialogue against the Fever Pestilence*, too, effective reading is aligned with Protestantism. But whereas Baldwin's anti-Catholicism is immediately apparent, Bullein's emerges more gradually

---

Kahn, *Rhetoric, Prudence, and Skepticism in the Renaissance* (Ithaca: Cornell University Press, 1985), 19–22.

[31] Erasmus, *De ratione studii*, tr. and ed. Brian McGregor, *Collected Works of Erasmus*, Vol. 24, *Literary and Educational Writings* 2 (Toronto: University of Toronto Press, 1978). For Colet and Lily, see J. B. Trapp, 'From Guarino of Verona to John Colet', in *Italy and the English Renaissance*, ed. Sergio Rossi and Dianella Savoia (Milan: Unicopli, 1989), esp. 46–7; Foster Watson, *The English Grammar Schools to 1660: Their Curriculum and Practice* (Cambridge: Cambridge University Press, 1908), 222–72; and Nicholas Orme, *English Schools in the Middle Ages* (London: Methuen, 1973), esp. 87–115.

[32] For the glossing of Erasmus' *Moria* and Chaloner's *Praise of Folie*, see Chapter 4 above.

[33] Cf. Bowers, 'Production and Communication of Knowledge', esp. 14–23.

from a text that initially appears to have a more immediate, practical end: the prevention of the plague. Bullein was a medical practitioner, whose previous publications included *The Government of Health* (1558), a medical miscellany under the title *The Bulwarke of Defence* (1562), and *A Comfortable Regiment against Pleurisi* (1562).[34] Written in response to a serious outbreak of the plague in London in 1563, in which up to a quarter of the population lost their lives, the title of the *Dialogue* suggests that it will fit comfortably into this list of medical works. It is notably more fictionalized, however. Its information on how to avoid the plague, lists of symptoms, and detailed recipes for medicines to treat it are almost swamped by a medley of other genres. It consists of a series of loosely connected conversations, set in two houses in plague-ridden London and in Hertfordshire. There are two distinct narrative strands: one following the householder Civis, his wife Susan, and their servant Roger as they attempt to flee the plague, the other focusing on the wealthy but dying Antonius and the corrupt doctors and lawyers who attend him. Narrative, however, takes second place to formal experimentation. The *Dialogue* progresses from complaint and estates satire through garden of the Muses and rogues' gallery to beast fable and Utopian travelogue, ending with scenes that take their inspiration from morality play and *ars moriendi*. It is also extensively glossed, and although in this respect, too, it resembles Bullein's previous works, the fictional nature of the *Dialogue* and the oblique relationship between text and gloss alter the impact of its glosses; the many voices of the text are complemented by further voices in the margins, as if the work's readers had also become characters with speaking parts.

Despite its multivocality, the *Dialogue* has a strong unifying theme, that of the collapse of social cohesion. Each man—whether rich man, sick man, doctor, apothecary, or lawyer—proves to be out for himself. Yet, as both Elizabeth McCutcheon and Jacqueline Proust have argued, the *Dialogue* is not so much a satire as an anatomy.[35] Bullein not only itemizes the failings of urban society in the sixteenth century, presenting the plague

---

[34] For Bullein's earlier works, see Catherine Cole Mambretti, 'William Bullein and the "Lively Fashions" in Tudor Medical Literature', *Clio Medica* 9 (1974), 285–97; R. W. Maslen, 'The Healing Dialogues of Doctor Bullein', *Yearbook of English Studies* 38 (2008), esp. 119–28; and Phil Withington, ' "For This Is True or Els I Do Lye": Thomas Smith, William Bullein, and Mid-Tudor Dialogue', in *Oxford Handbook of Tudor Literature*, esp. 462–7.

[35] Elizabeth McCutcheon, 'William Bullein's *Dialogue against the Fever Pestilence*: A Sixteenth-Century Anatomy', in *Miscellenea Moreana: Essays for Germaine Marc'hadour*, ed. Claire M. Murphy, Henri Gibaud, and Mario A. di Cesare (Binghamton: State University of New York, 1989), 341–59; and Jacqueline Proust, 'Le Dialogue de William Bullein à propos de la Peste (1564): Formulation d'une Thérapeutique pour l'Ame en Peril', in *Le Dialogue au Temps de la Renaissance*, ed. M. T. Jones-Davies (Paris: Jean Touzot Libraire-Editeur, 1984), 59–70.

as metaphorical retribution for the division between civil society and God, but also seeks to remedy the situation he describes. As well as providing a literal response to Civis' question 'Alas, what shall I doe to saue my life?', he addresses its metaphorical sense, not so much by providing direct instruction as by prompting the reader to engage with the text's indirections.[36] As a result, reading and interpretation, or what Victoria Kahn has called 'the effect of the text on the reader', become subjects of the work in their own right.[37] If anything, Bullein attaches a still greater importance to active, engaged reading than Baldwin does in *Beware the Cat*; whereas for Baldwin, good reading is a means of promoting the Reformation, for Bullein it is symbolic of the kind of good citizenship that would avert the divine punishment of the plague. The *Dialogue* offers its readers an opportunity to exercise just such interpretation.

Bullein's connection of reading with ethics appears from two episodes in particular: the description by the Doctor's assistant, Crispinus, of the elaborate sculpture in the garden outside Antonius' house, and Civis' interpretation of the allegorical wall hangings in the tavern where he and his wife pause in their flight from the city. Both sculpture and hangings take the form of emblems: allegorical representations in a visual medium accompanied by a motto or 'poesie', which combine to convey to the attentive reader a single, moral truth about the world. The first of these that we encounter is Crispinus' description of what he has seen on a pillar at the centre of the fountain in Antonius' garden: 'a Tyger fearfully hauyng a yonge childe in his armes readie to kill it; the childe [with] a croune of golde upon his head, and in his left hande a globe figuering the whole worlde, [. . .] called μικρόκοσμος [microcosm], about which was written *Globus conuersus est* [the world is upside-down].'[38] The message, clearly, is that the world is in parlous state, but the corrupt Doctor to whom Crispinus describes the emblem is unable to make any sense of it. We have already learned that he is defrauding his supposed friend Antonius, and his moral failings are re-emphasized by his inability to interpret the emblem.[39] His suggestion that the child holding the globe must be Antonius' coat of arms reveals that he views it as a sign of worldly success rather than of imminent danger. Still more tellingly, when Crispinus describes the other statues in the garden—the nine muses, and a number of Latin, English, and Scottish poets—the Doctor entirely fails to respond until Crispinus

---

[36] William Bullein, *A Dialogue against the Feuer Pestilence*, ed. Mark W. Bullen and A. H. Bullen, EETS e.s. 52 (London, 1888), 56. Unless otherwise specified, all quotations will be taken from this edition.
[37] Kahn, *Rhetoric*, 19. [38] Bullein, *Dialogue*, 15.
[39] For the Doctor and his real-life inspiration, see Mambretti, 'Bullein', 288–90.

mentions 'a faire Diall for this Orison, vnto whiche was added the howers of the Planettes: vpon the same was written in large letters of fine golde, *tempora labuntur*'. At this point he interrupts: 'There stop and lay a strawe; For *Tempora labuntur* is to say, by little and little tyme doth slip awaie. I will heare the reste of the matter at leasure. What is it a clocke?'[40] Despite translating the Latin phrase correctly, he fails to take account of its teaching. Emphasizing his own pressing business and equating the interpretation of the emblems with leisure activity, he refuses to acknowledge that the latter is potentially a way of gaining the self-knowledge necessary to save the commonwealth, and thereby his own soul.

In contrast, Civis' response to the complex emblems in the tavern affirms that good reading is a sign of good citizenship. Whereas the Doctor claims to have no time for contemplation, Civis makes profitable use of the interval in which he and his fellow travellers are waiting for their dinner, interpreting a large number of emblematic painted hangings for the benefit of his wife, Susan. The vast majority either illustrate general moral truths or attack instances of selfishness and social injustice. Their language is entirely familiar to Civis; he is able not only to interpret what he sees, but to amplify it. Thus, when Susan enquires the meaning of the 'straunge picture' showing 'a manne double, or in twoo, twinnes back to back; the one side is lustie, faire, riche, and yonge, and beautiful; the other side seemeth sicke, foule, poore, and olde; in the yong mannes hande was a grashopper, and in the old mannes an Ant without feete', Civis not only interprets it for her, but also gives a voice to the old man in the picture:

> In that table is liuely declared mankinde, both the tyme of his youth, in felicitie, with the careless grashopper, gatheryng nothing . . . and when age commeth hee would be thryftie, and then can get no more then the lame footeles ante. Then maketh he exclamation, saiyng, oh! what gooddes did my father leaue mee; what good counsaill my frendes gaue me; but I esteemed none of theim both, but in fine lost both riches and frendes, and now I am in great pouertie, sicknes, and age. Lette other men take example by mee, and remember the wisdome of Salomon, saiyng: *Vade ad formicum* [sic] *o piger et considera vias eius et disce sapientiam*, &c. Goe thou, idle bodie, to the Ante; consider, and marke well her waies, and learne wisdome; she hath not guide, prince, nor law geuer, but gathereth in somer to kepe her in winter, &c.[41]

By adding speech and quotation, Civis brings the tableau to life, rendering it quite literally a 'speaking picture'. He is equally at home with more contentious material, as when he explains the picture of a man in 'blacke, scholer like . . . with a Rake in his hande with teeth of golde . . . groping

---

[40] Bullein, *Dialogue*, 18–19.   [41] Bullein, *Dialogue*, 90–91.

belike in the Lake after some thyng that he would find' as that of a corrupt churchman who 'hath no vertue to prefer him to a liuyng, but onely the name of a priest or minister . . . [and] raketh with the Deuils golden rake, euen in the conscience of the coueitous patrons or conpounders hart'.[42] In each of these cases, what is of significance is not only the moral teaching locked up in the emblem, but Civis' ability to interpret it with such confidence, supplying the missing parts himself. He not only reconstructs a picture of what he has seen and read within his mind, but re-presents it to an audience of his own, thereby demonstrating that the sententious messages contained in the hangings have a specific and timely relevance. Although, as Rosalie Colie has argued, pithy verbal sayings or adages of the kind found in the statues and wall hangings were 'literally a common place, a convergence point of consensus [. . .] or [a convenient agent] of cultural transfer', the virtue of Bullein's emblems is not inherent in the commonplaces alone; rather, it derives from the process of interpreting them.[43]

Thus, although both Baldwin and Bullein give thematic importance to the spoken word, it seems that orality has a very different significance in their respective works. Baldwin draws attention to the disjunction between the printed and the spoken word, using the vagaries of the latter as a means of satirizing a number of Catholic practices and beliefs, yet *Beware the Cat* as a whole calls that theoretical distinction into question by using the printed word to encompass glosses that themselves amplify and divert the text. In contrast, Bullein begins from the position that the spoken word has a moral force. His character Civis breathes life into the formerly static emblems when he interprets them for his fellow travellers, and even the statues in his garden of the Muses are said to 'speak'; for Bullein, as Paul Ricoeur puts it, 'texts are meaningful insofar as they are returned to the condition of their originating authority in speech, which is the function of interpretative reading'.[44] Despite this difference, both works use glossing to reflect upon the role of the printed word in a Reformist context, proposing reading itself as a spiritual activity. Civis' ready explication of the emblems not only signals his own good citizenship—both his possession of shared values and the ability to formulate them for the benefit of others—but reveals how, if the *Dialogue*'s readers are prompted to imitate

---

[42] Bullein, *Dialogue*, 82–3.
[43] Rosalie L. Colie, *The Resources of Kind: Genre-Theory in the Renaissance* (Berkeley: University of California Press, 1973), 33. Cf. Laura Kendrick, *Animating the Letter: The Figurative Embodiment of Writing from Late Antiquity to the Renaissance* (Columbus: Ohio State University Press, 1999), 24–30.
[44] Paul Ricoeur, 'What Is a Text? Explanation and Interpretation', paraphrased in Elsky, *Authorizing Words*, 112.

his reading practices, Bullein's work may hold out hope for the restitution of his own society. As we shall see, its glosses are an important means of encouraging such imitation. However, they also reveal Bullein in the act of thinking about how a text means. They do not just contribute to a fictionalized representation of the contrast between orality and print but, in recording the process of bringing the text into being, reveal the idea of the 'finality' of print to be an oxymoronic one.

GLOSSING THE *DIALOGUE*: DIVERTING THE READER

As in Baldwin's *Beware the Cat*, the relationship between text and glosses in Bullein's *Dialogue* is analogous to that between the different parts of an emblem, creating a two-part meaning for the reader to make whole. Unlike Baldwin, however, it seems that Bullein only gradually becomes aware of his glosses' potential for encouraging such engaged reading. The earliest glosses in the *Dialogue* replicate the relatively straightforward glossing of Bullein's earlier medical works; thus, those surrounding the Doctor's list of remedies for the plague note its sources (Aristotle and Avicenna among them), provide short, indexing summaries that assist the reader in finding the remedy relevant to his own complaint, and translate into English those recipes which the Doctor provides only in Latin.[45] Despite the Doctor's dubious moral character, they contain nothing to suggest that his remedies should not be taken seriously. Including comments such as 'A goodly rule against the Plague', 'Note also that clisters are good before the opening of the veines', and 'Signs of the Plague', the glosses confirm that fiction has here ceded to the very serious business of prevention and cure.[46]

Other glosses have a less straightforward relationship to the text, however. When Crispinus enquires of a new character, the corrupt lawyer Ambodexter, 'What meaneth hee by winkyng like a Goose in the raine, and byting of his lippe?' and the Doctor replies that 'it is a good signe of a constant man', the gloss merely observes: 'a constant man by his looke'.[47] Accurately echoing the text, but entirely overlooking the Doctor's own

---

[45] In Bullein's *Bulwarke of Defence* the vast majority of the glosses index and give sources for, or provide additional information on, the diseases and remedies discussed in the text, though they do occasionally venture to point a general moral truth. In *The Government of Health*, where the glosses are of a similar kind, there is an interesting typographical experiment: glosses that give source references are in Roman type, while glosses that summarize the text are in black letter.

[46] Bullein, *Dialogue*, 39, 40, 45.   [47] Bullein, *Dialogue*, 20.

misinterpretation of Ambodexter's body language, it creates a startling lacuna; by repeating the words of the text verbatim, it reveals that not even a precisely reduplicated phrase carries the same meaning twice. Repetition makes the phrase appear parodic, and thus undermines the text, rather than underwriting it. This gloss occurs at a very early point in the work, before the first extensive block of glossing around the Doctor's remedies for the plague, and its parodic effect may be accidental. Later, however, equivalent effects are clearly achieved by design. For example, when Civis' servant Roger tells a barnyard fable that includes the rather elaborate observation 'at the water side the Drake with all the water foules did stoupe lowe and receiue their carriage, and when they were all cockehorse together, they wente into the water', the gloss reads simply 'Horsemen'.[48] It picks up an incidental metaphor without even noting that that is what it is, completely ignoring both the literal sense of the story and its moral; its conspicuous naïvety goads the reader to do better. In other glosses, a comparable lack of judgement appears not in relation to the content of the tale, but in relation to the character of the teller. Thus, when the traveller Mendax (whose name should be a warning) relates his incredible adventures abroad, the glossator seems to take his assertions at face value, noting simply 'Ambergrise as plentifull as claie' and 'Diamondes gathered with rakes'.[49]

Although here the naïvety of the glossator appears complete, other glosses assume an air of amused superiority, as when Susan expresses surprise that charcoal does not grow upon trees, and the margin declares: 'A wise cockney.'[50] As in *Beware the Cat*, such discrepancies in tone mean that the glosses obtrude, giving the impression of capturing impromptu and non-authoritative responses to the text. Recording a range of heterogenous voices, from responsible medical practitioner to worldly wise citizen, naïve lay reader, and theologian, they continue in the margins the conversations that characterize the main body of the work; although they constitute models of both good and bad reading, there is nothing to indicate which is which. Formally, there is no distinction between the glosses that surround the Doctor's remedies for the plague, which publish up-to-date medical advice, and those to Mendax's narrative or Susan's observation, which resemble the informal jottings of an individual reader or readers. The juxtaposition of such diverse kinds of gloss means that the *Dialogue*, like the emblems Civis interprets, is riddled with blanks; both the episodic

---

[48] Bullein, *Dialogue*, 66. The ducks are in the process of drowning some chickens under the pretext of teaching them to swim; the chickens, like the author of the gloss, are guilty of not looking for the subtext to their kind offer: guilty, that is, of not interpreting properly.
[49] Bullein, *Dialogue*, 99, 100.   [50] Bullein, *Dialogue*, 59.

nature of the text and the frequently oblique relationship between text and gloss deny the reader a fixed and reliable perspective, and thus prompt him to establish an interpretation of his own.

Both the inconsistency of the glosses and the consonance between gloss and emblem are most apparent in the tavern scene. Just as Civis interprets the painted hangings for Susan, the glosses mediate them for the reader—yet the two interpretations may contradict as well as complement each other. Text and gloss alike both supply and withhold information; on occasion, the gloss directs the reader back to the text by pointing out something he has missed, while at other times, Civis' words suggest that the gloss is incomplete. Thus, when Civis describes 'the picture or Effigium of a noble man, whiche in his daies serued a greate noble Kyng, and was like the cutter doune of Trees by the grounde . . . [who] if God had not vpon some secrete purpose preuented his labour in the woodde of Antichriste . . . would haue vtterly eradicated vp all Papistrie', it is the gloss that provides the crucial piece of information that this is 'The Lorde Crumwell'.[51] With the very next picture, however, the gloss is noticeably less forthcoming, putting the onus on the reader to find out what it implies. Considering the emblem of a man 'whiche hath a gray hore hed, a long goune, and a locke of Gold linkyng his lippes together, with manie goodlie bookes before hym, and a paire of blinde spectacles on his nose', Civis suggests that it is an allegory of 'the nobel Tallente of wisedome hidden'. The gloss both implies that it would be possible to be more precise, and refuses to be so; it states that 'This picture sygnifieth a great clerke euill occupied in kepyng silence'.[52] Coming immediately after the gloss in which Cromwell is identified, it gives rise to the suspicion that this clerk too is a highly specific portrait. It ostentatiously fails to go any further, however, instead demanding that the reader complete the text. Similarly, when Civis discusses the picture of the man angling after benefices with a gold-toothed rake, he introduces his interpretation with the warning to his wife that 'I dare saie but little to this matter to others, but to you I will speake a little, and not so much as I doe thinke'. From the description of the picture in the text it is not immediately obvious why Civis has suddenly become so circumspect, but the gloss provides a clue, even as it fails to provide an answer; in a rare shift into the first person, it insists 'I meane no honest or lerned man'.[53] The immediate effect of such a denial is of course to prompt the reader to consider whose might be a fitting foot for the

[51] Bullein, *Dialogue*, 81.   [52] Bullein, *Dialogue*, 82.
[53] Bullein, *Dialogue*, 82.

shoe. Such teasing glosses make of the printed page the textual equivalent of a pictorial emblem, creating the need for the reader to place together diverse parts in order to come to a complete understanding of what is portrayed—or even to stand in for one of Bullein's own characters, acting as part of the fictional national community.[54]

'THE BEST DOCTRIN IS GODES WOORDE': PLAIN INSTRUCTION IN THE *DIALOGUE*

The community which Bullein's readers are invited to join is a highly literary one. Like *Beware the Cat*, the *Dialogue* shows clear traces of humanist influence: Mendax's travelogue owes an obvious debt to More's *Utopia*, while More's glosses anticipate Bullein's in veering from useful to idiosyncratic; for example, his annotator does not just draw attention to the possibility that 'Disease and Filth Introduce the Plague into Cities', but also expresses an interest in 'A Remarkable Method of Hatching Eggs'.[55] Yet the *Dialogue* owes at least as much to vernacular models; indeed, it is clear from his description of the garden of the Muses that Bullein seeks to place his work in a specifically vernacular tradition of advice literature. The majority of the statues identified by Crispinus are English and Scottish writers, and the words that Bullein puts into their mouths posit them as the moral guardians of their nation. Chaucer, for example, is shown sitting:

> In a chaire of gold couered with Roses, writyng Prose and Risme [. . .] and [. . .] saied lamenting:
>
> Couetos men do catch al that thei may haue,
> The feeld & the flock, the tombe & the graue,
> And as they abuse riches, and their graues that are gone,
> The same measure they shall haue euery one.
> Yet no burial hurteth holy men though beastes them deuour,
> Nor riche graue preuaileth the wicked for all yearthly power.[56]

The statues of Skelton, Lydgate, Alexander Barclay, and David Lindsay also have such conceits put into their mouths.[57] Their 'sayings' are not true

---

[54] Cf. Roger Chartier (ed.), *The Culture of Print: Power and the Uses of Print in Early Modern Europe* (Cambridge: Polity Press, 1989), 5; and Elsky, *Authorizing Words*, 110–46.

[55] Thomas More, *Utopia*, ed. Edward Surtz, S. J., and J. H. Hexter (New Haven: Yale University Press, 1965), 139, 115.

[56] Bullein, *Dialogue*, 17.

[57] The idea of the 'speaking statue' has its origins as far back as the Greek epigram, which was originally an inscription on a statue or monument. Closer to Bullein's time, in 1501,

quotations, but sententious admonitions with which Bullein claims them as ancestors who share his concerns, and thus authorize his own writing as ethical advice for the commonweal.

These writers do not just provide an ideal community, but (like More) constitute a practical influence on Bullein's writing. As they journey away from London, Civis, Susan, and their servant Roger engage in wide-ranging conversation, in the course of which Roger observes that: 'In the olde tyme . . . Horses, Sheepe, Hogges, Dogges, Cattes, Rattes, and Mise did speake, and I dooe partlie beleue that, for as muche as our Parate will saie, Parate is a minion, and beware the Catte.'[58] This remark identifies two important pre-texts for Bullein's *Dialogue*: Skelton's *Speke Parrot*, whose protagonist is explicitly warned 'Ware the cat, Parrot, ware the false cat', and—of course—Baldwin's *Beware the Cat*.[59] It thus reveals much about the traditions within which Bullein viewed his work. A heteroglossic cacophony of parrots, ladies, authors, proverbs, adages, and commonplaces, with the epigraph 'Lectoribus auctor recipit opusculy huius auxesim' ['By his readers an author receives amplification of his little work'], Skelton's poem not only satirizes the state of the nation, but emblematically represents its disintegration through the form of his poem, and attempts to re-educate the reader as a means of restoring the nation to health. It is also one of the earliest English works to experiment with diverting glossing.[60] Baldwin's work is a still more significant influence on Bullein, in that it provides a precedent for using complex glossing as a means of exploring points of Reformist doctrine. Like Baldwin's, Bullein's sympathies are broadly anti-Catholic. Although he 'anatomizes' a wide variety of abuses, ranging from the Doctor's and lawyers' fleecing of their clients through the theft of the Doctor's mule to Roger's abandonment of Civis on his deathbed, Bullein implies several times that religious confusion is the underlying cause of the civic breakdown he portrays, and that the persistence of Catholic practices

---

a damaged statue was dug up in Rome, and the practice developed of attaching satirical epigrams to it. The statue was known as 'Pasquino' or 'Pasquillio'. In England the Italian tradition is reflected in literary use of the figure of Pasquin or Pasquil as a satirical mouthpiece, as for example in Sir Thomas Elyot's *Pasquil the Playne* (1533), and in the works of later writers such as Nicholas Breton.

[58] Bullein, *Dialogue*, 61.

[59] *Speke Parrot*, in *John Skelton: The Complete English Poems*, ed. John Scattergood (Harmondsworth: Penguin, 1983), l. 99; the poem was published three times between 1545 and 1560. Although no pre-1564 edition of Baldwin's work survives, Roger and Civis subsequently discuss stories of women who gave birth to cats in anti-Catholic terms that seem to echo Baldwin's, and further suggest that Bullein knew the work (*Dialogue*, 73).

[60] For *Speke Parrot* and its glosses, see Jane Griffiths, *John Skelton and Poetic Authority: Defining the Liberty to Speak* (Oxford: Clarendon Press, 2006), 79–100 and 111–117; and cf. John Scattergood, 'The Early Annotations to John Skelton's Poems', *Poetica* 35 (1992), 53–63.

is particularly to blame.[61] Antonius and the Doctor confess to one another that they are 'Nullafidians', or men of no faith at all, but their fear of being overheard by 'Protestants' suggests that their very lack of faith is a form of Catholicism.[62] So too, the beggar who visits Civis in the first scene is willing to say the Paternoster and what he calls the 'Debrafundis' in any form, English or Latin, that may please a potential benefactor.[63] Although here it seems at first that Bullein is targeting the opportunities offered to the unscrupulous by Reformation and counter-Reformation alike, on consideration this too proves to be a more partisan, Protestant passage: the first of many in the *Dialogue* that reflect on the consequences of obscuring or withholding information from a would-be reader. And this indicates a significant difference between Skelton and Baldwin on the one hand, and Bullein on the other. Although he seeks to locate his work in a tradition of cryptic, allusive social satire, and to ally himself with writers with Reformist associations, Bullein manifests uneasiness about some of the techniques which he learns from them.[64]

Whereas for Baldwin, debates over the translation and glossing of the Bible are one of several contexts that inform his experimentation with glosses, for Bullein they are themselves one of the main subjects of his work. Throughout the *Dialogue*, Bullein's interest in the plain word coexists uneasily with his faith in the complex emblem. A striking example occurs in the tavern scene when Civis replies to one of Susan's enquiries about the meaning of a tapestry with a strange mixture of elucidation and obfuscation:

> *Non hominis consuetudinem sed dei veritatem sequi oportet*: which is, It behoueth vs not to followe the constitutions or customes of men, but to followe the truthe of Godes woorde. And also there is a good saiyng followyng the same. *Doctrinis variis et peregrinis ne circumferamini*. That is, be not ledde or caried about with diuerse or straunge doctrine. Here is more folowyng written vpon the chimney, good wife, whiche I will kepe in store. Oh God, what serpentes thei are, lorde defende me from them! I will rede it to my self. *O mulier omne facinus ausa est plus quam omne, verum nihil est peius nec erit vnquam muliere inter hominum calamitatis*.[65]

---

[61] For the extent of religious confusion in the mid-sixteenth century, see Brigden, *London and the Reformation*, 378–457; and D. M. Palliser, 'Popular Reactions to the Reformation during the Years of Uncertainty 1530–70', in *The English Reformation Revisited*, ed. Christopher Haigh (Cambridge: Cambridge University Press, 1987), 94–113.
[62] Bullein, *Dialogue*, 14.   [63] Bullein, *Dialogue*, 6.
[64] Although Skelton was not, of course, a Reformist writer, he was appropriated as one shortly after his death. See further Griffiths, *Skelton and Poetic Authority*, 160–70.
[65] Bullein, *Dialogue*, 81. 'Oh! Woman is more given to misdeeds than anything else, but nothing is or ever will be a greater disaster than a woman among men.'

Civis here translates faithfully what it seems to him appropriate to tell his wife, but keeps to himself what it does not. In a passage that explicitly declares the importance of following God's word, it is difficult not to see him momentarily as a figure of an obfuscating priest. The glosses reinforce this message, stating that 'The truthe must be followed' and 'The best doctrin is godes Woorde', but Susan's response shows just how difficult it is to follow 'truth' when the word cannot be understood: 'Well, man, well; truth seketh no corners; I perceiue there is some noughtie matter that I know not, but by one thyng that I doe here you rede, make me thinke all the rest is not well, because the firste worde is starke nought, & that is *O Mulier*, which I am sure is nor neuer was good.'[66] The text seems to invite us to mock Susan for parroting the misogynist message she has only half understood; certainly this is a response encouraged by the gloss, which comments: 'Mulier is a naughtie [i.e. 'wicked'] woorde, saied the gentle-women.' Susan here nonetheless shows an ability to get the gist of something that both text and interpreter conspire to keep from her. Moreover, her sharp remark that 'truth seketh no corners' serves not only as a rebuke to Civis, but also as a comment on the (Catholic) practice of withholding the word of God from the common man or woman. What seems at first to be a comic exchange between a man and his wife proves to have a bearing on the question 'What shall I doe to save my life?' For someone—like Susan—who knows no Latin, it seems that the means of salvation are being withheld.

This concern is further reflected in the interplay between text and gloss. For example, when Ambodexter commends Bishop Bonner for being 'Quasi Leo rugiens querens quem deuoret' ['Like a roaring lion seeking whom to devour'], the gloss suggests that Bonner is 'As gentle as a Lion'.[67] For the reader without Latin, the gloss wholly misrepresents the text; it is only the bilingual reader who is able to appreciate the irony. For such a reader, the discrepancy between text and gloss implicitly criticizes not only opposition to the translation of the Bible but also, more generally, the use of any kind of foreign tongue or slant glossing in order to mislead. Of course, the same criticism might be levelled at Bullein's own glossing. As the Bonner example shows, it too presupposes a reader who is comfortable in Latin as well as in English, even inviting such a reader to align himself with Civis and treat all text as matter for the exercise of his ingenuity. For a moment Bullein seems to resemble Baldwin's G. B., blithely unconscious of the implications of his own practice.

---

[66] Bullein, *Dialogue*, 81.
[67] Bullein, *Dialogue*, 24. This gloss is not found in the 1564 edition.

Elsewhere, however, Bullein shows himself to be well aware of the resemblances between his own textual indirections and those for which he criticizes the Catholic Church. Thus, Ambodexter boasts to his colleague that:

> I am alone vpon gloses, I haue arte in store to Sophist, I was brought vp 3 yere with a Frier of Mont Piller: he taught me how to handle *prosa, obscurum, inordinatum,* and *barbarum*, with *genus* and *species* [. . .] I have many rotten rules whiche do serue for the purpose; I learned theim in Louen, they are written in an old barbarous booke.[68]

At first glance, Ambodexter's speech seems to refer purely to the way in which lawyers profiteer from their skilful interpretations; he goes on to declare: 'When wee are at more leasure I will shewe thee all my cunnynge, my gaines and profites'. On further consideration his speech proves to contribute to the text's anti-Catholic satire; the fact that Ambodexter has learnt his art from a friar connects his explicit deceptions with the Catholic *glossa ordinaria*, implying that it too is equally corrupt. When its marginal gloss is taken into account, however, the passage proves to reflect adversely on Bullein's own text as well. Taking the form of an indexing gloss, it reads simply 'gloses'. Although Ambodexter uses the word 'gloss' in its early sense of 'commentary', by virtue of its position in the margin the gloss cannot help but incorporate the secondary sense 'marginal note' as well.[69] It thus implicitly invites comparison of Bullein's glosses with Ambodexter's deceptions. This element of self-satire recurs in a subsequent scene, when Civis promises Roger to reward him for his good service if ever he is able, and the gloss comments: 'Note this note well'.[70] Although this is simply a variant on the common gloss 'Nota', the wordplay creates a startling reflexivity that functions like Ambodexter's 'gloses': if a gloss is liable to abuse not just as a blank signpost, but as a dead end, it calls into question the profitability of glossing at all.

Formalizing such conspicuously diversionary tactics as part of the printed text, glosses of this kind encourage the reader to think both about the way form affects meaning, and the extent to which he himself is in part responsible for making sense of the text. It nonetheless appears from the final episode in the *Dialogue* that Bullein is not wholly comfortable with the implications of his experimentation. Here he abandons the entertaining play between text and gloss, with its implicit trust in the efficacy of human artefacts, in favour

---

[68] Bullein, *Dialogue*, 25.

[69] For early senses of 'gloss' and 'commentary', and the fusion of the two, see Rita Copeland, 'Gloss and Commentary', in *The Oxford Handbook of Medieval Latin Literature*, ed. Ralph H. Hexter and David Townsend (Oxford: Oxford University Press, 2012), 171–91.

[70] Bullein, *Dialogue*, 67.

of providing direct, extra-textual instruction. When Death smites Civis with the dart of pestilence, Civis quickly reconciles himself to his fate; guided by the priest Theologus, he makes an exemplary end, professing his belief in 'all the Articles of my Christian faith', and declaring that 'the Father created me, the Sonne redeemed me, and the Holie Ghost sanctified me and inspired me, whereby I knowe that I am his elected'. His use of the term 'elected' implies that he is thinking in Calvinist terms, yet he nonetheless stresses that it is the unmediated word of God that has given him the certainty that he is chosen: 'One vndefiled mother, the churche, hath thus taught me in that blessed boke of Patriarkes, Prophetes, Martyres, and Jesus with his Apostles, which is Goddes worke.'[71] Civis' emphasis here is on the written word of the Bible, without any of the playfulness or enjoyment of his own interpretative abilities that we have previously seen.

This new plainness is reflected in the glosses as well. Those surrounding Theologus' sermon either provide straightforward summaries or quote Biblical chapter and verse. Thus, when Theologus exhorts us not to 'lamente for our frendes diyng, but rather by the example of their deathes to remember our ende', the gloss reaffirms 'Remember our ende'; when he asserts that 'wee haue not made our selues, wee are his vessels, and are in his sight, and cannot flie from his presence nor run beyonde that rase whiche he hath appoincted us', the gloss cites 'Genesis ii; Sapien. x, Job iii, and Math. xxv' in support.[72] The Biblical citations are remarkable for their succinctness; they do not include any quotation but, by being pared down to the minimum, encourage the readers to look up the exact wording of the Bible for themselves. They thus avoid the danger of partial, flawed, or skewed interpretation. Directing the reader away from Bullein's work towards the Bible, for the first time they reflect the position stated in one of the glosses in the tavern scene, 'The best doctrin is godes Woorde'.[73] They are not so much a continuation of Bullein's earlier method of instruction but, conversely, a reflection of the desire to return to a source that lies safely outside the mutable realm of Bullein's own text.

Like Baldwin, then, Bullein too raises the question to what extent it is possible to trust the written word at all, but whereas Baldwin implies that ultimately there is no such thing as the 'plain word', Bullein ends by reaffirming that there is. The formal diversity of the *Dialogue*, and notably its gestures towards genres with strong Catholic associations, such as the *Everyman*-type morality play, the *ars moriendi*, and even the Utopian

---

[71] Bullein, *Dialogue*, 128.
[72] Bullein, *Dialogue*, 131. In the 1564 edition the reference is to Job xiii. Neither seems unequivocally appropriate.
[73] Bullein, *Dialogue*, 81.

travelogue, may be understood both as part of its challenge to the reader to construct a single 'sentence' from multiple parts, and as an attempt to find viable forms in which to express a new understanding of man's responsibilities for himself, toward others, and toward God. The process of reworking and reclaiming existing genres is not unlike Civis' slanting of general moral precepts to give them a specifically Protestant application. It also posits Bullein's work in its entirety as a gloss, or human approximation; Bullein's suspicion of the very interpretative approach he has encouraged suggests the incompatiblity of saving one's life in this world and saving one's soul. His glossing is the means whereby he discovers that mutability, but the implication is that adages, emblems, and commonplaces are inadequate in the fact of death. Human artefacts and the ingenious diversion they afford are, ultimately, childish things that must be left behind.

TOWARDS A TRADITION: THE GLOSS AS EXPERIMENTAL FORM

Still more than Baldwin's skilful manipulation of the form, Bullein's inconsistencies show the process of working out the implications of glossing a text. Although Bullein too experiments with destabilizing glossing, he ultimately attempts to gloss in a way that provides an escape from the endless proliferations of the fictional text, referring the reader to the Bible as a final, non-negotiable authority. But despite this difference, Bullein's glossing resembles Baldwin's not only in the way it responds to contemporary religious controversy, but also in the way it explores the impact of print on the relations between writer and reader. In both the *Cat* and the *Dialogue*, the lacunae between text and gloss force the reader (as Gutierrez puts it) 'to pay attention not to *what* is being said but to *how* it is said'.[74] By standing physically apart from the text, the glosses draw the reader's attention to the page as object, while by standing metaphorically in an oblique relation to it, they prompt him to read the printed page in the same engaged, active fashion required by Bullein's statues or the hangings in his tavern scene. Both texts almost obsessively test the relationship between the printed and the spoken word. Both invoke the idea of textual stability (Baldwin through the persona of G. B., Bullein through having recourse to the word of God), while also demonstrating that, in the fallen human world, there is no such thing. Bullein implies that speech is necessary to activate the teaching of his emblems, while Baldwin suggests that

[74] Gutierrez, '*Beware the Cat*', 53.

even a printed text shares the instability of its oral sources. In the absence of any reliable point of reference, the onus to discriminate—both textually and religiously—is placed firmly on the reader, who is encouraged to read faithfully and Protestantly even when the word cannot keep faith itself. Thus Baldwin's work, like Bullein's, ultimately proposes reading not just as ethical activity in a general sense, but as a process that mirrors the state of the reader's soul.

For Baldwin and Bullein, then, the form of the text *is* its content. Both writers are at least as much interested in the process of making meaning as they are in the finished text. The way they use the interplay between text and gloss as a means of provoking reader engagement ensures that both the *Dialogue* and the *Cat* make visible on the page their authors' thinking *about* and *through* their own practice. Thus, although both writers reflect the views of writing and reading made current by the Latin humanist writing of the earlier sixteenth century, in which a seriously playful habit of amplification and self-contradiction requires an equivalently inventive response on the part of the reader, they also attest the emergence of diverting glossing in print as a form with its own (unconventional) conventions: a very material form of wit.

6

'Masking naked in a net'
Author and Text in the Works of Gascoigne and Harington

Whereas Baldwin's and Bullein's glossing directly addresses the way in which publication in the relatively new medium of print affects the meaning of a text, slightly later writers use glosses in ways that suggest they expected their readers to interpret them in the light of an established set of print conventions. One concomitant of the increasing use of paratextual material in sixteenth-century printed texts—including epistles to the reader, tables of contents, marginal glosses, and, in some cases, author portraits—was an emerging interest, among authors, in the way in which the format of a book shaped reception of the work it contained. For some, this interest found expression in the use of print conventions to fashion a distinct authorial persona. While Spenser's *Shepheardes Calendar* is the most familiar instance of this phenomenon, the works of George Gascoigne (1534/5–1577) and Sir John Harington (1560–1612) are two further cases in point.[1]

Perhaps unsurprisingly, these authors have not often been paired. Although both were authors and soldiers, Gascoigne was a professional lawyer as well as a writer and a mercenary, whereas Harington's authorship and military service were both the result of his exceptionally good connections: his father, whose first wife was Henry VIII's illegitimate daughter, was noted for his strong loyalty to Elizabeth prior to her succession, and their association was reaffirmed when Elizabeth became godmother to Harington junior, who was attached to the court from an early age.[2] Gascoigne's publication history clearly indicates that his writing was a commercial endeavour, whereas Harington's writings are presented as

---

[1] For the glossing of the *Shepheardes Calendar*, see the Introduction, note 7.
[2] For Gascoigne's early life, see Gillian Austen, *George Gascoigne* (Woodbridge: D.S. Brewer, 2008), 22–5; for Harington's life, see D. H. Craig, *Sir John Harington* (Boston: Twayne, 1985), 1–30; and cf. Jason Scott-Warren, *Sir John Harington and the Book as Gift* (Oxford: Oxford University Press, 2001), 18–20.

consummately amateur—even though they, just as much as Gascoigne's, are designed to further his career. Both writers, however, use their works to fashion a distinct textual identity, and do so in part through a creative use of print conventions. Whether working within the parameters of reader expectation, or going against them, both assume a common knowledge of the signals given by layout and paratexts about a work and its author, and use them to shape the face they present to the public.

For both writers, an interest in glossing is just one aspect of a wider interest in print publication. Both Gascoigne and Harington were actively engaged in the preparation of their works for the press. Gascoigne informs his readers of his attention to detail in the production of the woodcuts for *The Noble Art of Venerie* (1575) and of his determination that a servant should oversee the proofs of *The Dromme of Doomesday* (1576) when he was himself unwell; indeed, he does so in the context of apologizing for the fact that, in consequence, 'there have passed some faultes much contrary unto both our meanings and desires'.[3] Harington shows similar pride in the technical innovation of his 'pictures . . . all cut in brasse' in his *Orlando Furioso* (1591), while the surviving printer's copy-texts of both the *Orlando* and the later *New Discourse* (1596) include his handwritten instructions to the printer as to which typeface to use and how to deal with particular problems of page layout.[4] Both writers, too, are clearly aware of publication as a means of furthering their careers: for Gascoigne, by enabling him to fashion his life into a fable of moral instruction, and thereby quite literally invent himself as an author; for Harington, by drawing attention to his desire for preferment at court.[5] Yet both also show an awareness of the dangers as well as the benefits attaching to print publication—of poetry in particular. Their creative use of paratexts is intended largely to circumvent such dangers, and even turn them to their own ends.

The vexed status of poetry in the later sixteenth century is clearly apparent from the *Defence of Poetry* with which Harington prefaced his *Orlando Furioso*, as well as from Sidney's earlier *Apology for Poetry* (a. 1586, pub. 1595). For Harington, the problem is all in the minds of critics who 'terme all that is written in verse Poesie' and, refusing to distinguish between occasional songs

---

[3] George Gascoigne, *The Droomme of Doomes Day*, in *The Complete Works*, ed. John W. Cunliffe, 2 vols. (Cambridge: Cambridge University Press, 1907–10), 2: 215. For discussion, including the suggestion that Gascoigne's illness may have been a fiction, see Austen, *Gascoigne*, 169–70.

[4] John Harington, *Orlando Furioso*, ed. Robert McNulty (Oxford: Clarendon Press, 1972), 17. For Harington's involvement with his publishers, see further W. Greg, 'An Elizabethan Printer and his Copy', *The Library*, 4th ser., vol. iv (1923-24), 102–18; and Ruth Hughey, 'The Harington Manuscript at Arundel Castle', *The Library*, 4th ser., vol. xv (1935), 403–4.

[5] See further Austen, *Gascoigne*, 14–18 and 84–115; and Scott-Warren, *Harington*, 1–24.

and sonnets and serious heroic or allegorical writing, declare that poetry 'is a nurse of lies, a pleaser of fooles, a breeder of dangerous errors, and an inticer to wantonnes'.[6] Sidney had previously made a very similar case.[7] However, it is a third treatise, George Puttenham's *Arte of English Poesie* (1560s; pub. 1589), that is key to understanding the context in which the writing and printing of poetry was debated. Unlike either Sidney's or Harington's, Puttenham's treatise is a verse-writing manual, aimed specifically at the courtier and at the gentleman who would like to think himself one. What Puttenham says of his reasons for writing is oxymoronic: he claims both that it provides instruction in the necessary courtly art of versification and that the true courtier has no need of instruction in the art, because verse is artificial, and artifice is the courtier's natural condition. His professed endeavour is to create versifiers so skilled that they appear to have no skill at all; the courtly poet will have the ability 'when he is most artificial so to disguise and cloak it as it may not appear, nor seem to proceed from him by any study or trade of rules, but to be his natural'.[8] For Puttenham this kind of artificiality is not only a courtly accomplishment, but a metaphor for the courtier's character: as appears from his famous definition of allegory as 'the *courtly* figure . . . when we speak one thing and think another, and . . . our words and meanings meet not', writing verse and succeeding at court are both forms of feigning or dissembling dissembled to be no feigning at all.[9]

It is by showing how inextricably poetry and class were connected that Puttenham's treatise sheds light on the negative connotations of print publication. Puttenham's assertion that, for the courtier or aristocrat, verse must above all appear effortless, is clearly incompatible with going to the effort of commercial publication.[10] Although there is sufficient evidence of the publication of poetry and other literary works by 'gentlemen' to suggest that the 'stigma of print' was perceived rather than real, Puttenham's treatise nonetheless provides a potential rationale for it.[11] Both Gascoigne

---

[6] Harington, *Orlando*, 2, 4.

[7] Sir Philip Sidney, *A Defence of Poetry*, in *English Renaissance Literary Criticism*, ed. Brian Vickers (Oxford: Oxford University Press, 1999), 369–71.

[8] George Puttenham, *The Arte of English Poesie*, in *English Renaissance Literary Criticism*, 292. For the complex relationship between art and nature in Puttenham's treatise, see Derek Attridge, 'Puttenham's Perplexity: Nature, Art, and the Supplement in Renaissance Poetic Theory', in *Literary Theory/Renaissance Texts*, ed. Patricia Parker and David Quint, (Baltimore: Johns Hopkins University Press, 1986), 257–79.

[9] Puttenham, *Arte*, 247. The italics are mine.

[10] See further J. W. Saunders, 'The Stigma of Print: A Note on the Social Bases of Tudor Poetry', *Essays in Criticism* 1 (1951), 139–64; cf. also Scott-Warren, *Harington*, 32–5; and Richard Helgerson, *The Elizabethan Prodigals* (Berkeley: University of California Press, 1976), 1–15; and 44–57 on Gascoigne specifically.

[11] See further Steven W. May, 'Tudor Aristocrats and the Mythical "Stigma of Print"', *Renaissance Papers* (1980), 11–18.

and Harington are clearly aware of the issue: the courtier Harington finds courtly excuses for his writing, while the professional Gascoigne disguises himself, in the first instance, as a gentleman who has unwittingly been published by others.[12] For both writers the construction of a textual alter ego—an artificial self that appears to be entirely natural—is a means of negotiating the minefield of print publication.

Gascoigne's and Harington's creation of second selves in print is found in its most literal form in their respective uses of author portraits. On the title page of his *Orlando Furioso*, Harington's portrait appears as a small part of a large and elaborate design. Like the engravings that appear at the beginning of each canto, the title page is modelled on that of his source, the 1584 Francesco edition of Ariosto's *Orlando*. But although the elaborate architectural frame (including Corinthian columns, an ornate broken pediment, and Mars and Venus as caryatids) is reproduced in every detail, at the foot of the title page, where Ariosto has an image of the Muse, Harington substitutes a portrait of himself and his spaniel Bungey.[13] Thus, whereas Ariosto posits the Muse as his ultimate source, Harington focuses instead on his own position as enabler and disseminator of his work. But although he makes such an overt claim to the status of author, the inclusion of Bungey means that Harington presents himself not as a perfected, isolated figure, but as his everyday self, complete with dog, and complete with a degree of irreverence towards the mammoth work he has just translated. Simultaneously claiming ownership of the book and making light of the labour it involved, the title page is an embodiment of courtly sprezzatura.[14]

In contrast, Gascoigne's portrait in *The Steele Glass* and *Complaynt of Phylomene* (1576) appears both amateur and impressively serious.[15] Taking up an entire page, it too includes both a pictorial and a verbal

---

[12] For Harington's excuses, see *Orlando*, 13–15. There may be a wry reference to the 'stigma of print' in Gascoigne's *Dan Bartholmew of Bathe*, where the frustrated lover says to his lady: 'Thy love was light, and lusted styll to leape. / The rimes which pleased thee were all in print, / And mine were ragged, hard for to be read' (*Collected Works*, 1: 117); unfaithfulness appears to be equated with a preference for print over manuscript.

[13] Cf. Evelyn B. Tribble, *Margins and Marginality: The Printed Page in Early Modern England* (Charlottesville: University Press of Virginia, 1993), 88–9; and for other such elaborate frontispieces, see Margery Corbett and Ronald Lightbown, *The Comely Frontispiece: The Emblematic Titlepage in England 1550–1660* (London: Routledge, 1979), 1–47.

[14] As Scott-Warren has argued, the epigraph that Harington includes on his title page, 'Principibus placuisse viris non vltima est' ['to have won favour with the foremost men is not the lowest glory'], implies that he seeks to make a career out of service at court, and although the substitution of his own portrait for that of the Muse seems a bold assertion of authorship, it too may be read as prioritizing his role as courtier—that is, his 'real-life' self—over that of author (*Harington*, 52–5).

[15] Austen suggests that the woodcut may be a self-portrait (*Gascoigne*, 157–8).

element, showing the head and shoulders of the author, with the tools of war to one side of his head and a shelf of books to the other, and with Gascoigne's motto 'Tam Marti quam Mercurio' beneath. Whereas Harington's motto is only a small part of an elaborate title page, Gascoigne's is so prominent that his portrait immediately proclaims itself as an emblem. This has significant implications for the way in which the volume as a whole is understood. Contemporary emblems, such as those popularized by Geoffrey Whitney, typically included not only a woodcut and a motto, but also a short verse; the full meaning of the emblem was revealed by a simultaneous 'reading' of all three elements.[16] Gascoigne's use of a combined portrait and motto at the beginning of *The Steele Glass* and *Complaynt of Phylomene* thus implies that the volume as a whole takes the place of the verse; that is, that the writings it contains should be interpreted as the third element in his self-portrait. Not only does this suggest that Gascoigne, like Baldwin before him, is concerned to encourage active reading, but the book becomes an instance of what Douglas Bruster has defined as 'embodied writing', which granted 'a bodily presence to fictional characters, and a fictional identity to real bodies . . . mediated the imaginary and the actual [so that] the relation between person and print as characters, authors, and books became much closer to each other, and sometimes interchangeable.'[17] For Bruster, this phenomenon is traceable not just in the creation of fictional characters that only thinly veil their historical counterparts, but also in the independent existence achieved by characters such as John Lyly's Euphues and Nicholas Breton's Pasquil, which increasingly became identified with their authors.[18] Gascoigne's title page suggests a third way in which a book might come to 'stand for' its author. It thus establishes a different kind of authorial presence from

---

[16] Geoffrey Whitney, *A Choice of Emblems and Other Devices* (Leiden, 1586); and cf. George Wither, *A Collection of Emblemes* (London: John Grismond, 1635). For emblem books see further Michael Bath, *Speaking Pictures: English Emblem Books and Renaissance Culture* (London: Longman, 1994); for discussion of the different possible relationships between the pictorial and verbal elements of an emblem, cf. also David Graham, 'Pictures Speaking, Pictures Spoken To: Guillaume de la Perriere and Emblematic "Illustration"', in *Visual and Verbal Pictures: Essays in Honour of Michael Bath*, ed. Alison Saunders and Peter Davidson (Glasgow: Glasgow Emblem Studies, 2005), 69–88; and John Manning, *The Emblem* (London: Reaktion, 2002), esp. 80–140.

[17] Douglas Bruster, 'The Structural Transformation of Print in Late Elizabethan England', in *Print, Manuscript, and Performance: The Changing Relations of the Media in Early Modern England*, ed. Arthur F. Marotti and Michael D. Bristol (Columbus: Ohio State University Press, 2000), 50, 56.

[18] For Euphues, see *The Complete Works of John Lyly*, ed. R. Warwick Bond, 3 vols. (Oxford: Clarendon Press, 1902), 1: 177–375. Breton published four works under the persona of Pasquil in 1600: *Pasquils Mad-cap* (STC 3675 and 3676); *Pasquils Fooles-cap* (STC 3677.5); *Pasquils Mistresse* (STC 3678); and *Pasquils passe, and passeth not* (STC 3679).

Harington's. Whereas Harington introduces a vignette of his private, everyday self into his public, published work, Gascoigne implies that his entire book is an image of—or even a substitute for—himself. This difference is sustained throughout their writing and publication histories. Whereas Gascoigne constructs a series of riddles about the precise relationship of his writing to his life, Harington treats his work as an extension of his person. Gascoigne's and Harington's portraits are emblematic of two very different experiments with self-fashioning in print which—precisely because of their differences—provide an insight into print's 'mundus significans' in the late-sixteenth century: that is, its 'storehouse of signifying capacities potentially available to each member of a given community.'[19] Their glosses allow us to explore this further.

A CHAPTER OF SUPPOSES: THE GLOSSING OF GASCOIGNE'S *POSIES*

For Gascoigne, print provides the opportunity for both self-revelation and self-concealment. His first publication, *A Hundreth Sundrie Flowers* (1573), is ostensibly a collection of works by diverse hands, modelled on Tottel's *Songs and Sonets*; although the addition of Gascoigne's motto 'Tam Marti quam Mercurio' to several of the lyrics identifies him as one of the many supposed contributors, there is no suggestion that he is the sole author. As Elizabeth Heale has argued, this manner of publication gives the impression that Gascoigne was not himself seeking publicity by printing his works.[20] At the same time, the fact that he alone of all the gentlemen contributors is named in the table of contents implies that he is foremost in his coterie.[21] This strategy allows him to combine seeming modesty with actual self-promotion. It also enables the construction of the text in its entirety as a riddle. Like the *Songs and Sonets*, *A Hundreth* is constructed as what Austen has termed a 'reality game'.[22] The use of devices to identify the various contributors and the provision of contextualizing snippets of information about the situations supposedly giving

---

[19] Thomas M. Greene, *The Light in Troy: Imitation and Discovery in Renaissance Poetry* (New Haven: Yale University Press, 1982), 20.

[20] Elizabeth Heale, 'Songs, Sonnets, and Autobiography: Self-Representation in Sixteenth-Century Verse Miscellanies', in *Betraying Our Selves: Forms of Self-Representation in Early Modern English Texts*, ed. Sheila Ottway and Helen Wilcox (2000), 66–7; and cf. Wendy Wall, *The Imprint of Gender: Authorship and Publication in the English Renaissance* (Ithaca: Cornell University Press, 1993), 243–5.

[21] George Gascoigne, *A Hundreth Sundrie Flowers*, ed. G. W. Pigman (Oxford: Oxford University Press, 2000), 2.

[22] Austen, *Gascoigne*, 70.

rise to the lyrics suggest that the verses can be traced back to actual situations and relationships, and so reaffirm the pretence (which is key to the *Songs and Sonets* too) that the reader is being granted privileged access to writings that were formerly circulated only among friends.[23] There is an important difference, however: whereas the *Songs and Sonets* provide fictional information about real writers, in *A Hundreth* the authors, too, are so many fictional masks for Gascoigne himself. Here, for the first time, we see Gascoigne's simultaneous understanding and undermining of the 'language' of print: that is, of the implicit contract between author and reader as to how a text signifies. *A Hundreth* does not simply give an appearance of transgressing the boundary between public and private, as the *Songs and Sonets* do, but parodies that trope. The playfulness for which Gascoigne himself later condemned the content of *A Hundreth* is thus paralleled in its form: Gascoigne uses the printed text as a mask that, when removed, only reveals a further mask beneath.

The elaborate pretences of *A Hundreth* both anticipate the attention-seeking anonymity of Spenser's *Shepheardes Calendar* and serve as a means of circumventing the 'stigma' of print. Yet they are also play for play's sake. The relatively wide dissemination of a printed text creates the opportunity not just to imitate the intimacy of manuscript circulation, but to establish a new kind of intimacy, based on riddle: on what is *not* known by the readers about the author, rather than on what is. Gascoigne quite evidently delights in this opportunity. His interest in blurring the boundaries between public and private, and between truth and fiction, remained a constant throughout his career, even when (in his later works) he ostensibly sought to assert a much more sober identity. *The Posies* (1575), *The Steele Glass* (1576), and *The Dromme of Doomesday* (1576) all claim him as a reformed prodigal and moralist, whose experience gives him the authority to instruct, and whose repentance of his previous profligacy renders him worthy of patronage.[24] But in these works too, Gascoigne retains his interest in print as a means of concealment as well as revelation, and in calling into question which is which.

The Posies—a revised, and apparently simplified, version of *A Hundreth*—is a textbook example of the way in which the form of a text affects its meaning.[25] Although its contents are virtually identical to

---

[23] For the *Songs and Sonets*, see Arthur F. Marotti, *Manuscript, Print, and the English Renaissance Lyric* (Ithaca: Cornell University Press), 212–27; and cf. Wall, *Imprint*, 23–30.

[24] See further Austen, *Gascoigne*, 84–102 and 153–75; and cf. Arthur F. Kinney, *Humanist Poetics: Thought, Rhetoric, and Fiction in Sixteenth-Century England* (Amherst: University of Massachusetts Press, 1986), 89–117.

[25] For the relationship between the texts see Pigman (ed.), *Hundreth*, pp. xlv–lxv; and cf. Austen, *Gascoigne*, 85–6.

those of *A Hundreth*, the way in which they are framed is entirely different. The lyrics lose their contextualizing introductions, while several other poems gain marginal glosses, and the whole volume is prefaced by a large number of commendatory verses. Moreover, unlike *A Hundreth*, *The Posies* is unambiguously ascribed to Gascoigne. Not only does his name appear on the title page, but the first paratext a reader encounters is a letter from Gascoigne, in his own name, in which he confesses authorship of *A Hundreth* and claims that he is republishing it, in its revised form of *The Posies*, in order to tame its more licentious elements.[26] He repeatedly stresses his new division of the contents into 'Floures . . . more pleasant than profitable'; 'Hearbes', or 'morall discourses . . . more profitable than pleasant'; and 'Weedes'. He also goes out of his way to stress the instructive nature of his writing, arguing that even the 'Weedes' may benefit the reader by providing negative exempla.[27] Attention is redirected from individual works to the volume as a whole, and the latter is anchored to verifiable external reality both by the assertion that Gascoigne is its author and by the prefatory verses whose authors are identified by plain initials, rather than by riddling mottoes.[28] Just as these changes create a performance of openness, stressing the author's concern for his readers' edification, the provision of glosses, too, promises to bridge any gaps between author and reader. The paratext of *The Posies* confirms what Gascoigne says so emphatically in his prefatory letter: that this is a useful and profitable book.

Despite its language of profit and morality, the work does not necessarily reflect those qualities. To identify the 'Weedes' and place them together in a discrete section of the volume simply enables readers who so desire to avoid the moral parts of the text altogether, while the prefatory verses are so very numerous that the suspicion arises that Gascoigne authored some of them himself; it is especially suggestive that he draws attention to their vast number in a poem entitled 'The opinion of the auctor himself after all these commendations'.[29] Even as the verses and Gascoigne's response to them evince a clear awareness of how such commendations are meant to work—by incorporating within the book external judgements

---

[26] Ironically, it was *The Posies*, not *A Hundreth*, which was censored. See Austen, *Gascoigne*, 85–6.

[27] George Gascoigne, *Complete Works*, 1: 13. Gascoigne's re-presentation of his earlier work allows him to claim that he publishes *The Posies* as a 'reformed man' who seeks to correct the works of his 'deformed youth', but it also enables him unambiguously to assert his authorship of the very works of which he is repenting; his technique is comparable to that of Chaucer in the *Retraction* to the *Canterbury Tales*, where he lists his works in considerable detail under the pretext of repudiating those 'that sownen into sin'.

[28] At least some of these would have been instantly recognizable to Gascoigne's contemporaries; 'T. Ch.', for example, seems clearly to indicate the egregious Thomas Churchyard.

[29] Gascoigne, *Complete Works*, 1: 33.

on it—they raise the possibility that, in this case, the judgements themselves are fictional.

Such playfulness is also in evidence in the glosses to *The Posies*, which similarly call into question where authorial invention ends and 'reality' begins. As appears from his later works, Gascoigne was more than capable of glossing in a conventionally directive way; in *The Dromme of Doomesday*, for example, the majority of the glosses are indexing ones, supplemented by a large number of Biblical citation glosses.[30] Anchoring the teaching of the text in Scripture, these are unambiguously useful and profitable. Within *The Posies*, Gascoigne states that its glossing too is intended to be helpful; he asserts that the various literal glosses to the tragic play *Jocasta* were begun 'at request of a gentlewoman who understoode not poetycall words or termes', and declares his 'trust those and the rest of my notes throughout the booke, shall not be hurtfull to any reader'.[31] The implication is that his glossing, like his division of 'Weedes' from 'Hearbes' and 'Flowers', witnesses his consideration towards his readers; just as the licentiousness of *A Hundreth* has supposedly been made safe by articulating the 'true meaning' of the work, the glosses to *The Posies* will assist the reader who wishes fully to understand that meaning.

At first sight the glosses to *Jocasta* do indeed appear to be helpful, serving primarily to index the text and indicate its *sententiae*. As commonplaces in their own right, the majority draw attention to the 'herbal' morals that may be extracted from the work. Thus, one series of consecutive glosses teaches that 'Youth seeth not so much as age'; that 'Ambition doth destroye al: equalytie doth maynteyne al things'; and that 'If the head be evill the body cannot be good'.[32] In their implication that the text is a useful storehouse of universally applicable morals, they resemble glosses of the kind found in Copland's edition of the *Eneados*, and tacitly support Gascoigne's claim that this is a 'reformed' text. Yet just as Copland's glosses fail to account for the complexities of the *Eneados*, Gascoigne's too are problematic. Although *Jocasta* is a drama, its speeches are glossed without reference to the character of the speaker or the context in which they are speaking, and they are phrased unconditionally, asserting (for example) that 'Content *is* rich', not that content *is said to be* rich.[33] On at least one occasion this encourages a seriously misguided reading of the text. When

---

[30] For the *Dromme*, see further C. T. Prouty, *George Gascoigne: Elizabethan Courtier, Soldier, Poet* (New York: Columbia University Press, 1942), 260–77, and Austen, *Gascoigne*, 168–75.

[31] Gascoigne, *Complete Works*, 1: 326. The identity of the unknown gentlewoman itself becomes part of the 'reality game'.

[32] Gascoigne, *Complete Works*, 1: 272–3.

[33] Gascoigne, *Complete Works*, 1: 273. The italics are mine.

Etheocles cites Cicero in the course of a speech in which he illegitimately refuses to give up the kingdom of Thebes to his brother, a gloss notes that this is 'Tullyes opinyon' and, by identifying the source of Etheocles' speech, momentarily appears to authorize the use he makes of it.[34] With just a few exceptions, the glosses are essentially non-dramatic, treating the play not as dialogue, but as authoritatively monologic text.

These glosses of Gascoigne's thus recall Baldwin's experiment in making the spoken word 'book-like': providing single, extractable morals as an integral part of the printed text, they suggest the limitations of such an instructive approach. Although on the evidence of *Jocasta* alone, this effect could be accidental, from the glossing of the play *Supposes* it appears that such is not the case. Here the glosses are demonstrably parodic, and their parody depends for effect on Gascoigne's undermining of one of the assumptions that underpins conventional glossing: that glosses refer to an external, verifiable 'truth'. The action of *Supposes* involves numerous deceptions and assumptions of false identities, and the glosses at first appear to indicate each stage in the thickening of the plot; they identify 'The first suppose & grownd of all the suposes' and numerous instances of 'Another supose', 'A doltish supose', 'A stoute supose', 'A shamelesse supose', and so on.[35] The number of 'supposes' marked by the glosses considerably outnumbers those that materially affect the plot. Those identified in the margins prove also to include suppositions, conceits, and mistakes, in a continuation of the kind of punning that Gascoigne employs in the very first lines of his Prologue: 'I suppose you are assembled here, supposing to reape the fruite of my travayles: and to be playne, I meane presently to presente you with a Comedie called Supposes: the verye name wherof may peradventure drive into every of your heades a sundry Suppose, to suppose, the meaning of our supposes.'[36] Such repetition to the point of senselessness is replicated in the glosses, which not only ring the changes on the different possible senses of 'suppose', but in doing so parody the common use of glosses as a form of index. A second kind of parody is found in glosses that identify as 'supposes' expressions by individual characters of snippets of sententious or proverbial wisdom. For example, the exclamation 'Fye upon the Devill, it is a thing almost unpossible for a man nowe a dayes to handle money, but the mettal will sticke on his fingers' is glossed 'An other suppose'.[37] Such a gloss implies that a commonplace is

---

[34] Gascoigne, *Complete Works*, 1: 272.
[35] Gascoigne, *Complete Works*, 1: 191, 194, 200, 204, 207, 215, 216, 222, 223, 224, 226, and 227, to list but a few.
[36] Gascoigne, *Complete Works*, 1: 188.
[37] Gascoigne, *Complete Works*, 1: 215.

common only because it commonly goes unchallenged, and that what is accepted as common sense may not really be sense at all. It thus resembles the glossing of *Jocasta* in calling into question the validity of extracting universal morals from a particular text, but does so more ostentatiously. And not only do the text's morals vanish on investigation, so too does their author. The self-evidently unreliable and performative quality of the *Supposes* glosses invites the question 'who is speaking?', and although the most obvious answer might seem to be 'Gascoigne', the notorious glosses in *Dan Bartholmew of Bathe* reveal that, in *The Posies*, the author is far from being a stable figure external to the text. Rather, he is himself a textual construct.

The glosses in *Dan Bartholmew* complicate what is already an elaborate 'reality game' in the work. *Dan Bartholmew* is a narrative poem that records an unsuccessful courtship, and includes within it the love lyrics to which the courtship gives rise. The majority of its glosses are literal ones, providing interpretations of words that might give difficulty, but there are several that are conspicuously peculiar, and that are the more disconcerting for being interspersed among those that give direct practical assistance to the reader. The first of these oddities is attached to the lines where Dan Bartholmew recalls an encounter with his lover in which she claims he is the cause of her unfaithfulness. His lines are slightly cryptic; he recounts how:

> Not so content, thou furthermore didst sweare
> That of thy selfe thou never meant to swerve,
> For proofe wherof thou didst the colour weare,
> Which might bewray, what saint thou ment to serve.
> And that thy blood was sacrificed eke,
> To manyfest thy stedfast martyred mynde.

Far from elucidating the text, the gloss is more cryptic still; it comments that: 'These thinges are mistical and not to bee understoode but by Thaucthour him selfe.'[38] Subsequent glosses attached to references in the text to 'a trustie token', an unidentified 'noble face', and a certain 'Ippocrace' are equally elusive, each in turn identifying 'Another misterie', and ostentatiously withholding any further information.[39]

As Austen says, these glosses 'seem gratuitously provocative... [intended] to provoke speculation about the relation of the narrative to external reality'—not least about the identity of Dan Bartholmew himself.[40] Like the *Supposes* glosses, they become a running joke, but by implying that the

---

[38] Gascoigne, *Complete Works*, 1: 110.
[39] Gascoigne, *Complete Works*, 1: 112–13.
[40] Austen, *Gascoigne*, 96.

glossed lines of the text refer to people or incidents that might be recognized by readers in the know, they also contribute to Gascoigne's construction of an authorship puzzle that is more devious even than that of *A Hundreth*. The narrator of *Dan Bartholmew* is an anonymous 'Reporter', who insists that his story is the record of an actual sequence of events; he claims to know Dan Bartholmew, and to have attended him on his sickbed. There is something disingenous about his claim to be writing the literal truth, however. He several times refers to Dan Bartholmew as the 'Green Knight', and the Green Knight himself appears later in *The Posies* as the author of the poetic sequence 'The Fruite of Fetters', lamenting his misspent life in terms that suggest considerable overlap with Gascoigne's own biography.[41] If the Green Knight is a figure of Gascoigne as well as a figure of Dan Bartholmew, then the latter must also represent Gascoigne, and it becomes possible to attribute the various unsuccessful love affairs to the real man—with attendant questions, of course, about the identity of the ladies. The reality game of *A Hundreth* has thus been displaced from the paratext to the body of the text, and there is a teasing suggestion that *The Posies* in its entirety should be read as a roman à clef.

The 'misterie' glosses do not just replicate or draw attention to this puzzle, but add a further layer. In particular, the gloss that refers to 'Thaucthour him selfe' not only raises questions about the relation of various characters to the author, but also about the identity of the author *within* the book. Is the one who understands the 'misterie' Dan Bartholmew, to whose lyric the gloss is attached, the Reporter, who is responsible for making Dan Bartholmew's narration 'book-like', or Gascoigne, as creator of Dan Bartholmew and the Reporter alike? The fact that this allusion appears in a gloss, in a text where many other glosses are elucidating ones, raises the expectation that it will clarify such questions of identity. By ostentatiously withholding information where clarification might be expected, it makes very clear that the text cannot be verified by reference to anything outside itself. Although there is a strong possibility that Dan Bartholmew's amours are 'empty secrets', and that Gascoigne is more interested in giving the impression that he has something to hide than he is to hide it, the gloss nonetheless invokes the existence of an objective measure of 'truth' by

---

[41] Austen also draws attention to the connection between *The Fruit of Fetters* and the 'overtly autobiographical account' of Gascoigne's military service in *Dulce Bellum Inexpertis* (*Gascoigne*, 96–8), arguing that this sequence of correspondences might be extended to include the protagonist of *The Adventures of Master F.J.*, too. Gabriel Harvey made a similar connection, noting at the end of *Dulce Bellum* in his copy of *The Posies* (now Bodleian Library Mal. 792 (1)): 'The like pleasurable History of the Green Knight, p. 175. Item, Gascoignes Woodmanship, p. 156' (p. cxii).

which to judge the text, only to reveal that it, too, is unverifiable.[42] Thus, although Gascoigne's glossing depends largely on parody of indexing and sententious glosses, it goes beyond parody for parody's sake. Rather, it is part of a wilful misuse of the 'language' of print which renders his artificial printed self indistinguishable from his natural one; in Puttenham's terms, his textual self not only 'surmounts' his own identity, but is artful enough to be taken for the real thing.[43]

'YO[R] INTEREST IS MOCH IN THE WORK BECAUS YT IS MOSTE IN THE WRYTER': SIR JOHN HARINGTON'S PERSONAL GLOSSING

Whereas Gascoigne's reinvention of himself is possible only in print, Sir John Harington's takes the form of an attempt to negate the distance between himself and his readers. Gascoigne's books turn the relationship between his real and his printed selves into a riddle, but Harington implies that his book is a window on his innermost self; his joking description, mid-career, of his own writing as 'masking naked in a net' is in some ways a remarkably accurate one.[44] It is nonetheless as much a performance as Gascoigne's. In his first published work, his translation of Ariosto's *Orlando Furioso*, this is evident not only from his portrait on its title page, but also from the text of his translation and its apparatus. Providing both a commentary at the end of each canto and marginal glosses throughout (neither of which has a counterpart in Ariosto), Harington entirely reframes the work. As appears from his explanation of the different levels of interpretation in his commentary, he is specifically concerned to classicize it, applying the approach of academic commentary to his English translation of Ariosto's Italian text. He states that he will provide:

The Morall that we may apply it to our owne maners and disposition to the amendment of the same.

The Historie both that the true ground of the poem may appear (for learned men hold that a perfect poeme must be grounded in truth) (as I shew

---

[42] For 'empty secrets', see Richard Rambuss, *Spenser's Secret Career* (Cambridge: Cambridge University Press, 1993), 53.

[43] Puttenham, *Arte*, 293. Harvey's comment in his copy of *The Posies* suggests that Gascoigne's confidence in the sophistication of his readers may have been misplaced. Harvey criticizes the Green Knight as if he were a straightforward representation of the author, rather than one of a complex series of linked personae, noting darkly that 'leuity [is] his special faulte' (192).

[44] See below, note 69.

more at large on another place) as also to explane some things that are lightly touched by him as examples of all times, either of old or of late.

The Allegorie of some things that are meerely fabulous, yet have an allegorical sense which every bodie at the first shew cannot perceive.

The Allusion, of fictions to be applied to some things done or written of times past, and also where without offence applied to times present.[45]

Harington's emphasis in the usefulness of his work may have been intended to counteract the circumstances that gave rise to its composition; his translation of the scurrilous Canto XXVIII reputedly so offended the Queen that she commanded him to translate the entire epic.[46] The addition of the commentary asserts the seriousness with which he undertook the task. It also contains a memory of the self-authorizing strategies used by Gower, Douglas, and (more recently) by Spenser, serving as a visual claim to the status of the work and to Harington's own achievement in translating it.[47]

As Evelyn Tribble has argued, however, Harington quite systematically 'domesticates' Ariosto, introducing references to English rather than Italian landscapes, heroes, and histories, and—more significantly—including in both his translation and his commentary a large number of allusions to his own friends and family.[48] Far from classicizing or monumentalizing the work, these allusions have the opposite effect: they make it more familiar. Thus, Harington interrupts his allegorization of Rogero's flight from Alcyna: 'As soone is a temperat and moderat mind discovered in prosperitie as in adversitie, and (as Tully saith) a wise man is neither Adversis rebus oppressus nec elatus secundis; to which effect I remember a verse of my fathers.'[49] This he quotes in its entirety before recalling himself to the task in hand with the phrase 'But to proceede in the Allegorie . . .'. He thus both lends classical weight to his work by citing Cicero in its moralization and grants his father equivalent authoritative status, as the anecdote puts his father in the position of Cicero's wise man. As Tribble rightly suggests, such shifts from universal moral to private memory draw attention to the distance between Harington and the reader, allowing the reader to

[45] Harington, *Orlando*, 17.
[46] See *Nugae Antiquae* (1804), pp. x–xi, quoted in Harington, *Orlando*, p. xxv; see further Scott-Warren, *Harington*, 26–35.
[47] For Gower, see the Introduction; and for Douglas, see Chapter 3. For the presentation of the *Shepheardes Calendar*, see Steven K. Galbraith, '"English" Black-Letter Type and Spenser's *Shepheardes Calendar*', *Spenser Studies* 23 (2008), 13–40; Geller, 'You Can't Tell a Book by Its Contents: (Mis)Interpretation in/of Spenser's *The Shepheardes Calendar*', *Spenser Studies* 13 (1999), 23–64; Michael McCanles, '*The Shepheardes Calendar* as Document and Monument', *SEL* 22 (1982), 5–19; and Ruth Samson Luborsky, 'The Allusive Presentation of *The Shepheardes Calendar*', *Spenser Studies* 1 (1980), 29–68.
[48] Tribble, *Margins and Marginality*, 92–8.   [49] Harington, *Orlando*, 99.

approach a close-knit social circle without ever quite admitting him to it.[50] At the same time, however, they also afford a glimpse of Harington's thought-processes as he free-associates on the printed page. The effect is strangely intimate; like overhearing his speaking voice, it creates the momentary illusion of Harington's actual presence.

In contrast with the discursive text and commentary, Harington's marginal glosses at first appear to be limited to the provision of material directly relevant to the matter at hand, and thus to be less personal. He himself defines their role as a fairly restricted one, writing that:

> I have in the marginall notes quoted the apt similitudes and pithie sentences or adages with the best descriptions and the excellent imitations and the places and authors from whence they are taken.
>
> Further, where divers stories in this work seeme in many places abruptly broken off I have set directions in the margent where to find the continuance of every such storie.[51]

Unlike the appropriation of authority by Harington's intimates in the commentary, the kind of glosses outlined here leave the way clear for the reader to make the text his own. Yet despite Harington's clear definitions of the functions of gloss and commentary, in practice they are not wholly distinct; indeed, at the end of his description of the commentary, Harington himself admits that there is a certain degree of overlap when he writes that: 'if any other notes happen to come after, it is but for want of rome in the margent that they were faine to be put out of their due place'.[52]

The margins too show evidence of material that, according to Harington's own division of parts, has no business there. A number of glosses perpetuate the 'domesticating' tendencies of text and commentary in a way that anticipates the glossing of Speght's prefatory matter in his edition of Chaucer; thus, a reference in the text to the Bishop of Bath is glossed: 'The last Bishop, M. Godwin, a reverend man, told me that epitheton was unfit for the sea at that time'; and a reference to a bulwark in the river Poe elicits the comment 'the like is at London bridge'.[53] Harington frequently digresses into the provision of purely incidental information, as when he observes that: 'Many times wise men are readier to beleeve straunge

---

[50] Tribble, *Margins and Marginality*, 96. Tiffany Jo Werth argues that Harington's glossing in *Orlando Furioso* is a way of 'bridling' the morally dubious genre of romance and emphasizing its allegorical value, in what she convincingly interprets as a Protestant reframing of a Catholic genre (*The Fabulous Dark Cloister: Romance in England after the Reformation* (Baltimore: Johns Hopkins University Press, 2011), 103–14).

[51] Harington, *Orlando*, 15.   [52] Harington, *Orlando*, 17.

[53] Harington, *Orlando*, 118, 554. 'Epitheton' here appears to be used in the rare sense of 'cognisance' or heraldic device.

reports of credible persons than the foolish' or 'Comets or blasing for the most part cause great wondring'; and when he notes that: 'The red sea is indeed called the red sea because the sand is so red at the bottom as makes it cast red.'[54] Even glosses that seem designed simply to give a brief piece of factual information often shade into discursiveness, as Harington's own opinions intrude, for example when he writes: 'According as Boiardus the poet writes, whom, as I often alledge, my author followeth'; 'This is taken out of Catullus, but greatly bettered'; or 'I do not find that Eleonora was the mother he means here, for her he praises in the 13 booke, but rather the mother church that favoured not the Duke of Ferrara'.[55]

While the information such glosses provide may be useful, the personal tone diverts attention from their content to the person who provides them. In this respect they bear a striking resemblance to the glosses of Harington's last known work: a translation of Book IV of the *Aeneid*, produced for James I's eldest son Prince Henry, which was circulated exclusively in manuscript.[56] These too are highly personal in tone. Although, as Simon Cauchi has demonstrated, Harington made quite extensive use of Servius' commentary on the *Aeneid*, his glosses frequently stray away from explication of the text.[57] Thus, that to the line 'Your fleet prophaned ys with guilty blood' leads via a reference to pagan beliefs about murder to an aide memoire on the same subject attributed to 'some old Churchmen' and concludes with the anecdotal evidence that: 'The peeple of Ierland do report that yf any murder be committed within the hye water mark of the sea, that the very fysh will leave that coast for a longe tyme, and namely at Carlingford whear the herring fyshing suddenly fayld they askrybd yt to that occasyon.'[58] The equally extensive gloss on suicide is another case in point. Beginning with a defence of the priest who, condemned to be burned, concealed gunpowder under his shirt to shorten his suffering, it goes on to propose that: 'So by degrees hee that wear sewr to be hangd and quarterd tomorrow and wold to avoyd the shame & payn lep into ye tems to be drownd myght leav his damnacion disputable rather then determinable but of this I will say more in the end.'[59] These glosses are typical of Harington both in their free association and in their move from explication of Virgil's text to discussion of contemporary people and events. Like Harington's *Orlando*, his Virgil is glossed in an intensely sociable manner; there are references to the Countess of Pembroke, Ariosto, and Ascham,

---

[54] Harington, *Orlando*, 36, 49, 127.   [55] Harington, *Orlando*, 170, 24, 45.
[56] See further John Harington, *The Sixth Book of Virgil's Aeneid*, ed. Simon Cauchi (Oxford, Clarendon Press, 1991), pp. liv–lvii.
[57] Harington, *Aeneid*, 13. Unless otherwise specified, all further quotations will be taken from this edition.
[58] Harington, *Aeneid*, 17.   [59] Harington, *Aeneid*, 33.

as well as to Falstaff's dubious recruiting practices in Shakespeare's *Henry IV*, which (in a tone recalling that of Harvey's comments on Gascoigne's *Adventures of Master F.J.*) are treated as if they were historical fact.[60] What matters in each of these glosses is not so much what is said as the fact that it is Harington who says it. Thus, he observes of the myth of Orpheus 'I can make no great morall of this ficcion', and then goes on to speculate:

> I thinke beinge an excellent musycian or Poet hee made some kynde epitaph on his wyfe wch made her memory lyve on earth whearby they fayn hee recoverd her from hell or oblyvion. but one that comments on Ovids metamorphoses tells seryously that in germany one lost his wyfe in soche a manner and making great moan for her death, she came to lyfe agayn & told him that she was to stay wth him as longe as he wold keep him self from swearing & blaspheming wch hee was moche gevn to, and a few months after relapsing into the same fawlt she was taken owt of his syght.[61]

In both texts, Harington's associative glossing apparently seeks to replicate his conversation, providing a picture of the man and his mind to a potential patron. Just as his translation of *Orlando Furioso* was intended to placate Queen Elizabeth, his presentation of his translation of the *Aeneid* to King James was an attempt to regain royal favour—something which Harington had forfeited in consequence of his publication of the controversial *New Discourse* in 1596. The resemblance between the two sets of glosses seems to call into question Harington's awareness of there being a 'language' or 'etiquette' of print. Glossing that in the *Aeneid* seems entirely appropriate to its circulation as, essentially, a private document appears distinctly odd when put into wider circulation as part of a printed text: despite being presented as an integral part of the work, Harington's glosses to the *Orlando* resemble annotations intended only for the writer and his immediate circle. Their appearance there initially suggests that Harington's is the very opposite of a sophisticated use of print, and that his glossing reveals a blithe unawareness that a manuscript and a printed text are in any way different in kind.

This would be a misreading, however. Although Harington's tone implies that his glossing is essentially amateur, there are indications throughout his career that he is highly aware of both the practicalities and the connotations of print publication. Thus, it is clear from his instructions to the printer of *Orlando Furioso*, Richard Field, that his attention to the layout of his work was considerable; in a note on the printer's copy-text he writes: 'Mr Feeld I dowt this will not come in in the last page, and thearfore

---

[60] Harington, *Aeneid*, 9, 37, 35. For Harvey, see note 41 above.
[61] Harington, *Aeneid*, 15.

I wowld have immedyatly in the next page after the fynyshinge of this last booke, with some prety knotte to . . . set down the tytle, and a peece of the Allegory as foloweth in this next page.'[62] More broadly, with both the *Orlando* and the *Aeneid*, his choice of the medium of transmission reflects his concern that each of these texts should serve as an ambassador for himself. With *Orlando Furioso*, not only is the 'error' of his translation of Canto XXVIII subsumed in an epic, but the grandeur of the printed text goes beyond what the Queen had requested: at a court where performance was the measure of sincerity, the flamboyance of Harington's gesture is an important part of his appeal for rehabilitation. With the *Aeneid*, the reverse is the case. The two requests which Harington makes in his prefatory letter to James show clearly how he is using the work as an attempt to escape his former 'embodied self' and to substitute another. The first is: 'that nothing written by mee before yor Maties raign bee imputed to mee as a fawlt . . . The other that my former spending or rather mispending of so moch tyme vppon toys be no preiudyce to any future employment that my breeding hath made mee otherwyse capable of.'[63] The decision to circulate the work exclusively in manuscript adds weight to Harington's assertion in the epistle that he is a reformed character who should not be judged by former follies (or publications). Harington is apparently no longer seeking publicity either for himself or for his works, but writing for the King alone, and therefore the more to be trusted.

Harington's awareness of the boundary between public and private and of how to transgress it effectively are—ironically—most apparent in the work for which he became notorious: the *New Discourse*. This bizarre creation was published in three parts: the *Anatomie* (a practical treatise explaining how to construct Harington's pet invention, a flushing lavatory); the *Apologie*, in which the *Anatomie* is put on trial; and *A New Discourse of a Stale Subject* (a mock-encomium of 'a jakes', in which the loo is given a wide variety of heroic associations).[64] A genuinely useful treatise that requires widespread circulation in print fully to realize its potential is thus accompanied by two coterie publications. All three texts were published anonymously, as if to guard against the stigma of printing such matter, yet—for those who knew him—each contains clear indications that the author is Harington. In the encomium, a prefatory letter to the author 'Misacmos' drops heavy hints about Bath (the nearest town to Harington's

---

[62] Harington, *Orlando*, 557n.   [63] Harington, *Aeneid*, 3.
[64] All three texts have been edited in a single volume as *Sir John Harington's A New Discourse of a Stale Subject Called the Metamorphosis of Ajax*, ed. Elizabeth Story Donno (London: Routledge, 1962); for the relationship between them, see her discussion on pp. 11–48.

country house at Kelston) and there is a pointed reference to Ariosto, while in the *Apologie*, the jurors who decide the fate of the work at its trial are all personal friends of Harington's.[65] At the end of the *Anatomie*, an emblem appears that both conceals and reveals Harington's authorship (see Plate 6.1). It consists of a woodcut of a hare with a ring in its mouth sitting on a tun, encircled with the motto 'Gratia Dei Nobiscum', and followed by the verse:

> The (grace of God) guides well both age and youth,
> Fly sin with feare, as harmlesse (hare) doth hound,
> Like precious (ring) embrace, more precious truth,
> As (tunne) full of good juyce, not emptie sound,
> In these right scand, Mysacmos name is found.[66]

The joke, of course, is that the emblem is too easy to decipher. Like the rather blatant clues to Harington's identity in the prefatory epistle to the encomium, it makes a conspicuous fiction of the work's anonymity. Harington re-emphasizes this in the copy of the *Anatomie* which he presented to Gervase Markham by adding a helpful note elucidating the one element of the verbal riddle that might not be immediately obvious: 'Joannes signifies gracia Dei'.[67]

The transparency of the 'anonymous' author's identity is key to one of the work's two purposes. Whereas the professed, public-spirited aim of the *Anatomie* is to make the flushing lavatory available to the general public, the more elaborate mock-encomium and *Apologie* are aimed, once again, at Harington's rehabilitation. As Scott-Warren has argued, a letter to Lady Russell around the time of the publication of the *New Discourse* demonstrates that it was intended to remind his former fellow courtiers of his existence, after he had been a long time absent on his estate near Bath.[68] It is in joking acknowledgement of this motive within the text that Harington writes (in the persona of Misacmos): 'Some supposed, that because my writings now lay dead, and had not been thought of this good while; I thought . . . I wold send my Muse abroad, masking naked in a net . . . Of my honor that is not true. Will you deny it on your oth? No by our Lady, not for a thousand pounds.'[69] This impromptu fictional dialogue signals not only Harington's aim in publishing the *New Discourse*, but also

---

[65] *New Discourse*, 55–6, 225–42.   [66] *New Discourse*, 204.
[67] *New Discourse*, 204 n. Some of the printed glosses also provide clues to Harington's identity, for example that immediately preceding the woodcut and that which observes 'It seems the writer hereof would faine be thought a Justice of peace'; as Donno notes, Harington himself had been qualified as a Justice of the Peace since 1584 (*New Discourse*, 118).
[68] See Scott-Warren, 'The Privy Politics of Sir John Harington's *New Discourse of a Stale Subject, Called the Metamorphosis of Ajax*', *Studies in Philology* 93 (1996), 412–42.
[69] *New Discourse*, 211.

An vnequall Paralell.

none is our friēd so much to helpe vs to thē. We haue playd, and bene playd with, for our writings. *Si quis quod fecit, patiatur ius erit equū*. If you do take but such as you giue, it is one for another, but if they that play so, would giue vs but a peece of gold for euerie good verse we thinke we haue made; we should leaue some of thē, but poore felowes. But soft, if I shold tell all, he wold say, I am of kin to *Sauntus Ablabius*. It is no matter, since he makes me to write of *Sauntus Acacchius*.

But now, that you may know I haue bene a dealer in Emblemes, I will conclude with a deuise not sharpe in conceyt, but of venerable antiquitie, and yet by my masters owne computation, it is not so auncient as Dame *Cloacyna*, by 1800. yeares and more. Now riddle me what name is this.

8

Now if the man such prayse will haue. Thē what must he that keepes the knaues Dametas in Arcadya.

It is good to set a name to the booke: For a booke without name may be called a libell.

The (grace of God) guides well both age and youth,
Fly sin with feare, as harmlesse (hare) doth hound,
Like precious (ring) embrace, more precious truth,
As (tunne) full of good iuyce, not emptie found,
In these right scand, Mysacmos name is found.

Plate 6.1 Sir John Harington, *An Anatomie of the Metamorphosed Ajax* (London: Richard Field, 1596), sig. Lviii. Douce H.qi (2). Reproduced courtesy of The Bodleian Libraries, The University of Oxford.

the means by which he hopes to achieve his end. By speaking in his own person, and implying that he does so in 'real time', in the reader's present, Harington ensures that his work forms a lively reminder of his person. As with his glossing of *Orlando Furioso*, the incongruity of recreating his speaking self in print is an important part of his appeal: he seeks not just to remind his friends at court of his existence, but to remind them that he makes them laugh. Although the *Anatomie* is ostensibly aimed at an audience that will have a real use for the practical treatise, and is not much concerned about its author, it is also an elaborate pretext for two elaborately performative texts for whose intended audience its anonymity is a joke. Although it is clear that it proved in practice impossible effectively to manage such different registers in a single volume, or to control the reception of a private work in the public sphere, the *New Discourse* nonetheless constitutes a sophisticated attempt to play to the different kinds of readership that result from print publication, and to reveal to the more intimate of his readers that this is what he is doing.[70] It is indeed a performance of nakedness.

The glosses of the three related texts similarly range from the practical to the performative. Those surrounding the treatise on the construction of the lavatory are working notes; thus, where the text refers to 'a Cesterne . . . a small pype of leade . . . a vessell of an ovall forme', the glosses refer the reader to the relevant parts of the accompanying diagrams: 'This Cistern in the first plot is figured at the letter A. and so likewise in the second plot . . . The small pype in the first plot at D. in the 2. E, but it ought to lye out of sight . . . This vessell is exprest in the first plot H. M. N. in the 2. H. K.'.[71] They are entirely to the point, assisting the reader who wants to use the treatise in constructing a lavatory of his own, and even going so far as to include shopping instructions: 'These forces as also the great washer you shall buy at the Queenes Brasiers in Lothbery at the Bores head.'[72] Some of the glosses to the mock-encomium are almost equally straightforward. Consisting primarily of source glosses such as 'Ovid Meta. Lib. 12' and 'Rabbles lib. I. cap. 13', many provide chapter and verse from Harington's sources. Yet some purposefully wild aberrations are interspersed among them, including the deadpan gloss 'Liber Fictitius' to a reference to 'Rabbles . . . xiiii. book of his tenth Decad', and the gloss 'This may be omitted in reading' to Misacmos' assertion that his treatise is superior to a rival's on the grounds that 'I treate of the house [*sc.* the jakes] it self, & he

---

[70] As Colin Burrow writes, the publication of the *New Discourse* 'has enabled critics ever since to sneer at [Harington]' (*Epic Romance: Homer to Milton* (Oxford: Clarendon Press, 1993), 148).
[71] *New Discourse*, 192–3.   [72] *New Discourse*, 194.

but of part of that is to be done in the house, & that no essential part of the business' (see Plate 6.2).[73]

Still more than those to the *Orlando*, the sheer inconsistency of these glosses gives the impression that Harington is indiscriminately recording the entire contents of his head on the page, jokes and all, and that they are as much a portrait of the author as they are a source of information. Within just a single pair of facing pages, we find glosses that define 'teachers of all sorts' as 'Grammarians. Musitians. Daunsers. Fensers'; translate a quote from Cicero ('O matter slouenly to be seene, to be heard hatefull, etc.'); identify a syllogism and its constituent parts; name 'the incomparable Poet of our age' as 'Syr P. Sid.'; observe that the text records 'A good triall of what spirit a booke is written'; note that the line 'let me deale Sillogistice in moode and figure' is addressed 'to you that be Schollers'; and translate a commonplace, given in Latin in the text, as 'Egles stoope not at flyes'.[74] Some glosses even depend on the reader's having personal knowledge of the author, such as that in the 'Apologie' at the point where Harington writes that 'to shew a manifest evidence of intended love, where my autor very sparingly had praised some wives, I added of mine owne (   ) so much as more I thinke was never said for them', the gloss supplies the blank: 'Mine owne subauditur verse or wife which you will.'[75] Despite the work's supposed anonymity, the talkative, unsystematic, associative voice of both text and margins is witness to Harington's character: one of the signs by which he may be recognized and known, and a lively reminder of the reasons why he should be recalled to court in person.

Thus, whereas Gascoigne uses print for ostentatious performances of secrecy, Harington uses it to construct digressive and revealing portrayals of himself, and whereas Gascoigne's riddles would make no sense *except* in print, Harington's printed glosses do not differ significantly from those in his manuscript *Aeneid*. His desire to return print to the condition of manuscript is still more apparent from the handwritten annotations which he adds to several of his presentation copies of the *New Discourse*.[76] The majority name outright friends and family members who are otherwise identified only allusively, in a gesture that implies a degree of intimacy and trust between author and recipient; thus one note makes explicit that 'a grave & godlie Ladie, and grandmother to all my wives children' is 'the Lady Rogers somtyme caled the fayre Nonne of Cannington', and another provides a potentially more contentious elucidation of a covert reference

---

[73] *New Discourse*, 68–9, 64.
[74] *An Anatomie of the Metamorphosed Ajax* (London: Richard Field, 1596), [12–13]. STC 12772. Cf. *New Discourse*, 199–201.
[75] *New Discourse*, 256–7.   [76] See further Scott-Warren, *Harington*, 81–98.

tana Errate, which I hear will come forth shortly in English. 7. a seuenth (whom I would gesse by
his writing, to bee groome of the stoole to some
Prince of the bloud in Fraunce) writes a beastly
treatise onely to examine what is the fittest thing
to wipe withall, alledging that white paper is too
smooth, browne paper too rough, wollen cloth too
stiffe, linnen cloth too hollow, satten too slipperie,
taffeta too thin, veluet too thick, or perhaps too
costly: but he concludes, that a goose necke to bee
drawne betweene the legs against the fethers, is
the most delicate and cleanly thing that may bee.
Nowe it is possible that I may bee reckned after
these seuen, as sapientum octauus, because I wil
write of a Iakes, yet I wil chalenge of right (if the
Heralds should appoint vs our places (to go before
this filthie fellow, for as according to Aristotle, a
ryder is an Architectonicall *science* to a sadler,
and a sadler to a stirop maker &c. so my discourse
must needes be Architectonical to his, sith I treat
of the house it selfe, and he but of part of that is to
be done in the house, and that no essentiall part of
the busines: for they say there be three things that
" if one neglect to doe them, they wil do themselues;
" one is for a man to make euen his reconnings, for
" who so neglects it will be left euen iust nothing; an
" other is to mary his daughters, for if the parentes
" bestowe them not, they will bestowe themselues;
" the third is that, which the foresaid French man
" writes of: which they that omit, their lawndresses
" shall finde it done in their linnen. Which mishap

Margin notes:

This matter is discoursed by Rabbles in his 13. chapter of his fift book.

Vn moyen de me torcher le cul le plus Seigneurial, le plus excellent, le plus expedient que ia-mais fut veu.

This may bee omitted in reading.

Plate 6.2 Sir John Harington, *An Anatomie of the Metamorphosed Ajax* (London: Richard Field, 1596), sig. Avi[v]. Douce Hqi (1). Reproduced courtesy of The Bodleian Libraries, The University of Oxford.

to Leicester.[77] Still more striking is Harington's series of asides to the directions to his estate. These not only name its location outright, but also assume the reader's familiarity with the character of his wife:

You shall come to a towne that is more then a towne	Bathe
where be waters that be more then waters. But from	the hot bathes
thence, you shall passe downe a streame that seemes	becaus yt is so still
to be no streame, by corne fields that seeme no fields,	becaus they be so stony
downe a street no street, in at a gate no gate, over a	becaus they bee all so
bridge no bridge, into a court no court, where if I be	fanstasticall
not at home, you shall finde perhaps a foole no foole.[78]	becaus she ys so shrowd

What is odd about these additions is that they do not really provide any information about Harington's identity that the majority of his readers could not have gleaned from the printed text alone. It is not as if the recipient of this copy had been given a copy of the *Shepheardes Calendar* with a handwritten addition revealing Spenser as the new poet (or even the identity of E. K. himself), or as if Gascoigne had added a note to a copy of *A Hundreth* confessing his authorship of the entire volume. What is important is not the content of the annotations, but the presence of Harington's hand, and the fact that the notes are unique. Their function is something like that of a postcard or a text message without practical purpose; signalling 'I thought this might amuse you', they both imply and develop further a level of intimacy with the recipient.[79]

Just as the cod-anonymity of Harington's *New Discourse* parodies the use of anonymity as an attention-seeking device (even as it also exploits exactly the same technique), these additions to his presentation copies gently mock the use of genuinely revelatory handwritten additions to the text as a means of signalling intimacy, yet nonetheless perform a comparable function. They thus display a combination of artfulness and artlessness

---

[77] *New Discourse*, 84, 225. Harington's handwritten annotations in presentation copies of the *Orlando* are rather different in kind: not additions but corrections, within the text, of the errata identified by the printer at the end of the work. They are neatly, sometimes almost invisibly, done with Harington's handwriting matched to the letter-forms of the printed text. They do not seek to inscribe Harington's physical presence within the text; his primary concern appears instead to be for the correctness of the text, and ease of reading. These annotations are personal in that they are intended for specific recipients, but not in their form of expression. See further Scott-Warren, *Harington*, 49–55.

[78] *New Discourse*, 60.

[79] For the association of manuscript with personal presence, see D. F. McKenzie, 'Speech-Manuscript-Print', in *New Directions in Textual Studies*, ed. Dave Oliphant and Robin Bradford (Austin: Henry Ransom Humanities Research Center, 1990), 87–109.

Writing of the emergence of the footnote, Peter Cosgrove has argued that a 'genre' may be considered as established when it is possible to discern: 'The deliberate or de facto incorporation of a set of literary practices that writers may draw on in their work—in Hans Robert Jauss' terms, "rules of the game" which . . . can then be varied, extended, corrected, but also transformed, crossed out or simply reproduced.'[81] Gascoigne's and Harington's glosses suggest that Cosgrove's argument might be applied to the marginal gloss as well: their transformations reveal the extent to which glossing was becoming a familiar form, and the extent to which this enabled diversion.

---

[81] Peter Cosgrove, 'Undermining the Text: Edward Gibbon, Alexander Pope, and the Anti-Authenticating Footnote', in *Annotation and Its Texts*, ed. Stephen Barney (Oxford: Oxford University Press, 1991), 133.

which is characteristic of Harington. Although they apparently refuse t[o] recognize any distinction between glossing for a text that is to be circu[-]lated in manuscript and one that is intended for print, they nonethele[ss] reveal his easy familiarity with past uses of print that blur the bounda[ry] between public and private, and his own frequent transgression of th[at] boundary for the amusement of his friends. They thus also reveal a stri[k]ing confidence that what will interest people about his words is that th[ey] are *his* words, regardless of the medium of transmission; they confir[m] what he says in his handwritten dedication of one copy of the *Anatom[y]* and *Apologie*, that the main interest of the book may (for some reade[rs] anyhow) be the fact that it is the product of this particular author: 'y[our] interest is moch in the work becaus yt is moste in the wryter.'[80] What [is] implied by Harington's substitution of the playful portrait of himself f[or] that of the Muse on the title page of his *Orlando Furioso* is also appare[nt] from his glossing: he does not so much use paratextual or presentatio[n] devices to authorize himself as writer, as use his known character a[nd] personality to lend meaning and interest to his work. The highly p[er]sonal voice of the printed glosses suggests an attempt to replicate t[his] effect even for those readers who do not know him in person.

Harington's practice, then, is in many ways diametrically opposed [to] Gascoigne's, depending on an attempt to negate the distance between [the] author and the readers of his work in print, rather than exploiting it [for] purposes of self-reinvention. Whereas Gascoigne's paratexts substitute t[ext] for external reality, Harington's introduce reality firmly into the text. [In] their different ways, however, both writers treat their books as a form [of] self-portrait, and reveal a sophisticated understanding of print conv[en]tions in doing so. Each has an understanding of print decorum that all[ows] him to be *effectively* indecorous, and each depends on finding at least so[me] readers who share that understanding—even though Harvey's respo[nse] to Gascoigne's *Posies*, the formal censoring of the *Posies*, and the infor[mal] censure attracted by Harington's *New Discourse* all indicate that their f[aith] in that shared understanding was not necessarily justified. For both, [the] gloss is a natural extension of the text: for Gascoigne, an opportunit[y to] pursue the reality games that characterize so much of his writing, [and] for Harington a natural locus for speaking—ostensibly—off the rec[ord] and thus emphasizing the trope of his personal presence in the text. [In] their confident transgression of the boundaries between public and [pri]vate, both Harington and Gascoigne show to what extent glossing [is] becoming established as a phenomenon with its own particular 'langu[age]'

---

[80] *New Discourse*, 24.

7

'Playing the Dolt in Print'
The Extemporary Glossing of Nashe's *Pierce Penilesse his Supplication to the Devil*

Harington's use of the gloss as a means of conveying personal presence and Gascoigne's interest in print as a medium of concealment and revelation are taken to still further extremes in the work of Thomas Nashe. Nashe (1567–c. 1600) was above all a professional writer. He is known in a variety of different roles: as the author of the experimental prose fiction *The Unfortunate Traveller,* as the associate of Marlowe and the would-be associate of Greene, the original of the precocious page Moth in *Love's Labour's Lost,* Gabriel Harvey's opponent in a remarkably long-drawn-out quarrel about nothing in particular, and Jonson's collaborator on the notorious (and lost) *Isle of Dogs.*[1] But he is also known for his own virtuosity. He seems never to have written in the same genre twice; the only consistent factors in his writing are his repeated characterization of himself as protean and his creation of a style which he himself terms an 'endless argument of speech'.[2] This chapter will consider the glossing of *Pierce Penilesse* (1592) as a further manifestation of his restless invention and experimentation: a way of making his much-vaunted improvisation visible on the page. Its numerous different functions and switches in register echo a variety of glossing precedents, from the Marprelate tracts to William Bullein's *Dialogue against the Fever Pestilence* to Robert Crowley's edition of Langland's *Piers Plowman*. They thus also reveal the extent to which, for Nashe, the marginal gloss is a form with an established identity. At once part of the text and distinct from it, Nashe's glossing both reveals his thinking about the nature of the writing process and shows this to be inseparable from the material forms in which it is transmitted.

---

[1] See further Charles Nicholl, *A Cup of Newes: The Life of Thomas Nashe* (London: Routledge & Kegan Paul, 1984).
[2] Thomas Nashe, *The Works of Thomas Nashe*, ed. R. B. McKerrow, 5 vols. (Oxford: Basil Blackwell, 1966), 1: 245.

Nashe's *Pierce Penilesse his Supplication to the Devil* was an extremely popular work, running to three editions in 1592. It is also a thoroughly odd piece of writing. The premise is that Pierce, a penniless author, is in such dire straits that he has no option but to sell his soul to the devil. Yet the text is very far from working out that premise in a straightforward way. Instead it undermines the reader's expectations on all kinds of levels. As Lorna Hutson has argued, Pierce's initial characterization of himself seems to align him with the figure of the repentant prodigal familiar from the prefaces to George Gascoigne's satires, but Pierce swiftly departs from the expected treatment of the subject in order to blame potential patrons, rather than his own shortcomings, for his want of ready cash.[3] Characterizing them as ruled by a personified Greedinesse and his wife Dame Niggardize, he slips by degrees into a full-blown satire structured according to the topos of the seven deadly sins. Not only is this an unexpected way of complaining about the difficulty of making a living as a writer, but Pierce does not abide by the conventions of the sin topos either. Its demands are so conspicuously at odds with the interests of the writer who deploys it that the effect is something like hearing one tune sung to the words of another. Thus, although Pierce's discussion of Pride includes an attack on the standard target of painted ladies, it focuses primarily on Pierce's own rivals for potential sources of income, while the discussion of Wrath not only encompasses an extensive (and wrathful) attack on Gabriel and Richard Harvey, but veers off into a defence of poetry.[4] Pierce's anticipated appeal to the devil for patronage is never made explicitly, and it is not clear what he hopes to achieve by his writing, except perhaps the sheer feat of having made something out of nothing. Even the Knight of the Post who is to carry his appeal to the devil comments that this is the maddest supplication he ever saw, yet the Knight's own digressions and indirections are then made a part of the work: he trumps Pierce's exercise on the theme of the deadly sins with a satire in the form of an elaborate beast fable and a disquisition on the nature of spirits.[5] Pierce boasts that his writing is 'extemporall', and the rapidity with which the work shifts from genre to genre suggests that extemporizing or improvisation is in fact its organizing principle: not only at the level of the sentence or paragraph, but at the level of the work as a whole. Pierce's complaint about his want of patrons becomes the occasion for him to display both his competence in a diversity

---

[3] Lorna Hutson, *Thomas Nashe in Context* (Oxford: Clarendon Press, 1989), 172–96. This is a recurrent theme in Nashe's work; see for example Sherri Geller, 'Commentary as Cover-Up: Criticizing Illiberal Patronage in Thomas Nashe's *Summer's Last Will and Testament*', *English Literary Renaissance* 25 (1995), 148–78.
[4] Nashe, *Works*, 1: 187–99.   [5] Nashe, *Works*, 1: 217.

of genres and the ingenuity underlying that competence. In doing so, of course, he reveals Nashe to possess these qualities too. Although Pierce is not fully identified with Nashe, as a figure of the indigent professional writer he resembles him closely; just as Pierce's complaint demonstrates his willingness, like that of the Knight of the Post, to 'sweare you anything for twelue pence', it also shows how well Nashe himself can swear.[6] The work thus functions as an appeal for patronage at one remove: the request which Pierce never quite puts to the devil, Nashe makes indirectly to potential patrons among his readers.

The form as well as the content of the work is designed to display Pierce's (and thereby Nashe's) ingenuity. It consists of two main parts: an introduction in which Pierce describes his penury and the circumstances giving rise to his supplication, and the supplication itself. The first of these takes the form of an epistle to the reader, but it does not announce itself as such. Instead, the title of the work, 'Pierce Penilesse his Supplication to the Devil', appears as a running head above Pierce's confessional opening lines, so that the reader who encounters Pierce's vituperative, excitable complaint for the first time assumes that this *is* the supplication, and only gradually discovers that he himself, rather than the devil, is the addressee.[7] As Hutson has argued, Nashe intended to compound this confusion by presenting the text without any prefatory matter.[8] It was only due to the pre-emptive pirating of the work by the printer Richard Jones that *Pierce* first appeared in slightly more approachable form, with a title page that reassures readers as to the work's moral purpose and an explanatory letter from the printer in which he assures his readers that, despite the unfamiliar appearance of the text, 'if you vouchsafe the Reading, you shall finde . . . Dedication, Epistle, & Proeme to your liking'.[9] But even after such reassurances, the content of the work remains disconcerting. Haunted by fleeting, protean likenesses of familiar genres and topoi, it challenges the assumption that recognition of the genre of a work entails understanding of its meaning too. In the absence of clues as to how to interpret its constant shape-shifting, the natural tendency is for a reader to look for guidance to the only available element of paratext: the marginal glosses.

[6] Nashe, *Works*, 1: 164.
[7] Thomas Nashe, *Pierce Penilesse his supplicacion to the diuell* (London: Richard Jones, 1592), sigs. B1–B4ᵛ. STC 18371.
[8] Hutson, *Nashe*, 174–5.
[9] Nashe, *Works*, 1: 149, 150. For the argument that Nashe's placing of the dedicatory Epistle towards the end of the work is a parody of Spenser's practice in the *Faerie Queene*, see Andrew Wallace, 'Reading the 1590 *Faerie Queene* with Thomas Nashe', *Studies in the Literary Imagination* 38 (2005), 35–49; for back matter more generally, see William H. Sherman, 'Terminal Paratext and the Birth of Print Culture', in *Renaissance Paratexts*, ed. Helen Smith and Louise Wilson (Cambridge: Cambridge University Press, 2011), 65–87.

The glossing to *Pierce Penilesse* is remarkably inconsistent, however. The first few pages contain Latin glosses, primarily quotations from Ovid and Horace. The glossing then ceases almost completely, only to reappear at the beginning of Pierce's formal address to the Devil. Here, however, it takes a rather different form: the majority of the glosses are in English, and serve in the first instance as an index to the text, albeit a rather sporadic one. They thus resemble what is probably the most common kind of glossing in printed texts of the period, providing the reader with a useful series of place-finders by indicating topics such as 'The complaint of pride', 'The nature of an upstart', and 'The counterfeit politician'.[10] Yet interspersed among these tidily supplementary glosses are others, also in English, consisting of vigorous first-person responses and additions to the text. Many of these seem to represent a kind of *esprit d'escalier*, offering a wry critique of Pierce's pronouncements, and several—whose voice is unambiguously Pierce's own—appear not to be supplementary to, but inseparable from the text. Such juxtaposition of different kinds of gloss implies what is physically impossible: that the margins of the printed page record temporally distinct layers of annotation. Their unruly content is matched by a visual untidiness, too. Whereas the indexing glosses are spaced fairly evenly throughout the text, the first-person glosses tend to be concentrated in blocks, creating a sudden, excited-looking overcrowding of the margins. The glossing is by no means a 'silent' or transparent guide. Even on a purely visual level, it draws attention to itself.

The different types of gloss suggest quite different ways of approaching the text. The Latin glosses, the majority of which are drawn from Ovid's *Tristia* and Horace's *Epistles*, with additions from the *Metamorphoses*, the *Amores*, and Gellio's *Noctes Africae*, imply that *Pierce Penilesse* is a text with a weighty literary ancestry. Both the *Tristia* and the cited epistles have certain themes in common with Nashe's work. Horace's *Epistle* II.i contains a direct appeal to Caesar for patronage, and in his *Epistle* II.ii, Horace, like Pierce, firmly links writing with financial reward, cynically casting doubt on its moral value. Juxtaposing quotations from the *Epistles* with Pierce's complaint thus re-emphasizes the innate ambiguity of his position, as a prodigal whose repentance is occasioned less by genuine remorse than by the position to which his prodigality has reduced him. But even as they call the value of Pierce's writing into question, these quotations nonetheless constitute a kind of literary faith: a belief in a deep intertextuality, whereby new writing is grounded and validated by existing texts, gaining part of its meaning by reference to what is already known.[11] The resulting network

---

[10] Nashe, *Works*, 1: 168–9.
[11] For this view of writing, see Martin Irvine, '"Bothe Text and Gloss": Manuscript Form, the Textuality of Commentary, and Chaucer's Dream Poems', in *The Uses of*

of correspondences implies an underlying value system, tacitly reasserting what Pierce's resistance to generic conventions denies: the viability of reading his work in the light of a series of reference points shared between author and reader.

There is nonetheless something faintly ludicrous about the comparisons which the glosses invite. In particular, there is a conspicuous mismatch between Ovid's permanent banishment from Rome to the coast of the Black Sea and Pierce's little local financial difficulty. The two works share a conceit: Pierce's supplication, like Ovid's *Tristia*, will go where he cannot go himself, and make his case for him, but whereas Ovid's supplication is to the actual emperor, Augustus, Pierce fantastically supplicates to a devil who is clearly created in his own image; whereas Ovid develops the metaphor of the poet as a lost soul in order to stress the seriousness of his plight, by dicing with the devil Pierce simultaneously literalizes this metaphor and renders it farcical. The differences between their respective works are repeatedly re-emphasized in individual glosses. For example, the Ovidian gloss 'Est aliquid fatale malum per verba levare' ['it is something to lighten with words a fated evil'] sits oddly alongside the passage where Pierce explains that, having failed to make any money by his labours:

> I accused my fortune, raild on my patrones, bit my pen, rent my papers, and ragde in all points like a mad man. In which agony tormenting my selfe a long time, I grew by degrees to a milder discontent: and pausing a while over my standish, I resoPlved in verse to paint forth my passion: which best agreeing with the vaine of my vnrest, I began to complain in this sort:
>
>> Why ist damnation to dispaire and die,
>> When life is my true happinesse disease?
>> My soule, my soule, thy safetye makes me flie
>> The faultie meanes, that might my paine appease.
>> Diuines and dying men may talke of hell,
>> But in my heart, her seueral torments dwell.[12]

Although these lines propose that the agony caused by the failure of past writing may be remedied by new writing, compared to Pierce's previous prose description of his rage, they are remarkably formulaic. The gloss that sententiously proposes verse-writing as a means of alleviating distress is

---

Manuscripts in Literary Studies: Essays in Memory of Judson Boyce Allen, ed. Charlotte Cook Morse, Penelope Reed Doob, and Marjorie Curry Woods (Kalamazoo: Medieval Institute Publications, 1992), 81–109; Thomas M. Greene, *The Light in Troy: Imitation and Discovery in Renaissance Poetry* (New Haven: Yale University Press, 1982); and David Quint, *Origin and Originality in Renaissance Literature: Versions of the Source* (New Haven: Yale University Press, 1983); cf. also Timothy Hampton, *Writing from History: The Rhetoric of Exemplarity* (Ithaca: Cornell University Press, 1990).

[12] Nashe, *Works*, 1: 157.

thus singularly inappropriate; like many of the glosses to Copland's edition of the *Eneados*, it reads like a universal commonplace in a context that reveals it to be no such thing. Similarly, when Pierce rattles off a series of rhetorical questions as to why he, of all people, is unable to earn a living from his writing, the gloss from the *Metamorphoses*, 'Meritis expendite causam' ['judge the cause on its merits'], is entirely out of proportion to the text. Taken from the speech where Ulysses argues that he, rather than Ajax, should inherit Achilles' arms, it has an approximate relevance to Pierce's complaint—Pierce's run of rhetorical questions as to why he, specifically, is poverty-stricken, focuses on questions of birth and intelligence, just as Ulysses does—yet for Ulysses these questions lie at the very heart of his case and are explored in detail, whereas for Pierce they are merely a rhetorical flourish made in passing. The gloss is so clearly a borrowed gesture that it simultaneously reveals both Pierce's lack of integrity and his ability to gloss over this lack with a display of verbal fireworks; like Baldwin and Gascoigne, he renders the very idea of a commonplace absurd.

Of course, the effect of such glossing will vary from reader to reader, depending on whether they recognize the sources of the (unattributed) citations, whether they have sufficient recall of their original contexts to bring them to bear on Pierce's complaint, and even whether they have any knowledge of Latin at all. On the most general level, the allusions in the glosses seem aptly to lend authority to Pierce's appeal, but direct reference back to the sources shows them to have the opposite effect, to the extent that they not only reveal Pierce's predicament to be a relatively trivial one, but call into question the very thing their presence at first seems to imply: the validity of a reading that relies on intertextuality. Nashe's writing has been said to manifest a crisis of faith, in which the writer's knowledge that he is able to say anything undermines his belief that there is anything of value to say.[13] By encouraging intertextual readings that imply that there is such a thing as reading for profit, yet are just slightly beside the point, the glosses reflect that crisis. Pierce's sources have ceased to be sources in any meaningful sense of the word; they have instead been reduced to snippets and phrases which he uses at will. Although they give the appearance that his complaint is grounded in sources outside himself, they reveal that those same sources have been entirely recast in his own image.

Such appropriation is most strikingly visible in those glosses which introduce a first-person speaker. Like the other citation glosses, these too tend to be both approximately appropriate and entirely disproportionate

---

[13] See for example A. F. Kinney, *Humanist Poetics: Thought, Rhetoric, and Fiction in Sixteenth-Century England* (Amherst: University of Massachusetts Press, 1986), 304–62.

to the text. For example, when Pierce concludes the final stanza of his verse complaint with the lines 'In some far Land will I my griefes reherse . . . England (adieu) the Soyle that brought me foorth, / Adieu vnkinde, where skill is nothing worth', the Ovidian gloss 'Hei mihi, quam paucos haec mea dicta mouent' ['ah me, how few are moved by these words of mine'] at first glance adds resonance to his words, and on second thoughts implies that he is merely petulant.[14] Ovid's line is taken from a plea to be allowed to return to Rome, lamenting the fact that his previous pleas have gone unheeded. Pierce is merely expressing a decision to leave his country because he has been unable to persuade anyone to pay him for his writing. Moreover, the use of a quote which is spoken in the first person raises the question of how the 'I' of the gloss relates to the 'I' of the text. Should the gloss be understood as having been provided as a supplement to the text, inviting comparison of the *Tristia* and Pierce's supplication just as the other citation glosses do, or should Pierce be understood as having subsumed Ovid's voice entirely?

The inclusion of a number of English-language glosses which are undeniably in Pierce's voice suggests that the latter is the case. For example, when Pierce complains in the text that he hasn't received a penny in the last six months, the gloss intemperately adds: 'No: Ile be sworne vppon a book haue I not.'[15] At other times, although there is no explicit first-person speaker in the gloss, the gloss completes a sentence from the text as if both had been produced by the same hand; thus, when Pierce writes that 'he that hath neither comlinesse nor coine to commend him, vndoutedly strides ouer time by stratagems', the gloss adds: 'As by carrying tales, or playing the doutie Pandor.'[16] Elsewhere, the glosses contribute afterthoughts and quibbles, as when Pierce writes of those who have 'no eares but their mouths, nor sense but of that which they swallowe downe their throates', and the gloss adds the observation 'And that sence often maks them senceless'; or when Pierce refers in the text to portraits of women wearing make-up with the term 'counterfets', and the gloss comments that 'They may well be called counterfaites, since the beauty they imitate is counterfeyted'.[17] Others again remark on Pierce's own performance, as in the approving comment 'Marke these two letter-leaping Metaphors, good people' at the point where the phrase 'the lawne of licentiousness [and] the wheat of hospitalitie' appears in the text; or in the patently absurd 'Translated word for word, iuxta originalem' alongside Pierce's observation

---

[14] Ovid, *Tristia*, I.ix.36.   [15] Nashe, *Works*, 1: 165.
[16] Nashe, *Works*, 1: 176. Cf. *Works* 1: 160, where the gloss-like observation 'A good policy to suppresse superfluous liberalitie' is found in the text.
[17] Nashe, *Works*, 1: 180, 1: 181.

that 'Cucullus non facit Monachum: tis not their newe bonnets will keep them from the old boan-ache'.[18] Even within the text Pierce's writing is characterized by frequent bracketed interpolations, and these glosses appear to be an extension of the same self-reflexive technique.

At times, the lack of a clear distinction between the voice of the text and that in the margins spills over into outright parody of well-established glossing functions. For example, when Pierce inveighs against 'some tired Iade belonging to the Presse, whom I neuer wronged in my life [who] hath . . . accused me of want of learning', the gloss adds: 'I wold tell you in what booke it is, but I am afraid it would make his booke sell in his latter daies, which hetherto hath lien dead, and beene a great losse to the Printer' (see Plate 7.1).[19] This gloss not only allows Pierce to colonize the margins, but also raises (and then dashes) the expectation that a gloss will provide chapter and verse for a looser allusion in the text. Elsewhere, the play between the finished, considered layout of the page and the impromptu content of the gloss amounts to a challenge to the conditions of print publication itself. Thus, when Pierce describes an archetypal Danishman as one who has 'cheekes that sag like a womans dugs ouer his chin-bone, his apparel . . . puft vp with bladdres of Taffatie, and his back like biefe stuft with Parsly . . .', the gloss continues in the same vein: 'If you know him not by any of these marks, look on his fingers, & you shal be sure to find half a dozen siluer rings, worth thre pence a peece.'[20] Despite the fact that this is a mass-produced text, Pierce ('I') here appears to address the individual reader directly, as 'you'. The effect is comparable to that of the stage aside, when a character breaks away from the lines set down in his part in order to speak 'out of place'. The glosses thus establish, however spuriously, a sense of intimacy or even collusion between author and reader, refusing to acknowledge the distance between them in space and time, and—due to the illusion of being off the record—implying that they grant the reader access to the writer's true, private thoughts.

The unpredictable and oddly intimate quality of Nashe's glossing is a key part of his exploration of the possible relationships between writer, text, and reader. By extension, it is a key part of his thinking about what it is that he is doing when he writes. In minimizing the distance between reader and writer, the glosses to *Pierce Penilesse* are the visible counterpart of the equation of writing with speech which recurs throughout the work.[21] In the text, the recurrent interpolations 'quoth I', and 'quoth he',

---

[18] Nashe, *Works*, 1: 181, 1: 180, 1: 181, 1: 182.
[19] Nashe, *Works*, 1: 195. [20] Nashe, *Works*, 1: 178.
[21] Nashe's representation of writing as speech is illuminatingly explored by Neil Rhodes, 'On Speech, Print, and New Media: Thomas Nashe and Marshall McLuhan', *Oral Tradition* 24 (2009), 373–92.

Pierce Penilesse his

way with a Flea in mine eare, let him looke that I will rayle on him soundly: not for an houre or a day, whiles the iniury is fresh in my memory: but in some elaborate pollished Poem, which I will leaue to the worlde when I am dead, to be a liuing Image to all ages, of his beggerly parsimony and ignoble illiberaltie: and let him not (whatsoeuer he be) measure the weight of my words by this booke, where I write *Quicquid in buccam venerit*, as fast as my hand can trot: but I haue tearmes (if I be vext) laid in steepe in *Aqua fortis*, and Gunpowder, that shall rattle through the Skyes, and make an Earthquake in a Pesants eares. But

I would tell you in what booke it is, but I am afraid it would make his booke sell in his latter daies, which hetherto hath lien dead and beene a great losse to the Printer.

Gabriel Harvey.

Looke at the Chandlers shop, or at the Flaxwiues stall, if you see no tow nor Sope wrapt vp in the title page of such a Pamphlet, as Incerti Authoris Io. Pæan.

case (since I am not yet out of the Theame of Wrath) that some tired Iade belonging to the Presse, whome I neuer wronged in my life; hath named me expressely in Print (as I will not do him) and accused me of want of learning, vpbraiding me for reuiuing in an epistle of mine the reuerend memory of Sir Thomas Moore, Sir Iohn Cheeke, Doctor Watson, Doctor Haddon, Doctor Carre, Maister Ascham, as if they were no meate but for his Maisterships mouth, or none but some such as the sonne of a ropemaker were worthy to mention them. To shewe how I can rayle, thus would I begin to rayle on him. Thou that hadst thy hood turnd ouer thy eares when thou wert a Batchelor, for abusing of Aristotle, and setting him vp on the Schoole gates painted with Asses eares on his head: is it any discredit for me, thou great baboune, thou Pigmie Braggart, thou Pamphleter of nothing but * Peans, to bee censured by thee, that hast scorned the Prince of Philosophers; thou that in thy Dialogues soldst Hunny for a halpenie, and the choycest Writers exant for cues a pece, that cam'it to the Logicke Schooles when thou wert a Fresh-man and writst phrases; off with thy gowne and vntrusse, for I meane to lash thee mightily. Thou hast a Brother hast thou not, student in Almanackes, go too Ile stand to it, be father done of thy bastards (a booke I meane) which being of thy begetting was set forth vnder his name.

Gentlemen, I am sure you haue hearde of a ridiculous
Asse

Plate 7.1 Thomas Nashe, *Pierce Penilesse his Supplication to the Diuell* (London: John Busby, 1592), f. 18ᵛ. Mal. 566 (q). Reproduced courtesy of The Bodleian Libraries, The University of Oxford.

emphatically remind the reader that a large part of the supplication is in the form of reported speech; so too do such formulations as the reference to the readers as 'Auditores' and the statement 'I am at leasure to talke to thee [*sc.* the reader]'.[22] Still more striking is the frequent description of Pierce's own writing in terms of spoken utterance, as when Pierce writes of an anonymous opponent of poetry:

> If I bee euill intreated, or sent away with a Flea in mine eare, let him looke that I will raile on him soundly: not for an houre or a day, whiles the iniury is fresh in my memory, but in some elaborate, pollished Poem, which I will leaue to the world when I am dead, to be a liuing Image to all ages, of his beggerly parsimony and ignoble illiberalitie: and let him not . . . measure the weight of my words by this booke, where I write *Quicquid in buccam venerit*, as fast as my hand can trot.[23]

This passage both represents writing as speech, and speech as writing. The threatened 'railing' turns out to take the form not of an oral attack, but of an 'elaborate polished poem', while Pierce's translation of 'Quicquid in buccam venerit' ('whatever comes to the mouth') with 'as fast as my hand can trot' implicitly equates the speaking mouth with the writing hand. The same conflation appears in *Have With You to Saffron Walden* (1596), Nashe's most extensive contribution to the quarrel with the Harveys. When Nashe, writing in the persona of 'Piers Penilesse Respondent', declares that: 'You ly, you ly, *Gabriell*, I know what you are about to saye, but Ile shred you off three leaues at one blowe', he both images himself in spoken debate with Harvey, with each interrupting the other, and claims that he will have the last word by producing more writing ('leaues') than Harvey can. Shortly after, ventriloquizing Harvey, he enquires: 'Hath he spoken, printed, written, contriued, or imagined, or caused to be spoken, written, printed, contriued, or imagined, anie thing . . .?' as if imagination, speech, writing, and printing were exact equivalents, at once equally solid and equally evanescent.[24] There is no distinction between the thought and the representation of it, nor between the various modes that its representation might take.

In minimizing the distinction between the formal printed gloss and informal speech, Nashe's glossing bears a strong resemblance to William Baldwin's practice in *Beware the Cat*. Where Nashe differs, however, is in his identification of the glossator with the writer rather than the editor of the work: however bizarre, G. B.'s glosses are explicitly claimed as part of his preparation of Streamer's oration for the press, while those to *Pierce*

---

[22] Nashe, *Works*, 1: 217, 1: 199, 1: 239.
[23] Nashe, *Works*, 1: 195.
[24] Nashe, *Works*, 3: 118.

Penilesse seem to be part of its composition. They thus take their place among the constant references to speech in *Pierce Penilesse* and *Have With You* as an important part of Nashe's presentation of his writing as extemporary—and thus, as proof of the unlimited inventive powers of his mind. Nashe is evidently a writer for whom improvisation, or words breeding words, is the equivalent of inspiration: one for whom, in Terence Cave's words, 'the objective [is] to construct . . . a reproduction or representation so carried and animated by the authentic *spiritus* of the speaker that . . . it lives and breathes'.[25] As literal asides, and as visibly extemporized comments, his glosses are one of the means by which he achieves that end.

It would be tempting, then, to see Nashe's practice as a response to the kind of opposition which Walter Ong famously posits between the spoken and the printed word. In Ong's view, 'writing had reconstituted the originally oral, spoken word in visual space' and:

> Print embedded the word in space more definitively . . . Print . . . [like writing] situates utterance and thought on a surface disengaged from everything else, but it also goes farther in suggesting self-containment. Print encloses thought in thousands of copies of a work of exactly the same visual and physical consistency . . . The printed text is supposed to represent the words of an author in definitive or 'final' form. For print is comfortable only with finality.[26]

What the *Pierce Penilesse* glosses appear to be doing is seeking to return the text to the condition of speech, replicating in print what Ong calls 'the give-and-take of oral expression' and thus, in Ong's words again, presenting Nashe's text as 'a kind of utterance, an occurrence in the course of conversation, rather than as an object'.[27] If we follow this line of argument, we could make a plausible case that Nashe insists that he is extemporizing precisely because he is so aware of writing for print: for a text several degrees removed from the level of spontaneity he claims. Nashe thus anticipates Ong's belief in the distancing effect of print, and his intention in stressing his own spontaneity, and using glosses to represent that spontaneity on the printed page is to negate that effect, thereby ensuring that his readers are 'less closed off' from him than the readers of printed texts might otherwise be from their authors.[28] As D. F. McKenzie has argued: 'We know . . . that an important difference between talking and writing is what is now called "presence". The spoken text can be more sharply defined, and its

---

[25] Terence Cave, *The Cornucopian Text: Problems of Writing in the French Renaissance* (Oxford: Clarendon Press, 1979), 145.

[26] Walter J. Ong, *Orality and Literacy: The Technologizing of the Word* (London: Routledge, 2002), 121, 130.

[27] Ong, *Orality and Literacy*, 123.   [28] Ong, *Orality and Literacy*, 123.

authority enhanced, by the speaker's control of tone, nuance, gesture, and responsiveness to an audience.'[29] Nashe's glossing shows him attempting to replicate the conditions of spoken utterance on the printed page.

He does so, however, not by attempting to render print invisible, as Harington does, but by diametrically the opposite tactic: by drawing attention to the absurdity of his own attempt to create a shared present for himself and his readers. This is most conspicuous in *Have With You to Saffron Walden*. Here Nashe's refusal to distinguish between speech and writing finds expression not only in the glosses, but throughout the work. The title page itself heralds the conflation; after providing a run of alternative subtitles, each pointedly identifying Harvey as Nashe's target, it concludes: 'The Mott, or Posie, instead of *Omne tulit punctum: Pacis fiducia nunquam*, As much as to say, as I sayd I would speake with him' (see Plate 7.2).[30] Presenting the printed work as 'oral literature', it creates a very evident contradiction in terms, which is further emphasized by some decidedly idiosyncratic glosses.[31] The introductory Epistle to *Have With You* is glossed with a number of irreverent asides at Harvey's expense, but as soon as the protagonist (again named Piers) begins a dialogue with a number of exotically named interlocutors, the latter take over the role of undercutting and interpolating, and the glosses become increasingly infrequent; when glosses do reappear sporadically at later stages in the text, it is when Piers is again giving a lengthy and uninterrupted monologue.[32] It appears, then, that the substitution of dialogue within the text for an interplay between text and gloss is a conscious one; at one point, Piers even accuses the others of making 'too long gloses on the text', while later he exclaims: 'Supply mee with a margent note, some bodie that hath more idle leasure than I haue at the post hast hudling vp of these presents.'[33] The effect is to draw the making of the book itself into the realm of the impromptu, something which is re-emphasized when one of Piers' interlocutors calls out for 'More Copie, more Copie; we leese a great deale of time for want of Text.'[34] The implication is that the work is being extemporized even as it

---

[29] D. F. McKenzie, 'Speech-Manuscript-Print', in *New Directions in Textual Studies*, ed. Dave Oliphant and Robin Bradford (Austin: Henry Ransom Humanities Research Center, 1990), 89.

[30] Thomas Nashe, *Haue with you to Saffron-walden*. London: John Danter, 1596, title page. STC 18369.

[31] For the argument that oral and literate works are not always entirely distinct, see Ruth Finnegan, *Orality and Literacy: Studies in the Technology of Communication* (Oxford: Basil Blackwell, 1988); and cf. Adam Fox and D. R. Woolf, *The Spoken Word: Oral Culture in Britain, 1500–1850* (Manchester: Manchester University Press, 2002), 1–51.

[32] Nashe, *Works*, 3: 47, 3: 50. For the glossing of Piers' monologues, see e.g. 3: 85, 3: 90.

[33] Nashe, *Works*, 3: 44.

[34] Nashe, *Works*, 3: 50.

Haue vvith you to Saf-fron-vvalden.

OR,

Gabriell Harueys Hunt is vp.

Containing a full Answere to the eldest sonne of the Halter-maker.

OR,

Nashe his Confutation of the sinfull Doctor.

The Mott or Posie, in stead of *Omne tulit punctum*:

Pacis fiducia nunquam.

As much to say, as I sayd I would speake with him.

Printed at London by *Iohn Danter.*
1596.

Plate 7.2 Thomas Nashe, *Have with you to Saffron-walden* (London: J. Danter, 1596), title page. Douce N. 242. Reproduced courtesy of The Bodleian Libraries, The University of Oxford.

is being printed—or that, as Rhodes puts it, Nashe is using 'typography to reconstruct an apparently oral medium'.[35]

Despite all of this, Nashe manifests a very strong awareness of his work as created for the printed page, as appears most dramatically at the point where he interrupts his dedicatory epistle in order to insert a blank space, carefully contained within an ornate printed border.[36] He explains this unexpected and emphatic gap in the text as a space for the reader to contribute: 'Purposely that space I left, that as manie as I shall perswade they [sc. Gabriel Harvey and his brothers] are *Pachecoes, Poldauisses*, and *Dringles* may set their hands to their definitiue sentence.'[37] There is an intriguing contradiction in terms here. The explanation of the blank proposes the work as unfinished, showing how Nashe is using the completed, printed page in order to convey what is incomplete and impromptu. The framed white space could thus be said to 'stand for' the way in which Nashe's glossing works too: in using visual effects to represent thought-processes, blank and glosses alike make visible Nashe's extemporizing technique on the printed page.

Both blank and glosses, then, suggest that the arrangement of Nashe's pages exemplifies something of the habit of mind that underlies the use of emblems in William Bullein's *Dialogue against the Fever Pestilence*.[38] Nashe was clearly familiar with Bullein's work; in the Epistle to the Reader in *Have With You to Saffron Walden* he notes: 'Memorandum, I frame my whole Booke in the nature of a Dialogue, much like Bullen and his Doctor Tocrub.'[39] As witnessed by his inclusion of speaking statues and the way in which his character Civis 'voices' the emblems he describes, Bullein (like Nashe) has a clear interest in the boundaries between speech and writing, and in his case too this is connected to an interest in the creation of a work whose dialogue is between text and glosses as well as between characters within the text. However, where Bullein's work includes lengthy descriptions of emblems that contain both verbal and visual elements, re-presenting both statues and paintings through the medium of speech, Nashe's interest finds expression primarily through experimentation with the play between the content of his work and its layout on the page.

In *Have With You*, even the title page, with its reference to the 'Mott or Posie' of the work, presents the book in its entirety—like Gascoigne's *Steele*

---

[35] Rhodes, 'On Speech, Print, and New Media', 383.
[36] Cf. Rhodes, 'On Speech, Print, and New Media', 380–1.
[37] Nashe, *Works*, 3: 12.
[38] Cf. Juliet Fleming, *Graffiti and the Writing Arts of Early Modern England* (London: Reaktion Books, 2001), 9.
[39] Nashe, *Works*, 3: 20.

Glasse—as an emblem. But the habit of mind is manifest throughout both *Have With You* and *Pierce Penilesse* in Nashe's typographic experimentation, most notably in the use of printed glosses which serve as a means of what Juliet Fleming calls 'the translation of aural into visual shapes'.[40] These play with ideas of both space and time in the printed text. On the one hand, Nashe's typographic experimentation counters the common illusion identified by Joseph Grigely that whereas: 'art appears in contexts that are, quite literally, physical spaces . . . literature, perhaps because of language's iterability, has the illusion of occupying spaceless space'.[41] On the other hand, although the visual attention-seeking of the layout (including the use of framed blanks and the striking unevenness of the glosses) suggests that each page may be viewed as a single unit, emblematically as well as verbally, the content of the glosses emphasizes instead that the words captured on the page are not past, and immutable, but are part of an ongoing process of extemporizing.[42] Nashe thus plays the *idea* of the text as utterance against its physical reality. That is (despite his emphasis on the extemporary, speech-like qualities of his writing), he does not so much attempt to negate the perceived atemporality of print as to exploit its potential to assert two incompatible positions at once: both the text's extemporal quality and its fixed physical existence.[43]

One effect of such play is to foster engaged reading, just as Bullein's glossing does. The literal blanks on the page are analogous to the metaphorical blanks or lacunae between the content of text and gloss. Visually, like Bullein's characters in the garden and tavern scenes, who are faced with emblems that combine word and image, Bullein's and Nashe's readers are faced with pages that are divided between text and gloss, and must put the pieces together, anticipating in the most literal terms Wolfgang Iser's theory that the 'blank' is that on which communication depends, since it is what spurs the reader into action.[44] In Nashe's case, however, there is an additional effect. His protean glossing not only encourages active, interpretative reading, but also diverts by performing the impossible.

---

[40] Fleming, *Graffiti*, 14; and cf. McKenzie, 'Speech-Manuscript-Print', 104–5.

[41] Joseph Grigely, 'Textual Criticism and the Arts: The Problem of Textual Space', *Text* 7 (1994), 27.

[42] Cf. William N. West, 'Old News: Caxton, De Worde, and the Invention of the Edition', in *Caxton's Trace: Studies in the History of English Printing*, ed. William Kuskin (Notre Dame: University of Notre Dame Press, 2006), 241–74 (esp. 245–51).

[43] For the perceived atemporality of print, see Susan Noakes, *Timely Reading: Between Exegesis and Interpretation* (Ithaca: Cornell University Press, 1988), 34–5; and cf. Andrew Taylor, *Textual Situations: Three Medieval Manuscripts and their Readers* (Philadelphia: University of Pennsylvania Press, 2002), 15–18.

[44] Wolfgang Iser, 'Interaction between Text and Reader', in *The Reader in the Text: Essays on Audience and Interpretation*, ed. Susan R. Suleiman and Inge Crosman (Princeton University Press, 1980), 111–12.

His simultaneous equation of the gloss with the impromptu, speaking voice and his emphasis on the physicality of the printed page means that his glosses convey two conflicting messages: both 'this is a printed, mass-produced text' and 'I am talking to you directly, and to you alone, dear reader'. It is the impossibility that both these things should be true which seduces, inviting each reader in turn to believe that he is hearing a private voice in a public place, yet at the same time diverting him with the knowledge that this is ridiculous, so that the shared joke becomes another kind of intimacy. The page is not merely a blank which has impressed upon it something foreign to itself, in the form of Nashe's profusion of puns and digressions; rather, print prompts new ways of extemporizing, becoming a medium that not only expresses thought, but forms it.

PIERCE PENILESSE IN CONTEXT: THE MARPRELATE TRACTS

For all their idiosyncracy, Nashe's glossing practices have close relations in a variety of earlier and contemporary works. Those most frequently cited as an influence are the Marprelate tracts of 1588–9. *Pierce Penilesse* was the first work Nashe published after he had been employed by the Archbishop of Canterbury, John Whitgift, to refute the pseudonymous 'Martin Marprelate's' attacks on the established church, and both its reference to Martin by name and what appears to be a series of Martinist allusions within the beast fable told by the Knight of the Post suggest that the controversy was at the forefront of Nashe's mind at the time of writing.[45] Moreover, there are striking resemblances between (on the one hand) Martin's playful use of print conventions and his habit of addressing the reader directly, and (on the other) the tactics which Nashe deploys both in *Pierce Penilesse* and again in *Have With You to Saffron Walden*. The connection may not be a simple case of influence, however. Rather, Martin's works may be read alongside Nashe's as a response to a variety of previous print practices.

Characterized by an informal, talkative, frequently burlesque voice and by a far-reaching parody of print conventions, the six pamphlets published by the pseudonymous 'Martin Marprelate' in 1588 and 1589 have attracted as much critical attention for their style as for their substance. The work of an author, or a group of authors, whose identity has still not

---

[45] Nashe, *Works*, 1: 197. For allusions to Martin in the beast fable, see Donald J. McGinn, 'The Allegory of the "Beare" and the "Foxe" in Nashe's *Pierce Penilesse*', *PMLA* 61 (1946), 431–53.

definitively been established, they appear to have sprung from nowhere.[46] Their contribution to the ecclesiastical disputes of the day was not in itself ground-breaking; as Joseph L. Black has demonstrated, Martin's main challenge to the established church was the familiar Presbyterian one that the majority of church offices, including archbishops, bishops, deans, and archdeacons, were without foundation in the New Testament and should be replaced by a simple structure of just four offices, each with clearly defined responsibilities at parish level.[47] Yet, as Joseph Navitsky has argued, Martin's presentation of his material was designed to command the attention of a popular audience for arguments which might otherwise seem to have grown stale.[48]

Produced in response to the publication in 1587 of a treatise by John Bridges, Dean of Salisbury, *A Defence of the Government Established in the Church of Englande for Ecclesiasticall Matters*, the title page of Martin's first pamphlet, the *Epistle*, gives an instant indication of his methods. Beginning with an exhortation to 'read ouer D. John Bridges for it is a worthy worke', it seems to present the work as a supplement to Bridges' *Defence*.[49] This is confirmed by the lengthy description which follows, defining the pamphlet as: 'an epitome of the / fyrste Booke of that right worshipfull vo- / lume written against the Puritanes / in the defence of / the noble cleargie by as worshipfull a prieste John Bridges / Presbyter Priest or elder doctor of Diuillitie and Deane of / Sarum'.[50] The arrangement of these lines is conventional: they are set in decreasing sizes of type, so that the content of the first is considerably more conspicuous than that of the

---

[46] The names most frequently mentioned in connection with the tracts are the Puritans John Penry and Job Throkmorton. For their rival claims, see Donald J. McGinn, *John Penry and the Marprelate Controversy* (New Brunswick: Rutgers University Press, 1966); and Leland H. Carlson, *Martin Marprelate, Gentleman* (San Marino: Huntington Library, 1981). For an overview, see Joseph L. Black, *The Martin Marprelate Tracts: A Modernized and Annotated Edition* (Cambridge: Cambridge University Press, 2008), pp. xxxiv–xlvi.

[47] Black, *Marprelate Tracts*, pp. xviii–lxxiv. For the substance of the quarrel, see also Jesse M. Lander, *Inventing Polemic: Religion, Print, and Literary Culture in Early Modern England* (Cambridge: Cambridge University Press, 2006), 80–109; and cf. William Pierce, *An Historical Introduction to the Martin Marprelate Tracts* (London: Archibald Constable, 1908); *The Marprelate Tracts, 1588, 1589*, ed. William Pierce (London: James Clark, 1911), pp. xiii–xxviii; and Edward Arber, *An Introductory Sketch to the Martin Marprelate Controversy, 1588–90* (London: Archibald Constable, 1895).

[48] Joseph Navitsky, 'Disputing Good Bishop's English: Martin Marprelate and the Voice of Menippean Opposition', *Texas Studies in Language and Literature* 50 (2008), 177–200. Cf. also Black, *Marprelate Tracts*, pp. xv–xxxiv; and Lander, *Inventing Polemic*, 94–105.

[49] For discussion of Bridges, see Black, *Marprelate Tracts*, pp. xxii–xxiv; and cf. Raymond A. Anselment, *'Betwixt Jest and Earnest': Marprelate, Milton, Marvell, Swift and the Decorum of Religious Ridicule* (Toronto: University of Toronto Press, 1979), 33–4.

[50] *Oh read ouer D. Iohn Bridges, for it is a worthy worke* (East Molesey: Robert Waldegrave, 1588); STC 17453.

last.[51] But this standard layout is used to subversive effect. A reader who persists beyond the first three, prominent, lines discovers that this work is quite the opposite of what it at first appeared to be; it is in the smaller type size that Dean Bridges is given the Presbyterian equivalent of his title ('Presbyter') before he is acknowledged as 'Dean of Sarum', and then—in what could, in black letter, easily be overlooked as a blotchy bit of printing—claimed as 'doctor of Diuillitie' rather than Divinity.

The descriptive title thus effectively divides its readers into sheep and goats, giving very different information to those who read it in full than it does to those who do not. The decreasing type size functions like a whispered stage aside, proposing both the work and the title page itself as a hoax in which the alert reader may share. Moreover, the title page does not just semi-secretly convey the anonymous author's true opinion of the Dean, but goes on to reveal that it is itself not genuinely a title page at all. The work it so carefully describes as having been 'Compiled for the behoof and overthrow of the Parsons, Vicars, / and Curates, that have learnt their Catechisms, and are past Grace' proves to be not the *Epistle* that follows, but a different publication altogether: namely the *Epitome*, which 'is not yet published, but it shall be when the Bishops / are at convenient leisure to view the same. In the mean- / time, let them be content with this learned Epistle.' Publicizing a future work, rather than describing the work which it prefaces, this makes a nonsense of the purpose of a title page; it implies that the *Epistle* is not 'really' a work in its own right at all, but a version of the dedicatory epistle that frequently prefaced a printed work which has somehow become detached from the work it introduces. The colophon similarly defies its expected purpose, proclaiming publication of the *Epistle* to have occurred 'oversea in Europe Within two Fur- / longs of a Bounsing Priest'.[52]

The colophon's suppression of the name of the printer and place of publication was of course a necessary subterfuge. Martin's views were seditious ones; not only were they opposed to the Church's articles of faith but, in consequence of the doctrine of royal supremacy, opposition to the

---

[51] As Walter J. Ong has noted, this kind of layout, 'which often seems to us crazily erratic in [its] attention to visual word units', may suggest that 'well after printing was developed, auditory processing continued for some time to dominate the visible, printed text' (*Orality and Literacy*, 118–19). For the standard layout of a title page, see Joad Raymond, *Pamphlets and Pamphleteering in Early Modern Britain* (Cambridge: Cambridge University Press, 2003), 39–40.

[52] For dedicatory epistles, see Wendy Wall, *The Imprint of Gender: Authorship and Publication in the English Renaissance* (Ithaca: Cornell University Press, 1993), 169–226. For the fake colophon as a convention in its own right, see Raymond, *Pamphlets and Pamphleteering*, 40; and for that of the *Epistle*, see Marcy L. North, *The Anonymous Renaissance: Cultures of Discretion in Tudor-Stuart England* (Chicago: University of Chicago Press, 2003), 140, 143.

bishops was held to be the equivalent of opposition to the state. Martin's attention-grabbing and popular expression of these views thus made him the subject not just of printed refutations, but of a sustained attempt to identify, locate, and prosecute him. The consequences of discovery were severe; although the author or authors of the Marprelate tracts were never identified, one of the men whose name was most closely associated with them, John Penry, was indicted and found guilty of publishing other 'seditious' works, and was hanged for the offence.[53] But while the fake colophon was a necessity, the elaborate pseudo-title points to sheer delight at messing around in print. By assuming the same enjoyment on the part of its readers, it implicitly turns them into allies. It is a way of shaping them in Martin's own image: not persuading them by argument, but making them complicit with his own clever irreverence in a way that clearly anticipates Nashe's technique.[54]

Like Nashe, too, Martin glosses in such a way as to enhance this effect of intimacy, transgressing the boundary between text and gloss so as to suggest that his glosses are a record of the composition process. The clearest example of this occurs at a very early stage in the *Epistle*, where he allows the voices of his opponents to intrude into the text, and himself becomes a glossator commenting from the margins. At the point where a lengthy list of bishops in the text is 'interrupted' by the comment 'Now, I pray thee, good Martin, speak out', the gloss observes: 'What malapert knaves are these that cannot be content to stand by and hear, but they must teach a gentleman how to speak?'[55] This inversion of the expected relation between text and gloss is re-emphasized shortly after, in a gloss that gives voice to a speaker who is clearly not Martin; it observes: 'Master Marprelate, you put more than the question in at the conclusion of your syllogism' (see Plate 7.3). To this, Martin himself responds *in the text*: 'This is a pretty matter, that standers-by must be so busy in other men's games. Why, sauceboxes, must you be prattling? . . . But it is well that since you last interrupted me (for now this is the second time) you seem to have learnt your Cato *De Moribus*, in that you keep yourselves on the margent.'[56] By allowing comments in the margins to alter the direction of the text, this exchange flouts the convention that the

---

[53] See Black, *Marprelate Tracts*, pp. xxxvi–xxxvii.
[54] For Martin's deliberate indecorum, see Anselment, *'Betwixt Jest and Earnest'*; John Coolidge, 'Martin Marprelate, Marvell, and *Decorum Personae* as a Satirical Theme', *PMLA* 74 (1959), 526–32; and Kristen Poole, 'Facing Puritanism: Falstaff, Martin Marprelate, and the Grotesque Puritan', in *Shakespeare and Carnival: After Bakhtin*, ed. Ronald Knowles (London: Macmillan, 1998), 97–122.
[55] Pierce (ed.), *Marprelate Tracts*, 23.
[56] Pierce (ed.), *Marprelate Tracts*, 24–5. Tribble suggests that the voice in the margin is that of a bishop (*Margins and Marginality*, 110–11) but Lander argues convincingly that

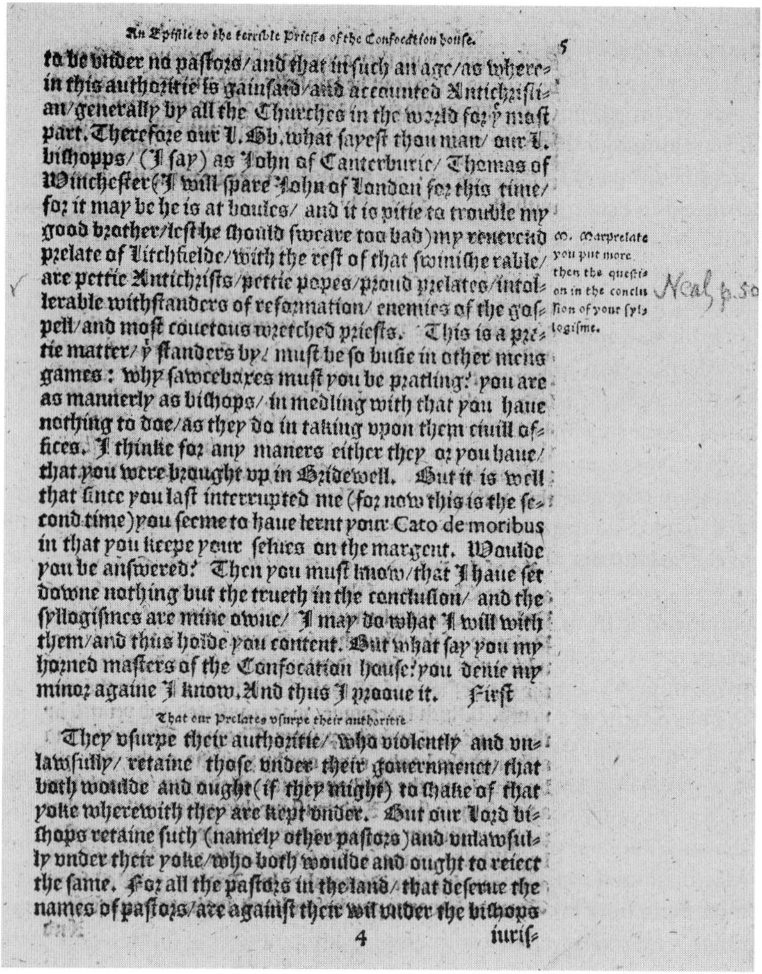

An Epistle to the terrible Priests of the Confocation house. 5

to be vnder no pastors/and that in such an age/as wherein this authoritie is gainsaid/and accounted Antichristi-
an/generally by all the Churches in the world for ÿ most
part. Therefore our L. Gb. what sayest thou man/ our L.
bishopps/ (I say) as Iohn of Canterburie/ Thomas of
Winchester (I will spare Iohn of London for this time/
for it may be he is at boules/ and it is pitie to trouble my
good brother/lest he should sweare too bad) my reuerend
prelate of Litchfielde/with the rest of that swinishe rable/
are pettie Antichrists/pettie popes/proud prelates/intol-
lerable withstanders of reformation/ enemies of the gos-
pell/and most couetous wretched priests. This is a pre-
tie matter/ ÿ standers by/ must be so busie in other mens
games: why sawceboxes must you be pratling? you are
as mannerly as bishops/ in medling with that you haue
nothing to doe/as they do in taking vpon them ciuill offices. I thinke for any maners either they or you haue/
that you were brought vp in Bridewell. But it is well
that since you last interrupted me (for now this is the second time) you seeme to haue lernt your Cato de moribus
in that you keepe your selues on the margent. Woulde
you be answered? Then you must know/that I haue set
downe nothing but the trueth in the conclusion/ and the
syllogismes are mine owne/ I may do what I will with
them/and thus holde you content. But what say you my
horned masters of the Confocation house? you denie my
minor againe I know. And thus I prooue it. First

M. Marprelate you put more then the question in the conclusion of your syllogisme.

That our Prelates vsurpe their authoritie

They vsurpe their authoritie/ who violently and vn-
lawfully/ retaine those vnder their gouernment/ that
both woulde and ought (if they might) to shake of that
yoke wherewith they are kept vnder. But our Lord bishops retaine such (namely other pastors) and vnlawful-
ly vnder their yoke/who both woulde and ought to reiect
the same. For all the pastors in the land/ that deserue the
names of pastors/are against their wil vnder the bishops

4 iuris-

Plate 7.3 Martin Marprelate, *Oh read ouer D. Iohn Bridges, for it is a worthy worke* (East Molesey, Surrey: Robert Waldegrave, 1588), 5. Douce PP 244. Reproduced courtesy of The Bodleian Libraries, The University of Oxford.

gloss is a supplement, added after the composition of the work; rather, as in Nashe's *Have With You*, text and gloss are presented as if they were part of a single, contemporaneous production process, in which the distinction between speaking, writing, and printing is also eroded.

Although Martin's tactics are startling, they have their origin in some fairly standard conventions in the printing of works of controversy. Martin's confusion of the voices of text and gloss parodies the layout of

Bridges' pages, whose glossing is exceptionally intricate. The *Defence* contains several different types of gloss, each carefully distinguished from the others by its own typeface. Italic glosses identify both passages in the text that are quoted from Beza's *Learned Discourse* and the point where Bridges' own refutation of each passage of Beza's begins. Smaller italic glosses provide citations of Biblical chapter and verse, while numerous small roman glosses give an orderly summary of each stage in the argument. In addition, italic running titles in an intermediate size of type appear in the margins at the head of each recto and verso, while within the text, Bridges' words appear in black letter, and quotations from the *Learned Discourse* appear in roman, frequently alternating several times in the course of a single sentence. This elaborate typography is used both to enable the page to represent multiple voices and—crucially—to keep them distinct.

The layout of Bridges' text exemplifies an arrangement that was common in printed controversies, in which quotations from the opponent's works were cited in a different typeface or a different position on the page from the main text, the better to be refuted.[57] Martin's practice, however, looks beyond the conventions of layout to what they imply about the relationship between text and gloss, and the extreme demands they place on both printer and reader. It then exaggerates his findings to the point of absurdity. This appears most clearly from one of the most elaborate glossing sequences in the Marprelate tracts, at the point in the *Epitome* where Martin cites passages from John Aylmer's contributions to Bishop Thomas Cooper's *Admonition to the People of England* (1589). Cooper's is an extraordinary work; it itemizes every last charge in Martin's *Epistle* in order to refute it, but by painstakingly denying, at length and with great circumstantial detail, such footling accusations as that the Bishop of London stole some cloth, or that he is a habitual swearer, it lays itself wide open to mockery.[58] In response Martin's *Epitome* quite literally runs

---

it is instead one of Martin's interested readers, so that the exchange between text and gloss allows Martin to pre-empt and answer questions his actual readers might wish to raise (*Inventing Polemic*, 90–92). Martin may here be parodying a confusion of speech and print that occurs in Bridges' own work when Bridges writes that 'Our Brethern say, they will not speake, of the confusion of voyces, which all speake at once', and a gloss notes 'Al speaking at once', as if the text *were* the confused speech (John Bridges, *A Defence of the Government* (London: Thomas Chard, 1587), 627).

[57] Cf. Benger, 'Authority of Writer', 212–13. For a comparison of Martin's layout with that of John Bale's editions of Thorpe, Oldcastle, and Askew, see Ritchie D. Kendall, *The Drama of Dissent: The Radical Poetics of Nonconformity, 1380–1590* (Chapel Hill: University of North Carolina Press, 1986), 180; and for the argument that Martin was influenced by humanist dialogue, see Navitsky, 'Disputing Good Bishop's English', 185.

[58] Thomas Cooper, *An admonition to the people of England vvherein are ansvvered, not onely the slaunderous vntruethes, reprochfully vttered by Martin the libeller, but also many other crimes by some of his broode* (London: Christopher Barker, 1589), 51–3, 61–3. STC 5682.

rings around the bishop. Parodying both Bridges' and Cooper's habit of quoting extracts from his own writings in their texts, Martin claims to be reproducing in turn not only extracts from their works, but the accompanying glosses as well. This is sufficiently complicated to require him to explain that: 'The particular sentences and marginal notes shall be set down, and where I set any note upon your book, there shall be an M. for difference' sake added thereunto.'[59] In fact, none of the glosses *are* citations from Cooper or Aylmer, but in the absence of an 'M.' claiming them as Martin's, glosses such as: 'The Queen deceived by her churchmen' and 'Spiritual men should not meddle with policies' appear to be attributable to the bishops.[60] The effect is not only to create severe visual overcrowding of the margins, but also to elide the distinction between different texts, or different 'voices'. The layout both assumes that its readers will understand how to negotiate the hierarchies, symbols, and differentiated typefaces of a printed text and, with deliberate indecorousness, utterly goes against that understanding.[61] Whereas the practice of marginal quotation and refutation generally invites the reader to enjoy the cleverness of the author as he demolishes his opponent's argument, Martin's version invites his readers to delight instead in the breakdown of that system.

A comparable diversion is effected by glosses that involve their readers directly, enquiring 'Will you be content, Bishop, it shall be so now?', and 'Doth he mean Watson, the pursuivant, trow you?'.[62] In each of these glosses, the 'you' is personal and immediate; in the former, it singles out one particular bishop from the wider readership, while in the latter, the fact that the 'you' is not identified means that it claims each of its readers as Martin's personal addressee. By seeming to address each reader personally, the question becomes non-rhetorical. Far from aiding the reader in interpretation of the text, it functions like the glosses that collapse the distinction between reading and writing, making him responsible for coming to his own understanding of the work and thus reinventing him as a collaborator. Although the *Epitome* professes to be a private letter to the

---

[59] Pierce (ed.), *Marprelate Tracts*, 147.
[60] Pierce (ed.), *Marprelate Tracts*, 147, 148.
[61] Such highly confrontational and visually bewildering glossing has precedents not only in the argumentative and multi-vocal glosses of the Matthew's Bible of 1536, which recapitulated previous interpretations of particular passages in order to refute them, but also in the glosses deployed by lay disputants. For the former, see Tribble, *Margins and Marginality*, 18–31; for the use of comparable techniques in the Grammarians' War of 1520–1, see Jane Griffiths, 'The Grammarian as "Poeta" and "Vates": Self-Presentation in the *AntiBossicon*', in *Self-Presentation and Social Identification: The Rhetoric and Pragmatics of Letter-Writing in Early Modern Times*, ed. Toon van Houdt, Jan Papy, and Gilbert Tournoy (Leuven: Leuven University Press, 2001), 317–36.
[62] Pierce (ed.), *Marprelate Tracts*, 149, 150.

clergy, these glosses draw in the readers of the printed text by implying that they are the textual equivalent of eavesdroppers: the privileged witnesses of Martin's dramatic and entertaining demolition of the bishops' point of view. Ostensibly making the reader privy to the writer's private, off-the-cuff thoughts, they replicate in print the effect of real authorial presence, and thereby establish a confidential alliance with their reader. In order to do so, however, they depend on their readers' familiarity with established typographic conventions, which they then subvert.

PIERCE PENILESSE IN CONTEXT: CROWLEY'S *PIERS PLOWMAN*

The fact that Martin's flamboyant glossing is not entirely his own invention, but depends in part on an established 'language' of print, suggests that Nashe's glossing too may be grounded in previous practice. Although the way in which Martin plays form against function clearly anticipates Nashe's technique, his is not the only influence on Nashe; rather, both are beneficiaries of existing traditions. Printed humanist and theological disputes are just one of these. Another is indicated by the name of Nashe's protagonist. Although the name 'Pierce' has long been recognized as a pun on 'Piers' and 'purse', it has generally been discussed as if 'purse' were the active component, in that it allows Nashe's protagonist to be identified wholly with his lack of cash.[63] However, the name Pierce also connects Nashe's treatise to the rich seam of vernacular, Reformist writing characterized by its use of the figure of 'Piers Plowman'.[64] With origins in Langland's *Piers Plowman* and the late-fourteenth-century *Piers the Plowman's Crede*, 'Piers' figures were common in radical religious writing of the mid-sixteenth century; their ancestry ensured that the name 'Piers' served as a shorthand for plainness and probity, and their function was generally to challenge Catholic practice or doctrine. The very titles of works that use a Piers-figure as their protagonist give an indication of their position; they include *The prayer and complaynt of the ploweman vnto Christ* (c. 1532), *A Godly dyalogue & dysputacyon betwene Pyers Plowman, and a popysh preest concernyng the supper of the Lorde* (c. 1550), *I playne Piers which can not flatter* (c. 1550), and *Pyers plowmans exhortation, vnto*

---

[63] See for example Niel K. Snortum, 'The Title of Nash's *Pierce Penilesse*', *Modern Language Notes* 72 (1957), 170–3.
[64] This connection has recently been noted by Mike Rodman Jones, *Radical Pastoral, 1381–1594: Appropriation and the Writing of Religious Controversy* (Farnham: Ashgate, 2011), 152–60.

the lordes, knightes and burgoysses of the Parlyamenthouse (c. 1550).[65] At least one of these later acquired a Marprelate association; the title page of the 1589 reprint of *I Playne Piers* exhorts its readers:

> O read me for I am of great antiquitie I plaine Piers which can not flatter, a plough man men me call, my speech is fowlle yet marke the matter now things may hap to fall, but now another Ile haue for mee, I thinke it is as fit say, if any my name doo craue, I am the gransier of Martin mareprelitte.

It continues in good parodic Martinist style with the assertion that it was: 'compiled afore yeaster day, for the behoofe and ouerthrow of all parsons, vikars, and curats, who haue learned their cathechismes and can not yet vnderstand them, although they be past their grace . . . Printed either of this side, or of that side of some the priestes.'[66] In the context of the Marprelate controversy the usefulness of claiming the virtuous and victorious outsider Piers as an ancestor is clear. In contrast, the wordy and indigent protagonist of Nashe's work seems at first sight to have little to do with his plain-speaking and innately virtuous namesakes. The one thing they have in common is their poverty, but for Nashe's Pierce this is far from serving as proof of his unworldliness; rather, it is an unfortunate condition which he is desperate to escape. Moreover, whereas the Piers of tradition is godly, the title of Nashe's work proclaims his protagonist to be the opposite. The allusion to Piers seems almost to be a mistake, as if the determination to create a pun on 'purse' had led Nashe astray.

On second thoughts, however, such reversals prove to be precisely the point: by raising certain expectations in the reader and then flamboyantly failing to meet them, Nashe's use of the name Pierce allows him to make two related satirical points. The fact that it is a *Piers*, of all people, who finds himself compelled to write a supplication to the devil re-emphasizes Nashe's point about the parlous state of society; the implication is that the character Piers can no longer be used as a figure of virtue because society has become such that his virtue has no place. As well as contributing to Nashe's social satire, the use of Pierce as protagonist enables Nashe to make a literary-satirical point too; if a Piers-figure can no longer be used in the conventional way, this implies that existing literary traditions themselves are bankrupt. The inevitable comparison between Nashe's Pierce and previous Piers figures thus provides fuel for the claim in *Pierce Penilesse* that the state of the literary nation is to blame for Pierce's (or

---

[65] See further Andrew N. Wawn, 'Chaucer, *The Plowman's Tale*, and Reformation Propaganda', *Bulletin of the John Rylands University Library of Manchester* 56 (1973), 174–92; and John N. King, *English Reformation Literature: The Tudor Origins of the Protestant Tradition* (Princeton: Princeton University Press, 1982), 323–6.

[66] See further Black, *Marprelate Tracts*, pp. xxix–xxx.

Nashe's) poverty: the dominance of the old, outworn genres means that truly virtuous writers (which for Nashe means truly virtuoso writers) go unrewarded. Nashe's revolutionary, inappropriate use of the name Pierce is thus a device comparable to the unexpected turn taken by Pierce's confession, the work's incorporation of a wide variety of genres, and its numerous bravura, 'extemporary' performances on set themes. Each is designed to startle readers (and potential patrons) out of their complacency, and into an acknowledgement that the work's own reinvention of literary traditions has innate value and thus deserves reward. It functions as a showcase for Pierce's (or Nashe's) virtuosity: a practical demonstration of his adaptability, and thus of his fitness to write for pay.

The majority of the 'Piers' works were printed in a cheap format, without glossing of any kind; it was not until 1606 that a related text, *The Ploughmans Tale*, was published with an extensive, radical commentary.[67] The notable exception is Langland's *Piers Plowman*. This was widely available in the sixteenth century, and was conspicuously popular; of the almost sixty surviving manuscripts of a complete form of the text, several are extensively annotated by sixteenth-century readers, while Robert Crowley's edition ran to three impressions in 1550, and was again reprinted by William Owen in 1561. Nashe's use of the name 'Pierce' in a work structured around the seven deadly sins suggests that his *Pierce Penilesse* does not allude only to Piers literature generally, but also, more specifically, to Langland's *Piers*. The confession of the seven deadly sins forms an important part of Passus V of Langland's work; as part of the A-text as well as the B- and C-texts, it was among the first parts of the poem to be composed, at a point where Langland was still writing in an established tradition of social satire, and had not begun to develop his intensely personal questioning of the nature of salvation and the extent of an individual's responsibility for the state of his own soul.[68] Although the sin topos had been in common use from the twelfth century onwards, personification of the sins was relatively rare outside drama, and personification in combination with a use of the sins that facilitates social satire, rather than treating the sins themselves as direct objects of attack, was highly unusual. Yet these are both features that Nashe's *Pierce Penilesse* shares with Langland's work.[69]

---

[67] *The plough-mans tale Shewing by the doctrine and liues of the Romish clergie, that the Pope is Antichrist and they his ministers* (London: Samuell Macham and Mathew Cooke, 1606), STC 5101.

[68] For the gradual evolution of *Piers Plowman*, see Malcolm Godden, *The Making of Piers Plowman* (Harlow: Longman, 1990).

[69] See further Morton W. Bloomfield, *The Seven Deadly Sins: An Introduction to the History of a Religious Concept* (Michigan: Michigan State College Press, 1952), esp. 157–201. It may also be significant that, like Nashe, Crowley consistently uses the spelling 'Pierce'.

Langland's *Piers Plowman* thus functions as a subtext to *Pierce Penilesse* in the way that Ovid's *Tristia* does, similarly illustrating Nashe's ability to work by contrast as well as comparison. Although Langland provides a precedent for using the sin topos as a means of social criticism, his sins are nonetheless engaged, however inadequately, in the process of confession; his treatment of them ends with Repentance, providing a vision of restored order and a reintegrated community unified in its search for Truth. Since both of these are signally lacking in Nashe's work, *Pierce Penilesse* gains a satirical edge by the absence of the expected resolution. Moreover, by presenting his protagonist Pierce so explicitly as an indigent *writer*, it is possible that Nashe is incorporating within his Piers-figure some of the doubts concerning the writer's moral authority, and the value of his work, which also beset the poet Will within Langland's poem. Characters that for Langland are opposites—one (Piers) so fully embodying the true Christian life that he becomes a figure of Christ, and the other (Will) beset with uncertainties about the moral value of his work as a writer—in Nashe's *Pierce Penilesse* are fused in the idle Pierce.[70] In effect, Nashe gives the name of one of Langland's characters to the sixteenth-century reincarnation of the other, and substitutes financial value for Christian value. When both works are kept simultaneously in mind, the effect is to strengthen further Nashe's theme of bankruptcy, stretching it to encompass not only society and patrons at large, but the author too, and perhaps even virtue itself. At the same time, however, the form in which Crowley presents Langland's work, and specifically his glossing, suggests ways in which print conventions might be used as a means of reinvigorating old literary forms, enabling them to provoke active engagement from their readers, and re-establishing the value of writing in all its senses. As its manuscripts attest, Langland's work had always attracted glosses from a diversity of readers.[71] The strangely uneven glossing of Crowley's edition is different in effect from such reader annotation, however. It both invites thought about the effects of including glosses as part of a printed text,

---

[70] For Will as a writer-figure, see James Simpson, 'The Power of Impropriety: Authorial Naming in *Piers Plowman*', in *William Langland's Piers Plowman: A Book of Essays*, ed. Kathleen M. Hewett-Smith (London: Routledge, 2001), 145–66; cf. also J. A. Burrow, *Langland's Fictions* (Oxford: Clarendon Press, 1993), 82–108; and John M. Bowers, *The Crisis of Will in Piers Plowman* (Washington, DC: Catholic University of America Press, 1986), 192–218.

[71] For readers' glosses, see C. David Benson and Lynne Blanchfield, *The Manuscripts of Piers Plowman: The B-Version* (Woodbridge: D. S. Brewer, 1997); and Carl Grindley, 'Reading *Piers Plowman* C-Text Annotations: Notes toward the Classification of Printed and Written Marginalia in Texts from the British Isles 1300–1641', in *The Medieval Professional Reader at Work: Evidence from Manuscripts of Chaucer, Langland, Kempe, and Gower*, ed. Kathryn Kerby-Fulton and Maidie Hilmo (Victoria: University of Victoria Press, 2001),

and suggests ways in which these might be exploited by writers (such as Nashe) self-conscious about their works' medium of transmission and the connotations of print publication.

Crowley's edition has generally been discussed as a means of appropriating a medieval text for Reformist ends, yet its glossing is much less consistent than this implies. Glosses that seek to claim *Piers Plowman* as a proto-Protestant text are relatively few in number.[72] The vast majority of Crowley's glosses are indexing ones, and Crowley is explicitly resistant to attempts to interpret Langland's work as a prophecy of the Reformation.[73] Where polemical glosses do appear, they frequently begin as summary. Thus, glosses such as 'High degre helpeth nothinge to heauenwarde', 'Friers did not seke þe bodi but the monie', 'Christe was pore', and 'Priesting was an occupation to lyue by' initially take their cues from the text, even though they then read it through a Reformist lens.[74] What is interesting about Crowley's glossing is less its consistency of purpose than what it reveals about the difficulty of glossing consistently. As appears from glosses such as 'What harme ye vitiliers do & what abucis in regratry', 'Drede maketh the gilty flee', and 'False can lack no maister', an element of either discursiveness or sententiousness is frequently necessary in order fully to convey the sense of the text.[75] Yet as with Copland's glosses to the *Eneados*, or Gascoigne's to *Jocasta*, sententiousness, in particular, frequently proves misleading. Because *Piers Plowman* contains so many speakers of such

---

73–141. Cf. also <http://www.rarebookschool.org/fellowships/rbs-uva/>, which provides all marginal annotations from twelve manuscripts of the B-text and all three of Crowley's prints.

[72] John N. King argues that Crowley's edition is polemically Protestant in other respects too ('Robert Crowley's Editions of *Piers Plowman*: A Tudor Apocalypse', *Modern Philology* 73 (1976), 342–52). His assertion that Crowley alters passages to make them doctrinally acceptable is convincingly refuted by J. R. Thorne and Marie-Claire Uhart, however ('Robert Crowley's *Piers Plowman*', *Medium Aevum* 55 (1986), 248–54).

[73] See further R. Carter Hailey, 'Robert Crowley and the Editing of *Piers Plowman* (1550)', *Yearbook of Langland Studies* 21 (2007), 143–70; Wendy Scase, 'Dauy Dycars Dreame and Robert Crowley's Prints of *Piers Plowman*', *Yearbook of Langland Studies* 21 (2007), 171–98; Rebecca L. Schoff, *Reformations: Three Medieval Authors in Manuscript and Moveable Type* (Turnhout: Brepols, 2007), 141–206; and Michael Johnston, 'From Edward III to Edward VI: *The Vision of Pierce Plowman* and Early Modern England', *Reformation* 11 (2006), 47–78. Cf. also Sarah A. Kelen, *Langland's Early Modern Identities* (Basingstoke: Palgrave MacMillan, 2007), 34–6; Barbara A. Johnson, *Reading 'Piers Plowman' and 'The Pilgrim's Progress': Reception and the Protestant Reader* (Carbondale: Southern Illinois University Press, 1992), 148–59; and Jane Griffiths, 'Editorial Glossing and Reader Resistance in a Copy of Robert Crowley's *Piers Plowman*', in *The Makers and Users of Medieval Books: Essays in Honour of A. S. G. Edwards*, ed. Carol M. Meale (Woodbridge: Boydell and Brewer, 2014), 202–13).

[74] *The Vision of Pierce Plowman* (London: R. Grafton for Robert Crowley [1550]), sigs. Nii^v, Oii, Oiii^v, Pi^v. Among these glosses are some that both contribute to and reflect the way in which Piers was becoming a universal figure of (Protestant) virtue, for example 'The plowman is Truthes seruaunt' (sig. Hi) and 'How Piers teacheth the waye to trueth' (sig. Hi^v).

[75] *Vision of Pierce Plowman*, sigs. Di and Ciii.

variable reliability, and because all pronouncements and discoveries in the text, even when offered by apparently authoritative figures such as Holy Church, prove to be provisional, even accurate summaries risk privileging a view that will shortly be shown to be compromised. Crowley's glossing thus reveals the potentially destabilizing effect of what is intended to be a useful and instructive apparatus, and provides a model against which Nashe's glossing reacts.

At the same time, Crowley anticipates the means by which Nashe will effect his challenging of assumptions of the stability of the printed text. A minority of the glosses make explicit the glossator's opinion, as for example the observation that 'He citeth a lye out of the Legend auri', or the sarcastic comment 'A good scholemaster' at the point where the text names Wrath as a priest.[76] Occasionally, Crowley also addresses the reader in person, inviting him to take responsibility for his own life and his own reading: thus we find 'Wo be to *you* þ^t turn the tithes to private use'; 'Bestowe *your* tythes as *you* are bounde to do'; 'Lerne to chose *the* a wife'; and 'The Legend of Sayntes, beleue it if *ye* luste'.[77] Like Cooper's and Bridges' works, then, Crowley's glossing both makes visible the potential pitfalls of overtly directive glossing and the potential of the printed text incongruously to formalize an informal aside. Both are tactics on which Martin and Nashe will draw, as they seek to encourage engagement with their works by entertaining rather than instructing their readers.

Nashe's glossing thus has a broader basis than has previously been suggested. His juxtaposition of different types of gloss suggests that his glossing is informed precisely by the incompatibility of a number of different models: by unlike as well as by like practice. On the one hand, Nashe's interest in the way the fixed medium of print can be made to represent the fluidity of speech, and his use of glosses that explore the relation between speech and print, recalls a tradition of experimentation with printed glosses of which Martin, too, was a beneficiary; on the other, the kind of glossing exemplified by Crowley both provides a theoretical standard from which to divert and reveals how even a relatively unself-conscious use of glosses may create a play of meaning outside the glossator's control. Like Nashe's transformation of familiar genres and topoi in the text of *Pierce Penilesse*, his glossing too depends on invoking and then re-inventing a familiar form. In this, his practice recalls that of many other diverting glossers. Specifically, Nashe revisits Baldwin's interest in challenging assumptions that print fixes and stabilizes a text by using techniques that

---

[76] *Vision of Pierce Plowman*, sigs. Bbii and Fii^v.
[77] *Vision of Pierce Plowman*, sigs. Lii^v, Liii, Liii^v, Xi^v (italics mine).

recall Harington's. They differ from Harington's, however, in that Nashe's asides do not represent an intrusion of the writer's self into the text, but a highly self-conscious *performance* of that self; like Gascoigne's elaborate (mis)use of paratextual conventions, they suggest that the figure of the writer is always a fiction: one that has no existence beyond the oxymoronic representation of the speaking voice on the printed page. Still more than those of previous diverting glossers, Nashe's glossing practices depend on his readers' recognition of the way they subvert expectations as to how glosses will relate to the text. They thus indicate the extent to which marginal glosses had become a familiar presence in printed texts of the period, yet also the extent to which they remained a locus of experimentation. For Nashe, as for experimental glossers for the previous two centuries, glosses both effect meaning, and make visible that they are doing so.

Afterword

Bringing us back to the 1590s, where the first chapter began, the glossing of Nashe's and Harington's works enables us to reappraise Speght's glossing of his edition of Chaucer. As Megan Cook has recently argued, both the form and the content of Speght's apparatus were demonstrably influenced by E. K.'s commentary on *The Shepheardes Calendar*.[1] The examples of Harington and Nashe, however, suggest that the apparently artless tone of Speght's glosses, as well as the substance of his observations, may be indebted not only to E. K. but also to a more widespread tendency in late-sixteenth-century glossing. As we saw in the first chapter, among the most striking characteristics of Speght's glossing is his use of an intimate first-person address to the reader, and this is something he shares not only with E. K., Nashe, and Harington, but also with a large number of other glossators of the late-sixteenth and early seventeenth centuries. Thus, a comparable voice is found in the glossing of works as diverse as Ben Jonson's masques, Michael Drayton's *Polyolbion*, and the polemical 1606 edition of *The Plough-man's Tale*.[2] Although each of these, in William Slights' term, seeks to 'edify' the reader, it does so less by overt direction than by covert persuasion; its 'creation and instruction of a community of readers' is performed through its confident assumption that it and they share a single perspective.[3]

In deploying an essentially private voice in a public medium, the glossing of these works bears a strong resemblance to diverting glossing. It differs, however, in that it displays no apparent sense of incongruity in doing so. That is why I have chosen to conclude this book with Nashe. The turn of the sixteenth and seventeenth centuries does not, of course, mark the end of

---

[1] Megan L. Cook, 'Marking and Managing the Page: Lexical Commentary in Spenser's *Shepheardes Calendar* (1579) and Chaucer's *Works* (1598/1602)', *Spenser Studies* 26 (2011), 179–222.

[2] For Jonson see Evelyn B. Tribble, *Margins and Marginality: The Printed Page in Early Modern England* (Charlottesville: University Press of Virginia, 1993), 130–57; for Selden's glossing of the *Polyolbion* see William W. E. Slights, *Managing Readers: Printed Marginalia in English Renaissance Books* (Ann Arbor: University of Michigan Press, 2001), 183–222 (esp. 201–3); Anne Lake Prescott, 'Marginal Discourse: Drayton's Muse and Selden's "Story"', *Studies in Philology* 88 (1991), 307–28; and Claire McEachern, *The Poetics of English Nationhood, 1590–1612* (Cambridge: Cambridge University Press, 1996), 173–87; for *The Plowman's Tale* see Paul J. Patterson, 'Reforming Chaucer: Margins and Religion in an Apocryphal *Canterbury Tale*', *Book History* 8 (2005), 11–36.

[3] Slights, *Managing Readers*, 19.

the marginal gloss; on the contrary, glossing remained a prominent feature of many printed texts for at least another century.[4] But as the incongruously personal voice that characterizes so many diverting glosses becomes mainstream, it ceases to be diverting.[5] Unlike Harington's or Nashe's, the personal speaking voice of Speght's or Jonson's glosses is not experimental; rather, it represents the confident use of a tried and tested, rhetorically effective trope. Selden's glossing of Drayton's *Polyolbion* and that of works by his fellow Spenserians may even constitute an appeal to an established vernacular glossing tradition as part of their nostalgic invocation of a past and more glorious England.[6] *The Plough-man's Tale*, too, appeals to precedent through its form as well as its content. The way in which its glossing recalls that of Crowley's *Pierce Plowman* functions analogously to the use of a ploughman figure within the text; just as the anonymous author positioned himself in relation to Langland's text, the glossator places himself in a tradition of Reformist glossing.[7] In neither case do the glosses prompt or present new discoveries about authorship; instead, they seek to authorize the texts to which they are attached by allusion to previous uses of the form with specific (nationalist or Reformist) connotations. The incongruously informal voice that was part of a radical challenge to print's connotations of fixity and stability has itself become a convention.

This is not to say that there was no further experimentation with glossing. In the quarto of *Sejanus* (1605), for example, Jonson takes the use of citation glosses to extremes, overcrowding the margins with references whose lengthy and quite impersonal lists of classical precedents and analogies were apparently designed to defend Jonson against charges of treason by the Privy Council.[8] Even in the glossing of his masques, where he too

---

[4] For the gradual replacement of the marginal gloss by the footnote, see Evelyn B. Tribble, '"Like a Looking-Glass in the Frame": From the Marginal Note to the Footnote', in *The Margins of the Text*, ed. D. C. Greetham (Ann Arbor: University of Michigan Press, 1997), 229–44; Anthony Grafton, *The Footnote: A Curious History* (Cambridge, MA: Harvard University Press, 1999); and Lawrence Lipking, 'The Marginal Gloss', *Critical Inquiry* 3 (1977), 625–7.

[5] This is not a remorselessly chronological development; for a late exception to the rule, see for example the glossing of John Bunyan, *The Holy War* (1682), discussed by Slights, *Managing Readers*, 21–2.

[6] For the nostalgia of Drayton and his contemporaries for late Elizabethan England, see Richard F. Hardin, *Michael Drayton and the Passing of Elizabethan England* (Lawrence: University Press of Kansas, 1973); and cf. Michelle O'Callaghan, *The 'Shepheards Nation': Jacobean Spenserians and Early Stuart Political Culture, 1612–1625* (Oxford: Clarendon Press, 2000); Richard Helgerson, *Forms of Nationhood: The Elizabethan Writing of England* (Chicago: University of Chicago Press, 1993), 125–47; and David Norbrook, *Poetry and Politics in the English Renaissance*, rev. ed. (Oxford: Oxford University Press, 2002), 173–98.

[7] Patterson suggests that the glossator may have been Anthony Wotton ('Reforming Chaucer', 27–30).

[8] See Tribble, *Margins and Marginality*, 146–57; and cf. Slights, *Managing Readers*, 28–33.

makes frequent use of the first person, he does so not in order to establish intimacy with his readers, but rather in order to authorize his work by impressing the readers with his learning. Jonson famously wrote in *Timber* that 'Language most shewes a man: speake, that I may see thee', and with their easy transition from colloquial English to Latin reference and quotation, the glosses to his masques imply that Jonson's innermost character is effortlessly erudite.[9]

The glossing of *Sejanus* and that of the masques serve as paradigms of the two contrasting functions of the gloss most frequently encountered in this study: authorization of the text by linking it to a verifiable external point of reference, and its destabilization by the introduction of an informal or unreliable voice that belies the timeless connotations of form in which it appears. Jonson's glossing thus perpetuates the connection that we have repeatedly encountered between glossing and reflection on the business of authorship. Both in manuscript and in printed texts we have seen a close correlation between the way in which glosses make visible the writing process on the page and a pronounced interest, on the part of the authors, in the relationship between thought and expression, and what that says about the writer's ownership of his work. Slights has argued that:

> A special sense of supplementarity is involved in notes whose purpose is to alter something in the centered text. The text is extended—or perhaps diverted—into new realms by notes that appropriate, correct, parody, preempt, or translate primary text. . . . From the most innocuous translation of a foreign term to the most devastating parody of an idea or a stylistic quirk, such notes take over a text from its author and deliver it to its readers as something quite transformed.[10]

Slights is here discussing third-party glossing—yet, as we have seen, the same effect occurs with self-glossing, too. In texts as diverse as Lydgate's *Siege of Thebes* and Harington's *Orlando Furioso* there is a reciprocal relationship between experiment with the form of the text and discovery of the writer's originary powers.

This inevitably raises the ghost of one of the questions with which I began. If self-consciously literary glossing can be traced, however sporadically, in fifteenth-century practice, how does print impact on its development? The question is the more pressing since playful annotation is not, of course, peculiar to *early* printed texts. Coleridge's *The Rime of the Ancient*

---

[9] *Ben Jonson*, ed. C. H. Herford and Evelyn Simpson, Vol. 8: *The Poems and Prose Works* (Oxford: Clarendon Press, 1947), 625. For Jonson's view of the masque as a serious literary form, see Richard Dutton, *Ben Jonson: To the First Folio* (Cambridge: Cambridge University Press, 1983), 93–102.

[10] Slights, *Managing Readers*, 64.

Mariner is just one obvious later example of highly self-conscious glossing, although this interestingly reverses the relationship between voices which we find in diverting glossing, as Coleridge supplements the personal voice of the text with that of an ostensibly objective annotator.[11] Closer analogies with diverting glossing may be found in a number of footnoted or end-noted texts: Pope's *Dunciad* is a case in point, as are Sterne's *Tristram Shandy*, Alasdair Gray's *Lanark*, and Eliot's *Wasteland*, and there is a further analogy in the elaborately experimental layout of Joyce's *Finnegan's Wake*.[12] Lawrence Lipking considers the move from marginal gloss to footnote to represent a shift from the equal representation of competing voices to a hierarchical arrangement in which the footnote is wholly subservient to the text, yet such talkative and digressive voices may be found in many periods, forms, and genres.[13] The kind of writer who responds to the requirement to present himself in print with the textual equivalent of Edward Lear's urge 'to giggle heartily and hop on one leg down the long gallery' is a remarkably persistent figure.[14]

Yet despite the recurrence of a diverting misuse of textual conventions across boundaries of period and genre, the early decades of printing in England witness a particular concentration of such formal experimentation. The explanation may perhaps be found precisely in the newness of the medium of print. Those sixteenth-century authors whose work we have considered share a strong awareness of the printed page as a visual medium rather than a transparent means of conveying a verbal message. Whereas, for glossators including Copland and Chaloner, print provided an opportunity to reinvent the ubiquitous but unsystematized form of the gloss as a vehicle for directing their readers, thus countering anxieties—themselves in part generated by print—over their texts' widespread dissemination, for diverting glossers it affected their use of the form in an entirely different way.[15] Richard Beadle recently suggested that the cult

---

[11] For the glossing of Coleridge's *Ancient Mariner*, see Lipking, 'Marginal Gloss', 613–24; and Wendy Wall, 'Interpreting Poetic Shadows: The Gloss of "The Rime of the Ancient Mariner"', *Criticism* 29 (1987), 179–95; cf. also Mark L. Barr, 'The Forms of Justice: Precedent and Gloss in *The Rime of the Ancient Mariner*', *ELH* 78 (2011), 863–89.

[12] See further Peter W. Cosgrove, 'Undermining the Text: Edward Gibbon, Alexander Pope, and the Anti-Authenticating Footnote', in *Annotation and Its Texts*, ed. Stephen A. Barney (Oxford: Oxford University Press, 1991), 130–51; Glyn White, 'The Critic in the Text: Footnotes and Marginalia in the Epilogue to Alasdair Gray's *Lanark: A Life in Four Books*', in *Ma(r)king the Text: The Presentation of Meaning on the Literary Page*, ed. Joe Bray, Miriam Handley, and Anne C. Henry (Aldershot: Ashgate, 2000), 55–70; Shari Benstock, 'At the Margin of Discourse: Footnotes in the Fictional Text', *PMLA* 98 (1983), 204–25; and Lipking, 'Marginal Gloss', 631–7.

[13] Lipking, 'Marginal Gloss', 626.

[14] See Vivien Noakes, *Edward Lear: The Life of a Wanderer*, rev. ed. (London: BBC, 1985), 34.

[15] For lack of an English glossing tradition, see the Introduction, note 21.

of handwriting is a feature of print culture: that, once the written word is destined for print, greater value is attached to the autograph manuscript as a way of recovering the lost 'presence' of the author.[16] Diverting glosses such as Gascoigne's, Nashe's, or Harington's have the capacity to function analogously, as a trace of authorial presence, speaking directly to the reader in denial of boundaries of time and space. What Shari Benstock has argued with reference to footnotes in fictional texts—that they compel a search for the author—is true of self-glossing too, and print is a necessary precondition for such a search: it enhances both the distance between author and reader, and the compulsion (on both sides) to bridge it.[17]

Diverting glossing thus reflects those discoveries about the 'timeliness' of the gloss—the realization of the gloss as material counterpart or visible sign of the processes of translation and imitation—which are found in Lydgate's and Douglas' writing and in *Reson and Sensuallyte*, but does it through the lens of the new medium of transmission. Both pre-print and print authors manifest a concern with authorship, with the gloss as genre, and with the intersection between the two, providing a reminder that, in Jerome McGann's words, 'discourse takes place in specific and concrete forms, and that those forms are by no means comprehended by the limits of language'.[18] Precisely because they are odd, awkward, and (in many cases) attention-seeking, both early experimental glossing and diverting glossing show how the form of the gloss may prompt as well as reflect developing ideas about authorship and an author's connection with his readers, and how theory is inseparable from the practice in which it is grounded. Both kinds of glossing thus allow a glimpse of the impossible: of a meaning that is still in the process of being made. As Lipking puts it: 'The text furnishes the occasion, but its value begins and ends with the activity of the mind. Margins. . . exemplify the infinite extension of thoughts, the profound white space, forever waiting to be filled, that supplies the necessary condition of mental life.'[19]

---

[16] Richard Beadle, 'Literary Autographs I: Fugitive Pieces', Lyell Lecture, University of Oxford, 25 April 2013.

[17] Shari Benstock, 'At the Margins of Discourse', 204–25.

[18] Jerome J. McGann, *The Beauty of Inflections: Literary Investigations in Historical Method and Theory*, quoted in Martin Irvine, ' "Bothe Text and Gloss": Manuscript Form, the Textuality of Commentary, and Chaucer's Dream Poems', in *The Uses of Manuscripts in Literary Studies: Essays in Memory of Judson Boyce Allen*, ed. Charlotte Cook Morse, Penelope Reed Doob, and Marjorie Curry Woods (Kalamazoo: Medieval Institute Publications, 1992), 82.

[19] Lipking, 'Marginal Gloss', 610.

Bibliography

MANUSCRIPTS

British Library MS Arundel 119
British Library MS Cotton Appendix xxvii
British Library MS Egerton 2864
British Library MS Harley 372
British Library MS Harley 1245
British Library MS Harley 1766
British Library MS Harley 2251
British Library MS Harley 3486
British Library MS Harley 4197
British Library MS Harley 4203
British Library MS Royal 14.E.v
British Library MS Royal 18.B.xxxi
British Library MS Royal 18.D.ii
British Library MS Royal 18.D.iv
British Library MS Royal 18.D.v
British Library MS Royal 18.D.vii
British Library MS Royal 20.C.iv
British Library MS Sloane 1710
British Library MS Sloane 4031
British Library MS Additional 5140
British Library MS Additional 16165
British Library MS Additional 18632
British Library MS Additional 18750
British Library MS Additional 21410
British Library MS Additional 29729
British Library MS Additional 39659
London, Lambeth Palace MS 117
London, Lambeth Palace MS 256
London, Lambeth Palace MS 742
Bodleian MS Arch. Selden B.24
Bodleian MS Bodley 263
Bodleian MS Bodley 265
Bodleian MS Bodley 638
Bodleian MS Bodley 776
Bodleian MS Digby 230
Bodleian MS e. Musaeo 1
Bodleian MS Fairfax 16

Bodleian MS Hatton 2
Bodleian MS Laud Misc. 416
Bodleian MS Laud Misc. 557
Bodleian MS Rawlinson C.48
Bodleian MS Rawlinson C.448
Bodleian MS Tanner 346
Oxford, Christ Church MS 152
Oxford, St John's College MS 266
Cambridge University Library MS Ff.1.6
Cambridge University Library MS Gg.4.27
Cambridge University Library MS Additional 3137
Cambridge University Library MS Additional 6864
Cambridge, Magdalene College MS Pepys 2006
Cambridge, Magdalene College MS Pepys 2011
Cambridge, Trinity College MS O.3.12
Cambridge, Trinity College MS O.5.2
Cambridge, Trinity College MS R.3.19
Cambridge, Trinity College MS R.4.20
Coventry City Record Office MS Acc. 325/1
Durham University Library MS Cosin V.ii.14
Edinburgh University Library MS Dc.1.43
Edinburgh University Library MS Dk.7.49
Glasglow University Library MS Hunter 5
Manchester University Library, MS Rylands English 2
Boston Public Library MS f. med. 94
New York, Columbia University Library MS Plimpton 255
New York, Pierpont Morgan Library MS M.4
New York, Pierpont Morgan Library MS M.124
Philadelphia, Rosenbach Library MS 439/16
Princeton University Library MS Garrett 139
Princeton University Library MS Taylor 2
Yale University, Beinecke MS 661

PRIMARY TEXTS

Anon. *Lystoire de Thebes*, in *Prose, Verse, and Truthtelling in the Thirteenth Century: An Essay on Form and Function in Selected Texts, Accompanied by an Edition of the Prose Thèbes as found in the Histoire ancienne jusqu'à César*. Ed. Molly Lynde-Recchia. Lexington, KT: French Forum, 2000.
Anon. *Sensuyt le Roman de Edipus. . . Nouuellement imprime a Paris*. [S.I., n.d.]
Anon. *The Late Medieval Religious Plays of Bodleian MS Digby 133 and e. Musaeo 160*. Ed. Donald C. Baker, John L. Murphy, and Louis B. Hall. London: Early English Text Society. Extra Series 183, 1982.
Anon. *The prayer and complaynt of the plowman vnto Christ*. London: T. Godfray, c. 1532. STC 20036.5.

Bibliography

Anon. *A Godly dyalogue & dysputacyon betwene Pyers Plowman, and a popysh preest concernyng the supper of the Lorde.* [London:] W. Copland, c. 1550. STC 19903.

Anon. *Pyers plowmans exhortation, vnto the lordes, knightes and burgoysses of the Parlyamenthouse.* London: Anthony Scoloker, c. 1550. STC 19905.

Anon. *I playne Piers which can not flatter.* London: N. Hill, 1550. STC 19903a.

Anon. *The plough-mans tale Shewing by the doctrine and liues of the Romish clergie, that the Pope is Antichrist and they his ministers.* London: Samuell Macham and Mathew Cooke, 1606. STC 5101.

Baldwin, William. *A maruelous hystory intitulede, beware the cat.* London: William Gryffith, 1570. STC 1244.

Baldwin, William. *[A maruelous hystory intitulede, beware the cat.]* London: Edward Allde, 1584. STC 1245.

Baldwin, William. *Beware the Cat.* Ed. William Ringler and Michael Flachmann. San Marino: Huntington Library, 1988.

[Baldwin, William.] *A Mirror for Magistrates.* Ed. Lily B. Campbell. 2 vols. Cambridge: Cambridge University Press, 1938.

Boccacio, Giovanni. 'De Genealogiae Deorum Gentilium.' Ed. Vittorio Zaccaria. In *Tutte le opere di Giovanni Boccaccio.* Gen. ed. Vittore Branca. Milan: Arnoldo Mondadori, 1998. Vols. 7–8.

Boccacio, Giovanni. *Boccaccio on Poetry: Being the Preface and the Fourteenth and Fifteenth Books of Boccaccio's Genealogia Deorum Gentilium in an English Version.* Tr. Charles G. Osgood. Princeton: Princeton University Press, 1930.

Breton, Nicholas. *Pasquils Mad-cap.* London: Thomas Bushell, 1600. STC 3675.

Breton, Nicholas. *Pasquils Fooles-cap.* London: Thomas Johns, 1600. STC 3677.5.

Breton, Nicholas. *Pasquils Mistresse.* London: Thomas Fisher, 1600. STC 3678.

Breton, Nicholas. *Pasquils passe, and passeth not.* London: John Smithick, 1600. STC 3679.

Bridges, John. *A Defence of the Government.* London: Thomas Chard, 1587. STC 3734.

Bullein, William. *A newe booke entituled the gouernement of healthe.* London: John Day, 1558. STC 4039.

Bullein, William. *Bulleins Bulwarke of Defence.* London: John Kingston, 1562. STC 4033.

Bullein, William. *A dialogue both pleasant and piety-full, against the fever pestilence.* London: John Kingston, 1564. STC 4036.

Bullein, William. *A Dialogue against the Feuer Pestilence.* Ed. Mark W. Bullen and A. H. Bullen. London: Early English Text Society. Extra Series 52. 1888.

Chaloner, Sir Thomas. *The Praise of Folie.* London: Thomas Berthelet, 1549. STC 10500.

Chaloner, Sir Thomas. *The Praise of Folie.* Ed. Clarence H. Miller. London: Early English Text Society. Original Series 257. 1965.

Chaucer, Geoffrey. *The Canterbury Tales.* Westminster: William Caxton, 1483. STC 5083.

Chaucer, Geoffrey. *The workes of Geffray Chaucer newly printed.* London: Thomas Godfray, 1532. STC 5068.

Chaucer, Geoffrey. *The woorkes of Geoffrey Chaucer, newly printed, with diuers addicions, whiche were neuer in printe before.* London: John White, 1561. STC 5076.
Chaucer, Geoffrey. *The workes of our antient and learned English poet, Geffrey Chaucer.* London: George Bishop, 1598. STC 5077.
Chaucer, Geoffrey. *The workes of our ancient and learned English poet, Geffrey Chaucer.* London: Adam Islip, 1602. STC 5080.
Chaucer, Geoffrey. *The Riverside Chaucer.* Ed. Larry D. Benson. Oxford: Oxford University Press, 1988.
Conty, Évrart de. *Le Livre des Eschez Amoureux Moralisés.* Ed. Francoise Guichard-Tesson and Bruno Roy. Montreal: CERES, 1993.
Cooper, Thomas. *An admonition to the people of England wherein are answered, not onely the slaunderous vntruethes, reprochfully vttered by Martin the libeller, but also many other crimes by some of his broode.* London: Christopher Barker, 1589. STC 5682.
Douglas, Gavin. *The xiii. Bukes of Eneados of the famose Poete Virgill Translatet out of Latyne verses into the Scottish metir bi the Reverend Father in God Mayster Gawin Douglas Bishop of Dunkel and vnkil to the Erle of Angus.* London: William Copland, 1553. STC 24797.
Douglas, Gavin. *The Poetical Works of Gavin Douglas.* Ed. John Small. 4 vols. Edinburgh: William Patterson, 1874.
Douglas, Gavin. *Virgil's Aeneid.* Ed. David F. C. Coldwell. 4 vols. Edinburgh: Scottish Text Society, 1957–64.
Douglas, Gavin. *The Palis of Honoure*, ed. David Parkinson. Kalamazoo: Medieval Institute Publications, 1992.
Erasmus, Desiderius. *Moriae Encomium.* Basel: Joannes Froben, 1516.
Erasmus, Desiderius. *Moriae Encomium.* Cologne: E. Ceruicornus, 1526.
Erasmus, Desiderius. *De ratione studii.* Ed. Jean-Claude Margolin. *Opera Omnia*, Vol. I: 2. Amsterdam: Koninklijke Nederlandse Akademie van Wetenschappen, 1971.
Erasmus, Desiderius. *De ratione studii.* Tr. and ed. Brian McGregor. *Collected Works of Erasmus*, Vol. 24: Literary and Educational Writings 2. Toronto: University of Toronto Press, 1978.
Erasmus, Desiderius. *Moriae Encomium.* Ed. Clarence H. Miller. *Opera Omnia*, Vol. IV: 3. Amsterdam: Koninklijke Nederlandse Akademie van Wetenschappen, 1979.
Erasmus, Desiderius. *The Praise of Folly.* Tr. Betty Radice. *Collected Works of Erasmus*, Vol. 27: Literary and Educational Writings 5. Toronto: University of Toronto Press, 1986.
Erasmus, Desiderius. *De copia verborum ac rerum.* Ed. Betty I. Knott. *Opera Omnia*, Vol. I: 6. Amsterdam: Koninklijke Nederlandse Akademie van Wetenschappen, 1988.
Erasmus, Desiderius. *De copia.* Tr. Betty I. Knott. *Collected Works of Erasmus*, Vol. 24: Literary and Educational Writings 2. Toronto: University of Toronto Press, 1978.
Gascoigne, George. *A hundreth sundrie flowres.* London: Richard Smith, 1573. STC 11635.

Gascoigne, George. *The Posies*. London: Richard Smith, 1575. STC 11637.
Gascoigne, George. *The Complete Works*. Ed. John W. Cunliffe. 2 vols. Cambridge: Cambridge University Press, 1907–10.
Gascoigne, George. *A Hundreth Sundrie Flowers*. Ed. G. W. Pigman. Oxford: Oxford University Press, 2000.
Harington, Sir John. *Orlando Furioso*. London: Richard Field, 1591. STC 746.
Harington, Sir John. *An anatomie of the metamorphosed Ajax*. London: Richard Field, 1596. STC 12772.
Harington, Sir John. *An apologie*. London: Richard Field, 1596. STC 12773.7.
Harington, Sir John. *A new discourse of a stale subject*. London: Richard Field, 1596. STC 12779.5.
Harington, Sir John. *Sir John Harington's A New Discourse of a Stale Subject Called the Metamorphosis of Ajax*. Ed. Elizabeth Story Donno. London: Routledge, 1962.
Harington, Sir John. *Orlando Furioso*. Ed. Robert McNulty. Oxford: Clarendon Press, 1972.
Harington, Sir John. *The Sixth Book of Virgil's Aeneid*. Ed. Simon Cauchi. Oxford: Clarendon Press, 1991.
Heyworth, Gregory, and Daniel E. O'Sullivan (eds). *Les Eschéz d'Amours: A Critical Edition of the Poem and Its Latin Glosses*. Leiden: Brill, 2013.
Horace, *Satires, Epistles, and Ars Poetica*. Tr. H. Rushton Fairclough. Cambridge, MA: Harvard University Press, 1970.
Jonson, Ben. *Ben Jonson*. Ed. C. H. Herford and Evelyn Simpson. Vol. 8: The Poems and Prose Works. Oxford: Clarendon Press, 1947.
Langland, William. *The Vision of Pierce Plowman now the seconde time imprinted*. London: R. Grafton for Roberte Crowley, [1550]. STC 19907.
Lydgate, John. *Here begynnethe the boke calledde Iohn bochas descriuinge the falle of princis princessis [and] other nobles*. London: Richard Pyson, 1494. STC 3175.
Lydgate, John. *Here begynneth the prologue of the storye of Thebes*. Westminster: Wynkyn de Worde, 1497. STC 17031.
Lydgate, John. *Here begynneth the testament of Iohn Lydgate*. London: Richard Pynson, 1520. STC 17035.
Lydgate, John. *Here begynneth the boke of Iohan Bochas, discryuing the fall of princes, princesses, and other nobles*. London: Richard Pynson, 1527. STC 3176.
Lydgate, John. *The fall of prynces*. London: John Wayland, 1554. STC 3177.5.
Lydgate, John. *The Minor Poems*. Ed. H. N. MacCracken. Vol. 1. London: Early English Text Society. Extra Series 107. 1911.
Lydgate, John. *The Fall of Princes*. Ed. Henry Bergen. 4 vols. London: Early English Text Society. Extra Series 121–124. 1924–7.
Lydgate, John. *Lydgate's Siege of Thebes*. Ed. Axel Erdmann and Eilert Ekwall. 2 vols. London: Early English Text Society. Extra Series 108 and 125. 1911 and 1930.
Lydgate, John. *Lydgate's Temple of Glass*. Ed. J. Schick. London: Early English Text Society. Extra Series 60. 1924.
Lydgate, John. *The Siege of Thebes*. Ed. Robert R. Edwards. Kalamazoo: Medieval Institute Publications, 2001.

[Lydgate, John.] *Lydgate's Reson and Sensuallyte*. Ed. Ernst Sieper, 2 vols. London: Early English Text Society. Extra Series 84 and 89. 1901 and 1903.

Lyly, John. *The Complete Works*. Ed. R. Warwick Bond. 3 vols. Oxford: Clarendon Press, 1902.

[Marprelate, Martin.] *Oh read ouer D. Iohn Bridges, for it is a worthy worke*. [East Molesey, Surrey: Robert Waldegrave, 1588]. STC 17453.

Marprelate, Martin. *The Martin Marprelate Tracts: A Modernized and Annotated Edition*. Ed. Joseph L. Black. Cambridge: Cambridge University Press, 2008.

Marprelate, Martin. *The Marprelate Tracts, 1588, 1589*. Ed. William Pierce. London: James Clark, 1911.

More, Sir Thomas. *Utopia*. Ed. Edward Surtz, S. J., and J. H. Hexter. New Haven: Yale University Press, 1965.

Nashe, Thomas. *Pierce Penilesse his supplicacion to the diuell*. London: Richard Ihones, 1592. STC 18371.

Nashe, Thomas. *Haue with you to Saffron-walden*. London: John Danter, 1596. STC 18369.

Nashe, Thomas. *The Works of Thomas Nashe*. Ed. R. B. McKerrow. 5 vols. Oxford: Basil Blackwell, 1966.

Ovid. *Metamorphoses*. Tr. Frank Justus Miller. 2 vols. 2nd ed. Cambridge, MA: Harvard University Press, 1958–60.

Ovid. *Tristia*. Tr. Arthur Leslie Wheeler and G. P. Goold. 2nd ed. Cambridge, MA: Harvard University Press, 1988.

Premierfait, Laurent de. *Laurent de Premierfait's Des Cas des Nobles Hommes et Femmes, Book I*. Ed. P. M. Gathercole. Chapel Hill: University of North Carolina Press, 1968.

Puttenham, George. *The Arte of English Poesie*. In: *English Renaissance Literary Criticism*. Ed. Brian Vickers. Oxford: Oxford University Press, 1999.

Quintilian. *De Institutio Oratoria*. Tr. Donald A. Russell. Cambridge, MA: Harvard University Press, 2001.

Skelton, John. *A ryght delectable treatyse upon a goodly garlande or chapelet of laurell*. London: Richard Faukes, 1523. STC 22610.

Skelton, John. *A replycacion agaynst certayne yong scolers, abiured of late*. London: Richard Pynson, 1528. STC 22609.

Skelton, John. *The Poetical Works of John Skelton*. Ed. Alexander Dyce. 2 vols. London: T. Rodd, 1843.

Skelton, John. *The Complete English Poems*. Ed. John Scattergood. Harmondsworth: Penguin, 1983.

Sidney, Sir Philip. *A Defence of Poetry*. In: *English Renaissance Literary Criticism*. Ed. Brian Vickers. Oxford: Oxford University Press, 1999.

Tottel, Richard (ed.). *Songs and Sonets*. London: Richard Tottel, 1557. STC 13861.

Virgil. *Aeneid*. Paris: Johannes Badus Ascensius, 1507.

Virgil. *Aeneid*. Tr. H. Rushton Fairclough. Rev. ed. Cambridge, MA: Harvard University Press, 1978.

Whitney, Geoffrey. *A Choice of Emblems and Other Devices*. Leiden, 1586.

William, Roy. *O read me for I am of great antiquitie I plaine Piers which can not flatter*. [S.I.] c. 1589. STC 19903a.5.
Wither, George. *A Collection of Emblemes*. London: John Grismond, 1635. STC 25900a.

SECONDARY SOURCES

Allen, Judson Boyce. *The Ethical Poetic of the Later Middle Ages: A Decorum of Convenient Distinction*. Toronto: University of Toronto Press, 1982.
Anselment, Raymond A. *'Betwixt Jest and Earnest': Marprelate, Milton, Marvell, Swift and the Decorum of Religious Ridicule*. Toronto: University of Toronto Press, 1979.
Arber, Edward. *An Introductory Sketch to the Martin Marprelate Controversy, 1588–90*. London: Archibald Constable, 1895.
Attridge, Derek. 'Puttenham's Perplexity: Nature, Art, and the Supplement in Renaissance Poetic Theory.' In: *Literary Theory/Renaissance Texts*, edited by Patricia Parker and David Quint, pp. 257–79. Baltimore: Johns Hopkins University Press, 1986.
Austen, Gillian. *George Gascoigne*. Woodbridge: D.S. Brewer, 2008.
Barr, Mark L. 'The Forms of Justice: Precedent and Gloss in *The Rime of the Ancient Mariner*.' *ELH* 78 (2011): 863–89.
Barthes, Roland. *S/Z: An Essay*. Tr. Richard Miller. London: Jonathan Cape, 1975.
Baswell, Christopher. 'Talking Back to the Text: Marginal Voices in Medieval Secular Literature.' In: *The Uses of Manuscripts in Literary Studies: Essays in Memory of Judson Boyce Allen*, edited by Charlotte Cook Morse, Penelope Reed Doob, and Marjorie Currie Woods, pp. 121–60. Kalamazoo: Medieval Institute Publications, 1992.
Baswell, Christopher. *Virgil in Medieval England: Figuring the Aeneid from the Twelfth Century to Chaucer*. Cambridge: Cambridge University Press, 1995.
Bath, Michael. *Speaking Pictures: English Emblem Books and Renaissance Culture*. London: Longman, 1994.
Bawcutt, Priscilla. *Gavin Douglas*. Edinburgh: Edinburgh University Press, 1976.
Beadle, Richard. 'Literary Autographs I: Fugitive Pieces.' Lyell Lecture, University of Oxford, 25 April 2013.
Benson, C. David, and Barry A. Windeatt. 'The Manuscript Glosses to Chaucer's *Troilus and Criseyde*.' *Chaucer Review* 25 (1990): 33–53.
Benson, C. David, and Lynne Blanchfield. *The Manuscripts of Piers Plowman: The B-Version*. Woodbridge: D.S. Brewer, 1997.
Benstock, Shari. 'At the Margin of Discourse: Footnotes in the Fictional Text.' *PMLA* 98 (1983): 204–25.
Bloomfield, Morton W. *The Seven Deadly Sins: An Introduction to the History of a Religious Concept*. Michigan: Michigan State College Press, 1952.
Bly, Siobhan. 'From Text to Man: Re-creating Chaucer in Sixteenth-Century Print Editions.' *Comitatus* 30 (1999): 131–66.
Blyth, Charles. *'The Knychtlyke Stile': A Study of Gavin Douglas' Aeneid*. London: Garland, 1987.

Boehrer, Bruce Thomas. *Animal Characters: Non-Human Beings in Early Modern Literature*. Philadelphia: University of Pennsylvania Press, 2010.

Boffey, Julia. 'The Reputation and Circulation of Chaucer's Lyrics in the Fifteenth Century.' *Chaucer Review* 28 (1993): 23–40.

Boffey, Julia. 'Annotation in Some Manuscripts of *Troilus and Criseyde*.' *English Manuscript Studies 1100-1700* 5 (1995): 1–17.

Boffey, Julia, and A. S. G. Edwards. 'Bodleian MS Arch. Selden B.24 and the "Scotticization" of Middle English Verse.' In: *Rewriting Chaucer: Culture, Authority and the Idea of the Authentic Text*, edited by Thomas A. Prendergast and Barbara Kline, pp. 166–85. Columbus: Ohio State University Press, 1999.

Boffey, Julia, and A. S. G. Edwards. *A New Index of Middle English Verse*. London: The British Library, 2005.

Boitani, Piero. *Chaucer and the Imaginary World of Fame*. Cambridge: D.S. Brewer, 1984.

Bonahue, Edward T. '"I Know the Place and the Persons": The Play of Textual Frames in Baldwin's *Beware the Cat*.' *Studies in Philology* 91 (1994): 283–300.

Bowers, John M. *The Crisis of Will in Piers Plowman*. Washington, DC: Catholic University of America Press, 1986.

Bowers, Terence. 'The Production and Communication of Knowledge in William Baldwin's *Beware the Cat*: Towards a Typographic Culture.' *Criticism* 33 (1991): 1–29.

Brigden, Susan. *London and the Reformation*. Oxford: Clarendon Press, 1989.

Brinton, Anna Cox (ed.). *Maphaeus Vegius and his Thirteenth Book of the Aeneid*. Bristol: Bristol Classical, 2002.

Brown, Cynthia J. *Poets, Patrons, and Printers: Crisis of Authority in Late-Medieval France*. Ithaca: Cornell University Press, 1995.

Bruster, Douglas. 'The Structural Transformation of Print in Late Elizabethan England.' In: *Print, Manuscript, and Performance: The Changing Relations of the Media in Early Modern England*, edited by Arthur F. Marotti and Michael D. Bristol, pp. 49–89. Columbus: Ohio State University Press, 2000.

Budra, Paul. *A Mirror for Magistrates and the De Casibus Tradition*. Toronto: University of Toronto Press, 2000.

Bühler, C. F. *The Fifteenth-Century Book: The Scribes, the Printers, the Decorators*. Philadelphia: University of Pennsylvania Press, 1960.

Burdon, Christopher. 'The Margin Is the Message: Commentary's Displacement of Canon.' *Literature and Theology* 13 (1999): 222–34.

Burrow, Colin. *Epic Romance: Homer to Milton*. Oxford: Clarendon Press, 1993.

Burrow, Colin. '"Full of the Maker's Guile": Ovid on Imitating and the Imitation of Ovid.' In: *Ovidian Transformations: Essays on the Metamorphoses and Its Reception*, edited by Philip Hardie, Alessandro Barchiesi, and Stephen Hinds, pp. 271–87. Cambridge: Cambridge Philological Society, 1999.

Burrow, John. 'The Poet and the Book.' In: *Genres, Themes, and Images in English Literature*, edited by Piero Boitani and Anna Torti, pp. 230–45. Tübingen: Gunter Narr Verlag, 1988.

Burrow, J. A. *Langland's Fictions*. Oxford: Clarendon Press, 1993.

Bushnell, Rebecca W. *A Culture of Teaching: Early Modern Humanism in Theory and Practice*. Ithaca: Cornell University Press, 1996.

Butterfield, Ardis. 'Mise-en-page in the *Troilus* Manuscripts: Chaucer and French Manuscript Culture.' *Huntington Library Quarterly* 58 (1995): 49–80.

Butterfield, Ardis. 'Articulating the Author: Gower and the French Vernacular Codex.' *Yearbook of English Studies* 33 (2003): 80–96.

Butterfield, Ardis. 'Rough Translation: Charles d'Orléans, Lydgate and Hoccleve.' In: *Rethinking Medieval Translation: Ethics, Politics, Theory*, edited by Emma Campbell and Robert Mills, pp. 204–25. Cambridge: D.S. Brewer, 2012.

Caie, Graham D. 'The Significance of the Early Chaucer Manuscript Glosses (with Special Reference to the *Wife of Bath's Prologue*).' *Chaucer Review* 10 (1975–6): 350–60.

Canitz, A. E. C. 'The Prologue to the *Eneados*: Gavin Douglas' Directions for Reading.' *Studies in Scottish Literature* 25 (1990): 1–22.

Canitz, A. E. C. 'From *Aeneid* to *Eneados*: Theory and Practice of Gavin Douglas' Translation.' *Medievalia et Humanistica* 19 (1991): 81–100.

Carlson, David, R. 'Thomas Hoccleve and the Chaucer Portrait.' *Huntington Library Quarterly* 54 (1991): 283–300.

Carlson, David R. 'A Theory of the Early English Printing Firm: Jobbing, Book Publishing, and the Productive Capacity in Caxton's Work.' In: *Caxton's Trace: Studies in the History of English Printing*, edited by William Kuskin, pp. 35–68. Notre Dame: University of Notre Dame Press, 2006.

Carlson, Leland H. *Martin Marprelate, Gentleman*. San Marino: Huntington Library, 1981.

Carruthers, Mary. *The Book of Memory: A Study of Memory in Medieval Culture*. 2nd ed. Cambridge: Cambridge University Press, 2008.

Cave, Terence. *The Cornucopian Text: Problems of Writing in the French Renaissance*. Oxford: Oxford University Press, 1979.

Chartier, Roger (ed.). *The Culture of Print: Power and the Uses of Print in Early Modern Europe*. Cambridge: Polity Press, 1989.

Clebsch, William. *England's Earliest Protestants, 1520–1535*. New Haven: Yale University Press, 1964.

Clogan, Paul M. 'Imaging the City of Thebes in Fifteenth-Century England.' In: *Acta Conventus Neo-Latini Hafniensis*, edited by Rhoda Schnur and Ann Moss, pp. 155–63. Binghamton, NY: Medieval and Renaissance Texts and Studies, 1994.

Colie, Rosalie L. *Paradoxia Epidemica*. Princeton: Princeton University Press, 1966.

Colie, Rosalie L. *The Resources of Kind: Genre-Theory in the Renaissance*. Berkeley: University of California Press, 1973.

Conté, Gian Bagio. *The Rhetoric of Imitation: Genre and Poetic Memory in Virgil and Other Latin Poets*. Ithaca: Cornell University Press, 1986.

Cook, Megan L. 'Marking and Managing the Page: Lexical Commentary in Spenser's *Shepheardes Calendar* (1579) and Chaucer's *Works* (1598/1602).' *Spenser Studies* 26 (2011): 179–222.

Coolidge, John. 'Martin Marprelate, Marvell, and *Decorum Personae* as a Satirical Theme.' *PMLA* 74 (1959): 526–32.

Cooper, Lisa H., and Andrea Denny-Brown (eds), *Lydgate Matters: Poetry and Material Culture in the Fifteenth Century*. Basingstoke: Palgrave MacMillan, 2008.

Copeland, Rita. *Rhetoric, Hermeneutics and Translation in the Middle Ages: Academic Tradition and Vernacular Texts*. Cambridge: Cambridge University Press, 1991.

Copeland, Rita. 'Gloss and Commentary.' In: *The Oxford Handbook of Medieval Latin Literature*, edited by Ralph H. Hexter and David Townsend, pp. 171–91. Oxford: Oxford University Press, 2012.

Corbett, Margery, and Ronald Lightbown. *The Comely Frontispiece: The Emblematic Titlepage in England 1550–1660*. London: Routledge, 1979.

Cosgrove, Peter. 'Undermining the Text: Edward Gibbon, Alexander Pope, and the Anti-Authenticating Footnote.' In: *Annotation and Its Texts*, edited by Stephen Barney. Oxford: Oxford University Press, 1991.

Craig, D. H. *Sir John Harington*. Boston: Twayne, 1985.

Crane, Mary Thomas. *Framing Authority: Sayings, Self and Society in Sixteenth Century England*. Princeton: Princeton University Press, 1993.

Cummings, Robert. '"To Cart the Fift Quheill": Gavin Douglas' Humanist Supplement to the *Eneados*.' *Translation and Literature* 4 (1995): 133–56.

Dane, Joseph A. 'In Search of Stow's Chaucer.' In: *John Stow (1525–1605) and the Making of the English Past*, edited by Ian Gadd and Alexandra Gillespie, pp. 145–56. London: The British Library, 2004.

Davis, John F. 'The Trials of Thomas Bylney and the English Reformation.' *Historical Journal* 24 (1981): 775–90.

Dearing, Bruce. 'Gavin Douglas' *Eneados*: A Reinterpretation.' *PMLA* 67 (1952): 845–62.

Dempster, Germaine. 'Chaucer at Work on the Complaint in the Franklin's Tale.' *Modern Language Notes* 52 (1937): 16–23.

Dempster, Germaine. 'A Further Note on Dorigen's Exempla.' *Modern Language Notes* 54 (1939): 137–8.

Dempster, Germaine. 'Chaucer's Manuscript of Petrarch's Version of the Griselda Story.' *Modern Philology* 41 (1943–4): 6–16.

Dobranski, Stephen B. *Readers and Authorship in Early Modern England*. Cambridge: Cambridge University Press, 2009.

Driver, Martha. 'Ideas of Order: Wynkyn de Worde and the Title Page.' In: *Texts and their Contexts*, edited by John Scattergood and Julia Boffey, pp. 87–149. Dublin: Four Courts Press, 1997.

Duffy, Eamon. *The Stripping of the Altars: Traditional Religion in England, c1400–c1580*. 2nd ed. Harvard: Yale University Press, 2005.

Dutton, Richard. *Ben Jonson: To the First Folio*. Cambridge: Cambridge University Press, 1983.

Ebin, Lois. 'Lydgate's Views on Poetry.' *Annuale Mediaevale* 18 (1977): 76–105.

Ebin, Lois. 'The Role of the Narrator in the Prologues to Gavin Douglas' *Eneados*.' *Chaucer Review* 14 (1980): 353–65.

Ebin, Lois. *Illuminator, Makar, Vates: Visions of Poetry in the Fifteenth Century.* Lincoln, NE: University of Nebraska Press, 1988.

Echard, Siân. 'With Carmen's Help: Latin Authorities in the *Confessio Amantis*.' *Studies in Philology* 95 (1998): 1–40.

Echard, Siân. 'Designs for Reading: Some Manuscripts of Gower's *Confessio Amantis*.' *Trivium* 31 (1999): 59–72.

Echard, Siân. 'Dialogues and Monologues: Representations of the Conversations of the *Confessio Amantis*.' In: *Middle English Poetry: Texts and Traditions in Honour of Derek Pearsall*, edited by A. J. Minnis, pp. 57–75. York: York Medieval Press, 2001.

Edwards, A. S. G. 'Lydgate's *Siege of Thebes*: A New Fragment.' *Neuphilologische Mitteilungen* 71 (1970): 133–6.

Edwards, A. S. G. 'John Lydgate, Medieval Antifeminism and Harley 2251.' *Annuale Medievale* 13 (1972): 32–44.

Edwards, A. S. G. 'The McGill Fragment of Lydgate's *Fall of Princes*.' *Scriptorium* 28 (1974): 75–7.

Edwards, A. S. G. 'The Influence of Lydgate's *Fall of Princes* c. 1440–1559: A Survey.' *Mediaeval Studies* 39 (1977): 424–39.

Edwards, A. S. G. 'Lydgate Manuscripts: Some Directions for Future Research.' In: *Manuscripts and Readers in Fifteenth-Century England: The Literary Implications of Manuscript Study*, edited by Derek Pearsall, pp. 15–26. Cambridge: D.S. Brewer, 1983.

Edwards, A. S. G. 'Beinecke MS 661 and Early Fifteenth-Century English Manuscript Production.' *Yale University Library Gazette* 66 (supp) (1991): 181–96.

Edwards, A. S. G. 'Chaucer from Manuscript to Print: The Social Text and the Critical Text.' *Mosaic* 28 (1995): 1–12.

Edwards, A. S. G. 'Bodleian MS Arch. Selden B.24: A "Transitional" Manuscript.' In: *The Whole Book: Cultural Perspectives on the Medieval Miscellany*, edited by Stephen G. Nichols and Siegfried Wenzel, pp. 53–67. Ann Arbor: University of Michigan Press, 1996.

Edwards, A. S. G. 'William Copland and the Identity of Printed Middle English Romance.' In: *The Matter of Identity in Medieval Romance*, edited by Phillipa Hardman, pp. 139–48. Cambridge: D.S. Brewer, 2002.

Edwards, Robert R. 'Translating Thebes: Lydgate's *Siege of Thebes* and Stow's Chaucer.' *ELH* 70 (2003): 319–41.

Eisenstein, Elizabeth. *The Printing Press as an Agent of Change: Communications and Cultural Transformations in Early Modern Europe*. Cambridge: Cambridge University Press, 1980.

Elsky, Martin. *Authorizing Words: Speech, Writing and Print in the English Renaissance*. Ithaca: Cornell University Press, 1989.

Erler, Mary C. 'Copland, William.' In: *The Oxford Dictionary of National Biography*. <http://www.oxforddnb.com/view/article/6266>.

Farrell, Thomas J. 'The Style of the "Clerk's Tale" and the Functions of Its Glosses.' *Studies in Philology* 86 (1989): 286–309.

Febvre, Lucien, and Henri-Jean Martin. *The Coming of the Book: The Impact of Printing, 1450–1800*. London: Verso, 1997.

Finnegan, Ruth. *Orality and Literacy: Studies in the Technology of Communication*. Oxford: Basil Blackwell, 1988.

Fleming, Juliet. *Graffiti and the Writing Arts of Early Modern England*. London: Reaktion Books, 2001.

Fletcher, Bradford Y. 'Printer's Copy for Stow's Chaucer.' *Studies in Bibliography* 31 (1978): 184–201.

Fox, Adam, and D. R. Woolf. *The Spoken Word: Oral Culture in Britain, 1500–1850*. Manchester: Manchester University Press, 2002.

Fox, Denton. 'Manuscripts and Prints of Scots Poetry in the Sixteenth Century.' In: *Bards and Makars. Scottish Language and Literature: Medieval and Renaissance*, edited by Adam J. Aitken, Matthew P. McDiarmid, and Derick S. Thomson, pp. 156–71. Glasgow: Glasgow University Press, 1977.

Galbraith, Steven K. '"English" Black-Letter Type and Spenser's *Shepheardes Calendar*.' *Spenser Studies* 23 (2008): 13–40.

Galloway, Andrew. 'Gower's *Confessio Amantis,* the *Prick of Conscience*, and the History of the Latin Gloss in Early English Literature.' In: *John Gower: Manuscripts, Readers, Contexts*, edited by Malte Urban, pp. 39–70. Turnhout: Brepols, 2009.

Gavin, J. Austin, and Thomas M. Walsh. '*The Praise of Folly* in Context: The Commentary of Gerardus Listrius.' *Renaissance Quarterly* 24 (1971): 193–209.

Gavin, Joseph A., and Clarence H. Miller. 'Erasmus' Additions to Listrius' Commentary on *The Praise of Folly*.' *Erasmus in English* 11 (1981–2): 19–26.

Geller, Sherri. 'Commentary as Cover-Up: Criticizing Illiberal Patronage in Thomas Nashe's *Summer's Last Will and Testament*.' *English Literary Renaissance* 25 (1995): 148–78.

Geller, Sherri. 'What History Really Teaches: Historical Pyrrhonism in William Baldwin's *A Mirror for Magistrates*.' In: *Opening the Borders: Inclusivity in Early Modern Studies*, edited by Peter C. Herman, pp. 150–84. Newark: Associated University Presses, 1999.

Geller, Sherri. 'You Can't Tell a Book by Its Contents: (Mis)Interpretation in/of Spenser's *The Shepheardes Calendar*.' *Spenser Studies* 13 (1999): 23–64.

Gellrich, Jesse M. *The Idea of the Book in the Middle Ages: Language Theory, Mythology, and Fiction*. Ithaca: Cornell University Press, 1985.

Ghosh, Kantik. '"The Fift Quheill": Gavin Douglas' Maffeo Vegio.' *Scottish Literary Journal* 22 (1995): 5–21.

Gillespie, Alexandra. 'Framing Lydgate's *Fall of Princes*: The Evidence of Book History.' *Mediaevalia* 20 (2001): 153–78.

Gillespie, Alexandra. '"Folowynge the trace of mayster Caxton": Some Histories of Fifteenth-Century Printed Books.' In: *Caxton's Trace: Studies in the History of English Printing*, edited by William Kuskin. Notre Dame: University of Notre Dame Press, 2005.

Gillespie, Alexandra. *Print Culture and the Medieval Author: Chaucer, Lydgate, and their Books, 1473–1557*. Oxford: Oxford University Press, 2006.

Ginsberg, David. 'Ploughboys versus Prelates: Tyndale and More and the Politics of Biblical Translation.' *Sixteenth Century Journal* 19 (1988): 45–61.

Godden, Malcolm. *The Making of Piers Plowman*. Harlow: Longman, 1990.
Grafton, Anthony. *The Footnote: A Curious History*. Cambridge, MA: Harvard University Press, 1999.
Grafton, Anthony, and Lisa Jardine. *From Humanism to the Humanities*. London: Duckworth, 1986.
Graham, David. 'Pictures Speaking, Pictures Spoken To: Guillaume de la Perriere and Emblematic "Illustration".' In: *Visual and Verbal Pictures: Essays in Honour of Michael Bath*, edited by Alison Saunders and Peter Davidson, pp. 69–88. Glasgow: Glasgow Emblem Studies, 2005.
Gray, Douglas. 'Gavin Douglas and "the gret prynce Eneas".' *Essays in Criticism* 51 (2001): 18–34.
Green, Richard Firth. *Poets and Princepleasers: Literature and the English Court in the Late Middle Ages*. Toronto: University of Toronto Press, 1980.
Greenblatt, Stephen. *Renaissance Self-Fashioning: From More to Shakespeare*. Chicago: University of Chicago Press, 1980.
Greene, Thomas M. *The Light in Troy: Imitation and Discovery in Renaissance Poetry*. New Haven: Yale University Press, 1982.
Greg, W. 'An Elizabethan Printer and his Copy.' *The Library*. 4th series, vol. iv (1923–4): 102–18.
Griffiths, Jane. 'The Grammarian as "Poeta" and "Vates": Self-Presentation in the *AntiBossicon*.' In: *Self-Presentation and Social Identification: The Rhetoric and Pragmatics of Letter-Writing in Early Modern Times*, edited by Toon van Houdt, Jan Papy, and Gilbert Tournoy, pp. 317–36. Leuven: Leuven University Press, 2001.
Griffiths, Jane. 'Text and Authority: John Stow's 1568 Edition of Skelton's Works.' In: *John Stow: Author, Editor and Reader*, edited by Ian Gadd and Alexandra Gillespie, pp. 127–34. London: British Library, 2004.
Griffiths, Jane. 'What's in a Name? The Transmission of "John Skelton, Laureate" in Manuscript and Print.' *Huntington Library Quarterly* 67 (2004): 215–35.
Griffiths, Jane. *John Skelton and Poetic Authority: Defining the Liberty to Speak*. Oxford: Clarendon Press, 2006.
Griffiths, Jane. 'Exhortations to the Reader: The Glossing of Douglas' *Eneados* in Cambridge, Trinity College MS O.3.12.' *English Manuscript Studies* 15 (2009): 185–97.
Griffiths, Jane. 'Editorial Glossing and Reader Resistance in a Copy of Robert Crowley's *Piers Plowman*.' In: *The Makers and Users of Medieval Books: Essays in Honour of A. S. G. Edwards*, edited by Carol M. Meale, 202–13. Woodbridge: Boydell and Brewer, 2014.
Griffiths, Jane. ' "In bookes thus I wryten fynde": Glossing Hoccleve's *Regiment of Princes*', forthcoming.
Grigely, Joseph. 'Textual Criticism and the Arts: The Problem of Textual Space.' *Text* 7 (1994): 25–60.
Grindley, Carl James. 'Reading *Piers Plowman* C-Text Annotations: Notes toward the Classification of Printed and Written Marginalia in Texts from the British Isles 1300-1641.' In: *The Medieval Professional Reader at Work: Evidence from Manuscripts of Chaucer, Langland, Kempe, and Gower*, edited by Kathryn

Kerby-Fulton and Maidie Hilmo, pp. 73–141. Victoria: University of Victoria Press, 2001.

Gutierrez, Nancy A. '*Beware the Cat*: Mimesis in a Skin of Oratory.' *Style* 23 (1989): 49–69.

Hailey, R. Carter. 'Robert Crowley and the Editing of *Piers Plowman* (1550).' *Yearbook of Langland Studies* 21 (2007): 143–70.

Hampton, Timothy. *Writing from History: The Rhetoric of Exemplarity*. Ithaca: Cornell University Press, 1990.

Hanna, Ralph. 'Annotation as Social Practice.' In: *Annotation and Its Texts*, edited by Stephen A. Barney. Oxford: Oxford University Press, 1991.

Hanna, Ralph, and A. S. G. Edwards. 'Rotheley, the De Vere Circle, and the Ellesmere Chaucer.' *Huntington Library Quarterly* 58 (1995): 11–35.

Hardin, Richard F. *Michael Drayton and the Passing of Elizabethan England*. Lawrence: University Press of Kansas, 1973.

Hardman, Phillipa. 'Lydgate's "Uneasy Style".' In: *John Lydgate: Poetry, Culture, and Lancastrian England*, edited by Larry Scanlon and James Simpson, pp. 12–35. Notre Dame: University of Notre Dame Press, 2006.

Heale, Elizabeth. 'Songs, Sonnets, and Autobiography: Self-Representation in Sixteenth-Century Verse Miscellanies.' In: *Betraying Our Selves: Forms of Self-Representation in Early Modern English Texts*, edited by Sheila Ottway and Helen Wilcox, pp. 11–35. Basingstoke: Macmillan, 2000.

Hecht, Jamey. 'Limitations of Textuality in Thomas More's *Confutation of Tyndale's Answer*.' *Sixteenth Century Journal* 26 (1995): 823–8.

Helgerson, Richard. *The Elizabethan Prodigals*. Berkeley: University of California Press, 1976.

Helgerson, Richard. *Forms of Nationhood: The Elizabethan Writing of England*. Chicago: University of Chicago Press, 1993.

Hellinga, Lotte, and J. B. Trapp (eds). *The Cambridge History of the Book in Britain 3: 1400–1557*. Cambridge: Cambridge University Press, 1999.

Hindman, Sandra, and James Douglas Farquhar. *Pen to Press: Illustrated Manuscripts and Printed Books in the First Century of Printing*. College Park: University of Maryland and Baltimore: Johns Hopkins University, 1977.

Hodnett, Edward. *English Woodcuts, 1480–1535*. London: The Bibliographical Society, 1935.

Hollander, Robert. 'The Validity of Boccaccio's Self-Exegesis in his *Teseida*.' *Medievalia et Humanistica* 8 (1977): 163–83.

Hudson, Anne. 'John Stow (1525?–1605)'. In: *Editing Chaucer: The Great Tradition*, edited by Paul G. Ruggiers, pp. 53–70. Norman, OK: Pilgrim, 1984.

Hughey, Ruth. 'The Harington Manuscript at Arundel Castle.' *The Library*. 4th series, vol. xv (1935): 388–444.

Huot, Sylvia. *The Roman de la Rose and Its Medieval Readers: Interpretation, Reception, Manuscript Transmission*. Cambridge: Cambridge University Press, 2007.

Hutson, Lorna. *Thomas Nashe in Context*. Oxford: Clarendon Press, 1989.

Irvine, Martin. '"Bothe text and gloss": Manuscript Form, the Textuality of Commentary, and Chaucer's Dream Poems.' In: *The Uses of Manuscripts in Literary Studies: Essays in Memory of Judson Boyce Allen*, edited by Charlotte Cook Morse, Penelope Reed Doob, and Marjorie Curry Woods, pp. 81–120. Kalamazoo: Medieval Institute Publications, 1992.

Iser, Wolfgang. 'Interaction between Text and Reader.' In: *The Reader in the Text: Essays on Audience and Interpretation*, edited by Susan R. Suleiman and Inge Crosman. Princeton: Princeton University Press, 1980.

Iser, Wolfgang. 'The Reading Process: A Phenomenological Approach.' In: *The Implied Reader*. Baltimore: Johns Hopkins University Press, 1974.

Jackson, H. J. *Marginalia: Readers Writing in Books*. New Haven: Yale University Press, 2001.

Jansen, J. P. M. 'Charles d'Orléans and the Fairfax Poems.' *English Studies* 70 (1989): 206–24.

Johns, Adrian. *The Nature of the Book: Print and Knowledge in the Making*. Chicago: University of Chicago Press, 1998.

Johnson, Barbara A. *Reading 'Piers Plowman' and 'The Pilgrim's Progress': Reception and the Protestant Reader*. Carbondale: Southern Illinois University Press, 1992.

Johnston, Michael. 'From Edward III to Edward VI: *The Vision of Pierce Plowman* and Early Modern England.' *Reformation* 11 (2006): 47–78.

Jones, Mike Rodman. *Radical Pastoral, 1381–1594: Appropriation and the Writing of Religious Controversy*. Farnham: Ashgate, 2011.

Kahn, Victoria. *Rhetoric, Prudence, and Skepticism in the Renaissance*. Ithaca: Cornell University Press, 1985.

Kaiser, Walter. *Praisers of Folly: Erasmus, Rabelais, Shakespeare*. London: Victor Gollancz, 1964.

Kamath, Stephanie A. Viereck Gibbs. 'Periphery and Purpose: The Fifteenth-Century Rubrication of the *Pilgrimage of Human Life*.' *Glossator* 1 (2009): 31–46.

Kamath, Stephanie A. Viereck Gibbs. 'John Lydgate and the Curse of Genius.' *Chaucer Review* 45 (2010): 32–58.

Kamath, Stephanie A. Viereck Gibbs. *Authorship and First-Person Allegory in Late Medieval France and England*. Cambridge: D.S. Brewer, 2012.

Kearney, James. 'Reformed Ventriloquism: *The Shepheardes Calendar* and the Craft of Commentary.' *Spenser Studies* 26 (2011): 111–51.

Keiser, George R. 'Serving the Needs of Readers: Textual Division in Some Late-Medieval English Texts.' In: *New Science Out of Old Books: Studies in Honour of A. I. Doyle*, edited by Richard Beadle and A. J. Piper, pp. 207–26. Aldershot: Scolar Press, 1995.

Kelen, Sarah A. *Langland's Early Modern Identities*. Basingstoke: Palgrave MacMillan, 2007.

Kendall, Ritchie D. *The Drama of Dissent: The Radical Poetics of Nonconformity, 1380–1590*. Chapel Hill: University of North Carolina Press, 1986.

Kendrick, Laura. *Animating the Letter: The Figurative Embodiment of Writing from Late Antiquity to the Renaissance*. Columbus: Ohio State University Press, 1999.

King, John N. 'Robert Crowley's Editions of *Piers Plowman*: A Tudor Apocalypse.' *Modern Philology* 73 (1976): 342–52.

King, John N. *English Reformation Literature: The Tudor Origins of the Protestant Tradition*. Princeton: Princeton University Press, 1982.

King, John N. 'Baldwin, William.' In: *The Oxford Dictionary of National Biography*. <http://www.oxforddnb.com/view/article/1171?docPos=1>.

King, Pamela M. 'Chaucer, Chaucerians, and the Theme of Poetry.' In: *Chaucer and Fifteenth-Century Poetry*, edited by Julia Boffey and Janet Cowan, pp. 1–14. London: King's College, 1991.

Kinney, A. F. *Humanist Poetics: Thought, Rhetoric, and Fiction in Sixteenth-Century England*. Amherst: University of Massachusetts Press, 1986.

Kinney, A. F. (ed.). *The Cambridge Companion to English Literature, 1500–1600*. Cambridge: Cambridge University Press, 2000.

Kinney, Clare R. 'Thomas Speght's Renaissance Chaucer and the Solaas of Sentence in *Troilus and Criseyde*.' In: *Refiguring Chaucer in the Renaissance*, edited by Theresa Krier, pp. 66–84. Gainesville: University of Florida Press, 1998.

Kinney, Clare R. 'Clamorous Voices, Incontinent Fictions: Orality, Oratory, and Gender in William Baldwin's *Beware the Cat*.' In: *Oral Traditions and Gender in Early Modern Literary Texts*, edited by Mary Ellen Lamb and Karen Bamford, pp. 195–207. Burlington, VT: Ashgate, 2008.

Kintgen, Eugene R. *Reading in Tudor England*. Pittsburgh: University of Pittsburgh Press, 1996.

Kirkham, Victoria. 'Decoration and Iconography of Lydgate's *Fall of Princes* (De Casibus) at the Philadelphia Rosenbach.' *Studi sul Boccaccio* 25 (1997): 297–310.

Kline, Barbara. 'Scribal Agendas and the Text of Chaucer's Tales in British Library MS Harley 7333.' In: *Rewriting Chaucer: Culture, Authority and the Idea of the Authentic Text*, edited by Thomas A. Prendergast and Barbara Kline, pp. 116–44. Columbus: Ohio State University Press, 1999.

Ko, Trudy. 'The Hybrid Text: Transformation of the Vernacular in *Beware the Cat*.' In: *The Transformation of Vernacular Expression in Early Modern Arts*, edited by Joost Keizer and Todd M. Richardson, pp. 207–27. Leiden: Brill, 2011.

Krochalis, Jeanne E. 'Hoccleve's Chaucer Portrait.' *Chaucer Review* 21 (1986): 234–45.

Lander, Jesse M. *Inventing Polemic: Religion, Print, and Literary Culture in Early Modern England*. Cambridge: Cambridge University Press, 2006.

Langdell, Sebastian. '"What worlde is this? How vndirstande am I?" A Reappraisal of Poetic Authority in Thomas Hoccleve's *Series*.' *Medium Aevum* 78 (2009): 281–99.

Lerer, Seth. 'Rewriting Chaucer: Two Fifteenth-Century Readings of *The Canterbury Tales*.' *Viator* 19 (1988): 311–26.

Lerer, Seth. *Chaucer and his Readers: Imagining the Author in Late-Medieval England*. Princeton: Princeton University Press, 1996.

Lewis, Robert E. 'Glosses to the *Man of Law's Tale* from Pope Innocent III's *De Miseria Humane Conditionis*.' *Studies in Philology* 64 (1967): 1–16.

Lipking, Lawrence. 'The Marginal Gloss.' *Critical Inquiry* 3 (1977): 609–55.

Littau, Karin. *Theories of Reading: Books, Bodies, and Bibliomania.* Cambridge: Polity Press, 2006.
Luborsky, Ruth Samson. 'The Allusive Presentation of *The Shepheardes Calendar*.' *Spenser Studies* 1 (1980): 29–68.
Lucas, Scott. *A Mirror for Magistrates and the Politics of the English Reformation.* Amherst: University of Massachusetts Press, 2009.
McCabe, Richard A. 'Annotating Anonymity, or Putting a Gloss on *The Shepheardes Calendar*.' In: *Ma(r)king the Text: The Presentation of Meaning on the Literary Page,* edited by Joe Bray, Miriam Handley, and Anne C. Henry, pp. 35–54. Aldershot: Ashgate, 2000.
McCanles, Michael. '*The Shepheardes Calendar* as Document and Monument.' *SEL* 22 (1982): 5–19.
McCutcheon, Elizabeth. 'William Bullein's *Dialogue against the Fever Pestilence*: A Sixteenth-Century Anatomy.' In: *Miscellenea Moreana: Essays for Germaine Marc'hadour,* edited by Claire M. Murphy, Henri Gibaud, and Mario A. di Cesare, pp. 341–59. Binghamton: State University of New York, 1989.
McEachern, Claire. *The Poetics of English Nationhood, 1590–1612.* Cambridge: Cambridge University Press, 1996.
McGinn, Donald J. 'The Allegory of the "Beare" and the "Foxe" in Nashe's *Pierce Penilesse*.' *PMLA* 61 (1946): 431–53.
McGinn, Donald J. *John Penry and the Marprelate Controversy.* New Brunswick: Rutgers University Press, 1966.
McKenzie, D. F. 'Speech-Manuscript-Print.' In: *New Directions in Textual Studies,* edited by Dave Oliphant and Robin Bradford, pp. 87–109. Austin: Henry Ransom Humanities Research Center, 1990.
McKinnon, Dana. 'The Marginal Glosses in More's *Utopia*: The Character of the Commentator.' *Renaissance Papers* (1970): 11–19.
McKitterick, David. *Print, Manuscript, and the Search for Order.* Cambridge: Cambridge University Press, 2003.
Machan, Tim W. 'Speght's *Works* and the Invention of Chaucer.' *Text* 8 (1995): 145–70.
Mambretti, Catherine Cole. 'William Bullein and the "Lively Fashions" in Tudor Medical Literature.' *Clio Medica* 9 (1974): 285–97.
Mann, Jill. 'The Authority of the Audience in Chaucer.' In: *Poetics: Theory and Practice in Medieval English Literature,* edited by Piero Boitani and Anna Torti, pp. 1–12. Cambridge: D.S. Brewer, 1991.
Manning, John, *The Emblem.* London: Reaktion, 2002.
Marotti, Arthur F. *Manuscript, Print, and the English Renaissance Lyric.* Ithaca: Cornell University Press, 1995.
Marzec, Marcia Smith. 'The Sources of Hoccleve's *Regiment* and the Use of Translations.' *Équivalences* 13 (1982): 9–21.
Maslen, Robert. '"The Cat Got Your Tongue": Pseudo-Translation, Conversion, and Control in William Baldwin's *Beware the Cat*.' *Translation and Literature* 8 (1999): 3–27.

Maslen, Robert. 'The Healing Dialogues of Doctor Bullein.' *Yearbook of English Studies* 38 (2008): 119–35.

Maslen, Robert. 'William Baldwin and the Tudor Imagination.' In: *The Oxford Handbook of Tudor Literature, 1485–1603*, edited by Mike Pincombe and Cathy Shrank, pp. 291–306. Oxford: Oxford University Press, 2009.

May, Steven W. 'Tudor Aristocrats and the Mythical "Stigma of Print".' *Renaissance Papers* (1980): 11–18.

Meyer-Lee, Robert J. *Poets and Power from Chaucer to Wyatt*. Cambridge: Cambridge University Press, 2007.

Miller, Clarence H. 'The Logic and Rhetoric of Proverbs in Erasmus' *Praise of Folly*.' In: *Essays on the Work of Erasmus*, edited by Richard L. De Molen, pp. 83–98. New Haven: Yale University Press, 1978.

Miller, Clarence H. 'Styles and Mixed Genres in Erasmus' *Praise of Folly*.' In: *Acta Conventus Neo-Latini Guelpherbytani*, edited by Stella P. Revard, Fidel Radle, and Mario A. Di Cesare, pp. 277–87. Binghamton: Medieval & Renaissance Texts & Studies, 1988.

Minnis, A. J. *Medieval Theory of Authorship: Scholastic Literary Attitudes in the Later Middle Ages*. 2nd ed. Aldershot: Wildwood House, 1988.

Minnis, A. J. 'De vulgari auctoritate: Chaucer, Gower, and the Men of Great Authority.' In: *Chaucer and Gower: Difference, Mutuality, Exchange*, edited by R. F. Yeager, pp. 36–74. Victoria: University of Victoria, 1991.

Minnis, A. J. *The Shorter Poems*, Oxford Guides to Chaucer. Oxford: Clarendon Press, 1995.

Minnis, A. J. *Magister Amoris: The Roman de la Rose and Vernacular Hermeneutics*. Oxford: Oxford University Press, 2001.

Minnis, A. J. *Translations of Authority in Medieval English Literature: Valuing the Vernacular*. Cambridge: Cambridge University Press, 2009.

Mooney, Linne R. 'A New Manuscript by the Hammond Scribe Discovered by Jeremy Griffiths.' In: *The English Medieval Book: Studies in Memory of Jeremy Griffiths*, edited by A. S. G. Edwards, Vincent Gillespie, and Ralph Hanna, pp. 113–23. London: The British Library, 2000.

Mooney, Linne R. 'Locating Scribal Activity in Late-Medieval London.' In: *Design and Distribution of Late Medieval Manuscripts in England*, edited by Margaret Connolly and Linne R. Mooney, pp. 183–204. Woodbridge: York Medieval Press, 2008.

Mooney, Linne R. 'A Holograph Copy of Thomas Hoccleve's *Regiment of Princes*.' *Studies in the Age of Chaucer* 33 (2011): 263–96.

Moore, Colette. *Quoting Speech in Early English*. Cambridge: Cambridge University Press, 2011.

Morgan-Straker, Scott. 'Deference and Difference: Lydgate, Chaucer, and the *Siege of Thebes*.' *Review of English Studies* 52 (2001): 1–21.

Mortimer, Nigel. *John Lydgate's Fall of Princes: Narrative Tragedy in Its Literary and Political Contexts*. Oxford: Clarendon Press, 2005.

Moss, Ann. *Printed Commonplace Books and the Structure of Renaissance Thought*. Oxford: Clarendon Press, 1996.

Nafde, Aditi. 'Deciphering the Manuscript Page: The Mise-en-Page of Chaucer, Gower, and Hoccleve Manuscripts.' Unpublished DPhil. thesis. University of Oxford, 2012.

Navitsky, Joseph. 'Disputing Good Bishop's English: Martin Marprelate and the Voice of Menippean Opposition.' *Texas Studies in Language and Literature* 50 (2008): 177–200.

Nelson, William. *John Skelton: Laureate.* New York: Columbia University Press, 1939.

Nicholl, Charles. *A Cup of Newes: The Life of Thomas Nashe.* London: Routledge Kegan Paul, 1984.

Noakes, Susan. *Timely Reading: Between Exegesis and Interpretation.* Ithaca: Cornell University Press, 1988.

Noakes, Vivien. *Edward Lear: The Life of a Wanderer.* Rev. ed. London: BBC, 1985.

Norbrook, David. *Poetry and Politics in the English Renaissance.* Rev. ed. Oxford: Oxford University Press, 2002.

North, Marcy L. *The Anonymous Renaissance: Cultures of Discretion in Tudor-Stuart England.* Chicago: University of Chicago Press, 2003.

Norton-Smith, John (ed.). *MS Fairfax 16: A Facsimile.* London: Scolar Press, 1979.

O'Callaghan, Michelle. *The 'Shepheards Nation': Jacobean Spenserians and Early Stuart Political Culture, 1612–1625.* Oxford: Clarendon Press, 2000.

Ong, Walter J. 'The Writer's Audience Is Always a Fiction.' *PMLA* 90 (1975): 9–21.

Ong, Walter J. *Orality and Literacy: The Technologizing of the Word.* London: Routledge, 2002.

Orme, Nicholas. *English Schools in the Middle Ages.* London: Methuen, 1973.

Owen, Charles A. 'The Alternative Reading of *The Canterbury Tales*: Chaucer's Text and the Early Manuscripts.' *PMLA* 97 (1982): 237–50.

Palliser, D. M. 'Popular Reactions to the Reformation during the Years of Uncertainty 1530-70.' In: *The English Reformation Revisited*, edited by Christopher Haigh, pp. 94–113. Cambridge: Cambridge University Press, 1987.

Parkes, M. B. 'The Influence of the Concepts of *Ordinatio* and *Compilatio* on the Development of the Book.' In: *Medieval Learning and Literature: Essays Presented to Richard William Hunt*, edited by J. J. G. Alexander, M. T. Gibson, and R. W. Southern, pp. 115–41. Oxford: Clarendon Press, 1976.

Partridge, Stephen. 'Glosses in the Manuscripts of Chaucer's *Canterbury Tales*: An Edition and Commentary.' Unpublished PhD. thesis. Harvard University, 1992.

Partridge, Stephen. 'Designing the Page.' In: *The Production of Books in England 1350–1500*, edited by Alexandra Gillespie and Daniel Wakelin, pp. 79–103. Cambridge: Cambridge University Press, 2011.

Partridge, Stephen. '"The Makere of this Boke": Chaucer's Retraction and the Author as Scribe and Compiler.' In: *Author, Reader, Book: Medieval Authorship in Theory and Practice*, edited by Stephen Partridge and Erik Kwakkel, pp. 106–53. Toronto: University of Toronto Press, 2012.

Patterson, Lee. *Chaucer and the Subject of History*. London: Routledge, 1991.
Patterson, Paul J. 'Reforming Chaucer: Margins and Religion in an Apocryphal *Canterbury Tale*.' *Book History* 8 (2005): 11–36.
Payne, Robert O. *The Key of Remembrance: A Study of Chaucer's Poetics*. New Haven: Yale University Press. 1963.
Pearsall, Derek. 'Thomas Speght (c. 1550–?).' In: *Editing Chaucer: The Great Tradition*, edited by Paul G. Ruggiers, pp. 71–92. Norman, OK: Pilgrim, 1984.
Pearsall, Derek. 'Gower's Latin in the *Confessio Amantis*.' In: *Latin and the Vernacular: Studies in Late Medieval Texts and Manuscripts*, edited by A. J. Minnis, pp. 13–25. Cambridge: D.S. Brewer, 1989.
Pearsall, Derek. 'John Stow and Thomas Speght as Editors of Chaucer: A Question of Class.' In: *John Stow and the Making of the English Past*, edited by Ian Gadd and Alexandra Gillespie, pp. 119–25. London: The British Library, 2004.
Pierce, William. *An Historical Introduction to the Martin Marprelate Tracts*. London: Archibald Constable, 1908.
Pinti, Daniel J. 'The Vernacular Gloss(ed) in Gavin Douglas' *Eneados*.' *Exemplaria* 7 (1995): 443–64.
Poole, Kristen. 'Facing Puritanism: Falstaff, Martin Marprelate, and the Grotesque Puritan.' In: *Shakespeare and Carnival: After Bakhtin*, edited by Ronald Knowles, pp. 97–122. London: Macmillan, 1998.
Prescott, Anne Lake. 'Marginal Discourse: Drayton's Muse and Selden's "Story".' *Studies in Philology* 88 (1991): 307–28.
Proust, Jacqueline. 'Le Dialogue de William Bullein à propos de la Peste (1564): Formulation d'une Thérapeutique pour l'Ame en Peril.' In: *Le Dialogue au Temps de la Renaissance*, edited by M. T. Jones-Davies, pp. 59–70. Paris: Jean Touzot Libraire-Editeur, 1984.
Prouty, C. T. *George Gascoigne: Elizabethan Courtier, Soldier, Poet*. New York: Columbia University Press, 1942.
Quint, David. *Origin and Originality in Renaissance Literature: Versions of the Source*. New Haven: Yale University Press, 1983.
Rambuss, Richard. *Spenser's Secret Career*. Cambridge: Cambridge University Press, 1993.
Raymond, Joad. *Pamphlets and Pamphleteering in Early Modern Britain*. Cambridge: Cambridge University Press, 2003.
Renoir, Alain. 'The Immediate Source of Lydgate's *Siege of Thebes*.' *Studia Neophilologica* 33 (1961): 86–95.
Rhodes, Neil. 'On Speech, Print, and New Media: Thomas Nashe and Marshall McLuhan.' *Oral Tradition* 24 (2009): 373–92.
Robinson, Pamela. *MS Bodley 638: A Facsimile*. Woodbridge: Boydell & Brewer, 1982.
Ruditsky, Peter. 'Ironic Textuality in *The Praise of Folly* and *Gargantua and Pantagruel*.' *Erasmus of Rotterdam Society Yearbook* 3 (1983): 56–103.
Ruggiers Paul G (ed.). *Editing Chaucer: The Great Tradition*. Norman, OK: Pilgrim, 1984.

Saenger, Paul, and Michael Heinlen. 'Incunable Description and its Implication for the Analysis of Fifteenth-Century Reading Habits.' In: *Printing the Written Word: The Social History of Books, circa 1450–1520*, edited by Sandra Hindman, pp. 225–58. Ithaca: Cornell University Press, 1991.

Saunders, J. W. 'The Stigma of Print: A Note on the Social Bases of Tudor Poetry.' *Essays in Criticism* 1 (1951): 139–64.

Scase, Wendy. 'Dauy Dycars Dreame and Robert Crowley's Prints of *Piers Plowman*.' *Yearbook of Langland Studies* 21 (2007): 171–98.

Scattergood, John. 'The Early Annotations to John Skelton's Poems.' *Poetica* 35 (1992): 53–63.

Schibanoff, Susan. 'The New Reader and Female Textuality in Two Early Commentaries on Chaucer.' *Studies in the Age of Chaucer* 10 (1988): 71–108.

Schnapp, Jeffrey T. 'A Commentary on Commentary in Boccaccio.' *South Atlantic Quarterly* 91 (1992): 813–34.

Schoff, Rebecca L. *Reformations: Three Medieval Authors in Manuscript and Moveable Type*. Turnhout: Brepols, 2007.

Scott-Warren, Jason. 'The Privy Politics of Sir John Harington's *New Discourse of a Stale Subject, Called the Metamorphosis of Ajax*.' *Studies in Philology* 93 (1996): 412–42.

Scott-Warren, Jason. *Sir John Harington and the Book as Gift*. Oxford: Oxford University Press, 2001.

Screech, M. A. *Ecstasy and The Praise of Folly*. London: Duckworth, 1980.

Seymour, M. C. 'Manuscript Portraits of Chaucer and Hoccleve.' *Burlington Magazine* 124, no. 955 (October, 1982): 618–23.

Sherman, William H. *Used Books: Marking Readers in Renaissance England*. Philadelphia: University of Pennsylvania Press, 2008.

Sherman, William H. 'Terminal Paratext and the Birth of Print Culture.' In: *Renaissance Paratexts*, edited by Helen Smith and Louise Wilson, pp. 65–87. Cambridge: Cambridge University Press, 2011.

Sieper, Ernst. *Les Echecs Amoureux: Eine Altfranzösische Nachahmung des Rosenromans und Ihre Englische Übertragung*. Weimar: Verlag von Emil Felber, 1898.

Silvia, Daniel S. 'Glosses to the *Canterbury Tales* from St Jerome's *Epistola Adversus Jovinianum*.' *Studies in Philology* 62 (1965): 28–39.

Simpson, James. '"Dysemol daies and fatal houres": Lydgate's *Destruction of Thebes* and Chaucer's *Knight's Tale*.' In: *The Long Fifteenth Century: Essays for Douglas Gray*, edited by Helen Cooper and Sally Mapstone, pp. 15–34. Oxford: Clarendon Press, 1997.

Simpson, James. 'The Power of Impropriety: Authorial Naming in *Piers Plowman*.' In: *William Langland's Piers Plowman: A Book of Essays*, edited by Kathleen M. Hewett-Smith, pp. 145–66. London: Routledge, 2001.

Simpson, James. 'The Economy of Involucrum: Idleness in *Reason and Sensuality*.' In: *Through a Classical Eye: Transcultural and Transhistorical Visions in Medieval English, Italian, and Latin Literature in Honour of Winthrop Wetherbee*, edited by Andrew Galloway and R. F. Yeager, pp. 390–414. Toronto: University of Toronto Press, 2009.

Slights, William W. E. *Managing Readers: Printed Marginalia in English Renaissance Books*. Ann Arbor: University of Michigan Press, 2002.

Smalley, Beryl. *The Study of the Bible in the Middle Ages*. Notre Dame: University of Notre Dame Press, 1964.

Smith, Lesley. *The Glossa Ordinaria: The Making of a Medieval Bible Commentary*. Leiden: Brill, 2009.

Smyth, Karen. *Imaginings of Time in Lydgate and Hoccleve's Verse*. Farnham: Ashgate, 2011.

Snortum, Niel K. 'The Title of Nash's *Pierce Penilesse*.' *Modern Language Notes* 72 (1957): 170–3.

Spearing, A. C. 'Lydgate's Canterbury Tale: *The Siege of Thebes* and Fifteenth-Century Chaucerianism.' In: *Fifteenth-Century Studies: Recent Essays*, edited by R. F. Yeager, pp. 333–64. Hamden, CT: Archon, 1984.

Stallybrass, Peter. 'Books and Scrolls: Navigating the Bible.' In: *Books and Readers in Early Modern England: Material Studies*, edited by Jennifer Anderson and Elizabeth Sauer, pp. 42–79. Philadelphia: University of Pennsylvania Press, 2002.

Stenger, Genevieve. 'The *Praise of Folly* and Its Parerga.' *Medievalia et Humanistica* 2 (1971): 97–117.

Strohm, Paul. *Politique: Languages of Statecraft between Chaucer and Shakespeare*. Notre Dame: University of Notre Dame Press, 2005.

Summit, Jennifer. ' "Stable in study": Lydgate's *Fall of Princes* and Duke Humfrey's Library.' In: *John Lydgate: Poetry, Culture, and Lancastrian England*, edited by Larry Scanlon and James Simpson, pp. 207–31. Notre Dame: University of Notre Dame Press, 2006.

Taylor, Andrew. *Textual Situations: Three Medieval Manuscripts and their Readers*. Philadelphia: University of Pennsylvania Press, 2002.

Thompson, John J. 'Reading Lydgate in Post-Reformation England.' In: *Middle English Poetry: Texts and Traditions*, edited by A. J. Minnis, pp. 181–209. York: University of York, 2001.

Thorne, J. R., and Marie-Claire Uhart. 'Robert Crowley's *Piers Plowman*.' *Medium Aevum* 55 (1986): 248–54.

Tinkle, Theresa. 'The Imagined Chaucerian Community of Bodleian MS Fairfax 16.' In: *Chaucer and the Challenges of Medievalism: Studies in Honor of H. A. Kelly*, edited by Donka Minkova and Theresa Tinkle, pp. 157–74. Frankfurt-am-Main: Peter Lang, 2003.

Tinkle, Theresa. 'The Wife of Bath's Marginal Authority.' *Studies in the Age of Chaucer* 32 (2010): 67–102.

Trapp, J. B. 'From Guarino of Verona to John Colet.' In: *Italy and the English Renaissance*, edited by Sergio Rossi and Dianella Savoia, pp. 45–54. Milan: Unicopli, 1989.

Tribble, Evelyn B. *Margins and Marginality: The Printed Page in Early Modern England*. Charlottesville: University Press of Virginia, 1993.

Tribble, Evelyn B. ' "Like a Looking-Glass in the Frame": From the Marginal Note to the Footnote.' In: *The Margins of the Text*, edited by D. C. Greetham, pp. 229–44. Ann Arbor: University of Michigan Press, 1997.

Trigg, Stephanie. 'Discourses of Affinity in the Reading Communities of Geoffrey Chaucer.' In: *Rewriting Chaucer: Culture, Authority and the Idea of the Authentic Text*, edited by Thomas A. Prendergast and Barbara Kline, pp. 270–91. Columbus: Ohio State University Press, 1999.

Wakelin, Daniel. *Humanism, Reading, and English Literature 1430–1530*. Oxford: Oxford University Press, 2007.

Wakelin, Daniel. 'Instructing Readers in Fifteenth-Century Poetic Manuscripts.' *Huntington Library Quarterly* 73 (2010): 433–52.

Wakelin, Daniel. 'Hoccleve and Lydgate.' In: *A Companion to Medieval Poetry*, edited by Corinne Saunders, pp. 557–74. Oxford: Wiley-Blackwell, 2010.

Wakelin, Daniel. 'Writing the Words.' In: *The Production of Books in England, 1350–1500*, edited by Alexandra Gillespie and Daniel Wakelin, pp. 34–58. Cambridge: Cambridge University Press, 2011.

Walker, Greg. *John Skelton and the Politics of the 1520s*. Cambridge: Cambridge University Press, 1988.

Walker, Greg. 'Saint or Schemer: The 1527 Heresy Trial of Thomas Bilney Reconsidered.' *Journal of Ecclesiastical History* 40 (1989): 219–38.

Wall, Wendy. 'Interpreting Poetic Shadows: The Gloss of "The Rime of the Ancient Mariner".' *Criticism* 29 (1987): 179–95.

Wall, Wendy. *The Imprint of Gender: Authorship and Publication in the English Renaissance*. Ithaca: Cornell University Press, 1993.

Wall, Wendy. 'Authorship and the Material Conditions of Writing.' In: *The Cambridge Companion to English Literature, 1500–1600*, edited by Arthur F. Kinney, pp. 64–89. Cambridge: Cambridge University Press, 2000.

Wallace, Andrew. 'Reading the 1590 *Faerie Queene* with Thomas Nashe.' *Studies in the Literary Imagination* 38 (2005): 35–49.

Warner, Lawrence. 'Langland's Collaborators and the Quick Brown Fox.' Paper delivered to the Medieval Research Seminar, University of Oxford, 24 April 2013.

Watson, Donald Gwynn. 'Erasmus' *Praise of Folly* and the Spirit of Carnival.' *Renaissance Quarterly* 32 (1979): 333–53.

Watson, Foster. *The English Grammar Schools to 1660: Their Curriculum and Practice*. Cambridge: Cambridge University Press, 1908.

Watt, David. '"I This Book Shall Make": Thomas Hoccleve's Self-Publication and Book Production.' *Leeds Studies in English* 34 (2003): 133–60.

Wawn, Andrew N. 'Chaucer, *The Plowman's Tale*, and Reformation Propaganda.' *Bulletin of the John Rylands University Library of Manchester* 56 (1973): 174–92.

Werth, Tiffany Jo. *The Fabulous Dark Cloister: Romance in England after the Reformation*. Baltimore: Johns Hopkins University Press. 2011.

West, William N. 'Old News: Caxton, De Worde, and the Invention of the Edition.' In: *Caxton's Trace: Studies in the History of English Printing*, edited by William Kuskin, pp. 241–74. Notre Dame: University of Notre Dame Press, 2006.

Wetherbee, Winthrop. 'Latin Structure and Vernacular Space: Gower, Chaucer, and the Boethian Tradition.' In: *Chaucer and Gower: Difference, Mutuality,*

Exchange, edited by R. F. Yeager, pp. 7–35. Victoria: University of Victoria, 1991.

White, Glyn. 'The Critic in the Text: Footnotes and Marginalia in the Epilogue to Alasdair Gray's *Lanark: A Life in Four Books*.' In: *Ma(r)king the Text: The Presentation of Meaning on the Literary Page*, edited by Joe Bray, Miriam Handley, and Anne C. Henry, pp. 55–70. Aldershot: Ashgate, 2000.

Whitehead, Christiania. *Castles of the Mind: A Study of Medieval Architectural Allegory*. Cardiff: University of Wales Press, 2003.

Winston, Jessica. '*A Mirror for Magistrates* and Public Political Discourse in Elizabethan England.' *Studies in Philology* 101 (2004): 381–400.

Withington, Phil. ' "For This Is True or Els I Do Lye": Thomas Smith, William Bullein, and Mid-Tudor Dialogue.' In: *The Oxford Handbook of Tudor Literature, 1485–1603*, edited by Mike Pincombe and Cathy Shrank, pp. 455–71. Oxford: Oxford University Press, 2009.

Wooden, Warren W. 'A Reconsideration of the Parerga of Thomas More's *Utopia*.' In: *Quincentennial Essays on St Thomas More: Selected Papers from the Thomas More College Conference*, edited by Michael J. Moore, pp. 151–60. Boone, NC: Albion, 1978.

Yeager, Robert F. 'English, Latin, and the Text as "Other": The Page as Sign in the Work of John Gower.' *Text* 3 (1987): 251–67.

Index

Plates are indicated in bold.

academic *accessus* 5, 65, 90, 108
academic commentary 7, 81–3, 85, 87, 89, 91, 107
annotations 40–1, 56–7, 77–8, 107, 167, 170, 172–3; *see also* marginalia
Ariosto 152, 161–2, 164
ars moriendi 146
Arthur, Thomas 1
Ascencius, Johnannes Badius 83–4, 87, 91, 95
Ascham, Roger 164
Augustine, St 89
Austen, Gillian 154, 159
author portrait 21, 50–1, 152
Aylmer, John 195

Baldwin, William 122, 143, 146, 149, 153, 158, 180
  works: *A Mirror for Magistrates* 124–5, 133, *A Treatise of Moral Philosophy* 124, 133, *Beware the Cat* 15–17, 123–6, **131**, 132–3, 135, 137–9, 141–2, 147, 184, *Wonderful News of the Death of Paul III* 124
Barclay, Alexander 141
Baswell, Christopher 78, 87
Bawcutt, Priscilla 87, 98
Beadle, Richard 208
Beaumont, Francis 21
Benstock, Shari 209
Beroaldus 83
Beza, Theodore 195
Bible:
  glossing of 123, 132
  see also *glossa ordinaria*
Bilney, Thomas 1–2
Black, Joseph L. 191
Boccaccio, Giovanni 34
  works: *De Casibus Virorum Illustrium* 36, *De Genealogiae Deorum Gentilium* 69, 89, *Teseida* 7
  see also 'Bochas'
'Bochas' 25, 34, 36–8, 71
Bonner, Edmund 144
Bracciolini, Poggio 95
Breton, Nicholas 153
Bridges, John 191–2, 195–6, 202
Bruster, Douglas 153

Bucer, Martin 108
Bullein, William 122, 149
  works: *A Comfortable Regiment against the Pleurisi* 134, *A Dialogue against the Fever Pestilence* 15–17, 123, 133–47, 175, 188–9, *The Bulwarke of Defence* 134, *The Government of Health* 134
Burrow, Colin 60

Caie, Graham D. 10
Cauchi, Simon 164
Cave, Terence 185
Caxton, William 92
Cecil, William, Lord Burghley 20
Chaloner, Sir Thomas:
  The Praise of Folie 13–15, 103, 114–22, 133, 208
Chaucer, Geoffrey:
  as speaking statue 141
  Speght's presentation of 20–3
  works: *Anelida and Arcite* 78, *Boece* 23, *The Book of the Duchess* 54, 57, 61, *The Canterbury Tales* 9–11, 30–2, 57–8, *The Complaint of Mars* 78, *The House of Fame* 9, 12, 15, 54–5, 57, 61–3, 69, 71, 75, 78, 127–8, *The Legend of Good Women* 45, 54, *The Parliament of Fowls* 54, *The Treatise of the Astrolabe* 23, *Troilus and Criseyde* 9, 23
Clanvowe, John 54
Coldwell, David F. 101
Coleridge, Samuel Taylor 207
Colet, John 133
Colie, Rosalie 106, 137
Colonne, Guido de 90
Conty, Évrart de 55, 65–6, 71–3
Cook, Megan L. 205
Cooper, Lisa 23
Cooper, Thomas 195–6, 202
Copeland, Rita 8, 45, 48, 63
Copland, William 13–15, 81, 92–7, 99, 101, 114, 157, 180, 201, 208
Cosgrove, Peter 174
Crowley, Robert:
  editions of *Piers Plowman* 17, 175, 199–202, 206

Dathus 83
Denny-Brown, Andrea 23
Donatus 83
Dorp, Martin 107–8
Douglas, Gavin:
  Eneados 12–13, 15, 81–99, **100**, 101–3, 110, 114, 162, 209
  Palice of Honour 89, 92, 96
Drayton, Michael 205–6
Dudley, Robert, Earl of Leicester 172

Ebin, Lois 33, 36
Echard, Siân 71
Edwards, A. S. G. 32
Edwards, Robert 49
Eliot, T. S. 208
Elizabeth I 149, 165
Elizabeth, Lady Russell 167
Elsky, Martin 129
emblem 137–8, 141, 147, 153, 167, 188–9
Erasmus:
  Adages 133
  De copia 105, 129
  De ratione studii 109, 119, 133
  Moriae Encomium 12–13, 103–13, **112–13**, 120–1, 123, 133
Everyman 146

Falstaff 165
Field, Richard 165
Fleming, Juliet 189

Gascoigne, George 16, 122, 149–61, 170, 173–6, 180, 203, 209
  involvement with printing of his works 150
  works: *A Hundreth Sundrie Flowers* 154–7, 160, 172, *Complaynt of Phylomene* 152–3, *Dan Bartholmew of Bathe* 159, *Jocasta* 157, 159, 201, *Supposes* 158–9, *The Adventures of Master F. J.* 165, *The Dromme of Doomesday* 150, 155, *The Noble Art of Venerie* 150, *The Posies* 155–7, 160, 173, *The Steele Glass* 152–3, 155, 188–9
Geddes, Matthew 82, 98
Gellius, Aulus 178
Gillespie, Alexandra 9, 37, 49, 50
glossa ordinaria 5, 145
glosses:
  categorization 3
  definition of 4–6
  'diverting' 4, 15–18, 123, 142, 148, 205, 208–9

history of 5–6
indexing 24, 35, 41, 51, 55, 76–7, 111, 157
transmission of 9, 13, 48–9
glossing:
  as experimental practice 8, 11–13, 17–18, 26–39, 43–5, 75–6, 79–80, 91, 102, 111, 202–3, 208–9
  as influence on theories of authorship 8, 11–13, 18, 33, 36, 38–9, 48, 64–5, 75–6, 207, 209
  as making visible the writing process 12, 16–18, 26, 30, 48, 52–3, 55, 63, 71, 76, 79, 81, 84–6, 90, 96–7, 121, 148, 175, 182, 184, 188, 209
  as means of conveying authority 7, 26, 70–1, 90
  as means of directing the reader 79, 93, 103, 114–18, 157
  as means of engaging the reader 17, 22, 90–91, 103, 109–10, 113, 122, 132–3, 139–40, 146–7
  as means of suggesting authorial presence 163–7, 169–70, 172–3, 180–2, 197, 209
  as means of stabilizing the text 13, 15, 97, 102
  connected to translation 8, 13, 28–30, 37–9, 44–5, 57–9, 62, 65, 67–73, 75–9, 81–91, 94–5, 107, 121
  'double' 112–13
  misleading 15, 93–4, 119–21, 128, 130, 132, 139–40, 157–61, 178–81, 195–7, 201–2
  in relation to Reformist writing 15, 17, 123, 126–7, 132–3, 137–8, 142–7, 201, 206
Gower, John:
  Confessio Amantis 7–8, 11–12, 26, 45, 48, 71, 162
grammar school teaching 95–6
Gray, Alasdair 208
Greene, Robert 175
Grigely, Joseph 189
Grindley, Carl James 6
Gutierrez, Nancy A. 132, 147

Hanna, Ralph 8, 32
Harington, Sir John 16, 122, 149–54, 161–7, 169–70, 172–5, 186, 203, 205, 209
  involvement with printing of his works 150
  works: *Anatomie* 166–7, **168**, 169, **171**, 173, *Apologie* 166–7, 173,

Index

New Discourse 150, 165–6, 169–70, 172–3, *Orlando Furioso* 150, 152, 161, 164–6, 169–70, 173, 207, translation of the *Aeneid* 164–6, 170
Harvey, Gabriel 161n, 175, 184, 186, 188
Heale, Elizabeth 154
Henry, Prince of Wales 164
Hoccleve, Thomas 7, 11–12, 54, 70
Homer 112
Horace 94, 178
Huot, Sylvia 9
Hutson, Lorna 176–7

Irvine, Martin 7, 15, 17
Iser, Wolfgang 15, 189

James I 164
Jauss, Hans Robert 174
Jonson, Ben 175, 205–7
Joyce, James 208

Kahn, Victoria 135
Kamath, Stephanie A. Viereck Gibbs 75
Kinney, A. F. 106

La Belle Dame sans Merci 23, 76n, 78
Landino, Cristoforo 87–8, 90
Langland, William 197, 199–200, 206
Lear, Edward 208
Les Echecs Amoureux 55, 63–6, 68–73, 76–7, 79
Lewis, Robert E. 10, 57
Lily, William 133
Lindsay, David 141
Lipking, Lawrence 3, 208–9
Listrius, Gerardus 107–10, 117, 120, 122
Livy 90
Lydgate, John 26–7, 54, 102, 209
 as speaking statue 141
 poetics 24–6, 32–6
 works: *Testament* 50–1, *The Fall of Princes* 7, 12, 17, 24–9, 35–52, **42**, **45-7**, 54, 69, 71, 81–2, 99, 107, *The Siege of Thebes* 7, 12, 17, 19, 23–4, 26–36, **31**, 39–40, 43, 48–9, 51–2, 54, 81–2, 207, *The Temple of Glass* 57, 78, *Troy Book* 24; see also *Reson and Sensuallyte*
Lyly, John 153
Lyra, Nicholas de 110–11, 121

Machan, Tim W. 21
Mann, Jill 59, 61
manuscripts:
 Beinecke MS 661 27n, Bodleian Library MS Arch. Selden B. 24 54, Bodleian Library MS Bodley 263 28n, Bodleian Library MS Bodley 638 54, 56, 78n, Bodleian Library MS Bodley 776 27n, Bodleian Library MS Digby 230 27n, **31**, 43, Bodleian Library MS e.Musaeo.1 28n, Bodleian Library MS Fairfax 16 12, 54–7, **60**, 63, **74**, 75, 77–9, 99, Bodleian Library MS Hatton 2 28n, Bodleian Library MS Laud Misc. 416 27n, Bodleian Library MS Laud Misc. 557 27n, Bodleian Library MS Rawlinson C.48 27, 43, Bodleian Library MS Rawlinson C.448 28n, Bodleian Library MS Tanner 346 54, 56, 78n, Boston Public Library MS f. med. 94 27n, British Library MS Additional 16165 78n, British Library MS Additional 18632 28, 43, British Library MS Additional 21410 28n, British Library MS Additional 39659 28n, British Library MS Arundel 119 27n, British Library MS Harley 372 76n, 78n, British Library MS Harley 1245 28n, 40, British Library MS Harley 1766 28n, 42, **47**, British Library MS Harley 2251 40–1, **42**, 99, British Library MS Harley 3486 28n, British Library MS Harley 4197 28n, 44, **47**, British Library MS Harley 4203 28n, 43, **45–6**, British Library MS Harley 4866 21, British Library MS Royal 18.B.xxxi 28n, British Library MS Royal 18.D.ii 27n, 43, British Library MS Royal 18.D.iv 28n, British Library MS Royal 18.D.v 28n, British Library MS Sloane 1710 78n, British Library MS Sloane 4031 28n, Cambridge Magdalene College MS Pepys 2006 56, 78n, Cambridge Magdalene College MS Pepys 2011 27n, Cambridge Trinity College MS O.3.12 81–2, 91, 93, 97–9, **100**, 101–2, Cambridge Trinity College MS O.5.2 27n, Cambridge Trinity College MS R.3.19 78n, Cambridge Trinity College MS R.4.20 27n, Cambridge University Library MS Additional 3137 27n, Cambridge University Library MS Additional 6864 40, Cambridge University Library MS Ff.1.6 78n,

manuscripts: *(cont.)*
  Cambridge University Library MS Gg.4.27 78n, Columbia University Library MS Plimpton 255 28n, Coventry City Record Office MS Acc. 325/1 27n, Durham University Library MS Cosin V.ii.14 27n, Glasgow University Library MS Hunter 5 28n, 44, Lambeth Palace MS 117 92, Lambeth Palace MS 742 27n, Manchester MS Rylands 2 28n, 38–9, 49, Oxford Christ Church MS 152 27n, Oxford St John's College MS 266 27n, 48, Pierpont Morgan Library MS M.4 27n, Pierpont Morgan Library MS M.124 28n, Princeton University Library MS Garrett 139 28n, Princeton University Library MS Taylor 2 28n, Rosenbach Library MS 439/16 28n, 37n
marginalia 3, 6, 97–8, 99, 101–2; *see also* annotations
Markham, Gervase 167
Marlowe, Christopher 175
'Marprelate, Martin' 190, 193, 196, 198, 202
  works: *Epitome* 192, 195–6, *Epistle* 191–3, **194**, 195
Marprelate tracts 17, 175, 190, 193
Mary, Countess of Pembroke 164
McCutcheon, Elizabeth 134
McGann, Jerome J. 209
McKenzie, Donald F. 18, 185
Meyer-Lee, Robert J. 32
Miller, Clarence H. 114, 119
Minnis, A. J. 59, 64–5
More, Sir Thomas 106, 123, 141–2
Moth 175
mouvance 48

Nashe, Thomas 16, 122, 175–7, 180, 182, 188, 193, 201–3, 205–6, 209
  works: *Have With You to Saffron Walden* 184–6, **187**, 188, 190, 194, *Pierce Penilesse his Supplication to the Devil* 176–82, **183**, 184–5, 189–90, 195, 197–200, 202
Navitsky, Joseph 191
Nelson, William 1
Noakes, Susan 14, 91, 96, 102
Norton-Smith, John 56

Ong, Walter J. 185
Ovid:
  Heroides 78
  Metamorphoses 56–7, 59–61, 178, 180

Remedia Amoris 66
Tristia 178–9, 200
Owen, Charles A. 10
Owen, William 199

Partridge, Stephen Bradford 10, 11
Pearsall, Derek 8
Penry, John 193
'Piers' pamphlets:
  A Godly dyalogue & dysputacyon between Pyers Plowman, and a popysh preest concernyng the supper of the Lorde 197
  I playne Piers which can not flatter 197–8
  Piers the Plowman's Crede 197
  The Plough-man's Tale 199, 205
  The prayer and complaint of the ploweman vnto Christ 197
  Pyers plowmans exhortation, vnto the lordes, knightes and burgoysses of the Parlyamenthouse 197–8
Pinti, Daniel J. 89
Pope, Alexander 208
Premierfait, Laurence de 28–9, 35–6
print:
  as means of self-fashioning 149–52, 154–5, 161, 170
  effect on glossing practices 4, 13, 96–7, 121–2, 207–9
  effect on meaning of the text 16, 51–3, 124, 190
  relationship to manuscript 14, 48–53, 96–7, 165–6, 170, 172, 182, 184–6, 209
  relationship to orality 15, 122, 125–8, 137–8, 146–7, 190, 202
  'stability' of 14–16, 52, 102, 206
  'stigma' of 151, 155, 166
Proust, Jacqueline 134
Puttenham, George 151
Pynson, Richard 12, 49–51

Quintilian 105

reading as ethical practice 93, 136–8
'reality game' 154, 160
Reson and Sensuallyte 12, 54–5, **60**, 63–73, **74**, 76–7, 79, 81, 84, 209
Rhodes, Neil 188
Romance of the Rose 59
Roman de la Rose 9, 63–4

Scheurer, Matthew 107
Schnapp, Jeffrey T. 13
Scott-Warren, Jason 167
Selden, John 206

self-glossing 4, 7–9, 11–13, 17–18, 79, 81, 110, 209
Servius 83, 85–8, 91, 164
Sidney, Sir Philip 150
Silvia, Daniel S. 10, 57
Skelton, John 143
  antagonism towards Cardinal Wolsey 1–2
  as speaking statue 141
  glossing practices 1–3
  works: *A Garlande of Laurell* 2, 50, *A Replycacion* 1–2, 34, *Speke Parrot* 2, 142
Slights, William W. E. 3–4, 205, 207
speaking picture 136
Spearing, A. C. 30
Speght, Thomas:
  editions of Chaucer 12, 19–23, 26, 49, 63, 163, 205–6
Spenser, Edmund:
  Shepheardes Calendar 3, 149, 155, 162, 172, 205
Stallybrass, Peter 6
Sterne, Lawrence 208
Stow, John 12

edition of Chaucer 12, 19–20, 23, 49

Taylor, Andrew 14
Tottel's *Songs and Sonets* 154–5
translatio 59–60, 62, 71
Tribble, Evelyn B. 162
Tyndale, William 126

Valla, Lorenzo 95
Virgil:
  Aeneid 56–8, 62, 81, 83, 85–7, 89–90, 112, 164

Wakelin, Daniel 4, 9, 96
Wall, Wendy 16
Warner, Lawrence 57
Whitchurch, Edward 128
Whitgift, John 190
Whitney, Geoffrey 153
Wolsey, Cardinal 1–2, 50
Worde, Wynkyn de 12, 48–9

Zumthor, Paul 39